Rethinking Globalizations
Edited by Barry K. Gills, University of Newcastle, UK

This series is designed to break new ground in the literature on globalization and its academic and popular understanding. Rather than perpetuating or simply reacting to the economic understanding of globalization, this series seeks to capture the term and broaden its meaning to encompass a wide range of issues and disciplines and convey a sense of alternative possibilities for the future.

1. Whither Globalization?
The vortex of knowledge and globalization
James H. Mittelman

2. Globalization and Global History
Edited by Barry K. Gills and William R. Thompson

3. Rethinking Civilization
Communication and terror in the global village
Majid Tehranian

4. Globalization and Contestation
The new great counter-movement
Ronaldo Munck

5. Global Activism
Ruth Reitan

6. Globalization, the City and Civil Society in Pacific Asia
Edited by Mike Douglass, K.C. Ho and Giok Ling Ooi

7. Challenging Euro-America's Politics of Identity
The return of the native
Jorge Luis Andrade Fernandes

8. The Global Politics of Globalization
"Empire" vs "Cosmopolis"
Edited by Barry K. Gills

9. The Globalization of Environmental Crisis
Edited by Jan Oosthoek and Barry K. Gills

10. Globalization as Evolutionary Process
Modeling global change
Edited by Geroge Modelski, Tessaleno Devezas and William R. Thompson

11. The Political Economy of Global Security
War, future crises and changes in global governance
Heikki Patomäki

12. Cultures of Globalization
Coherence, hybridity, contestation
Edited by Kevin Archer, M. Martin Bosman, M. Mark Amen and Ella Schmidt

13. Globalization and the Global Politics of Justice
Edited by Barry K. Gills

14. Global Economy Contested
Power and conflict across the international division of labor
Edited by Marcus Taylor

15. Rethinking Insecurity, War and Violence
Beyond savage globalization?
Edited by Damian Grenfell and Paul James

16. Recognition and Redistribution
Beyond international development
Edited by Heloise Weber and Mark T. Berger

17. The Social Economy
Working alternatives in a globalizing era
Edited by Hasmet M. Uluorta

18. The Global Governance of Food
Edited by Sara R. Curran, April Linton, Abigail Cooke and Andrew Schrank

19. Global Poverty, Ethics and Human Rights
The role of multilateral organisations
Desmond McNeill and Asunción Lera St. Clair

20. Globalization and Popular Sovereignty
Democracy's transnational dilemma
Adam Lupel

21. Limits to Globalization
North-South divergence
William R. Thompson and Rafael Reuveny

22. Globalisation, Knowledge and Labour
Education for solidarity within spaces of resistance
Edited by Mario Novelli and Anibel Ferus-Comelo

23. Dying Empire
U.S. imperialism and global resistance
Francis Shor

24. Alternative Globalizations
An integrative approach to studying dissident knowledge in the global justice movement
S. A. Hamed Hosseini

25. Global Restructuring, Labour and the Challenges for Transnational Solidarity
Edited by Andreas Bieler and Ingemar Lindberg

26. Global South to the Rescue
Emerging humanitarian superpowers and globalizing rescue industries
Edited by Paul Amar

27. Global Ideologies and Urban Landscapes
Edited by Manfred B. Steger and Anne McNevin

28. Power and Transnational Activism
Edited by Thomas Olesen

29. Globalization and Crisis
Edited by Barry K. Gills

30. Andre Gunder Frank and Global Development
Visions, remembrances and explorations
Edited by Patrick Manning and Barry K. Gills

31. Global Social Justice
Edited by Heather Widdows and Nicola J. Smith

32. Globalization, Labor Export and Resistance
A study of Filipino migrant domestic workers in global cities.
Ligaya Lindio-McGovern

33. Situating Global Resistance
Between Discipline and Dissent
Edited by Lara Montesinos Coleman and Karen Tucker

34. A History of World Order and Resistance
The Making and Unmaking of Global Subjects
André C. Drainville

35. Migration, Work and Citizenship in the New Global Order
Edited by Ronaldo Munck, Carl-Ulrik Schierup and Raúl Delgado Wise

36. Edges of Global Justice
The World Social Forum and Its 'Others'
Janet Conway

37. Land Grabbing and Global Governance
Edited by Matias E. Margulis, Nora McKeon and Saturnino Borras Jr.

38. Dialectics in World Politics
Edited by Shannon Brincat

39. Crisis, Movement, Management: Globalising Dynamics
Edited by James Goodman and Jonathan Paul Marshall

40. China's Development
Capitalism and Empire
Michel Aglietta and Guo Bai

41. Global Governance and NGO Participation
Charlotte Dany

Global South to the Rescue

Emerging Humanitarian Superpowers and Globalizing Rescue Industries

Edited by
Paul Amar

Routledge
Taylor & Francis Group
LONDON AND NEW YORK

First published 2013
by Routledge
2 Park Square, Milton Park, Abingdon, Oxon, OX14 4RN

Simultaneously published in the USA and Canada
by Routledge
711 Third Avenue, New York, NY 10017

Routledge is an imprint of the Taylor & Francis Group, an informa business

This book is a reproduction of *Globalizations*, vol. 9, issue 1. The Publisher requests to those authors who may be citing this book to state, also, the bibliographical details of the special issue on which the book was based.

British Library Cataloguing in Publication Data
A catalogue record for this book is available from the British Library

ISBN13: 978-0-415-57795-3

Typeset in Times New Roman
by Taylor & Francis Books

Publisher's Note
The publisher would like to make readers aware that the chapters in this book may be referred to as articles as they are identical to the articles published in the special issue. The publisher accepts responsibility for any inconsistencies that may have arisen in the course of preparing this volume for print.

Contents

Foreword

There is little doubt at this point that we have moved well beyond the end of the end of history! The first crucial rupture was associated with the choice to respond to the 9/11 attacks by launching a global-scale war against those that would challenge the global supremacy of the United States. This ongoing war, episodes of which are often justified as humanitarian interventions, refuses to defer to the territorial sovereignty of independent states in the South and is increasingly accompanied by revolutionary drone-attack technology with its promise of zero casualties. Then in 2011 the Arab Spring combined with the Occupy Movement disclosed a new phase of international turbulence challenging the pro-Western established order within and above states and throughout the oil rich Middle East. This monumental eruption of the forces of globalization-from-below is already transformative, although its full historical impact and national outcomes remain highly uncertain and likely various. In this period the most probable scenarios stress an ebb-and-flow rhythm between counter-revolutionary restorations of authoritarian rule and periodic reassertions of revolutionary demands for democracy and economic justice. This meta-narrative of 21st-century world order is a work in progress that will require frequent reappraisals as the future unwinds in ways that we cannot anticipate at this time.

In other respects the profound restructurings of world order today are less opaque. It is evident that a series of emerging non-Western states are redrawing the geopolitical map in ways that mainstream academic scholarship has yet to assimilate due to its lingering Orientalist approach to global policy issues. The hegemonic texts in the International Relations field remains doggedly West-centric, although there are some acknowledgements of non-Western challenges, mainly those mounted by Islam and the extraordinary Chinese surge. At the same time, academic custodians of Western dominance are quick to chide countries like Brazil and Turkey for not 'staying in their lane,' that is, not deferring to Washington's geopolitical (mis)management of hard power diplomacy in the Middle East and elsewhere. The quaintest feature of this Old Geopolitics is that it overrides geographic proximity by instructing a country such as Turkey that it is exceeding its role as a bit part actor by trying to circumvent American-led coercive diplomacy with soft power initiatives that might actually resolve the conflict involving Iran without bloodshed. An important development that has not yet made its way into the American mindset is that territorial sovereignty and regional autonomy are increasingly significant features of the post-colonial era, and if not recognized, will deepen conflict and give added strength to worldwide anti-American resentment.

Not much further in the background are the multiple inclusions and exclusions arising from the dynamics of globalization leading countries to open and close their borders, seeking both the benefits of participation in the world economy and avoiding unwanted persons, products, and ideas diluting the fragile realities of sovereignty and independence, and above all cultural identity. Both the repressions of colonialism and the hierarchical alliance relations of the Cold War period suppressed many forms of wider activism in world politics. What has been evolving in the last few decades are new routes and modes for gradually enhanced participation in global policy issues, especially under the guidance of internationally ambitious political leaderships in such key countries as Mahathir's Malaysia, Lula's Brazil, and Erdogan's Turkey. Such assertiveness is combined with a series of parallel developments of great consequence for the domestic quality of life, including especially the privatization of many security and policing functions previously exclusively associated with sovereign states.

It is against this kind of background that we should enthusiastically welcome the publication of this brilliant series of essays expertly edited by Paul Amar. This volume addresses many of the most problematic global policy issues, including especially peacekeeping and humanitarian intervention, as seen from a variety of country perspectives. The chapters analyzing the behavior of what Amar identifies as 'emerging humanitarian superpowers' are very illuminating, with such unexpected commonalities as the quest for higher status on the global stage being achieved by recourse to soft power diplomacy, through struggles in and around the UN Security Council, participating in regional and global peacekeeping operations, and providing good offices for the mediation of regional conflicts. Such patterns contrast happily with the alternative path to global ascendancy, namely the accelerated buildups of hard power capabilities in the form of weaponry, armies, navies, and foreign bases, and at the extreme, acquisition of nuclear weaponry. This reliance on a soft power approach to attaining an enhanced global status is one of the more hopeful contributions being made by these pivotal states, and may help shape the geopolitical climate in more constructive directions in the years ahead. And maybe it will even have an impact on dysfunctional warmongering being spearheaded by the United States, and having only a string of defeats to show for it. This frustration of American militarism has occurred despite spending almost as much as the whole world combined on its defense budget. The country is in tears about its deficit, and has yet to comprehend that in this young century military superiority is not the most effective mechanism to retain a firm hold on global leadership and is not effective in lessening vulnerability to the most serious security threats. Of course, there is the danger that this predatory militarism of the United States will induce others to invest more in weaponry so as to deter Washington's interventionary adventurism.

This volume does much more than depict the rise of the South. It gives an array of insights into the ways in which police and the military in the global south are reallocating security assignments, as well as how the private sector is taking over from the state in managing traditional governmental functions with respect to security. As well, several innovative chapters explore gender and sexuality dimensions of policing and peacekeeping, which inevitably refer to the growing relevance of human rights as a site of conflict and a zone within which perceptions of legitimacy and illegitimacy are being formed and deformed in novel ways.

I find the most exhilarating contribution of this collection of original essays is the fact that it provides new analytical tools and a wealth of case-study data for those of us who are trying to understand the dynamics of the de-Westernizing of world order, a dialectical process that has been unfolding for more than the past half century. The West under the aegis of American militarism, increasingly relying on the NATO framework, is continuing to project its power globally, often futilely yet with devastating human results. Western ideas and practices also continue to dominate global economic policy whether shaped by the Group of 20 (G-20) or at the Davos World Economic Forum. The persistence of the neoliberal consensus, even in the face of the revelations surrounding the global recession, keeps in place the discriminatory constraints and burdens on trade, investment, and developmental potentialities in the most disadvantaged regions of the global south. This incipient battle to control the future of world order is far from over, but as this book shows, new patterns of non-Western assertiveness are raising hopes for global justice, and should be taken into account in our interpretations of 21st century geopolitics. *Global South to the Rescue* helps us to *see* from southern perspectives and not merely *look* at the world through a habitual but increasingly anachronistic Western optic.

Richard Falk
March 4, 2012

Richard Falk is Albert G. Milbank Professor Emeritus of International Law at Princeton University and since 2002 Visiting Distinguished Professor in Global and International Studies at the University of California, Santa Barbara. His most recent books are *Achieving Human Rights*(2009) and the co-authored *Path to Zero: Dialogues on Nuclear Disarmament* (2012). In 2001, he served on a three person Human Rights Inquiry Commission for the Palestine Territories that was appointed by the United Nations, and previously, on the Independent International Commission on Kosovo. He is the author or co-author of numerous books, including *Religion and Humane Global Governance; Human Rights Horizons; On Humane Governance: Toward a New Global Politics; Explorations at the Edge of Time; Revolutionaries and Functionaries; The Promise of World Order; Indefensible Weapons; Human Rights and State Sovereignty; A Study of Future Worlds; This Endangered Planet;* co-editor of *Crimes of War*. He serves as Chair of the Nuclear Age Peace Foundation's Board of Directors and as honourary vice president of the American Society of International Law. Falk also acted as counsel to Ethiopia and Liberia in the Southwest Africa Case before the International Court of Justice. He received his BS from the Wharton School, University of Pennsylvania; LLB. from Yale Law School; and JSD from Harvard University. In March 2008, the United Nations Human Rights Council appointed Falk to a six-year term as a UN Special Rapporteur on Palestinian human rights.

INTRODUCTION

Global South to the Rescue: Emerging Humanitarian Superpowers and Globalizing Rescue Industries

PAUL AMAR

University of California, Santa Barbara, CA, USA

ABSTRACT *The introductory essay offers a brief overview of current trends in critical globalization studies and international relations scholarship that shed light on three intersections: between imperialism and humanitarianism, between neoliberal globalization and "rescue industry" transnationalism, and between patterns of geopolitical hegemony and trajectories of peacekeeping internationalism. These research agendas have been generative and politically useful, but have tended to neglect the forms of humanitarian and peacekeeping agency emanating from the global south. In order to address this gap, this introduction lays out a new research agenda that combines interdisciplinary methods from global studies, gender and race studies, critical security studies, police and military sociology, Third World diplomatic history, and international relations. This introduction also theoretically situates the other contributions and case studies gathered here, providing a framework of analysis that groups them into three clusters: (I) Globalizing Peacekeeper Identities, (II) Assertive "Regional Internationalisms," and (III) Emergent Alternative Paradigms.*

On 28 March 2011, the *Financial Times* exclaimed "Libya, a last hurrah for the west?" (Rachman, 2011) and on 1 September, the *Telegraph* warned "Libya could be the last place where the West is allowed to intervene" (Joshi, 2011). Although the year 2011 offered a wealth of political-economic and diplomatic evidence that the foundations of global north/west hegemony were rapidly eroding, the period also featured an airstrike campaign against the Qaddhafi regime that seemed to prove, spectacularly, that Western geopolitical and military dominance was still secure. The UN Security Council authorized NATO to use "all necessary measures to protect civilians [in Libya] ... and provide full humanitarian access to those in need" (UN News Centre, 2011). This militarized humanitarian intervention took the form of a new kind of operation, "the first real test of the Responsibility to Protect Doctrine since its formal adoption by the United Nations in 2005" (Politics & Polity, 2011). But from the perspective of many observers based in emerging global-south countries, these interventions seemed more like a return to the past. How could a colonial-era style bombardment of North African cities by French, Italian, and US air forces fit into an age of multipolarism and "liberal peace?" How could a Cold War-type "contra" insurgency supported by US covert intelligence operators reconcile itself with the early-twenty-first-century universe of non-violent uprisings and vibrant new media solidarities?

Although NATO launched the intervention in Libya after seeking not just a UNSC authorization but also the consent of the once radical Cairo-based Arab League and the collaboration of the solidly reactionary Saudi-centered Gulf Cooperation Council, these global-south security communities did not design or direct the intervention. When the airstrikes did succeed in bringing down Qaddhafi and ushering into power Libya's rebel National Transitional Council in October 2011, NATO gloated and insisted that the new Council in Libya suspend the oil, trade, infrastructure, and industrial contracts won by Russia, Brazil, and South Africa who had not championed NATO's intervention. Abdeljalil Mayouf, information manager at the Libyan rebel oil firm Agoco, told Reuters "we don't have problems with Western countries like the Italians, French and UK companies. But we may have some political issues with Russia, China and Brazil" (RT News, 2011). These kinds of statement generated an enraged backlash and "very strong resistance" from these emerging global south powers including Brazil, South Africa, and India "which aspire to become permanent members of an expanded Security Council" (Charbonneau, 2011). The BRICS group promised either to never support another Security Council resolution of this kind or to control the character and terms of such humanitarian interventions, themselves, in the future. "Russia, China, Brazil, India and South Africa have repeatedly complained that the NATO intervention in Libya has gone far beyond the U.N. mandate approved by the council in March to protect civilians from violence by the government. They say they do not want the same thing to happen in Syria" (ibid). As an alternative, BRICS countries began pushing discussions for the scrapping of the UN authorization of force system and for a new set of mechanisms similar to those articulated by UN Rapporteur Richard Falk: "In the end, what becomes obvious is that such protective undertakings to achieve credibility in the future must be detached from geopolitics. The best mechanism for reaching such a goal would clearly involve the establishment of a UN Emergency Force that could be activated by a two-thirds vote in either the Security Council or General Assembly, and not be subject to the veto. Such UNEF would need to be funded independently, possibly by finally imposing some sort of UN revenue raising tax on international flights or currency transactions" (Falk, 2011).

Indeed, the massively militarized and global-north orchestrated humanitarian intervention in Libya (March-October 2011) interrupted a year of extraordinary shifts in patterns of globalization and international security that were pointing world order toward other horizons of possibility. The pro-democracy uprisings of the Arab Spring challenged neoliberal policies and deposed officials who had pushed radical forms of privatization and security policies that favored the West. The increasingly organized and influential African Union and South America's revolutionary Bolivarian Alliance generated and aggressively advocated consensus- and global-south-based alternatives to Western and UN humanitarian militarism. And the rising economic and geopolitical powerhouses of Russia, China, India, and Brazil increased their degree of autonomy in and around the Security Council, IMF, and other UN commissions and agencies. The emerging influence of global-south powers that had been gaining momentum for a decade reached a tipping point in 2011, inverting essential pillars of global hierarchy. Via internationalist mechanisms and institutions, emerging powers began establishing a degree of sway over the same northern countries that had once been their colonial masters. In 2011, China and Brazil proposed to channel money through the IMF to prop up the Eurozone economy, demanding favorable trade concessions and currency rates in exchange for their aid (Childress, 2011; Reuters, 2011). And while the US and Eurozone continued to fret about what they referred to as the "global" financial crisis, the finances of most of the global south just kept getting better, as economic growth shot up and debt burdens fell in Brazil, China, and even in much of Africa.

In terms of the growth of global-south participation in and leadership of humanitarian and peacekeeping interventions during this tumultuous year, the NATO-in-Libya model seemed an outlier that strayed far from the trend line. Indeed, alternative models and evidence of new kinds of frameworks constituted by the global south came from every continent. Brazil redeployed its military peacekeepers (who had led the UN MINUSTAH operations) from Haiti to the narcotrafficker-occupied slum communities of Rio de Janeiro to "pacify" the city for the upcoming World Cup and Olympic Games. Ethiopian and Nigerian humanitarian troops poured into the new border between North and South Sudan, substituting for Western operations. Venezuela again provided affordable oil to impoverished and unemployed US and European households during the record-cold winters that bracketed the year and provided disaster relief and humanitarian aid in Africa and South Asia. And Turkey and Indonesia seemed to be the only powers able to establish stable peacekeeping and humanitarian operations in Afghanistan, with Ankara also leading international efforts to grapple with the humanitarian impact of civil strife in Syria, the nuclear program in Iran, and the devastating blockade of Gaza.

In the wake of the changes witnessed by this tumultuous year of humanitarian interventions, global-south uprisings, and peacekeeping innovations, this collection asks: What new roles are emergent powers of the global south playing in shaping new globalizing security industries, humanitarian interventions, and internationalist "peace enforcement" practices today?

Reviewing Traditions of Scholarship

In the twenty-first century, globalizing development agendas have become inseparable from internationalized, militarized, "securitized" interventions: aid missions embed themselves in walled police compounds (Duffield, 2001, 2007), international financial organizations focus on quelling insurgencies (Fox, 2008; Higate and Henry, 2009; Jones, 2008; Rosenau, 2009), and private investments flood the humanitarian intervention and protection sector (Abrahamson and Williams, 2010; Mandel, 2002). Recent studies have argued that this merging of developmentalism and securitization has been legitimized by the blending of discourses of humanitarianism and human security with neo-colonial metaphors of tutelage and protection (Doty 1996; Mamdani, 2010, 2011; Orford, 2003, 2011). This kind of humanitarianism, at the nexus of globalizing development and military intervention, increasingly demands that international enforcement (rather than mechanisms of entitlement or redistribution, for example) be mobilized regardless of the consent of its "recipient" populations (Orford, 1999; Amar, 2012).

Before this critical scholarship emerged, traditions of research on humanitarian intervention in political science, international relations, socio-legal studies, and global sociology focused on delimiting the red lines that national sovereignty must not cross. This literature provided legal or technical expertise, proposing to get the balance right or assess the predicament or dilemma posed by the clash between international humanitarian imperatives and the sovereignty rights enjoyed by independent states in the international system (Ayoob, 1995). Constructivist accounts have mapped the origins of transformative dynamics emanating from below and outside state and legal institutions. The best of this important work grounds the emergence of interventionism in particular civil society mobilizations, class interests, cultural value flows, and elite actor networks (Hehir, 2008; Kaldor, 2007; Santos and Rodrigues-Garavito, 2005). Another productive set of debates has explored the nature of transnational norm-dissemination practices and patterns of ideological contestation (Adamson, 2005; Acharya, 2004). Historically oriented work has identified three ages of humanitarianism: the age of nineteenth century Abolition through the World War I age of minority protection and ethno-national self-determination (Brown, 2006; Rodogno, 2011); the age of World War II justice and post-War humanitarian law codifications (Aksar, 2004); and the post-Cold War era when militarized humanitarian interventions have proliferated (Barnett, 2005; Razack, 2004). Scholarly research on these three ages of humanitarian intervention have tended to focus on the agents and agendas of global-north powers and humanitarian social movements emanating from metropolitan capitals.

Since 2000, a new body of scholarship has revealed the imperialist dynamics behind the wave of new humanitarian interventions unleashed since the Cold War ended. One group has elaborated a critique of new appropriations of the Kantian doctrine of "liberal peace." The contemporary version of this doctrine asserts that the protection of individual liberties and human rights trumps the traditional Realpolitik sanctification of state security and national sovereignty. This new wave of critical scholarship has argued that global-north powers since the end of the Cold War have used the doctrine of "liberal peace" to launch, paradoxically, an unending series of new wars. Despite the fact that they are labeled as humanitarian interventions, these deployments reveal the resurging imperial ambitions of US and European military powers (Barkawi and Laffey, 2006; Chandler, 2004; Falk, 1995, 1999; Lidén, 2009). Complementing these conversations, a group of more theoretically oriented scholars has explored the constitution of discourses and subjects of power around the "liberal peace" regime, drawing upon the work of Michel Foucault and profiling the biopolitical, disciplinary, paternalistic, and "therapeutic" dimensions of new kinds of humanitarian militarism (Dillon and Reid, 2001; Esmeir, 2007; Pupavac, 2005). In parallel, another group of "globalization studies" researchers has analyzed the political-economic structures that have enabled these new kinds of humanitarianized globalization and domination (Harvey, 2003; Nederveen Pieterse, 2004). Related the scholarship on "the development/security nexus" has focused its critique on European or North American interventions, particularly in states occupied in times of war, or in so-called "failed states" that require "nation building" where national sovereignty is weak and imperial legacies are strong (Bilgin and Morton, 2002; Bøås and Jennings, 2007; Chesterman, 2005; Duffield, 2007; Fearon and Laitin, 2004; Krasner, 2004; Pouigny, 2005). Together, these sets of projects have provided useful correctives and cautions that offer powerful alternatives designed to counter the arguments of a highly visible and influential group of intervention cheerleaders. Since 2001, these intervention advocates have established a troubling space of consensus between prominent figures of the human-rights left and the neoconservative right (Hitchens et al., 2008; Ignatieff, 2003).

However, what this cluster of research agendas have left relatively unexamined is the role of global-south states and "Third World"-originating transnational formations. Global-south actors are neglected as agents of innovation and are largely seen as the recipients or victims of Eurocentric agendas. Meanwhile, the great majority of new studies that have committed to highlighting the rise of the global south have focused overwhelmingly on general issues of economic growth and market expansion, especially on the BRICs' (Brazil, Russian, India, and China and sometimes South Africa) state-coordinated development and trade policies. The few but important exceptions to this economistic trend have examined the rise of "middle powers" (Joordan, 2003), "global rebalancing" (Nederveen Pieterse, 2011), the return of historical patterns of global south power (Korany, 1994), and the rise of new emancipatory models of global governance coming from the south (Al Attar and Miller, 2010; Gill, 2008; Lidén et al., 2009). In order to build on this nascent set of conversations and to address these gaps in the literature on humanitarian intervention, peacekeeping, and the security/development nexus, we in this collection focus on emergent powers in the global south that are transforming and deploying distinct internationalist security and militarized humanitarian development models. This collection aims to introduce globalization studies to new trends in police and military studies, highlight the cultural and political complexities of the global south, and develop new frameworks that articulate the best of feminist, political-economic, international relations, and ethnographic perspectives.

Objects and Methodologies of Analysis

The studies grouped together here will highlight three units of analysis: *Pivotal countries in the global south* (India, Brazil, Indonesia, Turkey, Nigeria, etc.) that have developed an internationalist profile and are asserting themselves increasingly as humanitarian, peacekeeping, and "policekeeping" actors on the world stage in ways that also promote their own economic globalization agendas and shift transnational patterns of norms diffusion; *global-south based transnational private networks of security-and-development contractors* that bring together elites and subaltern personnel from sites which served as laboratories for anti-communism and extreme neoliberalism (Fiji, Iraq, Colombia, El Salvador); and *community, paramilitary, and insurgent groupings in the global south* (Afghanistan, Haiti, Iraq, Indonesia) whose agency in engaging or resisting security-and-development missions has transformed the terms and aims of the international frameworks of humanitarianism as well as the globalizing "rescue industry."

This collection showcases a group of scholars who have been shaped by extensive first-hand experience in the global south. This group is unusual because each member has worked within security-development missions and/or in international institutions and has done interviews and participatory fieldwork among community members, aid recipients, state actors, and international humanitarian officials. This multi-dimensional experience means that our work does not idealize the humanitarian aims of interventions, nor does it romanticize possibilities for resistance or agency on the part of the clients or targets of these missions. On the other hand, these studies also resist the urge to see these operations as reproducing, wholesale, any singular, imperial, global logic. In order to capture the complexity of structural forces and agency dynamics that make the rescue industry in the global south so interesting, many of these projects combine ethnography with political-economic or social-historical analysis, providing clearer understandings of transnational forms of class identity and domination, militarized masculinity and femininity, as well as fetishized ethnic and minority identities. Each piece offers evidence of the shifting logics of security states in the global south. This collection, although resisting any neat narratives of imperialism, does not hesitate to examine how security institutions in the south engage with local and global forms of capitalism, dispossession, exploitation, and occupation. And we provide new insights on how states in the global south are shifting the terms of political internationalism and economic globalization through their projects for police reform, military civilianization, and humanitarian deployment.

Arrangement of Contributions

These studies are arranged into three subsections: (I) Globalizing Peacekeeper Identities, (II) Assertive "Regional Internationalisms," and (III) Emergent Alternative Paradigms. The first group of authors takes as its unit of analysis not individual global-south countries, but the identities and subjectivities of peacekeeping troops themselves. These multinational groupings are analyzed as they cross borders, interact with officers from other countries, assume and challenge forms of power, and respond to (or precipitate) conflict. The three studies in this group analyze the gender dimensions of peacekeeping troops coming from the global south and their insertion into global hierarchies of labor, race, and post-colonial identity. This section builds on the extraordinary contributions of feminist and critical race theory scholars to the study of humanitarian intervention and critical security studies (Ackerly and True, 2008; Carey, 2001; Cohn, 2008; Enloe, 2004; Gill 2008; Shepherd, 2010; Whitworth, 2004).

Marsha Henry's study of female peacekeeping troops from India and Uruguay sent to Liberia and Haiti opens this collection because its findings serve as a caution against utopian readings of new kinds of internationalism articulated by global-south powers. Henry offers a fine-grained analysis of interventions that explicitly represent themselves as new and emancipatory kinds of internationalism. These interventions are led by women soldiers from the global south, and they are charged with realizing a gender-sensitive human-security mission. As implied by the provocative title of her piece, "Peacexploitation," Henry is skeptical of the emancipatory claims asserted by the organizers of these missions. She reminds us that global race/gender geographies of neoliberalism have systematically hyper-exploited women's work within new global divisions of labor. Outsourcing work to Indian women is a central pattern of contemporary production chains. So when the humanitarian rescue industry operates along the same lines as transnational corporations and shifts jobs to South Asian women, why should we assume this is an emancipatory move free of globalized patterns of exploitation? Henry takes seriously the possibility that there is no geopolitical shift toward counter-hegemony going on here, nor any significant trend toward gender empowerment. However, Henry does not simply return us to a totalizing critique of neoliberal globalization or imperialist humanitarianism. Her nuanced reading of films, news reports, and the efforts of women soldiers and police officers, along with her analysis of mobilizations and subjectivities of women "aid recipients" in Liberia and Haiti, reveals that new subjects of gendered power and struggle are indeed emerging. In this light, we can imagine possible intersections that can challenge the hierarchies that militarized humanitarianism is now fostering under the guise of "global sisterhood" and "global-south emergence."

Paul Higate's analysis interrogates the revival of colonial notions of "martial race" and the production of novel, global forms of "militarized masculinity" in and around the mercenary sector (a.k.a. the "private security contractor" sector or "private military company" sector). Many books and articles have traced the increasing roles played by mercenary firms, such as the company formerly known as Blackwater, in the context of Iraq and Afghanistan wars and occupations (Pelton, 2007; Scahill, 2008). Studies sympathetic to the private security/military sector celebrate their efficiency and flexibility, while critics underline their propensity to feed into war profiteering, participating in protection racketeering, and generating violence against civilians in a climate of economic deregulation and juridical impunity. These transnational mercenary firms are highly likely to be viewed with suspicion if not loathing by civilian populations as well as by their underpaid and overworked colleagues in the uniformed military. This study focuses on the disaster response, pacification operations, and humanitarian interventions deployed by these private security forces, identifying particular national subgroups from Fiji,

Chile, and El Salvador that are overrepresented within the armed personnel of these companies. Complementing, but going in a different direction from Henry's piece above, Higate theorizes how male soldiers from these three countries make an "ethnic bargain," that is, they cash in on colonial or dictatorship-era notions of predatory masculinity and atavistic raciality that in their home countries are banished to a dark past of death squads and repression. But in the global mercenary economy, Higate argues, these abjected, martial, racialized masculinities become valuable currency exchanged for high wages in the private-sector warrior economy. This provocative case study demonstrates that the most anti-democratic forms of "global south to the rescue" are renaturalized, commodified, and rendered globally powerful through the racial and gender logics of the mercenary sector.

Ryerson Christie also highlights forms of ambivalence and the persistence of coloniality in his study of the gendering of Canadian Provincial Reconstruction Teams and the racialized feminization of their supposedly "helpless" aid recipients in Afghanistan. Christie's study maps the liberal logic of intervention and its necessarily gendered grammar, as it inserts local aid recipients into discourses of gendered dependency. Recipients' roles as converted insurgents are represented ideally as passive and controllable when confronted with a Western military occupation that has shifted from a "kinetic" kill-oriented mission to a humanitarian intervention. The shift from kinetic to humanitarian is also understood to incorporate the Western male soldier in a process of feminization. This supposed feminization of the military is represented by counterinsurgency discourse as driven by the agency of global south actors, that is, by the occupied populations themselves. Their voices, languages, needs, and cultural claims are represented as driving and shaping the actions of the PRTs. These humanitarian counterinsurgency teams come to play the nodal role of channeling these southern voices and needs toward counterinsurgency goals and in redirecting the militarized masculinities of occupiers toward development aims that are more culturally appropriate. Christie's analysis provocatively reveals perhaps the most hollowed-out form of "global south to the rescue," where the PRTs wholly stage subaltern agency and stretch fabricated humanitarian doctrines to the breaking point in order to justify the extension of a futile and unpopular occupation.

The *second group* of analyses provides case studies of the growing importance of emergent middle powers that have begun shaping new kinds of internationalism, primarily through interventions concentrated in their own regional or continental context. Through these newly framed and innovatively justified forms of cooperation and intervention, these mid-sized global-south powers have redefined not just humanitarianism, but also shifted patterns of economic and social globalization as well as the norms and identities of transnational religious communities.

Reşat Bayer and Fuat Keyman's study of Turkey profiles that country's increasingly autonomous role in defining peacekeeping, humanitarian intervention, and post-crisis security and development aid in the Mediterranean, Middle East, and Central Asian regions. Ankara's new forms of internationalism and humanitarian leadership have begun to break down what were regarded as irreconcilable antinomies: European integration versus Islamic solidarity, global-south ascendance versus NATO stability, and neo-Ottoman nostalgia versus a commitment to internationalist secular-modernism. This study places in context recent high-profile controversies attached to Turkey's new wave of internationalism and interventionism, including its stand-off with Israel over the blockade of Gaza and the commando raid on Turkish aid boats sent to help Palestinians, and the deal made by Turkey and Brazil to block sanctions against Iran for its nuclear program. Bayer and Keyman's analysis also provides a historical and political framework for analyzing the evolution of newly assertive forms of Turkish humanitarian internationalism through a study of Turkey's participation in recent peacekeeping operations in Afghanistan.

Alice Hills focuses on the cultures and behavior of West African police and peacekeeping officers and thus returns to some of the themes raised in the first set of "practitioner-focused" studies above. But she applies her findings to a broader national-level assessment of the role of Nigeria, a large and increasingly influential regional power. Hills's piece investigates the degree to which Nigerian peacekeeping police forces articulate a global security culture consonant with liberal internationalist norms. Through a careful examination of individual interventions associated with Nigeria's "big brother" role in conflict resolution in the region of West Africa, Hills finds that Nigeria's humanitarian and peacekeeping practices represent a hybrid and ultimately conjunctive fabric woven from four clusters of elements: site-specific pragmatic adaptations, the individual ambitions of rent-seeking leaders, institutional yearnings to accumulate expensive equipment and prestigious training, and state-level tactics aimed at achieving short-term foreign policy objectives. Nigeria's case, Hills argues, underlines the need for scholars and policymakers to look beyond the transnational rescue industry's celebration of liberal-norm globalization and human-security consensus. We must look critically at the notion that there exists a globalizing security culture or humanitarian system of norms and remain very cautious as we examine the possibility that major global-south participation in these interventions will either change this global culture in the long term or invent a new internationalist framework.

Jonathan Agensky and Joshua Barker's in-depth analysis of Indonesia cautiously argues, in contrast to Hills's piece, that emerging regional global-south powers are indeed reshaping dynamic patterns of norm globalization, in more than just short-term or narrowly instrumentalist ways. As depicted here, Indonesia's military, police, and diplomatic elites today are contributing to the erection of new multilateral and ultimately international forms and norms of humanitarianism and peacekeeping. Paradoxically, conflict within and between *illiberal* institutions and organizations (police services, military forces, ethno-religious militant groups, etc.) drive Indonesia's participation in and reconceptualization of the global structure of "liberal peace." Agensky and Barker's analysis places Indonesia's new regional and international assertions into historical context. They review the legacy of the Bandung Conference and Indonesia's role in the rise of Third Worldism in the 1950s (and the revival of Bandung nostalgia in the current moment). Agensky and Barker also examine the relatively success of the Association of South-East Asian Nations in peacekeeping activities during the late-twentieth century. And they trace the rise of entrepreneurialism and transnational circulation of Indonesian police and military forces since the Asian financial crisis of 1997.

Jan Bachmann offers a groundbreaking study of Kenya which is, like Indonesia, an emerging regional power with increasing international visibility. As in the Indonesia case, this analysis explores how the push and pull of the more illiberal tendencies of globalization animate participation in regional peacekeeping and counterterrorism operations. Bachmann's methodology carefully mixes an economic and political geography of Kenyan political elites with a history of Kenya's position as a hub of globalization and of violent cross-border trade and exchange. In this context, "globalization" is described not primarily as a means for disseminating a system of normative and international-law constraints that limit or inform national sovereignty. Instead, globalization represents structures of opportunity within which postcolonial polities position themselves to consolidate "stateness" and some form of sovereignty in the contentious global market and hierarchical international arena. And, in this case, this form of stateness is more repressive, economically oligarchic, and less politically liberal (providing military training to Somali youth and using counterterrorism tactics against its own civilians in Kenya, for example) precisely because of the state's insertion into humanitarian and peacekeeping interventions. Bachmann's study of Kenya reminds us that the ascendance of global-south agency in the transnational rescue industry and the global humanitarian order may render Third World states more powerful, but does not necessarily take us any farther down the road toward the democratization of global governance.

The *third group* of contributions gathered here takes us to three emergent or re-emergent internationalist powers: the "Bolivarian Bloc" (consisting primarily of Venezuela, Cuba, Ecuador, Nicaragua, and Bolivia), Brazil, and Egypt. These new or renewed internationalists claim, explicitly, to be in the business of generating new, counter-hegemonic frameworks for humanitarian militarism and international order. Research presented in each of these studies assesses these claims carefully and sets them into historical and institutional context, drawing upon in-depth familiarity with military cultures, diplomatic histories, and globalization patterns that inform these emergent forms of assertiveness.

Thomas Muhr's study explores the attempts of the Bolivarian Alliance for the Peoples of Our Americas (ALBA) to generate a military wing that espouses a radical form of humanitarian interventionist ideology. Until now, ALBA has served primarily as an economic and ideological grouping that aims to channel profits from Venezuelan oil sales toward social projects in politically sympathetic countries. As Muhr argues, the new aims of ALBA on the humanitarian-peacekeeping front are not to simply enlarge or refine international missions so that the group can provide more durable peace or more effective disaster relief. Instead, ALBA's aim is to fundamentally transform the notion of humanitarian internationalism so that it aims for long-term, emancipatory structural transformation. Standing against the paternalistic, self-serving, and dependency-producing notions of protection and aid fostered by the transnational rescue industry's liberal-imperialist agenda, ALBA advocates a new humanitarian internationalism based on assuring economic and social rights for all and constructing a New International Economic Order. ALBA sees the ultimate source of conflict and humanitarian disaster as the acute poverty caused by "totalitarian" forms of capitalist globalization.

Although often identified with the leftist-populist "Pink Wave" that has swept Latin America since the late 1990s, Brazil has committed to vastly expanded roles in global humanitarian operations and peacekeeping missions that are quite distinct from those proposed by ALBA. Brazil's new internationalist practices and doctrines reflect, in part, the legacies of the military dictatorship of the 1960s and 1970s as well as the older embedded "imperialist" economic interests that derive from its historic connections to other former Portuguese colonies in Africa and the East Indies. Alejandro Nieto's detailed study takes us inside the diplomatic and commercial negotiations, political-institutional bargains, and strategic compromises that have driven Brazil's highly visible roles in peacekeeping in East Timor and in humanitarian aid and pacification in Haiti, where Brazil led the UN military operations between 2004 and 2011. In order to set these missions in context, Nieto reviews the country's Imperialist Period, which began when the Brazilian Empire became independent of Portugal in 1822 and extended through the first decades of the plantation-centered republic until the 1930s. Nieto then notes the transformations that occurred (and the continuities that persisted) as expansionist imperial culture adapted to the socialist-statism of the Estado Novo, participated in Allied expeditions during World War II, and exerted repressive power during the military dictatorship at home from 1964–1985. In this historical light, Nieto offers a more cautious reading of Brazil's participation in contemporary peacekeeping missions and ambition to become a permanent member on the Security Council. Although recognizing the importance of history, Nieto insists that the mix of new nationalism and revived interests in expansionism and interventionism that characterize Brazil's participation in humanitarian missions cannot be understood as merely an echo of the past. Driven by new domestic and transnational social movements that challenge imperialist legacies and the military's participation in politics, and endowed with a strong sense of solidarity with developing countries' dilemmas (particularly those of Africa and the black nations of the West Indies), Brazil promises to play a truly transformative role, advocating new forms of globalization and interventionism in the years ahead.

In the final contribution in this collection, we turn to Egypt, which moved to the center of concerns about the social impact of globalization and the role of the military in "rescuing" civilian populations from severe repression during the mass uprisings, the Tahrir Square demonstrations, and the frustrated revolution of 2011. Paul Amar's analysis provides a detailed history of the rise and fall (and, perhaps, rise again) of forms of "Egyptian Globalism" that have thrived at the intersection of military institutions, cosmopolitan legalist cultures, and social movements backing broader processes of decolonization and "Third Worldist" non-alignment. This piece reminds the reader that the first UN peacekeeping mission, the UN Emergency Force, was created in Egypt after the Tripartite Agression of 1956 with the explicit aim of enabling decolonization (and preventing the militarized recolonization) of Egypt. Tracing the military history of Egyptian international interventions in Africa, the Arabian Peninsula, the Middle East, and Mediterranean Europe, Amar highlights the moments where Egypt pushed the formation of new norms of Third Worldism, socialism, and Pan-Arabism in the mid-twentieth century, and then of militarized neoliberalism and new forms of humanitarian paternalism in the late-twentieth and early-twenty-first centuries. Amar also examines the post-Camp David, pre-2011 Revolution period during which Egypt's militarized humanitarianism turned inward, as its armed forces focused on entrepreneurial and development activities at home. During that period, Egyptian Globalism continued to thrive and shape world politics through the agency of assertive UN-system leaders from Egypt. By recovering these histories, and tracing the contentious politics between developmentalism and internationalism in and around the armed forces, the findings presented here reveal the origins of the Egyptian military's oligarchical economic self-interest and, thus, the institutional cultures driving its severely repressive actions against anti-corruption and pro-democracy protesters. But on a more optimistic note, this study also provides insights into the country's capacity to generate powerful, transnationally linked humanitarian and human-rights movements and alternative normative regimes that could, perhaps, push significant sections of the military and diplomatic elites in new directions in the years to come.

Acknowledgements

I am grateful to Bristol University's Department of Politics and Global Insecurities Center and particularly to Professor Terrell Carver for supporting my work and for hosting the ground-breaking workshop in May 2009 where most of these contributors gathered to share drafts and where we founded this collaborative network. I would also like to thank the University of California, Santa Barbara's Global & International Studies Program and the Institute for Social and Behavioral Research for support that enabled the completion of this collection, and Professors Richard Falk and Hilal Elver for their generous input. Finally, I would like to thank Tess Popper for her superb work as a research assistant and for her skill and patience in copyediting and formatting.

References

Abrahamsen, R. & Williams, M. C. (2010) *Security Beyond the State: Security Privatization and International Politics* (Cambridge: Cambridge University Press).

Acharya, A. (2004) How ideas spread: Whose norms matter? Norm localization and institutional change in Asian regionalism, *International Organization*, 58(2), pp. 239–275.

Ackerly, B. & True, J. (2008) An intersectional analysis of international relations: recasting the discipline, *Politics and Gender*, 4(1), pp. 156–173.

Adamson, F. B. (2005) Global liberalism versus political Islam: competing ideological frameworks in international politics 1, *International Studies Review*, 7(4), pp. 547–569.

Aksar, Y. (2004) *Implementing International Humanitarian Law* (London: Psychology Press).

Al Attar, M. & Miller, R. (2010) Towards an emancipatory international law: the Bolivarian reconstruction, *Third World Quarterly*, 31(3), pp. 347–363.

Ayoob, M. (1995) *The Third World Security Predicament: Statemaking, Regional Conflict, and the International System* (Boulder, CO: Lynne Rienner).

Barkawi, T. & Laffey, M. (2006) The postcolonial moment in security studies, *Review of International Studies*, 32(2), pp. 329–352.

Barnett, M. (2005) Humanitarianism transformed, *Perspectives on Politics*, 3(4), pp. 723–740.

Bilgin, P. & Morton, A. D. (2002) Historicising representations of 'failed states': beyond the Cold War annexation of the social sciences? *Third World Quarterly*, 23(1), pp. 55–80.

Bøås, M. & Jennings, K. (2007) 'Failed states' and 'state failure': threats or opportunities? *Globalizations*, 4(4), pp. 475–485.

Brown, C. L. (2006) *Moral Capital: Foundations of British Abolitionism* (Chapell Hill, NC: University of North Carolina Press).

Carey, H. F. (2001) 'Women and peace and security': the politics of implementing gender sensitivity norms in peacekeeping, *International Peacekeeping*, 8(2), pp. 49–68.

Chandler, D. (2004) The responsibility to protect? Imposing the 'liberal peace', *International Peacekeeping*, 8(1), pp. 1–19.

Charbonneau, L. (2011) Russia, China resist UN sanctions push: envoy, 26 August. http://www.reuters.com/article/2011/08/26/us-syria-un-idUSTRE77P4X920110826.

Childress, S. (2011), Brazil may aid in Eurozone crisis, 28 October. http://www.globalpost.com/dispatches/globalpost-blogs/que-pasa/brazil-may-aid-euro-zone-crisis.

Chesterman, S. (2005) *You, the People: The United Nations, Transitional Administration, and State-Building* (New York: Oxford University Press).

Cohn, C. (2008) Mainstreaming gender in UN security policy: a path to political transformation, in S. M. Rai & G. Waylen (eds.) *Global Governance: Feminist Perspectives* (New York: Palgrave Macmillan), pp. 185–206.

Dillon, M. & Reid, J. (2000) Global governance, liberal peace, and complex emergency, *Alternatives*, 25(1), pp. 117–143.

Dillon, M. & Reid, J. (2001) Global liberal governance: biopolitics, security and war, *Millennium: Journal of International Studies*, 30(1), pp. 41–66.

Doty, R. L. (1996) *Imperial Encounters: The Politics of Representation in North-South Relations* (Minneapolis: University of Minnesota Press).

Duffield, M. (2001) *Global Governance and the New Wars: The Merging of Development and Security* (London: Zed).

Duffield, M. (2007) *Development, Security and Unending War: Governing the World of Peoples* (Cambridge: Polity).

Enloe, C. (2004) *The Curious Feminist: searching for women in a new age of empire* (Berkeley, CA: University of California Press).

Esmeir, S. (2007) The Violence of Non-Violence: Law and War in Iraq, *Journal of Law and Society*, 34(1), pp. 99–115.

Falk, R. (1995) *On Humane Governance: Towards a New Global Politics* (University Park, PA: Pennsylvania State University Press).

Falk, R. (1999) *Predatory Globalization: A Critique* (Cambridge: Polity Press).

Falk, R. (2011), Libya after Gaddafi: A dangerous precedent. AL-Jazeera, 22 October. http://www.responsibilitytoprotect.org/index.php/component/content/article/35-r2pcs-topics/3723-richard-falk-libya-after-gaddafi-a-dangerous-precedent.

Fearon, J. D. & Laitin, D. D. (2004) Neotrusteeship and the problem of weak states, *International Security*, 28(4), pp. 5–43.

Fox, G. (2008) *Humanitarian Occupation* (Cambridge: Cambridge University Press).

Gill, S. (2008) *Power and Resistance in the New World Order*, 2nd ed. (New York: Palgrave/Macmillan).
Harvey, D. (2003) *The New Imperialism* (Oxford: Oxford University Press).
Hehir, A. (2008) *Humanitarian Intervention after Kosovo* (Hampshire, UK: Palgrave and Macmillan).
Higate, P. & Henry, M. (2009) *Insecure Spaces: Peacekeeping, Power and Performance in Kosovo, Liberia and Haiti* (London: Zed Press).
Hitchens, C et al. (2008) *Christopher Hitchens and his Critics: Terror, Iraq and the Left* (New York, NY: New York University Press).
Ignatieff, M. (2003) The Burden, *New York Times*, 5 January.
Jones, S. (2008) *Counterinsurgency in Afghanistan* (Santa Monica, CA: RAND).
Joshi, S. (2011) "Libya could be the last place where the West is allowed to intervene", *Telegraph*, 1 September.
Joordan, E. (2003) The concept of a middle power in international relations: distinguishing between emerging and traditional middle powers, *Politikon: South African Journal of Political Studies*, 30(2), pp. 165–181.
Kaldor, M. (2007) Human Security: reflections on globalization and intervention, (Malden, MA: Polity Press).
Korany, B. (1994) End of history, or its continuation and accentuation? The global South and the 'new transformation' literature, Third World Quarterly, 15(1), pp. 7–15.
Krasner, S. D. (2004) Sharing sovereignty: new institutions for collapsed and failing states, *International Security*, 29(2), pp. 85–120.
Lidén, K. (2009) Building peace between global and local politics: the cosmopolitical ethics of liberal peacebuilding, *International Peacekeeping*, 16(5), pp. 616–634.
Lidén, K., MacGinty, R. & Richmond, O. P. (2009) Introduction: beyond Northern epistemologies of peace: peacebuilding reconstructed? *International Peacekeeping*, 16(5), pp. 587–598.
Mamdani, M. (2010) *Saviors and Survivors: Darfur, Politics and the War on Terror* (New York: Random House).
Mamdani, M. (2011) Responsibility to protect or right to punish? in P. Cunliffe (ed.) *Critical Perspectives on the Responsibility to Protect: Interrogating Theory and Practice* (London: Routledge).
Mandel, R. (2002) *Armies Without States: the Privatization of Security* (Boulder, CO: Lynne Rienner Publishers).
Nederveen Pieterse, J. (2004) *Globalization or Empire?* (London: Psychology Press).
Nederveen Pieterse, J. (2011) Global Rebalancing: Crisis and the East-South Turn, *Development and Change*, 42(1), pp. 22–48.
Orford, A. (1999) Muscular humanitarianism: reading the narratives of the new interventionism, *European Journal of International Law*, 10(4), pp. 679–711.
Orford, A. (2003) *Reading Humanitarian Intervention: Human Rights and the Use of Force in International Law* (Cambridge: Cambridge University Press).
Orford, A. (2011) *International Authority and the Responsibility to Protect* (Cambridge: Cambridge University Press).
Pelton, R. Y. (2007) *Licensed to Kill: Hired Guns in the War on Terror* (New York, NY: Broadway Books).
Politics & Polity (2011), Libya presents a test case for humanitarian intervention, 4 April. http://www.northbynorthwestern.com/story/libya-presents-test-case-for-humanitarian-interven/.
Pouligny, B. (2005) Civil society and post-conflict peacebuilding: ambiguities of international programmes aimed at building 'new' societies, *Security Dialogue*, 36(4), pp. 495–510.
Pupavac, V. (2005) Human security and the rise of therapeutic governance, *Conflict, Development and Security*, 5(2), pp. 161–182.
Rachman, G. (2011) "Libya, a last hurrah for the west?" *Financial Times*, 28 March.
Razack, S. (2004) *Dark Threats and White Knights: The Somalia Affair, Peacekeeping and the New Imperialism* (Toronto: University of Toronto Press).
Reuters (2011), Political Stalemate after China's EU aid offer, 11 November. http://www.cnbc.com/id/45253119/Political_Stalemate_After_China_s_EU_Aid_Offer_Sources.
Rodogno, D. (2011) *Against Massacre: Humanitarian Interventions in the Ottoman Empire 1815-1914* (Princeton: Princeton University Press).
Rosenau, W. (2009) *Corporations and Counterinsurgency* (Santa Monica, CA: RAND).
RT News (2011). Rebels might redraw Libya's oil contracts, 23 August 2011. http://rt.com/news/oil-contracts-libya-russia-645/.
Santos, B. D. S. & Rodríguez-Garavito, C. A. (2005) B.D.S. Santos & C.A. Rodríguez-Garavito (eds.), *Law and Globalization from Below* (Cambridge: Cambridge University Press).
Scahill, J. (2008) *Blackwater: The Rise of the World's Most Powerful Mercenary Army* (New York, NY: Nation Books).
Shepherd, L. (ed.) (2010) *Gender matters in global politics: a feminist introduction to international relations* (London: Taylor & Francis).

UN News Centre (2011) Libya: Ban welcomes Security Council authorization of measures to protect civilians. http://www.un.org/apps/news/story.asp?NewsID=37809&Cr=libya&Cr1. 18 March.

Whitworth, S. (2004) *Men, Militarism and UN Peacekeeping: A Gendered Analysis* (Boulder, CO: Lynne Rienner Publishers).

Paul Amar, Associate Professor in the Global & International Studies Program at the University of California, Santa Barbara, specializes in international security studies, political sociology, global ethnography, theories of the state, and theories of gender, race, and postcolonial politics. His research, publishing and teaching focuses on the areas of state institutions, security regimes, social movements, and democratic transitions in the Middle East and Latin America, and traces the global/local origins and intersections of new patterns of police militarization, security governance, humanitarian intervention, and state restructuring in the megacities of the global south.

Peacexploitation? Interrogating Labor Hierarchies and Global Sisterhood Among Indian and Uruguayan Female Peacekeepers?

MARSHA HENRY

London School of Economics, UK

ABSTRACT *As a result of UNSCR 1325, the UN has been eager to decrease incidents of sexual exploitation and abuse in peacekeeping operations, improve local women's security, and balance out the number of women and men in the police and military at both local and international levels. As peacekeeping missions begin to include more female peacekeepers, questions are raised about what this means for women in national militaries, local women in peacekeeping missions, and soldiers or militarized laborers from the 'developing' world. While countries such as Uruguay have been sending increasing numbers of female peacekeepers to various UN missions, it was not until 2007 that an all-female contingent was first deployed from India to Liberia and hailed as a gendered success. But in altering the gendered landscape, will the UN merely continue to exploit the cheap military labor of the global South? Will countries like India and Uruguay (major troop-contributing countries to UN peacekeeping operations) continue to bear the burden of providing security? This article examines the limits of a conventional interest in gender and gender relations in thinking about peacekeepers and advocates for an intersectional approach to the issue of female peacekeepers, importantly including the role of geography (and therefore 'race', empire and colonialism) in the thinking through the social, cultural, and political effects of peacekeeping deployments.*

Introduction

Multiple axes of power—among them gender, class, race, postcoloniality, and media visibility—intersect around the figures of militarized labor deployed in peacekeeping missions by the emergent powers of the global South. Thus, it is critical that scholarship consider both the politics of gender as well as the geography of global class and racial formations in thinking about the peacekeeping industry and its primary laborers. In Liberia and Haiti, female peacekeepers are providing an important form of outsourced labor which carries additional significance in relation to gender initiatives. That is, their embodiment as women and the cachet this may hold in terms of their international reputation can be seen as resource for themselves and the UN. As such, their unique presence as females within a male-dominated institution means that their signification within the UN's discursive public relations regime is different than that of their male counterparts. But is their labor contribution evidence of a gendered success or of globalized exploitation?

In this article, I explore peacekeeping as a project inserted within the international division of labor and propelled by the dynamics of middle-class aspirations and mobility in the postcolonial world, rather than as simply a benign response to global conflict. Peacekeeping has previously been conceptualized as central to the liberal peace agenda or as a civilizing mission (Duffield, 2001; Paris, 2001; Pugh, 2004; Razack, 2004). In this frame, uniformed as well as non-governmental or missionary sectors of the 'rescue industry' are seen through a common lens—as instrumentalizing the figure of 'global South women' as they construct objects and vehicles for legitimate intervention and designate those who are able to be the rescuers and those in need of rescue (Agustin, 2007; Amar, 2012). Thus, the gendered figure of humanitarian rescuer becomes central to today's rearticulation of global power relations, captured by UN peacekeeping discourses and practices. I propose that considering the intersectional, complex, and multiple aspects of power relations is essential for unpacking the ways in which power is manifested in discourse and provides for a more comprehensive and critical examination of the deployment of female peacekeepers from the global South.

The discussion above is considered in relation to a number of 'gender' developments set out by the United Nations (UN) since 1999. For example, the UN passed Resolution 1325 in 1999, which established a plan for gender mainstreaming and suggested improvements within the organization of the UN and post-conflict settings more generally, addressing a number of issues mostly relating to women and girls in peacekeeping missions (Carey, 2001; Cohn et al., 2004; Henry, 2007; Shepherd, 2008). The Resolution proposed that the UN should increase the number of women in peacekeeping roles, especially those at the top of the military and civil administrative command structures (Olsson, 2000). Subsequently, the UN and some troop-contributing countries introduced gender sensitivity training pre- and post-deployment, attempted to increase the number of women in military and civilian police ranks eligible for mission work, and appointed gender representatives in every unit possible within a Peace Support Operation (PSO) (Mazurana, 2003; Stiehm, 2001).

Although the Resolution was set out in 1999 (passed in 2000), state responses have been somewhat slow to develop and take on board the call to take gender seriously in post-conflict contexts (Cohn, 2008; Puechguirbal, 2010; Willet, 2010). There has been a steady response by many countries that have contributed female peacekeepers both in larger numbers than previously (India, Uruguay, South Africa) as well as at more senior ranks (Canada, Sweden, the Netherlands). However, one interesting and unique response to 1325 came in early 2007. India, one of the UN's largest troop contributors, deployed a 100-plus strong unit of female militarized police to the UN Mission in Liberia (UNMIL) (Beri, 2008). Although female peacekeepers have been playing an important role in peacekeeping operations over many years (De Groot, 2001; Fox, 2001; Haaland, 2008; Harris and Goldsmith, 2010; Karame, 2001; Mazurana, 2003; Olsson, 2000), this effort was the first of its kind on such a scale, and both India and the

UN promoted the deployment as unprecedented and potentially transformative.[1] It is not entirely evident what precipitated the decision by India to establish the all-female unit (Beri, 2008), but it is clear that the UN was hopeful that the deployment, along with other gender-mainstreaming initiatives (Barnes, 2006; Bridges and Horsfall, 2009), would positively alter the conditions for local girls and women as a direct consequence of numerous reports of sexual exploitation and abuse (SEA) by male peacekeepers in a number of PSOs (Higate, 2004; Martin, 2005) and encourage local women to join the national police service within Liberia.[2] In any event, the UN's reputation would have been uplifted by this measure in light of media accounts of peacekeeping misconduct and ineffectiveness which have dominated peacekeeping news since at least 2003 (Higate, 2004, 2007; Higate and Henry, 2009; Jennings, 2010; see also Whitworth, 2004 for discussion on historical legacies in Cambodia).

In June 2007, the British Broadcasting Corporation (BBC) aired a short documentary, which followed the first rotation of the all-female unit in Liberia. The 30-minute film, entitled *Girl Squad*, provides some background to the women's training, their everyday activities, and explores some of the individual peacekeeper's experiences of being deployed to a UN mission. In both the academic and popular literature, little is known about the impact and effectiveness of such deployments, partly because gender-mainstreaming initiatives are so recent and the numbers of women in military and police postings with the UN is still relatively low (Bridges and Horsfall, 2009; Simić, 2010). Importantly, this documentary is one of the few sources of data on this unique group of peacekeepers and some of their experiences. As such, it is crucial that the documentary be critically examined in order to gain some insight into Indian women peacekeeper's accounts as well as to interrogate the ways in which these female peacekeepers, and their experiences as gendered subjects, may be represented (or misrepresented) in popular form. The close reading of the film reveals contradictory narratives of gender at work that suggest that female peacekeepers are both different from, *and* the same as, their male counterparts. This is illustrated in the film through narration, the accounts of the individual officers interviewed, and the choice of different representational images of Indian women peacekeepers pre- and post-deployment.

I use the example of the Indian women peacekeepers, and their particular depiction within the documentary film, in comparison to another group of female peacekeepers who have generally been absent from studies or popular accounts of female peacekeepers. While multiple militaries from Asia and Africa have been steadily sending more women police into the peacekeeping field, Latin American militaries have been rapidly incorporating women into their militaries, although not in the grand gesturing style of recent all-female contingents, and these women are being deployed to peacekeeping missions as their national militaries have an increasing presence in the peacekeeping scene (Donadio, 2008). Thus, the second example introduced later in the article utilizes data obtained during a study conducted with a group of female peacekeepers from Uruguay who were stationed in the UN mission in Haiti (MINUSTAH) in 2006. The aim of this study was to explore the gendered experiences of a small group of women peacekeepers, deployed within a conventional male-dominated military battalion posted to international duty. In the article, I juxtapose the two cases, despite their significant methodological difference and history, as exemplar catalysts for raising questions and building a critique of gendered *and* racialized assumptions embedded in policies for promoting the participation of female peacekeepers. Both non-parallel examples serve as illustrations of some of the difficulties that arise in gender equality and mainstreaming initiatives, which implicitly view the inclusion of women in male-dominated institutional practices as adequate measures to address 'gender' problems. The power of comparing these two accounts lies in the way in which different narratives by female peacekeepers reveal similarly contradictory expectations of gender in male-dominated institutions such as the military and police, as well as the ways in which notions of sisterhood are both rejected and strengthened by different groups of women from the global South. Thus, what both examples do is suggest a theoretical and practical need to meticulously examine the presence of other axes of power such as class, 'race', and nationality in thinking about the purpose and effectiveness of female peacekeepers in peacekeeping contexts.

Who Ya Gonna Call? Global South Military Labor and UN Peace Support Operations

Where does the UN go when it needs troops to deploy to peacekeeping missions? Despite the visibility of Northern Security Council powers (US, Russia, China, France, UK) in deliberations about international military–humanitarian deployments, it is the countries of the global South that contribute the most troops to UN Peace Support Operations around the world. Currently, the top suppliers are South Asia, notably India (8,757), Pakistan (10,764), Bangladesh (10,427), Nepal (4,311) and Sri Lanka (1,070), despite ongoing civil unrest, longstanding border disputes and the presence of UN missions within these countries themselves.[3] As the second largest military in the world, India has consistently ranked in the top three of the most troops contributed to missions in any one year. Influenced during the colonial and postcolonial period by British models, the current Indian Army is highly professionalized and generally well-equipped and thus an 'ideal' troop contributor (Cohen, 1990; Kundu, 1998; Rosen, 1996). India's domination of outsourcing in other industries due to English proficiency and experience with the West because of its colonial past contributes to its growing power and place in the world economy. Yet, India's military spending power cannot adequately be compared to a country such as the US. However, India, alongside its South Asian neighbors, has a distinct advantage in that it has a readily available surplus military labor supply. Having one of the largest armed forces in the world with over 1 million soldiers registered as active, India has the ability to deploy numerous contingents to PSOs in need of 'boots on the ground'. Currently, on average about 10,000 soldiers are supplied for various peacekeeping missions (most of which are situated in the global South). However, the colonial legacies of British rule are still manifested in the representation of ethnic and caste minorities within the Indian military today with a majority of those from Hindu and 'martial races' background (Sikhs) being recruited from northern states and Muslims still remaining marginal within the institution (Cohen, 1969; Enloe, 1980; Khalidi, 2001; Kundu, 1994). Thus, the contemporary Indian military has embedded within the institution its own hierarchical structure, galvanizing those who are middle class and upper caste to occupy senior positions while those who do the bulk of the manual soldiering are those in class and caste positions with more scope for upward mobility.

This is on par with contributions made by other 'developing' countries such as Pakistan, Bangladesh, and Nigeria. Similarly, Ghana, Rwanda, Jordan, and Uruguay contribute over 3,000 on average, placing them high on the list of major troop contributors. In contrast, most Western nations renowned for peacekeeping duty such as Canada, Norway, and the Netherlands contribute fewer than 2,000 troops in total per year. Interestingly, countries in the global South with a history of military dictatorships have now remade themselves as quintessential peacekeeping nations—these include countries from the Southern Cone such as Chile, Argentina, and Uruguay (but also Brazil and Peru). Uruguay, often known as the Switzerland of Latin America because of its considerable banking industry and welfare policies, has channeled its once 'notorious' military into a professional peacekeeping force with significant postings in the Democratic Republic of Congo (DRC) and Haiti. With a number of economic upheavals in the southern region of South America in the early 2000s, the military has become a much sought after employment opportunity for those squeezed out of the market by the economic downturn in Argentina and neighboring Uruguay. The financial crash of this period has paradoxically provided an opportunity for the military to rebuild itself with renewed purpose: that of international humanitarian duty (see, for related discussions, Marcella, 1994; Sotomayor, 2010). After the fall of various military dictatorships in this area during the 1980s, many governments were keen to decrease the power of military institutions and their subsequently negative image in the minds of the general public and thus began directing military labor towards peacekeeping activities. Despite being the smallest country in the region, Uruguay makes the highest contribution of troops from the southern region of South America. Unlike Brazil, one of the largest 'middle-powers' in the region, Uruguay's less visible racial and patriarchal history has meant that gender and race have not been seen as significant in recruitment; nevertheless, overall patterns demonstrate that both women and minorities (such as Afro-descendant and Indigenous peoples) are marginalized within the general workforce (Bucheli and Porzecanski, 2008; Instituto Nacional de Estadística, 1998; Lewis, 2003; Rodriguez, 2003). Despite their own racialized and differentiated genealogies, 'developing' countries' militaries are making the central and essential labor contribution to the UN's peacekeeping operations.

However, there is a disproportionate amount of value given for different activities within the peacekeeping industry (Krishnasamy, 2001). While the US contributes small numbers of troops for UN peacekeeping duty, their financial contribution to peacekeeping is among the highest of the members of the Security Council. Thus, there is a marked division between those countries that make substantial financial contributions and those that contribute in the form of labor. In analyzing India's contribution to international peacekeeping, Krishnasamy suggests there are a number of motivating factors in making such impressive labor contributions, namely the hope that India will eventually receive recognition in the form of a permanent Security Council seat (2001). To date, this has not happened for any of the major troop contributors. According to Krishnasamy, another motivation is the hope that India's reputation as a major player within peace support operations may result in more appointments of senior Indian military figures to commanding posts in missions. There has been some success on this front in the previous mission in Rwanda and in the recent mission to the DRC (2001). However, recognition has not translated into important appointments within the Department of Peacekeeping Operations itself, and there has been criticism leveled at the lack of transparency in UN recruitment strategies and procedures (Krishnasamy, 2001). India, along with other 'developing' countries, has argued that the UN's appointment system still favors and rewards representatives from Western nations.

Like India, Uruguay has had ambitions for a more active role in international governance. As one of the original members of the UN, the country has sought to reverse its tarnished image from the 1970s and early 1980s when much of the Southern Cone was under military dictatorships (Aguero, 1998; Loveman, 1994; Pion-Berlin, 1992). Uruguay as an emerging or transitional democracy, has refashioned its military from a weapon of the regime to a more civic-minded and philanthropic outfit. This has partially been about democratizing previous authoritarian institutions and remodeling national images. However, it is not just image that Uruguay and other Southern Cone countries have been concerned with, but rather corporate and economic gains. Acquiring up-to-date technology paid for by the UN has been an additional benefit for countries with small armies such as Uruguay (Peláez, 2007; Ulery, 2005). With a decrease in support for the military following the military dictatorships, as well as more recent left-wing political governments within the region, the prospects for acquiring new weapons and equipment would otherwise be limited. Because the UN reimburses troop-contributing countries for related military equipment, the Uruguayan forces are in a position to acquire new items, thus replacing old and outdated machinery and enabling them to maintain a professional and technologically advanced force (Ross, 2004).

In addition, although many countries are motivated to participate in peacekeeping operations for financial gain, individual peacekeeper's salaries may vary from country to country. For example, it is estimated that most Indian officers receive in the region of US$1,000–1,500 a month, in addition to their salary, which is about one-third of this amount.[4] Despite the disadvantages of being away from home and family, for most officers a one-year tour may be financially rewarding. This is especially true in the case of Uruguay, where an 'officer receives ten times his [*sic*] usual salary' (Ulery, 2005, p. 60). In 2007, Peláez estimates that Uruguayan peacekeepers earn US$1,000 per month, and possibly up to US$3,000 a month in additional field pay (Peláez, 2007, p. 297). Because of the substantial differences in salary as a result of overseas duty, peacekeeping remittances have increased the economic income of Uruguay both nationally and individually (Peláez, 2007; Ulery, 2005). However, academic and popular accounts suggest that many peacekeepers from 'developing' countries are not always paid their salaries by their national militaries and, worse, are oftentimes ill-equipped (Buillon, 1997; Krishnasamy, 2001). Although the UN supplies much of the equipment used by troops once deployed (such as uniforms), this is not always evident in missions where troops have been known to be under-resourced (Higate and Henry, 2009). Although the UN may have uniform and 'fair' procedures for distributing payments and compensation, it is not within the institution's remit to enforce equality of salary across the troop-contributing countries. Furthermore, there are stark differences between individual military staff (especially between officers and contingent staff). The largest cohort of soldiers, the contingents, are the majority of bodies in the mission, and yet their rank and status means that they often receive the least financial gain from international duty. These differences have not only a great impact on the peacekeepers themselves, but on the local population, too, as they influence the micropolitics of peacekeeping economies. Clearly, Indian peacekeepers, as well as the Indian state and military, benefit from peacekeeping deployments in uneven ways from other military nations such as Canada, Sweden, and the Netherlands. And Uruguayan soldiers may be gaining larger salaries, but often for missions with a much higher security, and therefore, casualty risk (Pouligny, 2006). As such, questions are raised about the labor sourced from the 'developing' world. Is the UN indirectly exploiting the global South, by using its cheaper militarized 'manpower' as a form of security provision? While evidence suggests that the financial burden of peacekeeping is being disproportionately borne by the global North (Khanna et al., 1998), it is worthwhile recognizing other important contributions made by troops in the form of embodied labor. In addition, the process of electing representatives to the Security Council or to the Department of Peacekeeping Operations need to be transparent, providing opportunities for interrogating the power sharing in the UN and examining the global division of labor in regard to peacekeeping body work.

As the nature of peacekeeping has shifted from more neutral practices involving borders and monitoring buffer zones to more complex forms in the aftermath of 'new wars' (Duffield, 2001; Kaldor 1999), different types of peacekeepers have been required. Known more for 'humanitarian' work than 'muscular' peacekeeping, Indian peacekeepers have cultivated a unique reputation for themselves as hard-working and compassionate (Higate and Henry, 2009; Krishnasamy, 2001). They have been commended for their work in a number of missions where they have contributed positively to the social and physical reconstruction of post-conflict regions (Krishnasamy, 2001). Uruguay has also been praised by the UN, for their varied work in Western Sahara right through to recent deployments in Lebanon (Peláez, 2007). Uruguay has been recognized as a credible peacekeeping nation and its peacekeepers have been viewed as highly educated and professionalized (Sotomayor, 2010; Ulery, 2005). Yet both India and Uruguay's embodied commitment to peacekeeping has resulted in casualties, as in Somalia and the DRC, where a number of Uruguayan and Indian peacekeepers were killed in the line of duty (along with peacekeepers from other countries) (Pouligny, 2006).

Despite their positive reputations, there have also been negative accounts of their work. Historically India's involvement in Sri Lanka was viewed as a significant failure of regional peacekeeping, and more recently their conduct has come under scrutiny in the DRC, where there have been accusations of criminal activity and of contributing to local girls' and women's insecurity. A recent BBC exposé found that Indian peacekeepers were implicated in gold and arms smuggling in the DRC.[5] Just prior to this another media investigation was carried out in a number of missions (including Liberia, Haiti, and the DRC) where it was discovered that peacekeepers were involved in SEA.[6] Among the troops allegedly involved in these illicit activities were a handful of Indian peacekeepers. The negative publicity resulted in a campaign by members of the local population to oust Indian peacekeepers from the DRC.[7] Although there was bad press, the UN's reliance on South Asian military labor superseded any possibility of withdrawing large numbers of troops from any of the missions.

Similarly, Uruguayan troops have been at the epicenter of debates about the DRC.[8] First implicated in cases of SEA, Uruguayan peacekeepers also gained a reputation for being passive in face of atrocity (similar to accusations against the Dutch peacekeepers in Srebrenica, see Sion, 2007) or even perpetuating crimes (Marks, 2007). Because of the specific peacekeeping mandates, Uruguayan peacekeepers in militarized zones of the DRC could not engage in combat in order to stop violence and conflict in 2003. Without authorization, Uruguayan peacekeepers appeared ineffectual and perhaps even callous (Roessler and Prendergast, 2006). After the UN altered the mandate in the DRC, French troops were able to enter the DRC and use force to quell various rebel groups. Consequently, the Uruguayan military had a mixed reception within the DRC.[9]

Thus, it is obvious that the UN, India, and Uruguay would welcome initiatives that emphasize the positive side of the armed forces and restore their reputation as quintessential peacekeeping nations. One of the motivating factors for sending an all-female contingent may be directly related to recent reports of SEA in peacekeeping missions (Higate 2004, 2007; Martin, 2005; Zeid 2005). The initiative, on the surface, suggests that India is at the forefront of progressive gender politics, especially when the numbers of women in the Indian military are so low. Yet, the accounts of male peacekeepers involved in corruption, misconduct and SEA may contradict the positive image put forth by other gender-mainstreaming measures which may demonstrate a certain 'progressive' gender thinking. Either way, the accounts of peacekeepers from the global South need to be studied carefully. Accounts of peacekeepers' behavior should be analyzed alongside studies of the politics of ethnicity, 'race' and nationality in the context of international military deployments. In doing so, analysis could include a consideration of the historical legacies of colonialism and the enduring gender stereotypes of particular groups of military men (D'Amico, 1999, 2000; Higate and Henry, 2009; Razack, 2004; Sinha, 1995). For example, Orientalist accounts of South Asian men have long posited them as morally corrupt, sexually predatory, and paradoxically effeminate and weak (Said, 1982). Colonial stereotypes of Latin American men as 'lazy' and inherently macho also play a central role in how Uruguayan peacekeepers might be figured in different accounts (Torres et al., 2002).

Projects of Europeanization and whitening have their own unique histories in South Asia and Latin America, and play an important role in determining contemporary perceptions of Indians and Uruguayans (Minority Group Rights, 1995; Mizutani, 2009; Sinha, 1995; Wade, 1997). As such, both groups of military men are situated within internal and external hierarchies of nationality, ethnicity, class, caste, and 'race' and as such any 'quality' assessment of peacekeepers implicitly based on racial hierarchies needs to be critically interrogated. How can we understand issues of gender inequality, violence, and exploitation without losing sight of the racialization of certain troops, alongside their depiction in colonial and stereotypical ways? Under such conditions, who can be a rescuer and who is in need of rescue?

Prioritizing Gender: Problems and Questions

The BBC documentary *Girl Squad* (2007) provides important insights into some of the experiences of the first contingent of militarized police women deployed to UNMIL.[10] The film opens by showing a group of uniformed Indian women, participating in their daily routines on their training base in Delhi. They are filmed doing a number of soldierly duties, such as a taking part in the routine fitness and exercise regime and practicing using heavy weaponry at a firing range. According to the narrator of the film, the women chosen for duty in Liberia have been handpicked and have spent three months preparing for their overseas deployment. The women, who are members of the Central Defense Forces, are militarized police officers (also known as a rapid action force) and have experience in riot and crowd control. Centrally featured in the film, Seema Dhundia, the contingent commander, states that the women selected have had extensive martial experience in insurgency areas and are adept sportsmen [*sic*] who have basic communication skills—making them ideal for peacekeeping work. Dhundia also claims that women are the 'best option' for the post-conflict scenario because they are 'by nature caring, tender' and can therefore implement peacekeeping mandates. She says that when these women put on their uniform they are 'empowered' and that 'strength' comes automatically. Another senior officer interviewed about the suitability of women soldiers, Poonam Gupta, the chief operations officer, claims that the 'female has less distraction, apart from family', whereas 'men can have many distractions: liquor, women, all sorts of things'. In praising women's unique qualities she finds that 'women are more disciplined, more task-oriented and more dedicated' in comparison to men. In capturing these senior officers' opinions, the film also provides some context to these officers' family backgrounds. Seema is shown collecting her two children from school and preparing a meal for them while discussing her upcoming tour of duty. It is revealed that Seema's husband, who is also in the forces, will take care of them while she is away. Her daughter and son tell the camera that they do not want their mother to leave, and Seema seems to understand their feelings but states that she has to 'prepare them' adequately for her absence. Later in the film, Seema is shown carrying on a chat conversation over the web with her children while in Liberia. When asked about her feelings, she states that she does get 'emotional' when she thinks about her children, but that 'it isn't very good for police to get emotional'. Similarly, Poonam, an unmarried officer, is shown with her family before her departure. The film captures her having dinner with her parents, her sister, and her sister's children. The family is shown performing a religious ceremony, where collective worship is centered on Poonam's impending journey to Liberia. When her family is consulted about her abilities and their feelings, her sister characterizes Poonam as a hard worker who is emotionally very strong. Poonam responds to her sister's comments by stating that although she is anxious about the security situation in Liberia, she is 'ready to die' because after all, '[she's a] soldier'.

The first half of the documentary already raises a number of issues. As Segal argues, 'the social construction of gender, the importance attached to gender differences and cultural interpretations of gender has considerable implications for the inclusion and participation of women in the military' (Segal, 1995, p. 770). On the one hand, the film emphasizes the physical robustness and sophistication of the officers' militarized training. The footage of the women's physical prowess demonstrates that not only have they achieved parity with their male peers as far as bodily competence, but they have surpassed conventional military standards by becoming skilled beyond that of a regular police officer. As the narrator in the film states, with their advanced weapons training they are part of an 'elite' squad. Similarly, officers Dhundia and Gupta are shown to be disciplined and strict commanders, as footage of them overseeing a series of firing drills and shouting commands conveys their senior and authoritative presence. Yet, the squad can be viewed in a number of different ways. Both Dhundia and Gupta suggest that women are different from men, although they focus on attributes they believe are connected with women and which are useful to peacekeeping situations. The maternalist narratives they rely on propose that women are inherently suited to peace-promoting activities (Ruddick, 1980). To emphasize the idea that women are inherently more peaceful, the officers are shown interacting with their families in the private spaces of their homes. Seema is shown cooking for her children and Poonam expressing affection for her young nephew. As such, both officers are revealed to be emotionally tied to the domestic space as well as kin-bound. In this way they are depicted as 'feminine', despite being in 'masculine' occupations.

Another way in which a distinctive, yet conventional, form of femininity is constructed is in relation to women's historical association with virtue and men's with vice (Davidoff and Hall, 2002; Walkowitz, 1982). The two officers suggest that women are ideal peacekeepers because they are more emotionally skilled and are less likely to be distracted by stereotypical military temptations such as alcohol and prostitution. Although the women are under the same disciplinary regime as their male counterparts would likely be subject to—that is, while on overseas duty they are not allowed to leave the base except to attend church or temple services—there is an assumption, embedded within both the film and wider beliefs by the UN, that there will not be incidents of SEA simply because the peacekeepers are women. (A point left unexplored is whether this disciplinary measure is actually in place to protect women peacekeepers from sexual advances from the local population or other peacekeepers.) In the case of male peacekeepers, it has never been clear whether conduct measures such as restricting freedom of movement is to protect the reputation of the soldiers, or to protect the local population from misconduct that the soldiers might be tempted to engage in as part of military masculinity rituals (Patel and Tripodi, 2007; Whitworth, 2004).

If Boys will be Boys . . .

It is widely known that the presence of mostly male peacekeepers in a mission can have detrimental effects on the local female population (Bridges and Horsfall, 2009; Harrington, 2010; Higate and Henry, 2004; Simic, 2010; Whitworth, 2004). For example, 'peacekeepers have been responsible for rape and sexual assaults on women and children in host nations . . . HIV and AIDS have also presented as major problems, with peacekeepers contracting and passing on the disease from engaging in sexual assault and prostitution' (Bridges and Horsfall, 2009, p. 2). Studies have demonstrated that the introduction of female peacekeepers can have many positive effects, especially on the local population (Carey, 2001; Cockburn and Hubic, 2002). In particular, Bridges and Horsfall argue that 'a more balanced force of males and females on peacekeeping missions could reduce these crimes against women and children, coming closer to providing the environment necessary to meet positive and successful peacekeeping objectives', and furthermore 'increasing female participation will increase the effectiveness of such missions, engendering trust in host nations and decreasing the level of misconduct, and sometimes unlawful behavior, on the part of peacekeeping forces' (2009, pp. 2–3). Thus, the multiple aims of deploying such a group may include a desire to decrease incidents of SEA of local women and girls by peacekeepers and thus increase positive attitudes towards peacekeepers and the UN; encourage local women to join the national police force in order to move towards gender parity; and to provide girls and women who have suffered sexual abuse with women officers and representatives among whom they may feel more comfortable. Furthermore, equal numbers of men and women in peacekeeping units has been noted to have an impact on group cohesion within the military (Bridges and Horsfall, 2009).

Nevertheless, female officers in the military and police still face discrimination and marginalization (Harris and Goldsmith, 2010; Heinecken, 2002; Natarajan, 2008; Strobl, 2008; Valenius, 2007). In written accounts accompanying the airing of the film in June 2007, the female peacekeepers were portrayed by a few journalists in belittling ways. First, the film is problematically titled 'Girl Squad', which trivializes and demeans *women's* contribution to peacekeeping and national military service more generally. Second, in a BBC article promoting the film, one journalist focused on some of the more sensational aspects of the women's deployment. In an interview with Joanna Foster from UNMIL who helped to coordinate the female squad's tour of duty, the journalist quotes the gender advisor who states that 'being pretty is a disadvantage here. Indian women are pretty so they are going to be whistled at and all sorts of things but they will have to take it in their stride.' The journalist then went on to say 'but don't be deceived by the looks. I saw an enthusiastic salute by one of the Indian peacekeepers almost knock a journalist's microphone half-way to Mumbai. Stand back—these women are serious.'[11] The journalist's concluding statement in the article chimes with the sentiments of the film's title. The subject of women in the military seems to be a topic of juvenile amusement. Yet, at the same time as women's contribution might be undermined, gender seems to be a significant concept to be used in promoting the UN's reputation. Ban Ki-Moon recently commented on the all-female squad stating that the:

> Indian civil police unit in Liberia [is] a possible model. I believe that successful initiative serves as an excellent example of the unique contribution that female personnel can make. Through their sheer presence, the members of that Indian contingent are showing Liberian women that they, too, can play a role in law enforcement. We have the numbers to prove it. Since the female Blue Berets were first deployed, there has been a marked increase in the number of women applying for jobs with the Liberian police.[12]

Thus, while on the one hand the presence of female peacekeepers is treated as trivial in some contexts, it gives the UN greater leverage 'in advocating the inclusion of women in national police forces' in another.[13]

The documentary exposes the many contradictions involved in trying to marry the UN idea of gender equality and mainstreaming with the practical deployment of female personnel. The film suggests that women are as militarily capable as men, and yet distinctly different in their gendered disposition and character. The dichotomy implicitly reinforced is between ideas of masculinity and femininity as embedded in 'biology'. Thus, although women can be 'trained' like traditional male soldiers, there are still aspects of their embodied gender 'character' that cannot be 'erased' for the purposes of militarized duty. In fact, these characteristics, that at certain times might generally be considered negative, are made positive as they pertain to the peacekeeping context. Thus, competing ideas about gender are conveyed both in the content of the women's accounts and in the depiction of Indian women peacekeepers in the film.

Aren't all 'Third World' Women the Same?

I suggest that some of the basis for their deployment to Liberia is that there is a popular assumption of shared sisterhood among women from the global South. Although the UN has little choice in the women that they can deploy because of low recruitment numbers overall, perhaps wider social beliefs about commonalities on the basis of gender have enabled a focus on the deployment as an already successful venture. Yet the impact of female peacekeepers is a central concern—if one of the reasons for deploying an all-female unit is to enable better relations between the local civilian population and foreign military staff. But how do the female peacekeepers themselves experience gender and other relations while on duty? As 'third world' women, the Indian officers might be perceived to be predisposed to understand the plight of Liberian women, who face many of the obstacles to well-being that women in most 'developing' countries might face. This is revealed within the second half of the film, which shows the women leaving India, saying goodbye to their families and arriving to a warm reception in West Africa. The peacekeepers are quickly shown participating in a variety of security activities, such as providing close protection for officials such as the president of Liberia, Ellen Johnson-Sirleaf, and 'back-up' for the Liberian national police force. In one scene, Dhundia arrives at a site to check on the women under her command. She consults with them about whether they are feeling alright and whether they have eaten enough and taken their breaks. Engaging in a form of emotional labor (Martin, 1999), Dhundia demonstrates that there is a need to take care of peacekeepers' psychic and physical state, to ensure operational effectiveness and force protection (Higate and Henry, 2009).

However, the emotional labor involved in peacekeeping work does not extend to the relationships cultivated with the local population. Although Dhundia states that the female peacekeepers' presence is intended to reassure the local people that the war is over, the documentary and the women interviewed reveal that there is little direct contact with the local population. As one soldier interviewed suggests, they often think about women in Liberia and wonder how they survive. Despite this curiosity, the female peacekeepers also keep their distance and 'do their jobs'. But why should they 'naturally' gravitate to the local population when their training discourages them from social engagement? The women are trained to a high technical degree and are used to dealing with combative situations that require psychological and physical skills for resolving public conflicts. They have no specific training or knowledge in the history and politics of the Liberian conflict, post-conflict contexts and traumatized individuals more generally, or in training police officers. Why have they been deployed to such a mission, and what is their likely impact? What are the actual benefits of deploying women in a formed unit such as the one established in Liberia (Agordzo, 2009)? Although their presence may pave the way for women's empowerment (Gizelis, 2009) by encouraging Liberian women to join the national police force, their lack of connection with the local people may also hinder possible positive effects.

Further conversations with a few officers reveal that there are significant geopolitical differences between the female officers and women in the local population. One officer shares that she finds Liberia familiar: the climate (tropical) is similar and that food and fruit, like that 'from

India', can be easily sourced. But this seems to be the extent of any connection. When two peacekeepers are asked about their impressions of the local population, they share with the filmmaker that they feel 'embarrassed' by the ways in which Liberian men and women behave in public spaces. The two peacekeepers say that they felt that their 'culture' was better than that of Liberia, because women and men generally did not behave in a 'sexual' manner in public. During this sequence the camera captures a group of Liberian youths standing nearby. Within the group a young woman and man are embracing in public view.

Many of the Indian female peacekeepers briefly shown in the film appear to come from lower-class and caste groups (with the exception of senior officers who are mostly middle class and upper caste) and will have been exposed to a sex-segregated family and work life in India (personal communication, September 2010). The documentary portrays the peacekeepers as 'respectable' and hard-working women who have earned their place in the military through physical strength and mental toughness. The women deployed have their identity as 'respectable' women reinforced through the film, which depicts them in domestic and heteronormative backdrops while Liberian women are shown to be poor, vulnerable, and victimized by both conflict and heteropatriarchy. And while Liberian women clearly face many of the problems conventionally associated with post-conflict societies such as unemployment and homelessness, the film also contributes to a set of constructions where some women are represented as agents of security, 'upstanding' and 'respectable', and another as victims of insecurity, 'fallen' and 'damaged'. Surprisingly the documentary reveals that global class categories feature to reinforce ideas about difference between the peacekeepers and the local women over potential shared understandings and experiences of gender. And as such, questions about geopolitics need to be raised.

Same Difference: Uruguayan Women Peacekeepers' Accounts of Equality and Community Relations

In this section, I introduce general comments by a small group of women interviewed during a fieldwork trip to Haiti in 2006. These accounts, situated alongside the Indian women's portrayal in the film *Girl Squad*, highlight similarities and differences in the way in which women may view themselves vis-à-vis their male colleagues and the local communities that they are posted to help.

The interview cohort consisted of 13 contingent staff and two female officers who were part of one battalion at a base located outside of Port-au-Prince, in the UN mission in Haiti (MINUSTAH). The battalion's main purpose, at the time of research, was to facilitate the election process and to carry out basic surveillance and monitoring duties within the area. This battalion and base had 15 women peacekeepers, which was exceptional among all the military contingents and provided a unique opportunity understand these women's experiences and their potential impact within the mission (Donadio, 2008).

The Uruguayan women relied on similar narratives to their Indian female counterparts in Liberia. Overwhelmingly, this group of women asserted their equality with men in terms of emotional and mental states and treatment by international and national senior military and civilian officials. The women, including the two officers who were trained in medical fields, reiterated that they felt that they were no different to their male colleagues and that they were not treated differently. Importantly, during one focus group, all 13 members of the contingent agreed unanimously that unequal treatment of women did not exist within their military. Despite in-depth probing about gender-based inequalities in workplaces, the women in the study group stated that they did not experience 'everyday' forms of 'prejudice and discrimination' (Maria).[14] Their feeling of equality, they suggested, was mirrored in their home societies where women 'drive taxis and work in construction' (Elena). The women demonstrated that they were given equal tasks to their male colleagues; for example, all soldiers, regardless of rank and gender, had to participate in preparing food for the battalion and thus women soldiers were not 'ghettoized' (Ana). Physical fitness was an important aspect of their daily life, and all peacekeepers were given scheduled times at which it was expected that they would participate in group sport or individual training. Unlike for the Indian officers, physical prowess was not a central component of their previous duties in Uruguay, and as such none of the female soldiers had to acquire 'exceptional' skills in this regard. Because the atmosphere on the base was gender mixed, it might be expected that there was a level of tension between the male and female soldiers. However, sexist jokes and sexual harassment were not common practice within the battalion as one of the officers revealed when discussing social and leisure time in the mess hall. Maria recounted an incident where on a film night in the officers' mess hall the men had catcalled at the screen during a sex scene and that some officers discussed various aspects of their romantic and family lives, but that this sort of behavior and conversation was 'never brought into the office space'. Furthermore, the women did admit that they felt shortchanged when it came to promotions as Cara claimed that 'women soldiers did not move up the ranks as quickly as men' and her own slow progress compared to her colleagues was proof of this type of inequality. These narratives are not uncommon among military women more generally, and issues of integration, assimilation, and conformity have been known to arise in discussions of women's introduction to the forces (Basham, 2008; Kummel, 2002).

There are a number of interesting findings from this small study. Despite the fact that these female peacekeepers had virtually no contact with local women in the mission, they still had formed divergent opinions of, and attitudes towards, local Haitian women. Like their Indian counterparts in Liberia, the female peacekeepers formed opinions not from direct dialogue with local women and men, but from observing social relations in public and everyday contexts. Their duties were strictly limited (as were their male colleagues'), and not having French or Kreyol language skills made the possibility of interacting in a direct manner with local people even more challenging (one or two translators were often available). In contrast to the Indian women in Liberia, who shared linguistic skills of English with locals, these Spanish-speaking peacekeepers were severely limited in their ability to communicate with the local population. However, the female peacekeepers volunteered commentary on Haitian women's general condition, when asked questions about their perceptions about the gendered basis of insecurity in Haiti. But the bulk of their commentary was not framed in regard to expectations of sexual propriety as in the case of Liberia, but more in regard to 'race' and socio-economic positioning.[15]

The issue of 'race' emerged in a unique way. Although Uruguay has a different history of race relations and current attitude towards its indigenous population than most South American nations (Instituto Nacional de Estadística, 1998; Lewis, 2003), the female members of the contingent considered themselves to be Southern women, like Haitian women. One of the contingent staff stated that 'Haitian women are like us—they work hard to support their children' (Maria). Although these soldiers did not identify themselves as black (and there were no ethnically black members of the study group), they also did not identify themselves as 'white' or 'Western'. Rather they saw themselves as economic citizens of the '[global] South' and 'who were not like the wealthy Scandinavian women' who occupied positions of privilege within the civilian administration (Elena). They viewed themselves as being 'better off' than the Haitian women within their locale, but not significantly different in terms of the geopolitics of 'race' and the desire to protect family. In their few observations of women's daily life in Haiti, they saw 'themselves' *in* the local women, but '10–15 years back in time' (Cara). Although their evolutionary language was problematic and could be interpreted as colonialist, they did not share views that judged or depicted Haitian women as victims of a sexually 'immoral' society, as was the case with the Indian female peacekeepers in Liberia who implied that local women were in need of both rescue and re-education. Different ideas about sexuality influenced they ways in which the Uruguayan women perceived Liberian women. Similarly, they showed sympathy for Haitian women's daily struggles to support their families and their confrontation with a 'machismo' culture with which they were all too familiar. In addition, the contingent staff were from similar backgrounds as the Indian contingent staff, that is, from working-class backgrounds where they had 'made good' by finding a respectable and secure form of work.[16] The fixedness of their own class backgrounds may go some way in explaining their partial allegiances with local women; whereas the Indian women who came from predominantly upwardly mobile class backgrounds felt it necessary to construct themselves as very different from Liberian women. In addition, some have argued that racial politics in Uruguay have evolved in somewhat ambiguous ways compared to other countries in Latin America, where processes of whitening and Europeanization were taken on board more forcefully and uncritically (Rodriguez, 2003; Wade, 1997).

The two contexts also reveal that gender-mainstreaming initiatives do not always incorporate critical perspectives on women's and men's 'traditional' roles within institutional cultures such as the police and military, and may even perpetuate problematic understandings of gender. Both examples also illustrate that it is essential to look at other axes besides gender. Clearly the way in which these women might categorize themselves and others in nationality, class, caste, ethnic, and 'race' terms is crucial to understanding the intersectional nature of peacekeeping identities and experiences. It appears that respectability—a key concept for female peacekeepers and local women—not only stems from gender identities, but from the other modes of citizenship in the global South (Berhman et al., 2003). Consequently, after a detailed analysis of the film, I have briefly introduced a few examples from the Uruguayan women peacekeepers' accounts that highlight their own perception of working within the context of Haiti. I do so in order to further denaturalize assumed gendered alliances between women from the global South. Ultimately, using these examples provides an opportunity to question other aspects of peacekeepers' identities.

Conclusion: Using an Intersectional Approach?

How can we understand these extraordinary deployments? A conventional gendered approach might ask if the deployment of female peacekeepers is a triumph for feminist campaigners, or merely a superficial public relations stunt on the part of the UN. An analysis of the introduction of an all-female unit, or to a significant cohort of female personnel, to the traditionally masculine peacekeeping spaces often focuses on the advantages and disadvantages of gender initiatives. While there is much to be discussed in relation to gender, there has been a consistent neglect of thinking about the geopolitics of such decision-making and action. Accounting for gender alone is simply not enough. Thinking about both the economic and geopolitical power relations at stake in such initiatives reveals that there are multiple interpretations and effects. One possible interpretation is that these deployments are further evidence of exploitative labor conditions for 'developing' countries who contribute military personnel without subsequent recognition at the level of global governance. Indian and Uruguayan women, then, become a sub-pool of cheap labor that can be utilized to do both the manual work of peacekeeping and the public relations work needed to appease local populations and critics of military masculinity. Another interpretation is that a female unit, and the presence of female peacekeepers more generally, does not challenge conventional understandings of femininity and masculinity. Rather, women are continually seen to be associated with problematic notions of peace, and men are continually seen to be associated with war (Hutchings, 2008b). In this way, the presence of women does little to challenge patriarchal relations or to adequately improve the lives of women and men in host societies. The third interpretation that I have explored in this piece relates to the ways in which global class categories and the politics of geography challenge notions of shared sisterhood among countries of the global South. Rather than share in common the experience of 'development', Indian peacekeepers and local Liberian women were divided by patriarchal notions of respectability in contrast to Uruguayan women who saw Haitian women as similar to them, but separated by economic circumstances and time.

In the case of the Indian contingent, the divide resulted in a sedimentation of the categories of rescuer and rescue. And what is problematic about this categorization is that it contributes to justifications for the peacekeeping industry. Thus the 'need' to intervene in the lives of people from the global South, without consideration of the categories of gender, 'race', and class gives authority and credibility to the peacekeeping/rescue industry and erases its embeddedness within contemporary forms of empire. And yet, the rescue industry is highly implicated in the unequal effects of globalization, especially as it relates to the use of Southern 'laboring' bodies as they are geographically and socially positioned alongside those Southern 'victimized' bodies.

An intersectional approach might be an important place to begin to push an analysis of gender to its necessary limits (Ackerly and True, 2008; Hutchings, 2008a; McCall, 2005; Valentine, 2007; Yuval-Davis, 2006). An approach that recognizes the multiplicity of gender and gendered relations as they intersect with other forms of subjectivity, identity, and positionality is necessary if analyses of women's and men's locatedness in peacekeeping is to be truly critical. If gender is prioritized without consideration of other facets of power and hierarchy within such sensitive spaces as peacekeeping missions, then other types of processes may be left unquestioned. For example, in practical terms, an intersectional approach allows researchers to examine those other categories and processes that are often ignored when gender-mainstreaming initiatives take center stage. Razack, in her study of peacekeeping, argues that a framework of research and analysis that combines patriarchy, colonialism, and capitalism is necessary for understanding the dimensional sides of power in post-conflict and development contexts (Razack, 2004). By invoking such a theoretical and methodological lens, gender does not become a tool of the UN liberal project (without a critique at least), nor does it become a marketing ploy for the Indian armed forces to present themselves as the ultimate 'modern' military without taking into account issues of gender equity and balance. In addition, acknowledging the different ways in which sameness and difference can be strategically introduced into situations might eventually enable more fruitful outcomes for 'third world' women as peacekeepers, and as peacekeeping recipients.

Notes

1 During the writing of this article, Bangladesh has launched a similar initiative in Haiti: http://news.bbc.co.uk/1/hi/world/south_asia/8678561.stm.

2 http://www.un.org/Pubs/chronicle/2007/webArticles/071807_gender_equality.htm.

3 http://www.un.org/en/peacekeeping/contributors/2009/dec09_1.pdf.

4 http://www.hindustantimes.com/StoryPage/StoryPage.aspx?sectionName=NLetter&id=90c05c2d-8e25–404c-92de-2774e861d1f7&Headline = Government + underpays + peacekeepers.
5 http://www.guardian.co.uk/world/2008/apr/28/congo.unitednations.
6 http://news.bbc.co.uk/1/hi/world/americas/6195830.stm.
7 http://www.bbc.co.uk/worldservice/documentaries/2008/04/080424_panorama_un.shtml.
8 http://www.washingtonpost.com/wp-dyn/articles/A15363-2004Nov26.html.
9 As the percentage of women peacekeepers is so low, these accounts have exclusively involved male peacekeeping personnel.
10 http://news.bbc.co.uk/1/hi/programmes/this_world/6223246.stm
11 http://news.bbc.co.uk/1/hi/world/africa/6316387.stm.
12 http://www.peacewomen.org/un/sc/Open_Debates/Sexual_Violence08/UN.SecretaryGeneral.pdf.
13 http://www.womensenews.org/article.cfm/dyn/aid/3944.
14 All interviewee names are pseudonyms. Due to the small number of female peacekeepers, dates, and locations are not provided so as to ensure anonymity.
15 In addition, because of the security situation in Haiti at the time of the study, patrols of the area were generally done by international police, and the high presence of females in the Uruguayan military would therefore not have been as visible to local women in order to provide positive role models. Nevertheless, this is not significantly different from the case of the Indian peacekeepers who had somewhat of a presence during the day, but were curfewed in their barracks during the night.
16 Class backgrounds there were 'read' from their low ranking status combined with their age. They entered the military without higher education, unlike the higher ranking officers who almost all had higher education qualifications.

References

Ackerly, B. & True, J. (2008) An intersectional analysis of international relations: recasting the discipline, *Politics and Gender*, 4(1), pp. 156–173.

Agordzo, B. K. (2009) Filling the 'security gap' in post-conflict situations: could formed police units make a difference? *International Peacekeeping*, 16(2), pp. 287–294.

Aguero, F. (1998) Legacies of transitions: institutionalization, the military, and democracy in South America, *Mershon International Studies Review*, 42(2), pp. 383–404.

Agustín, L. (2007) *Sex at the Margins: Migration, Labor Markets and the Rescue Industry* (London: Zed Books).

Amar, Paul (2012) Global South to the rescue: emerging humanitarian superpowers and globalizing rescue industries: introduction to special issue, *Globalizations*, 9(1), pp. 1–13.

Barnes, K. (2006) Reform or more of the same? Gender mainstreaming and the changing nature of UN peace operations, *YCISS Working Paper*, Number 41, pp. 1–26.

Basham, V. (2009) Effecting discrimination: operational effectiveness and harassment in the British Armed Forces, *Armed Forces and Society*, 35(4), pp. 1–17.

BBC (2007) *Girl Squad*, Documentary, BBC2, 21 June, 23:20.

Beri, R. (2008) India's role in keeping peace in Africa, *Strategic Analysis*, 32(2), pp. 197–221.

Berhman, J., Gaviria, A. & Székely, M. (eds) (2003) *Who's In and Who's Out: Social Exclusion in Latin America* (Washington, DC & Baltimore: Johns Hopkins University Press).

Bridges, D. & Horsfall, D. (2009) Increasing operational effectiveness in UN peacekeeping: toward a gender-balanced force, *Armed Forces & Society*, 10(10), pp. 1–11.

Bucheli, M. & Porzecanski, R. (2008) Racial inequality in the Uruguayan labor market: an analysis of wage differentials between Afrodescendants and whites, *Documentos de Trabajo*, (working papers) 1508, Department of Economics—dECON.

Bullion, A. (1997) India and UN peacekeeping operations, *International Peacekeeping*, 4(1), pp. 98–114.

Carey, H. F. (2001) 'Women and peace and security': the politics of implementing gender sensitivity norms in peacekeeping, *International Peacekeeping*, 8(2), pp. 49–68.

Cockburn, C. & Hubic, M. (2002) Gender and the peacekeeping military: a view from Bosnian women's organizations, in C. Cockburn & D. Zarkov (eds.) *The Postwar Moment: Militaries, Masculinities and International Peacekeeping* (London: Lawrence and Wishart), pp. 103–121.

Cohen, S. P. (1969) The untouchable soldier: caste, politics and the Indian Army, *Journal of Asian Studies*, 28(3), pp. 453–468.

Cohen, S. P. (1990) *The Indian Army: Its Contribution to the Development of a Nation* (Delhi: Oxford University Press).

Cohn, C. (2008) Mainstreaming gender in UN security policy: a path to political transformation, in S. M. Rai & G. Waylen (eds.) *Global Governance: Feminist Perspectives* (New York: Palgrave Macmillan), pp. 185–206.

Cohn, C., Kinsella, H. & Gibbins, S. (2004) Women, peace and security, *International Feminist Journal of Politics*, 6(1), pp. 130–140.

DPKO (2006) *Enhancing the Operational Impact of Peacekeeping Operations: Gender Balance in Military Forces and Police Services Deployed to PKOs Policy Dialogue 28–29 March 2006—Background Paper*, http://www.peacewomen.org/resources/Peacekeeping/DPKO/women_in_peacekeeping.pdf.

D'Amico, F. (1999) Women workers in the United Nations: from margin to mainstream, in M. Meyer & E. Prugl (eds.) *Gender Politics in Global Governance* (London: Rowman and Littlefield), pp. 19–40.

D'Amico, F. (2000) Citizen-soldier? Class, race, gender, sexuality and the US Military, in S. Jacobs, R. Jacobson & J. Marchbank (eds.) *States of Conflict: Gender, Violence and Resistance* (London: Zed Books), pp. 105–122.

Davidoff, L. & Hall, C. (2002) *Family Fortunes: Men and Women of the English Middle-Class, 1780–1850*, 2nd ed. (London: Routledge).

DeGroot, G. (2001) A few good women: gender stereotypes, the military and peacekeeping, *International Peacekeeping*, 8(2), pp. 23–38.

Donadio, M. (2008) The incorporation of women in peace operations: a regional perspective for Latin America and the Caribbean, *Pearson Papers*, 11(2), pp. 42–61.

Duffield, M. (2001) *Global Governance and the New Wars: The Merging of Development and Security* (London: Zed Books).

Enloe, C. (1980) *Ethnic Soldiers: State Security in Divided Societies* (Atlanta: University of Georgia Press).

Fox, M. (2001) The idea of women in peacekeeping: Lysistrata and Antigone, *International Peacekeeping*, 8(2), pp. 9–22.

Gizelis, T. (2009) Gender empowerment and United Nations peacebuilding, *Journal of Peace Research*, 46, pp. 505–523.

Haaland, T. (2008) Invisible women and friendly war-fighters: perceptions of gender and masculinities in the Norwegian armed forces, *Norma: Nordic Journal for Masculinity Studies*, 3(2), pp. 167–181.

Harrington, C. (2010) *The Politicization of Sexual Violence: From Abolitionism to Peacekeeping* (London: Ashgate).

Harris, V. & Goldsmith, A. (2010) Gendering transnational policing: experiences of Australian women in international policing operations, *International Peacekeeping*, 17(2), pp. 292–306.

Heinecken, L. (2002) Affirming gender equality: the challenges facing the South African Armed Forces, *Current Sociology*, 50, pp. 715–728.

Henry, M. (2007) Gender, security and development, *Conflict, Security and Development*, 7(1), pp. 61–84.

Higate, P. (2004) Gender and peacekeeping case studies: the Democratic Republic of the Congo and Sierra Leone, *ISS Monograph Series*, No. 91.

Higate, P. (2007) Peacekeepers, masculinities, and sexual exploitation, *Men and Masculinities*, 10, pp. 99–119.

Higate, P. & Henry, M. (2004) Engendering (in)security in peacekeeping operations, *Security Dialogue* (special issue on Gender and Security), 35(4), pp. 481–498.

Higate, P. & Henry, M. (2009) *Insecure Spaces: Peacekeeping, Power and Performance in Kosovo, Liberia and Haiti* (London: Zed Press).

Hutchings, K. (2008a) 1988–1998: contrast and continuity in feminist international relations, *Millenium: Journal of International Studies*, 37, pp. 97–105.

Hutchings, K. (2008b) Making sense of masculinity and war, *Men and Masculinities*, 10, pp. 389–404.

Instituto Nacional de Estadística (1998) *Encuesta Continua de Hogares: Módulo de raza* (Montevideo: Instituto Nacional de Estadística).

Jennings, K. (2010) Unintended consequences of intimacy: political economies of peacekeeping and sex tourism, *International Peacekeeping*, 17(2), pp. 229–243.

Kaldor, M. (1999) *New and Old Wars: Organised Violence in a Global Era* (Cambridge: Polity Press).

Karame, K. H. (2001) Military women in peace operations: Experiences of the Norwegian battalion in UNIFIL 1978–1998, *International Peacekeeping*, 8(2), pp. 85–96.

Khalidi, O. (2001) Ethnic group recruitment in the Indian Army: the contrasting cases of Sikhs, Muslims, Gurkhas and others, *Pacific Affairs*, 74(4), pp. 529–552.

Khanna, J., Sandler, T. & Shimizu, H (1998) Sharing the financial burden for U.N. and NATO peacekeeping, 1976–1996, *The Journal of Conflict Resolution*, 42(2), pp. 176–195.

Krishnasamy, K. (2001) 'Recognition' for Third World peacekeepers: India and Pakistan, *International Peacekeeping*, 8(4), pp. 56–76.

Kummel, G. (2002) When boy meets girl: the 'feminization' of the military, *Current Sociology*, 50(5), pp. 615–639.

Kundu, A. (1994) The Indian Armed Forces' Sikh and Non-Sikh officers' opinions of Operation Blue Star, *Pacific Affairs*, 67(1), pp. 46–69.
Kundu, A. (1998) *Militarism in India: The Army and Civil Society in Consensus* (London: Taurus Academic Studies).
Lewis, M. (2003) *Afro-Uruguayan Literature: Postcolonial Perspectives* (Lewisburg, PA: Bucknell University Press).
Loveman, B. (1994) 'Protected democracies' and military guardianship: political transitions in Latin America 1978–1993, *Journal of Interamerican Studies and World Affairs*, 36(2), pp. 105–189.
McCall, L. (2005) The complexity of intersectionality, *Signs: Journal of Women, Culture and Society*, 30(3), pp. 1771–1800.
Marcella, G. (ed) (1994) Warriors in peacetime: future missions of the Latin American armed forces, *Warriors in Peacetime: The Military and Democracy in Latin America* (Portland, OR: Frank Cass).
Martin, S. E. (1999) Police force or police service? Gender and emotional labor, *The Annals of the American Academy of Political and Social Science*, 561, pp. 111–126.
Marks, J. (2007) The pitfalls of action and inaction: civilian protection in MONUC's peacekeeping operations, *African Security Review*, 16(3), pp. 67–80.
Martin, S. (2005) *Must Boys be Boys? Ending Sexual Exploitation and Abuse in UN Peacekeeping Missions* (Washington, DC: Refugees International).
Mazurana, D. (2003) Do women matter in peacekeeping: women in police, military and civilian peacekeeping, *Canadian Woman Studies*, 22(2), pp. 64–71.
Minority Rights Group (ed) (1995) *No Longer Invisible: Afro-Latin Americans Today* (London: Minority Rights Group Publications).
Mitzutani, S. (2009) Contested boundaries of whiteness; public service recruitment and the Eurasian and Anglo-Indian Association, 1876–1901, in H. Fischer-Tiné & S. Gehrmann (eds.) *Empires and Boundaries: Rethinking Race, Class and Gender in Colonial Thinking* (London: Routledge), pp. 86–106.
Natarajan, M. (2008) *Women Police in a Changing Society* India: Ashgate Press.
Olsson, L. (2000) Mainstreaming gender in multidimensional peacekeeping: A field perspective, *International Peacekeeping*, 7(3), pp. 1–16.
Patel, P. & Tripodi, P. (2007) Peacekeepers, HIV and the role of masculinity in military behaviour, *International Peacekeeping*, 14(5), pp. 584–598.
Peláez, A. (2007) Country survey XX: defense spending and peacekeeping in Uruguay, *Defense & Peace Economics*, 18(3), pp. 281–302.
Paris, R. (2001) Echoes of the Mission Civilisatrice: peacekeeping in the post-Cold War era, in E. Newman & O. Richmond (eds.) *The United Nations and Human Security* (London: Palgrave).
Pion-Berlin, D. (1992) Military autonomy and emerging democracies in South America, *Comparative Politics*, 25(1), pp. 83–102.
Pouligny, B. (2006) *Peace Operations Seen from Below: UN Missions and Local People* (Bloomfield, CT: Kumarian Press).
Puechguirbal, N. (2010) Discourses on gender, patriarchy and Resolution 1325: a textual analysis of UN documents, *International Peacekeeping*, 17(2), pp. 172–187.
Pugh, M. (2004) Peacekeeping and critical theory, *International Peacekeeping*, 11(1), pp. 39–58.
Razack, S. (2004) *Dark Threats, White Knights* (Toronto: University of Toronto Press).
Rodriguez, R. (2003) *Racismo y derechos humanos en Uruguay* (Montevideo: Organizaciones Mundo Afro).
Roessler, P. & Prendergast, J. (2006) Democratic Republic of the Congo, in W. J. Durch (ed.) *Twenty-First-Century Peace Operations* (Washington, DC: United States Institute of Peace).
Rosen, S. P. (1996) *Societies and Military Power: India and Its Armies* (Ithaca, NY: Cornell University Press).
Ross, J. (2004) The changing role of the military in Latin America, *Focal Policy Paper* (Ottawa: Canadian Foundation for the Americas), pp. 1–11.
Ruddick, S. (1980) Maternal thinking, *Feminist Studies*, 6(2), pp. 342–367.
Said, E. (1982) *Orientalism* (New York: Vintage).
Segal, M. (1995) Women's military roles cross-nationally: past, present and future, *Gender and Society*, 9(6), pp. 757–775.
Shepherd, L. J. (2008) Power and authority in the production of United Nations Security Council Resolution 1325, *International Studies Quarterly*, 52(2), pp. 383–404.
Simić, O. (2010) Does the presence of women really matter? Towards combating male sexual violence in peacekeeping operations, *International Peacekeeping*, 17(2), pp. 188–199.
Sinha, M. (1995) *Colonial Masculinity: The 'Manly Englishman' and The 'Effeminate Bengali' in the Late Nineteenth Century* (Manchester: Manchester University Press).

Sotomayor, A. (2010) Why some states participate in UN peace missions while others do not: an analysis of civil-military relations and its effects on Latin America's contributions to peacekeeping operations, *Security Studies*, 19(1), pp. 160–195.
Stiehm, J. H. (2001) Women, peacekeeping and peacemaking: gender balance and mainstreaming, *International Peacekeeping*, 8(2), pp. 39–48.
Strobl, S. (2008) The Women's Police Directorate in Bahrain: an ethnographic exploration of gender segregation and the likelihood of future integration, *International Criminal Justice Review*, 18(1), pp. 39–58.
Torres, J. B., Solberg, V. S. H. & Carlstrom, A. H. (2002) The myth of sameness among Latino men and their machismo, *American Journal of Orthopsychiatry*, 72, pp. 183–181.
Ulery, E. (2005) The Uruguayan Armed Forces and the Challenge of 21st Century Peacekeeping Operations, Unpublished thesis (MA), Naval Postgraduate College, Monterey, California, https://www.nps.edu/Academics/Centers/CCC/Research/StudentTheses/Ulery05.pdf.
Valenius, J. (2007) A few kind women: gender essentialism and Nordic peacekeeping operations, *International Peacekeeping*, 14(4), pp. 510–523.
Valentine, G. (2007) Theorising and researching intersectionality: a challenge for feminist geography, *The Professional Geographer*, 59(1), pp. 10–21.
Wade, P. (1997) *Race and Ethnicity in Latin America* (London: Pluto Press).
Walkowitz, J. (1982) Male vice and feminist virtue: feminism and the politics of prostitution in nineteenth-century Britain, *History Workshop*, 13, pp. 79–93.
Whitworth, S. (2004) *Men, Masculinities and UN Peacekeeping: A Gender Analysis* (Toronto: Lynne Rienner).
Willet, S. (2010) Introduction: Security Council Resolution 1325: assessing the impact on women, peace and security, *International Peacekeeping*, 17(2), pp. 142–158.
Yuval-Davis, N. (2006) Intersectionality and feminist politics, *European Journal of Women's Studies*, 13(3), pp. 193–209.
Zeid, Prince Ra'ad Zeid Al-Hussein (2005) *A Comprehensive Strategy to Eliminate Future Sexual Exploitation and Abuse in the United Nations Peacekeeping Operations*, Study undertaken for the Secretary-General by the Permanent Representative of Jordan, A/59/710, 24 March 2005.

Marsha Henry is a lecturer in the Gender Institute, London School of Economics. Her research has looked at various aspects of gender in South Asia, focusing on connections between the developed and developing worlds. Her recent research examines perceptions of security in peacekeeping missions: P. Higate and M. Henry *Insecure Spaces* (Zed Press, 2009).

Martial Races and Enforcement Masculinities of the Global South: Weaponising Fijian, Chilean, and Salvadoran Postcoloniality in the Mercenary Sector

PAUL HIGATE

School for Sociology, Politics and International Studies, University of Bristol, Clifton, Bristol BS8 1TY, UK

ABSTRACT *Set against the backdrop of the occupations of Iraq and Afghanistan, the private militarised security industry has grown rapidly over the last decade. Its growth into a multi-billion dollar enterprise has attracted the interest of scholars in international relations, legal studies, political science, and security studies who have debated questions of regulation and accountability, alongside the state's control on the monopoly of violence. While these contributions are to be welcomed, the absence of critical sociological approaches to the industry and its predominantly male security contracting workforce has served to occlude the gendered and racialised face of the private security sphere. These dimensions are important since the industry has come increasingly to rely on masculine bodies from the global South in the form of so-called third country and local national men. The involvement of these men is constituted in and through the articulation of historical, neocolonial, neoliberal, and militarising processes. These processes represent the focus of the current article in respect of Fijian and Latin American security contractors. Their trajectories into the industry are considered in respect of both 'push' and 'pull' factors, the likes of which differ in marked ways for each group. Specifically, states and social groups in Fiji, Chile, and El Salvador are appropriating what is described in the article as an ethnic bargain as one way in which to make a contribution to the global security sector, or—in direct regard to the Latin American context—to banish its more dangerous legacies from the domestic space. In conclusion, it is argued that the use of these contractors by the industry represents a hitherto unacknowledged gendered and racialised instance of the contemporary imperial moment.*

Contractors Creed

I am a U.S. contractor. I look out for myself, the operators to my left and right, and no one else. I will always take advantage of the fact that I can finally tell military officers to pound sand, and will do so at every opportunity. I am my country's scapegoat, the 'plausible deniability' warrior, and I love it. Less than $700 dollars a day is unacceptable. I am trained to eat things that would make a billy goat puke, but will refuse anything less than 60 dollars per diem because I am greedy. I care not for ribbons and awards for valor. I do this job for the opportunity to kill the enemies of my country, and to finally get that boat I've always wanted. I will be in better shape than 99% of the active duty personnel, although this is not hard. I will equip myself with the latest high speed gear, and will trick out my M4 until it weighs more than 24lbs, not because it works better, but because it looks cool in the photographs. I will carry more weapons, ammunition, and implements of death on my person that an infantry fire team, and when engaged I will lay waste to everything around me. In any combat zone, I will always locate the swimming pool, beer, and women, because I can. I will deploy on my terms, and if it ever gets too stupid, I will simply find another company that pays more.

Cited in Pelton (2006). Originally taken from an email circulated on contractor channels.

Introduction

Fuelled by a lethal mix of alcohol and undiagnosed post traumatic stress disorder (PTSD), a British private security contractor[1]—veteran of the British Army—reaches for his weapon and shoots dead two fellow employees of the private militarised security company (PMSC)[2] ArmorGroup in Baghdad's Green Zone in August 2009.[3] Once again, PMSC contractors are in the news, and this story follows on the heels of the murder and mutilation of four contractors in Fallujah in 2004 by unknown 'insurgents',[4] the shooting dead in 2007 of 17 Iraqi civilians, including children and women by Blackwater contractors,[5] the alleged shooting at civilian vehicles and their occupants in 2005 by contractors making a 'trophy video',[6] and most recently, the alleged involvement of the founder of Xe (formerly Blackwater), Erik Prince, in murder and weapons smuggling.[7] Over time, these incidents have occluded the everyday restraint and professionalism exercised by the majority of contractors and instead have engendered two normative positions within academic scholarship and more widely—either that PMSC should be stringently regulated,[8] or that they must be outlawed altogether as morally reprehensible excesses of the 'market for force'.[9]

A constellation of forces underpin the rapid growth of the PMSC sphere facilitated in no small measure by the dominance of post cold war markets that have fuelled a strong tendency to outsource traditional government functions. Simultaneously, national militaries have been downsized, providing a large number of men trained in 'the legitimate discharge of violence' ripe for recruitment by well-paying PMSC (Holmqvist, 2005). In addition, massive arms stocks have become available to the open market, helping to fuel intrastate conflict (Singer, 2008, p. 54). Other factors fuelling the demand for the services of contractors include the mass demobilisation of national military troops, a significant proportion of whom have gone on to be involved in conflict in 'weaker states' as demand for their services grows (Singer, 2008, p. 38). Few predicted the growth of a well-organised and determined insurgency in both Iraq and Afghanistan, a challenge to overstretched national militaries that—in conjunction with the exigencies of vast reconstruction budgets and allied security activities—provide for the services of around 240 PMSC employing 76,000 contractors across both countries. US- or British-run companies in Iraq have a preference for veterans of elite forces including the Special Air Service (SAS), the Special Boat Service (SBS), the US SEALS, Delta, and Rangers, and as noted above, third country national (TCN) and local national (LN) men. The dramatic burgeoning of the private security sector has led commentators to describe it as the new business face of warfare in the contemporary period, underscoring its significance both now and into the future (Avant, 2005; Kinsey, 2007; Mandel, 2002; Singer, 2008).

Yet, aside from the important work being developed by Chisholm on 'Ghurka' contractors (2011), the scholarship engaging PMSC remains underdeveloped, not least in its failure to consider the gendered and racialised[10] contexts of the industry where an increasing proportion of TCN and LN men comprise the diverse security contracting workforce. The central attraction of hiring these contractors is their premium cost as a consequence of their location on the periphery of the global economy. These men[11] tend to come from war-torn regions of the globe; Xe, for example, has been seeking 'conflict labor' in the guise of ex-combatants from Liberia envisaged as ideal soldiers because of their ability to fight wars, alongside their inability to secure employment in their home country. Uganda is also apposite in this respect and has mobilised large numbers of men (and fewer women) for employment in the private security industry with around 10,000 working as private security guards in Iraq in 2006. The country is said to be awash with potential recruits and its government was one of the original members of Bush's 'coalition of the willing'. The export of private security contractors to Iraq is the latest chapter in this story within the context of the 20-year insurgency in Uganda and the glut of experienced army veterans available to the PMSC industry (Delany, 2009, p. 1).

Given these developments, PMSCs represent a rich site through which to critically examine the nexus linking intra- and inter-gender relations, globalisation and militarisation as they play out in the legal spaces of exception characteristic of the Iraqi and Afghan contexts. How can we begin to make sense of the industry's turn to the global South for its manpower? Explaining the appeal men from the global South hold for recruiters together with the 'pull' of the industry for men drawn to its professional possibilities are the key concerns of the current article. Specifically, I argue that representational practices framing particular men from the global South are shaped by their assumed embodied disposition to employment in the industry as a result of the close articulation of neocolonial, political-economic, and political processes. I also argue that the need or 'choice' for these men to trade their occupational skills plays out within, and is productive of, their subjugation in a wider, masculine gender hierarchy. Here, those from the global South are required to strike an ethnic bargain[12] weighted in favour of white, former special forces contractors from the global North with whom their subaltern status is relationally constituted. In sum, and set against the backdrop of the 'war on terror' played out in and through the contemporary development wars,[13] analysis of transnational migration of the contractor workforce tends to have overlooked their neocolonial and political-economic dimensions.

Given that PMSCs are thoroughgoing masculine spaces, contextual discussion turns first to a brief overview of the masculinities literature before moving on to develop the concept of privatised enforcement masculinities as they manifest themselves in national-racial terms. Next, I consider the deeper drivers to the recruitment of Fijian and Latin American contractors—invoking the martial race category in the former and the articulation of the political and personal aspects of 'security expertise' in the latter. The overall subaltern position of both groups within a wider gender hierarchy where men from the global South are discursively and materially disadvantaged is then examined within a discussion of the ethnic bargain. A brief conclusion follows.

Theoretical Context: Masculinities, Race, Mercenaries

Over the last 30 years the literature on masculinities has grown exponentially across the social sciences. With a focus on the sociological and political science canon, this work has illuminated the hidden, naturalised power-practices of a diverse cluster of relational values, beliefs, performances, and ideologies known as 'masculinity', manifest from the everyday to the international in the global North and the global South (Brittan, 1989; Carver, 2004; Cleaver, 2002; Cockburn and Zarkov, 2002; Connell, 1987, 1995, 2005; Cornwall and Lindisfarne, 1994; Enloe, 2000; Hearn, 1998; Hooper, 2001; Kimmel, 2000; Messerschmidt, 2004; Morgan, 1992; Parpart and Zalewski, 2008; Pease and Pringle, 2001; Seidler, 1997; Whitehead and Barrett, 2001).

Hegemonic masculinity is one of the most influential and increasingly contested concepts to have been used in the critical men's studies literature, formulated to make sense of power, plurality, and positionality in respect of intra-masculine identity (Connell, 1995; Morrell and Swart, 2005, p. 91). It connotes a privileged and privileging gender identity that shapes individual and institutional possibilities according to one's relationship to its temporal, situational, and cultural expression. While masculinity is extremely difficult to define (Plummer, 1999, p. 47), in the final analysis its key feature is that it is *not femininity* (Hutchings, 2008), and that it signifies a common denominator in 'manhood acts', specifically the ways that men's practices sustain patriarchy and create inequality (Shrock and Schwalbe, 2009, p. 286). Masculinity, however, has a tendency to be used imprecisely. Here, it should be noted that masculinity is not a thing, a noun that names, but rather invokes configurations of contingent, sometimes contradictory, diverse social practices constituting particular gender identities, gender orders, and gender regimes (Connell, 1995) turning on attempts to control others (Schrock and Schwalbe, 2009). Boys learn to be men, and as such are encouraged to conform to a cluster of expectations—albeit with some cultural variability—framed in the following terms:

> A growing boy should not be a baby; he should observe clear differentiation from girls; he should express affinity with groups of other boys; he should become increasingly physically competent and mature . . . [T]hese requirements expose the yardsticks of 'normative' or 'hegemonic' masculinity. (Plummer, 1999, p. 86)

Ongoing processes of socialisation shaped by militarist norms from the youngest of ages (Dawson, 1994) are central to the gendered life-course and develop in articulation with broader influences where Western masculinities are shaped by 'macro-social structures . . . and in their interaction with dominant hegemonic masculinities . . . [alongside] race and class hierarchies' (Huggins and Haritos-Fatouros, 1998, p. 31). Moving from the macro-state level, (masculine) identities are also shaped in their recursive relationship with institutions (Giddens, 1991) and employment where the bread winner role remains central to masculine sense of self (Morgan, 1992).[14]

With a focus on masculinities, it is important to acknowledge a good deal of plurality in contractor's gendered-occupational identity, since these men are involved in diverse roles that tend *not* to require them to use violence in a direct sense, including, for example, the role of static compound guard, security sector reform work and allied training, and the provision of logistical and support functions to military operations. Greater likelihood of actual violence lies with missions involving several factors: convoy security; close protection of dignitaries; combat operations; and in direct regard to the US company Xe, locating and assassinating Al Qaeda operatives.[15] As noted above, a significant number of contractors in these roles will import military-embodied skill capitals into the private security sphere that extend to the competent use of firearms, and as such invoke the concept of militarised masculinities (Arkin and Dobrofsky, 1974; Barrett, 1996; Goldstein,

2001; Higate, 2006; Higate et al., 2003; Hutchings, 2008; Morgan, 1994; Whitworth, 2004). Having carried out military service, a number of contractors may be marked by masculine subcultures that 'militarize feelings' (Karner, 1998, p. 220) where aggression could be encouraged against the backdrop of how well they 'as men . . . measure up to these particular standards of manliness' (Karner, 1998, p. 216); though again, this observation needs to be balanced with the professionalism of the majority who may not see the use of violence as an act of manhood (Shrock and Schwalbe, 2009). Yet, for many, military institutions are where one's family resides, and consequently, where fraternal bonds can fuel homoerotic and narcissistic cultures (Leed, 1989). At times these can percolate into the private militarised security sphere, underscored in 2009 by the 'hazing incident' involving the contractor guard force at the US Embassy in Kabul (Higate, 2010). After discharge from the military, many may experience a sense of loss and frustration in 'adrenaline-lite', existentially vacuous, civilian occupations, craving instead the adventure of risk, danger, and, for the tiny minority, the chance to kill.[16] Others escaping the constraints of life in the armed forces may relish the opportunity to work in professions close to their sense of being and doing, while able to 'walk away [from their contracts] at any time' (Fainaru, 2008, p. 60). Yet, it would be inappropriate to conflate the diversity of privatised enforcement masculinities with the routine use of violence, since running alongside the newsworthy incidents of transgression are the everyday, unremarkable moments of restraint, caution, and measured response of heavily armed men living and working in hostile territory, as they might see it.[17]

However, not only are masculinities popularly believed to 'control' men's social practice (Hearn, 1996), but the term has a tendency to be used ethnocentrically in regard to its white, Western hegemonic (Beasley, 2008) and ahistorical form. Drawing on the postcolonial masculinities literature, Hokowhitu (2004, p. 1) highlights the racialised/coloniser masculinity dialectic in the exemplary context of the 'Maori man' against whom:

> . . . the colonists perceived . . . [themselves] as superior and normal and consequently Māori and *tikanga Māori* (Māori culture) as inferior and abnormal . . . Missionaries, for example, with little propensity to understand the complexities of Māori culture, simply described practices as barbaric . . . [and] as inherently inferior . . . dominant racist representations of Māori men grew out of this mentality . . . while 'civilized white men were the most manly ever evolved—firm of character; self-controlled; protectors of women and children' Māori men were physical, whimsical, unsophisticated, childlike, ruled by passion—and therefore in need of enlightenment through civilisation.

The resonance of these material and discursive framings can be found within the PMSC sphere where TCN and LN men from the global South (1) receive less pay than their white, Western peers from the global North, (2) are frequently subject to greater risk, and (3) have little scope to transform their subaltern status. In this respect, though power does *tend* to accrue to masculinities as a consequence of the patriarchal dividend that turns in the broader context on the overall subordination of women (Connell, 1995), the benefits of the dividend are mediated by processes of racialisation,[18] a point exemplified in the case of TCN and LN men and the intra-masculine hierarchies within which they are employed.

Hierarchies of Racialised Masculinities in the PMSC: Striking the Ethnic Bargain

Experienced in relation to a continuum of polar opposites, the labour market is the exemplary bargaining forum. At one extreme is the highly insecure employer who has little or no say in her level of remuneration, contractual obligations, or working conditions, while at the other is the worker who can name her, (or more likely) his price. Schultz and Yeung (2005, pp. 13–14) note that:

> Workers recruited by Middle Eastern labour brokers hail from impoverished countries such as Bangladesh, Nepal and the Philippines; they do menial labour for Private Security Companies, such as cooking, serving food and cleaning toilets. Other contractors, former combatants from countries such as Fiji and Uganda and from all over Latin America, more typically take up dangerous physical protection and military support duties.

As a microcosm of wider industrial relations, this employer–employee dynamic is replicated in the PMSC sphere noted here, where TCN and LN men are positioned at the lowest reaches of a masculinised and racialised hierarchy, with their bargaining ability severely curtailed in contrast to their white, former special forces peers from the global North. In turn, TCN and LN have necessarily to strike an ethnic bargain trading on assumptions around their embodied identities in return for material reward (Sa'ar, 2005, p. 681). Like women from the global South, TCN and LN men 'strategize to materialize whatever limited benefits they may extract from their disadvantaged position in the liberal order' (Sa'ar, 2005, p. 681). This strategising plays out against the backdrop of the essentialising of the ethnicity/race nexus and its corollary, the structural conditions of employment possibility (Sa'ar, 2005, p. 783) configuring the PMSC industry where TCN and LN men are disadvantaged spatially, materially, and discursively. Mohanty's (1999) work on Third World women who have necessarily to present as docile, heterosexual, and feminine (or in the case of the TCN and LN contractor workforce), heterosexual, manly, compliant and even reverential to the contractor hierarchy, underscores the potency of racialisation across the genders. And contractors' gendered and racialised 'suitability' to the industry often results from the dialogic interplay of colonised and coloniser in respect of the gendered identities to which [particular] historical and contemporary interactions give rise (Stanovsky, 2007, p. 493). In turn, 'hybrid masculinities' are created 'through the fusion of global [warrior] diasporas' (Stanovsky, 2007, p. 494). The representation of these men 'thus become an arena for the dissemination of colonial control' (Stanovsky, 2007, p. 494) shaped by 'first world discourses about . . . essentialised . . . and homogenized . . . third world masculinities . . . that reinforce . . . first world norms of masculinity and heterosexuality' (Stanovsky, 2007, p. 494). While they are co-opted into the geopolitics of the former colonisers, their investment into the ethnic bargain is shaped by a highly instrumental economic rationality. They 'are working for short-term gains . . . while avoiding conflictive emotional investments' (Sa'ar, 2005, p. 683) through trading their occupational skills alongside their 'ascribed traits' (Sa'ar, 2005, p. 684). From the static guarding of compounds, through riding 'shotgun' on security convoys and onto the torturing of 'insurgents', the role of TCN and LN men in the neoliberal project 'exists in articulation with male domination' instantiated through extra-state mechanisms (Sa'ar, 2005, p. 684). Yet, as a consequence of the Iraq 'war-rush', contractors from the global South *are* noted to generate relatively high incomes in the PMSC sphere, reaffirming the point that these 'ethnicized . . . men are not necessarily absent from the core of liberal society' (Sa'ar, 2005, p. 687). Scahill sees the recruitment of subaltern men from the global South as serving the needs of privileged nations when he argues that:

> The Iraq war has ushered in a new system. Wealthy nations can recruit the world's poor, from countries that have no direct stake in the conflict, and use them as cannon fodder to conquer weaker nations. (Scahill, 2007, p. 1)

Wages in the PMSC sector have been falling steadily since their peak during the occupation of Iraq in the immediate aftermath of Bush's notorious proclamation, 'mission accomplished'. Competition from other developing countries in Africa[19] and the Indian subcontinent has seen minimum incomes fall from $1,300 to $600 a month. That compares with the $15,000 that an industry insider estimated an American guard could make each month at the height of the Iraq bubble, although this figure is also in decline. As one Ugandan security contractor was reported to say: 'If I am earning $600 a month . . . these companies are making billions . . . it is not fair.' (Delany, 2009). Domestic interest in the plight of contractors from Uganda has been described as 'fierce' with some commentators comparing this kind of servitude with 'slavery' and 'human trafficking' (Delany, 2009). In contrast, contractors from the global North are discussed and represented in terms that, while engaging the national-racial dimension, are nonetheless qualitatively different from the TCN and LN cohort. For example, an article in the 'magazine for mercenaries', *Soldiers of Fortune* written by a former SAS warrant officer, relies on a narrative of quintessential British reserve even when shooting-up 'insurgents' in a following car. In a calm voice, and through a pall of fresh cordite, the ex-special forces British contractor turns towards the charges in his own vehicle, rudely awakened by the incessant clattering of his AK47, and urges them (with due nonchalance) to 'go back to sleep, guys' (Geddes, 2008). A recent documentary on the work of PMSC in Iraq by a Canadian film-maker perpetuates stereotypical portrayals of contractors where Italian operatives are preoccupied with hairstyle and clothing, and the British remain understated, pragmatic, and reserved[20] (Bicanic and Bourke, 2006). US contractors of the firm Blackwater have a particular status here and are invariably presented as hyper-masculine narcissists, who intimidate local populations as well as other contractors through their aggressive driving on convoy protection duties, their heavily armed appearance, and overall arrogance (Pelton, 2006). These somewhat stereotypical representations of US contractors turn on identities where—albeit in an ironic sense—'looking good in the photographs' depends on 'buying-the-look' of the all-American warrior, as framed here through journalistic prose discussing two contractors working out of the Green Zone in Baghdad:

> T-boy stands off by himself 'zoning', as he calls it, staying focused on the dangerous return trip to the Green Zone. T-Boy looks like he has adopted a style of generic death—black helmet, black shirt, black mask, black goggles, with a large skull and crossbones chalked on the back of his armor vest and another drawn on his Kevlar helmet. All the gear covers the skull tattoos. (Pelton, 2006, p. 8)

> Square jawed and built low, Pete resembles a real-life white-skinned version of the Incredible Hulk. In his early thirties, he originally hails from the Midwest and spent over a decade in the Special Forces as a weapons specialist. (Pelton, 2006, p. 75)

National identity is significant in other ways, too, and has been used by contractors as a way to distance themselves from both the Blackwater 'cowboys' and the distorted impression that the industry is inhabited solely by war-mongering mercenaries[21] stirring up trouble in order to justify their occupation of particular countries and the associated income generating possibilities it brings. Crucially, however, representations that canonise contractors in these kinds of ways tend to be reserved for men heading the informal masculinised and racialised hierarchy. And even when TCN are revered, there may be a sense in which these narratives are inflected with racial undertones.[22] Now that we have dealt with questions of gender and race, what of the controversial label 'mercenary'? How might we think through the analytical complexities of the term as it articulates in the contemporary period with questions of masculinity, politics, security, and the market?

Contractors, Mercenaries, and Privatised Enforcement Masculinities

The ways that the PMSC sector attempts to 'distance the market from mercenarism' (Leander, 2009, p. 11) has resulted in a stress on the market's links 'to peace and democracy rather than war and the military' (Leander, 2009, p. 11). A prime example of this discursive strategy is noted in the International Peace Operations Association (IPOA) that

> lobbies vigorously for the legitimacy and involvement of the private security industry in international peace and stability . . . [that] consistently tie it to peace, human security, ethical behaviour and democracy.[23] (Leander, 2009, p. 11)

However, given that a disproportionate number of PMSC contractors have backgrounds in all-volunteer or conscript militaries and/or police forces, and consequently are trained in the instrumental use of violence,[24] it is unsurprising that influential organisations including the United Nations (UN) should conceive of the industry's employees as 'mercenaries'. In challenging the mercenary moniker that paints private security in a dim light, the industry stresses a contractor's political relevance in respect of his 'professional' and increasingly important role in the development of a liberal-democratic state.[25] Industry representatives and (the majority of) contractors argue that modern day employers differ sharply from their mercenary predecessors who, motivated solely by financial gain, were 'willing to sell [their] military skills to the highest bidder, no matter what the cause' (Kinsey, 2007, p. 19). Thus, the traditional mercenary figure[26] driven purely by self-interest is one element of the broader aim of 'winning hearts and minds' and 'spreading democracy',[27] as might be inferred from the industry's recent representational practices.

Rather, those acting for the 'greater good' are described as private security contractors—in the main, highly trained professionals among whom one will occasionally find a 'bad apple'. Yet, 'bringing democracy' to 'failed states' often relies on the use of violence (Dillon and Reid, 2008) supported—ultimately—by tax-payers' money as noted above. Set against this backdrop, both 'mercenary' and 'private security contractor' lack analytical purchase on the contemporary imperial moment and the social practices underpinning its specific political-economic configurations. Instead, I argue for the plural term 'privatised enforcement masculinities' to better capture the articulation of everyday 'contractor' activity with the geopolitical and geostrategic imperatives driving their employment. In breaking the term into its component parts, it is noted that (1) in contrast to invoking endless questions of the market and asking whether or not security should be a public or a private good, the point here is that the *privatised* work of these men in spaces of exception (like Iraq and Afghanistan) is largely unaccountable in ways that can exacerbate insecurity, (2) that these men are tasked in a variety of ways to *enforce* the peace in ways that resonate with the UN Chapter VII mandate of 'peace enforcement', and that (3) those assumed to be most suited to security work of this kind are invariably believed to embody particular kinds of masculinity—frequently military or militarised masculinity. We move now from theoretical to substantive concerns in respect of two racialised categories of privatised military masculinity, those of the Fijian and Latin American.

Privatised Enforcement Masculinities: Fijian 'Warriors'

The recruitment of Fijian men into private security in Iraq is noted to be a growing source of revenue for the families of this warrior diaspora, and by mid-2005 there were more than 1,000 Fijians working in both Iraq and Kuwait as soldiers, security guards, and drivers (Maclellan, 2006, p. 50). The Fijian military (RFMF) is closely linked with mercenaries and private security as noted here:

> The Fijian military . . . is extremely well 'connected' to international power brokers . . . the government allows soldiers, particularly officers, to transit from military service to join private security firms, which in turn pay [the military] a fee.[28]

Soldiers, ex-soldiers, and non-military Fijians' employment overseas is welcomed by the domestic government in Fiji because of the healthy remittances dispatched to families back home. The extent to which these individuals' martial skills have been commodified in the global market place is due in part to the global resonance of Fijian 'warrior culture'. Warrior culture in Fiji is noted to engage ideological and cultural roots, in particular the links between 'Fijian ideologies of "lotu" (Christianity and Methodism), "turagaism" (a belief in chiefly rights to leadership) and militarism' (Maclellan, 2006, p. 51). In Fiji it is argued that masculinity, rugby, religion, and the 'bati' or warrior culture influence one another (Teaiwa, 2005). The genesis of Fijian warrior culture can be traced to the islands' pre-colonial past.

As Teaiwa (2005, p. 202) reminds us 'martial life in pre-colonial Fiji emerged out of deeply embodied notions of masculinity, spirituality, and society.' She further argues that in contemporary times 'the cultures that thrive in Fiji are permeated by militarized discourses and symbolism' that chime with the coloniser's earlier presence alongside other key events such as fighting the Japanese in World War II alongside the British, as well as later conflicts in Malaya, Borneo, and Oman.[29] The commodification of Fijian's 'security-skill' capital reinforces the wider militarisation of the cultural, political, and economic spheres in Fiji, compounded in the contemporary period by the 'military-led government . . . [that has reinforced] the relationship between hegemonic masculinity and militarization' (George, 2008, p. 180).

Fijians as a Martial Race

Trajectories shaping Fijians' recruitment into the private security industry resonate with their construction as members of a martial race, with lines of continuity reaching back to the intervention of the imperial powers who, mirroring the Kamba tribe in Kenya, recruited into the British army 'believed that certain sections of their subject populations had inherent combative and militaristic qualities that made them naturally suited for military service' (Parsons, 1999, p. 675). In this respect, the Fijian martial race joins a long list of others including Ghurkhas, Bedouin, Scots, Sikhs, Ibans, Berbers, Cossacks, Maori, Mongols, Kurds, Zulus, Irish, Montenegrins (Enloe, 1980, p. 26), the 'Buffalo Soldiers' (Billington, 1991), and the Mestizos (Nash, 1995). Men deemed to be disposed to fighting on account of their ethnic, cultural, and embodied dispositions through which they are racialised have been co-opted into state volunteer, conscript, and colonial militaries over at the last two centuries (Enloe, 1980; Henderson, 1989; Kirk-Greene, 1980; Parsons, 1999; Streets, 2004). Martial race identities are argued to flow from the 'military imagination' (Caplan, 1991) and understandings rooted in scientific theories of race around the end of the nineteenth century (Dimeo, 2002, p. 79) where the categories of 'tribes, clans, and castes [were developed] for administrative purposes' (Parsons, 1999, p. 672). Here it was understood that hardiness, industriousness, and embodied resilience were characteristics of those living in challenging climactic conditions that, in turn, came to be seen as valuable, embodied traits for the martial races. Political calculations made by military policymakers around martial races' loyalty, or indeed potential for unrest (Enloe, 1980), together with perceived military competence of certain communities in the pre-colonial historical record, also underpinned martial race identities (Enloe, 1980). In an intra-masculine sense, martial race identities were constructed in relation to subaltern men where, for example 'Punjabi Sikhs [from the north] were . . . "a fine martial race", whose admirable traits were "steadfast loyalty, dogged tenacity, and dauntless courage"', in opposition to their southern counterparts who were 'soft, lazy, weak . . . the physical organisation of the Bengalee is feeble even to effeminacy . . . his limbs delicate, his movements languid' (Dimeo, 2002, p. 79). However, unlike the compromises made by other racialised groups seeking employment with Western companies in the (over)-developed countries, the Fijian martial races do not 'leave their histories behind', nor are their 'histories ignored' (Sa'ar, 2005, p. 687). Indeed, these men successfully reconcile pre-colonial masculinity with that imported and mobilised by the (neo-)colonisers' racialised discursive framings in ways that bring material benefits.

Though constrained by the conservatives in Fiji 'who have made concerted efforts to ensure that the limits of tolerance regarding acceptable masculine ideals remain narrowly defined' (George, 2008, pp. 181–2), nonetheless, oppositional masculinities have challenged the militarised masculine hegemon. For example, in October 2002, gay male activists struggling for equal rights in Suva began wearing the sulu, a tailored wrap-around garment of considerable importance to the identity of Fiji's indigenous police force and military, an act of appropriation argued to be of considerable political significance (George, 2008, pp. 176–8). In the final analysis, Fijian security contractors recruited because they are both 'tough and loyal' (Teaiwa, 2005) are just as likely to join companies for reasons of economic necessity as they are for 'higher values' as noted in the context of other martial races enlisting into foreign militaries (Kirk-Greene, 1980; Parsons, 1999).

Evidence for the kind of ethnic bargain these Fijians have necessarily to make was highlighted in 2003 within the context of the British-based Global Risks Strategies which established a branch in Fiji that would pay $1,700 per month, which is high within the context of the Fijian labour market. However, it was reported that companies recruiting Fijian men have been slow to pay their employees or, more seriously, have been involved in fraud. As Maclellan records:

> Up to 15,000 people may have paid a registration fee of Fiji 150 dollars to 'Meridian' [name of intermediary] in order to be listed for work in Kuwait. Fijian journalist Samisen Pareti reported that villagers used development funds to pay application fees, and that Meridian's recruitment drives have drawn on Methodist church networks using church funds to pay for applications fees, with the money to be repaid if a job is found in Kuwait. (Maclellan, 2006, p. 54)

Yet, the intermediary had arranged only 2,000 jobs, and had failed to reimburse those who had paid the registration fee.

Privatised Enforcement Masculinities: Latin Americans

As we have seen, Fijians' trajectory into private security is shaped in part by their status as members of a martial race, against the backdrop of a colonial history that resonates with the current demand for low cost contractors. Another category of contractor that has attracted commentary in recent years is that of the Latin American, and it is to men from this region—employed mainly in Iraq and to a lesser extent Afghanistan—that attention now turns.

Privatised Enforcement Masculinities with 'Murky' Backgrounds?

Newspapers in Chile have estimated that approximately 37 Chileans working as contractors in Iraq are seasoned veterans of the Pinochet era (Nevaer, 2004: 1).[30] A recruiter known as Pizarro was alleged to have hired these Chileans for *Xe* through Neskown, a firm he set up in Uruguay while using a different company called *Global Guards* registered in Panama for his business with another major PMSC, *Triple Canopy*.[31]

This strategy was intended to circumvent Chilean law, which prohibits 'the act of providing or offering the services of private armed guards, in any form or designation, by a natural or artificial person' (Stoner, 2008, p. 1). And, since paramilitary activity is also banned in Chile, the limited training that recruits received was argued to have taken place in either Amman, Jordan, or in Iraq (Stoner, 2008, p. 1). A former political prisoner who was tortured under the dictatorship in Chile told the investigative journalist Scahill that the Chileans working for firms in Iraq 'are valued for their expertise in kidnapping, torturing, and killing defenceless citizens'.[32] Framed in a broader, strategic sense in respect of covert operations, one former high ranking Latino officer stated:

> The idea of using 'Latin American men' who could easily be assimilated into a mid-eastern environment with a little bit of cultural and language training, with the right clothing and growing of facial hair[33] . . . may also be an asset.[34]

As another Blackwater representative was alleged to have said, 'We scour the ends of the earth to find professionals—the Chilean commandos are very, very professional and they fit within the *Blackwater* system' (Franklin, 2004).[35] Further allegations that right-wing paramilitaries may be sought by some in the industry is suggested here:

> '*Blackwater* USA has sent recruiters to Chile, Peru, Argentina, Colombia and Guatemala for one specific reason alone,' said an intelligence officer in Kuwait who requested anonymity. 'All these countries experienced dirty wars and they have military men well-trained in dealing with internal subversives. They are well-versed in extracting confessions from prisoners.' (Nevaer, 2004, p. 2)

It was further reported that, on 12 October 2003, a discreet ad was placed in the Chilean newspaper *El Mercurio* inviting former members of the military, preferably ex-commandos:

> to sign up to provide security services abroad . . . the ad, placed by the Grupo Tactico, *Blackwater's* local representative, awakened the interest of at least 400 Marines and 'Black Berets'—the Chilean army's special operations forces—who retired early in the past few years.[36]

In light of these developments, activities that 'should be a national shame', argues the journalist Stoner, 'are transformed into market assets . . . as a consequence of the privatization of the Iraq war' (Stoner, 2008, p. 2). Thus, in addition to the stereotypical, pumped-up, 'hard stance' Blackwater 'cowboy' noted above, there appears to be demand—albeit to an unknown degree given the limited empirical evidence—for privatised enforcement masculinities fostered in the 'dirty wars' of Latin America. It is telling that one commentator should frame contractors from this region as having 'different bodies, different mentalities . . . different language [and a] different professional attitude' (Vail, 2008, p. 2). Here, specific kinds of privatised enforcement masculinities get reproduced where the category of 'non-combatant' and process of 'extraordinary rendition' underscore profound changes (as former British Prime Minister Tony Blair and others have put it) 'to the rules of the game'.[37] In turn, these transformed conditions may be imagined by some as the 'natural preserve' of those with specific biographies, attitudes, and practices functional for the altogether less accountable and secretive elements of the wider industry.

Democratisation and the Legacy of US Latin American Engagement

It is also important to note that this migration of Latin American men into certain, more murky corners of the PMSC industry speaks to the impact of political modernisation in the region, where democratic consolidation has grown apace over the last 30 years (Aguero and Stark, 1998). These developments have included several features: reform of militaries (D'Araujo, 2004); recognition of the repressive past (Harris and Reilly, 1998); bringing those responsible for repression to justice (Lutz and Sikkink, 2001); and, ultimately, the increasing 'obsolescence' of particular men seen as 'tainted' on account of their association with former authoritarian regimes. The 122 Chileans now in Iraq also form part of those *displaced* from active duty by a plan for the modernisation of the armed forces applied in the army be General Luis Emilio Cheyre, the current army chief.

Thus, part of the explanation for why a number of 'rougher' Latin American men have become increasingly available to transnational security companies is that they are being excluded at home.[38] Anecdotal evidence suggests that a significant number of recruiters and their affiliates deceived contractors through the use of lengthy and opaque contracts. Rights for legal recourse are waived against subsidiary companies and employers, even in cases where 'loss, damage, personal injury or death is caused or contributed to any manner [by the company]' (del Prado, 2008, p. 3). Noteworthy examples of legal get-out clauses predominate across the sector particularly in respect of men from the global South. For example, Mario Urquia, a 30-year veteran of the special forces in Honduras, was hired by Triple Canopy to guard the US Embassy in Iraq for a year. He claims the company promised him US citizenship once he completed his contract. Not only did this promise ring hollow, but he was never paid. 'Not a single penny' he told the *Salt Lake Tribune*. Urquia filed a complaint against the PMSC Your Solutions with the Honduran authorities, as have at least 16 others. Another Honduran guard badly injured his foot while in Iraq. Despite signing a contract that states the employer is responsible for providing medical and hospital insurance, he was not declared unfit for work and had little choice but to man [*sic*] his lookout tower on crutches. According to the UN Working Group on the Use of Mercenaries, the Hondurans who went to Iraq with Triple Canopy reported 'irregularities in contracts, harsh working conditions with excessive working hours' and 'wages partially paid or unpaid, ill-treatment, isolation, lack of basic facilities such as medical treatment'.[39] Problems do not end there, with the legacy of dangerous and financially insecure employment impacting on family members in the form of PTSD or disability, further exacerbated by the absence of welfare provision in home countries.

However, the broader context for the focus on Latin American contractors intermeshes with US involvement in Latin America over numerous decades, as noted in the example of the Western Hemisphere Institute for Security Cooperation (WHINSEC)[40] and also, most recently, the so-called 'Salvador Option' described here in *Newsweek* (Hirsch and Barry, 2005) as a Pentagon proposal to:

> send Special Forces teams to advise, support and possibly train Iraqi squads, most likely hand-picked Kurdish Peshmerga fighters and Shiite militiamen, to target Sunni insurgents and their sympathizers, even across the border into Syria . . . It remains unclear, however, whether this would be a policy of assassination or so-called 'snatch' operations, in which the targets are sent to secret facilities for interrogation. The current thinking is that while US Special Forces would lead operations in, say, Syria, activities inside Iraq itself would be carried out by Iraqi paramilitaries.

And, as noted in 2005:

> There are far more Americans in Iraq today—some 140,000 troops in all—than there were in El Salvador, but US soldiers are increasingly moving to a Salvador-style advisory role. In the process, they are backing up local forces that, like the military in El-Salvador, do not shy away from violence . . . excesses of [torture and death] were endemic in Latin America. . . . (Maass, 2005, p. 3)

It is striking to note that Colonel Jim Steele, a leader of the US Military Advisory Group to El Salvador between 1984 and 1986, had overall responsibility for training 'Police Commandos' to 'quell insurgency' in Iraq. It is argued that these operations have resulted in massacres where 'many . . . killings have taken place since the Police Commandos became operationally active

. . . [and that they] often correspond with areas where they have been deployed.'[41] Linking a key theme of this article, turning on the representation of contractors with the legacy of US training and a heritage reaching back to some of the worst excesses of violence perpetrated in the Latin American context, the Iraqi Commandos are described as 'cultivating a vaguely menacing look. They wear camouflage uniforms, but also irregular clothing, like black leather gloves and balaclavas'; this is not to 'hide their identities but to inspire fear among the enemy'. The author goes on to note that 'it is a look I saw among the Serbian paramilitaries who terrorised Croatia and Bosnia during the Balkan war in the 90s, and it is the look of the paramilitaries that operated in Latin America a decade earlier.'[42]

Conclusion

To reiterate the principal arguments of this article, (1) Fijian men's recruitment into the private security industry can be partly explained by their historical status as members of a martial race, (re)constituted, harnessed, and deployed in contemporary times to meet the needs of neoliberal, military-imperialist demands for low-cost privatised enforcement masculinities; (2) the appeal of a small, but not insignificant number of Latin American contractors for the private security industry may well lie in their association with politically repressive regimes believed to have fostered enforcement masculinities disposed to the privatised exigencies of the 'war on terror' as they interface with changing political conditions at home; and (3) in a broader sense, as men from the global South, both Fijian and Latin American security contractors are relatively disadvantaged in relation to their hegemonic, white, Western, former special forces contractors, though all are prone to representation through the national-racial dimension. In sum, the employment of men from the global South on the basis of their suitability to the PMSC sphere is an ironic yet largely *non-conscious* outcome of the ongoing processes of 'accumulation through dispossession' (Harvey, 2005) allied to the threat of, and actual use of violence. It is for that reason that a critical scholarship needs to be further developed in respect of the PMSC industry, as one way to counter its *increasing* normalisation that goes hand in glove with its *decreasing* visibility. My hope is that through foregrounding the articulation of race, gender, and violence in a specific context of growing importance, this article represents a modest attempt in that direction.

Notes

1 For reasons of brevity, the word 'contractor' is used throughout the remainder of the article.
2 I opt for the term private *militarised* security company, the rationale for which is provided in Higate (2011).
3 See http://www.independent.co.uk/news/uk/home-news/lsquoi-will-either-get-shot-there-or-kill-myselfrsquo-1771862.html (accessed 26 August 2009).
4 See http://www.newsobserver.com/news/story/630475.html (accessed 26 August 2009).
5 See http://www.harpers.org/archive/2007/11/hbc-90001669 (accessed 27 August 2009).
6 See http://news.bbc.co.uk/1/hi/uk/4490494.stm (accessed 26 August 2009).
7 See http://www.thenation.com/doc/20090817/scahill (accessed 26th August 2009).
8 Though, it has been argued that: 'the regulation of private military security should be understood as the *facilitation* rather than the restraint of those markets . . . [here] states are playing a formative role in the expansion of private military markets' (Whyte, 2003, p. 575; emphasis added).
9 Deborah Avant (2005) has coined this term, though her work is inclined towards regulating the industry.
10 I use the terms racialised/racialising and gendered in this article to draw attention to the primacy of race and gender in interpreting 'who' particular men from the global South are 'thought to be' and in turn, the martial traits they are believed to embody.

11 While there are occasions on which clients request female contractors (for example, as part of personal security details), overwhelmingly the industry is constituted by men with special forces backgrounds and/or from military combat branches (both of which tend to remain closed to women). Figures detailing gender breakdown in the industry are, to my knowledge, unavailable.

12 The gendered and racialised character of the migration flows facilitated by the PMSC sector have a good deal in common with labour migration of other kinds (see Pessar and Mahler, 2003) as I discuss further in the closing sections of the article.

13 I use the term development wars to capture the hybridised mix of conflict, violence, and reconstruction within the broader frame of the so-called 'liberal peace' (Chandler, 2004).

14 And, increasingly, women.

15 See http://www.nytimes.com/2009/08/20/us/20intel.html (accessed 26 August 2009).

16 By no means generalisable to the wider PMSC industry, the journalist Steve Fainaru discussing the 'mercs' he met in Iraq comments 'Sometimes . . . the mercs sat around and talked about killing . . . it made some operators uneasy . . . [but according to another merc] . . . 'there was a certain group of guys who were always trying to measure their weiners based on how many times they fired' (Fainaru, 2008, pp. 19–20).

17 I would like to thank Eric Herring and Joanna Tidy for drawing this to my attention.

18 The literature dealing with race is extensive; though in the case of men and masculinities from the global South, see Cornwall (2000), Dollimore (1997), Large (1997), Marriott (1996), and Morrell (2001).

19 At the time of writing, the British company Sabre was recruiting a significant number of 'West Side Boys' from Sierra Leone through their office in Freetown. A representative of the company (a former member of the SAS) was reported to have said that the West Side Boys were 'well equipped' and 'well disciplined'. Clues to the Sierra Leonian government's facilitation of their recruitment can be found in the West Side Boys' potential to destabilise the fragile peace in this post-conflict country.

20 British special forces operatives are represented in the movie *Hurtlocker* as quintessentially 'English', as calm under fire and understated unlike their jumpy, gun-toting American compatriots.

21 From interviews conducted with British contractors in September 2009.

22 As noted by the former SAS contractor John Geddes, who in commenting about another 'blade' (former SAS) Fijian states: 'Picture a muscular, broad-shouldered Polynesian warrior, who's polite, softly spoken and invariably gentle with his family and friends. But when his fighting blood is roused Tak is the most terrible of enemies.' (Geddes, 2006 , p. 190)

23 Similarly, and with a touch of irony, it is argued that NATO has worked hard to transform its image from that of a military alliance, to one that is 'peace loving' (Kuus, 2007). The IPOA is now known as the International Stability Operations Association (ISOA).

24 This is particularly the case for the ex-military men involved in Executive Outcome's 'successful' yet controversial operations in Angola and Sierra Leone (see Kinsey, 2007: 12).

25 The President of the ISOA, Doug Brooks has stressed this point numerously both privately (personal communication, August 2009) and publicly.

26 One approach here is to seek out evidence from contractors' own identity-work in relation to the label of 'mercenary'. There is variation here with the former SAS warrant officer Bob Shepherd writing in his book *The Circuit*, 'I see myself as a patriot and a security adviser. Never call me a mercenary' (2008 , p. 3). In contrast, Simon Low, author of *The Boys from Baghdad*, states: '. . . we took the money, the bullets . . . Mercenary might be an embarrassing term in the military world, but that's what we were . . . Dress us up as romantic soldiers of fortune . . . or post-fucking-modern euphemised PMC's, but it wouldn't alter the facts: we worked for large sums of money to be possibly killed and, if necessary, kill others. Enough said.' (2008, p. 71)

27 On 'hearts and minds', the security contractor Simon Low states: 'Hearts and minds was for uniformed armies, paid by governments to rid the world of evil dictators . . . and those who like to teach the world to sing in perfect harmony. I mean, do you really think that when answering the call for "ex-military types for interesting work in Iraq", the desire to win hearts and minds was what got the boys on the phone?' (2008, p. 31)

28 See http://www.japanfocus.org/-Andre-Vltchek/2863 (accessed 27 January 2010).

29 See http://www.timeout.com/london/features/1923/London_Lives-The_Fijian_soldier.html (accessed 27 January 2010).

30 Though an inconsequential number—their recruitment may have a disproportionate impact on those in receiving countries, as well as hint in a speculative sense at a more prevalent, hitherto unreported trend to recruit individuals 'skilled at torture' against the backdrop of the 'war on terror'. It should also be noted that these men are likely to be well into their 50s or older by now.

31 A US veteran of the Vietnam war told me that 'I have long suspected that U.S. Hispanic soldiers and others from Latin America are undercover in places like Iraq and Afghanistan' (email to author dated 22 February 2010).

32 This focus is not intended in any way to racialise men from Latin America, but to highlight how they could be imagined by some within the PMSC industry. It is also important—though outside the scope of the current article—to shine a light on the links between racialised and gendered discourses shaping how both the British and Americans have been implicated in torture. For example, in respect of the former, see http://www.guardian.co.uk/uk/2009/may/26/mi5-new-torture-allegations (accessed 24 March 2010).

33 Email to author, 23 February 2010.

34 A contact (see note 31 above) said that 'I imagine that Arab-looking Latinos serving U.S. interests can be an asset in Iraq and other places.' (Email to author dated 22 February 2010).

35 The broader context for approaches to 'tackling insecurity' that may invoke more potentially oppressive approaches is also flagged in the contract dispute involving Dyncorps concerning the increasing militarisation of the Afghan National Police, with the US military pushing for the inclusion of 'more counterinsurgency and tactical training' with recruits 'getting more instruction from military specialists including NATO advisers' (see http://www.huffingtonpost.com/2010/02/22/military-training-of-afgh_n_471519.html; accessed 24 March 2010).

36 See http://ipsnews.net/news.asp?idnews=23224 (accessed 24 March 2010).

37 The discourse of the 'war on terror' though fading from popular use, has nevertheless resonated strongly with the sentiment that 9/11 'changed everything', including the 'rules of the game'. Notably, the British Prime Minister Tony Blair invoked a change to the 'rules of the game' in his speech on security in 2005. See http://www.number10.gov.uk/Page8041 (accessed 20 November 2009).

38 One of the dynamics driving the export of now-redundant players in the torture and coercion industries is the improved accountability of the domestic context. The logic driving this migration is paralleled in cases as diverse as South African 'mercenaries' active during the Apartheid years, through, in an organizational sense, to the export of cigarette factories from the US to sub-Saharan Africa in light of the smoking ban. As accountability in domestic contexts increases, those trained in repressive techniques may look to rather less accountable contexts within which to sell their labour.

39 See http://www.unhchr.ch/huricane/huricane.nsf/view01/F8B77250C05361F3C125731A004B0E6D? (accessed 27 January 2010).

40 Known formerly as the School of the Americas, WHINSEC has trained tens of thousands of Latin American police officers and troops over the previous five decades, a proportion of whom have been implicated in human rights abuses (see Blakeley, 2009).

41 See http://www.globalresearch.ca/articles/FUL506A.html (accessed 25 March 2010).

42 See http://www.petermaass.com/articles/the_salvadorization_of_iraq/ (accessed 25 March 2010).

References

Aguero, F. & Stark, J. (eds) (1998) *Fault Lines of Democracy in Post Transition Latin America* (Miami: University of Miami).

Arkin, W. & Dobrofsky, L. R. (1978) Military socialization and masculinity, *Journal of Social Issues*, 34, pp. 151–168.

Avant, D. (2005) *The Market for Force: The Consequences of Privatizing Security* (Cambridge: Cambridge University Press).

Barrett, F. (1996) The organizational construction of hegemonic masculinity. The case of the US Navy, *Gender, Work and Organization*, 3(3), pp. 129–142.

Beasley, C. (2008) Rethinking hegemonic masculinity in a globalizing world, *Men & Masculinities*, 11(1), pp. 86–103.

Billington, M. L. (1991) *New Mexico's Buffalo Soldiers, 1866–1900* (Colorado: University Press of Colorado).

Bicanic, N. & Bourke, J. (2006) *Shadow Company*. DVD produced by Purpose Built Films.

Blakeley, R. (2009) *State Terrorism and Neo-Liberalism: The North in the South* (London: Routledge).

Brittan, A. (1989) *Masculinity and Power* (Oxford: Blackwell).

Caplan, L. (1991) 'Bravest of the brave': representations of the 'Ghurkha' in British military writings, *Modern Asian Studies*, 25(3), pp. 571–597.

Carver, T. (2004) *Men in Political Theory* (Manchester: Manchester University Press).

Chandler, D. (2004) The responsibility to protect? Enforcing the liberal peace, *International Peacekeeping*, 8(1), pp. 1–19.

Chisholm, A. (2011) Marketing militarised masculinities: An ethnographic account of racial and gendered practices in private security contractors in Afghanistan, paper presented at International Studies Association Annual Conference, Montreal, Canada.

Cleaver, F. (ed) (2002) *Masculinities Matter! Men, Gender and Development* (London: Zed Press).

Cockburn, C. & Zarkov, D. (2002) *The Post-War Moment: Militaries, Masculinities and International Peacekeeping* (London: Lawrence and Wishart).

Connell, R. (1987) *Gender and Power* (Palo Alto, CA: Stanford University Press).

Connell, R. (1995) *Masculinities* (Cambridge: Polity Press).

Connell, R. (2005) Globalization, imperialism, and masculinities, in M. Kimmel, J. Hearn & R. W. Connell (eds.) *Handbook of Studies on Men and Masculinities* (London: Sage), pp. 71–89.

Cornwall, A. & Lindisfarne, N. (1994) *Dislocating Masculinity: Comparative Ethnographies (Male Orders)* (London: Routledge).

Cornwall, A. (2000) Missing men? Reflections on men, masculinities and gender in GAD, *IDS Bulletin*, 31(2), pp. 60–67.

D'Araujo, M. C. (2004) Democratic governments and the military in Latin America: Brazil in a comparative perspective, *Security and Defence Studies Review*, 4(2), pp. 256–271.

Dawson, G. (1994) *Soldier Heroes* (London: Routledge).

Delany, M. (2009) Why 10,000 Ugandans are eagerly serving in Iraq, *The Christian Science Monitor Online*, http://www.csmonitor.com/2009/0306/p04s02-woaf.html.

Del Prado, G. (2008) *Impact on Human Rights of Private Military and Security Companies' Activities*, Online resource of Global Research, http://www.globalresearch.ca/index.php?context=va&aid=10523.

Dillon, M. & Reid, J. (2008) *The Liberal Way of War. Killing to Make Life Live* (London: Routledge).

Dimeo, P. (2002) Colonial bodies, colonial sport: 'martial' Punjabis, 'effeminate' Bengalis and the development of Indian football, *The International Journal of the History of Sport*, 19(1), pp. 72–90.

Dollimore, J. (1997) Desire and difference: homosexuality, race and masculinity, in H. Stecopoulos & M. Uebel (eds.) *Race and the Subject of Masculinities* (Durham, NC: Duke University Press), pp. 17–44.

Enloe, C. (1980) *The Ethnic Soldier: State Security in Divided Soldiers* (Athens, GA: University of Georgia Press).

Enloe, C. (2000) *Maneuvers* (Berkeley, CA: University of California Press).

Fainaru, S. (2008) *Big Boys Rules: America's Mercenaries Fighting in Iraq* (Philadelphia: Da Capo Press).

Franklin, J. (2004) US contractor recruits guards for Iraq in Chile, *Guardian*, 5 March, http://www.guardian.co.uk/world/2004/mar/05/iraq.chile.

Geddes, J. (2006) *Highway to Hell* (London: Century Books).

George, N. (2008) Contending masculinities and the limits of tolerance: sexual minorities in Fiji, *The Contemporary Pacific*, 20(1), pp. 163–189.

Giddens, T. (1991) *Modernity and Self Identity: Self and Society in the Late Modern Age* (Cambridge: Polity Press).

Goldstein, J. (2001) *War and Gender* (Cambridge: Cambridge University Press).

Harris, P. & Reilly, P. (eds) (1998) *Democracy and Deep Rooted Conflict: Options for Negotiators* (Stockholm: International Institute for Democracy and Electoral Assistance).

Harvey, D. (2005) *The New Imperialism* (Oxford: Oxford University Press).

Hearn, J. (1996) Is masculinity dead? A critique of the concept masculinity/masculinities, in M. Mac an Ghaill (ed.) *Understanding Masculinities: Social Relations and Cultural Arenas* (Buckingham: Open University Press), pp. 202–217.

Hearn, J. (1998) *The Violences of Men* (London: Sage).

Henderson, D. (1989) *Highland Soldiers: A Social Study of the Highland Regiments* (Edinburgh: John Donald Publishers Ltd).

Higate, P. et al. (ed) (2003) P. Higate, *Military Masculinities: Identity and the State* (Westport, CT: Praeger Press).

Higate, P. (2006) Theorizing continuity: from military to civilian life, *Armed Forces and Society*, 24(3), pp. 443–460.

Higate, P. (2011) In the business of (in)security? Mavericks, mercenaries and masculinities in the private security company, in A. Kronsell, E. Svedberg (eds.) *Making Gender, Making War. Violence, Military and Peacekeeping Practices* (London: Routledge), pp. 182–196.

Hirsch, M. & Barry, J. (2005) The Salvador option, *Newsweek*, 5 January, http://www.newsweek.com/2005/01/07/the-salvador-option.html.

Hokowhitu, B. (2004) Tackling Māori masculinity: a colonial genealogy of savagery and sport, *The Contemporary Pacific*, 16(2), pp. 259–284.

Holmqvist, C. (2005) *Private Security Companies: The Case for Regulation.* SIPRI Policy Paper No. 9 (Stockholm: SIPRI).

Hooper, C. (2001) *Manly States: Masculinities, International Relations and Gender Politics* (New York: Columbia University Press).
Huggins, M. K. & Haritos-Fatouros, M. (1998) Bureaucratizing masculinities among Brazilian torturers and murderers, in L. Bowker (ed.) *Masculinities and Violence* (London: Sage), pp. 29–54.
Hutchings, K. (2008) Making sense of masculinity and war, *Men & Masculinities*, 10(4), pp. 389–404.
Karner, T. X. (1998) Engendering violent men: oral histories of military masculinity, in L. Bowker (ed.) *Masculinities and Violence* (London: Sage), pp. 197–232.
Kimmel, M. (2000) *The Gendered Society* (Oxford: Oxford University Press).
Kinsey, C. (2007) *Corporate Soldiers and International Security: The Rise of Private Military Companies* (London: Routledge).
Kirk-Greene, A. H.? M. (1980) Damnosa hereditas: ethnic ranking and martial race imperatives in Africa, *Ethnic and Racial Studies*, 11, pp. 393–414.
Kuus, M. (2007) 'Love, peace and NATO': imperial subject-making in Central Europe, *Antipode*, 39(2), pp. 269–290.
Large, J. (1997) Disintegration conflicts and the restructuring of masculinity, *Gender and Development*, 5(2), pp. 23–30.
Leander, A. (2009) *Security: A Contested Commodity*, Working paper organised for The Centre for Security Economics and Technology, the University of St Gallen and the Geneva Centre for the Democratic Control over Armed Forces. Geneva, 2 & 3 November 2009.
Leed, E. J. (1989) Violence, death and masculinity, *Vietnam Generation*, 1(3–4), pp. 168–189.
Lifton, R. J. (1986) *The Nazi Doctors: Medical Killing the Psychology of Genocide* (New York: Basic Books).
Low, S. (2008) *The Boys from Baghdad* (London: Mainstream Publishing).
Lutz, E. & Sikkink, K. (2001) The justice cascade: the evolution and impact of foreign human rights trials in Latin America, *Chicago Journal of International Law*, 1(1), pp. 1–33.
Maass, P. (2005) The way of the commandos, *NY Times Magazine online*, http://www.nytimes.com/2005/05/01/magazine/01ARMY.html?pagewanted=1.
Maclellan, N. (2006) From Fiji to Fallujah: the war in Iraq and the privatisation of Pacific security, *Pacific Journalism Review*, 12(2), pp. 47–65.
Mandel, R. (2002) *Armies Without States: the Privatization of Security* (Boulder, CO: Lynne Rienner Publishers).
Marriot, D. (1996) Reading black masculinities, in M. Mac an Ghaill (ed.) *Understanding Masculinities* (Buckingham: Open University Press), pp. 185–201.
Messerschmidt, J. W. (2004) *Flesh and Blood: Adolescent Gender Diversity and Violence* (Lanham, MD: Rowman and Littlefield).
Morgan, D. (1992) *Discovering Men* (London: Routledge).
Morgan, D. (1994) Theater of war: Combat, the military and masculinities, in H. Brod & M. Kaufman (eds.) *Theorizing Masculinities* (London: Sage).
Morrell, R. (ed) (2001) *Changing Men in Southern Africa* (Pietermaritzburg: University of Natal Press).
Morrell, R. & Swart, S. (2005) Men in the Third World: postcolonial perspectives on masculinity, in M. Kimmel, J. Hearn & R. Connell (eds.) *Handbook of Studies on Men and Masculinities* (London: Sage), pp. 90–113.
Nash, G. (1995) The hidden history of Mestizo America, *The Journal of American History*, 82(3), pp. 941–964.
Nevaer, L. (2004) Here come the death squad veterans, http://www.alternet.org/world/18967.
Parpart, J. & Zalewski, M. (2008) J. Parpart, *Rethinking the Man Question: Sex, Gender and Violence in International Relations* (London: Zed Books).
Parsons, T. H. (1999) 'Wakamba warriors are soldiers of the queen': the evolution of the Kamba as a martial race, *Ethnohistory*, 46(4), pp. 671–701.
Pease, B. & Pringle, K. (eds) (2001) *A Man's World? Changing Men's Practices in a Globalized World* (London: Zed Press).
Pelton, R. Y. (2006) *Licensed to Kill: Hired Guns in the War on Terror* (New York: Three Rivers Press).
Pessar, P. R. & Mahler, S. J. (2003) Transnational migration: bringing gender in, *International Migration Review*, 37(3), pp. 812–846.
Plummer, D. (1999) *One of the Boys: Masculinity, Homophobia and Modern Manhood* (New York: Harrington Park Press).
Sa'ar, A. (2005) Postcolonial feminism: the politics of identification, and the liberal bargain, *Gender and Society*, 19(5), pp. 680–700.
Scahill, J. (2007) The mercenary revolution: flush with profits from the Iraq War, military contractors see a world of business opportunities, http://www.bibliotecapleyades.net/sociopolitica/sociopol_blackwater08.htm.
Schultz, S. & Yeung, C. (2005) *Private Military Security Companies and Gender*, Report prepared for Geneva Centre for the Democratic Control of Armed Forces (DCAF: component of Gender and SSR toolkit, tool #10).

Seidler, V. (1997) *Man Enough—Embodying Masculinity* (London: Routledge).

Shepherd, B. (2008) *The Circuit* (London: Pan).

Schrock, D. & Schwalbe, M. (2009) Men, masculinity and manhood acts, *The Annual Review of Sociology*, 35, pp. 277–295.

Singer, P. W. (2008) *Corporate Warriors: The Rise of the Privatized Military Industry* (New York: Cornell University Press).

Stanovsky, D. (2007) Postcolonial masculinities, in M. Flood et al. (eds.) *International Encyclopaedia of Men and Masculinities* (London: Routledge), pp. 34–47.

Stoner, E. (2008) Outsource the Iraq War: mercenary recruiters turn to Latin America, http://www.commondreams.org/archive /2008/07/14/10347.

Streets, H. (2004) *Martial Races: The Military, Race and Masculinity in British Imperial Culture 1157–1914* (Manchester: Manchester University Press).

Teaiwa, T. (2005) Articulated cultures: militarism and masculinities in Fiji during the mid 1990s, *Fijian Studies*, 3(2), pp. 201–222.

Vail, M. (2008) Blackwater: peacekeeping mercenaries?, http://www.thought-criminal.org/article/node/1434.

Whitehead, S. & Barrett, F. (eds) (2001) *The Masculinities Reader* (Cambridge: Polity Press).

Whitworth, S. (2004) *Men, Militarism and UN Peacekeeping: A Gendered Analysis* (Boulder, CO: Lynne Rienner Publishers).

Whyte, D. (2003) Lethal regulation: state-corporate crime and the United Kingdom government's new mercenaries, *Journal of Law and Society*, 30(4), pp. 575–600.

Paul Higate is Reader in Gender and Security in the School for Sociology, Politics and International Studies at the University of Bristol in the UK. He has authored, co-authored, and edited publications including *Military Masculinities: Identity and the State* (Praeger International) and *Insecure Spaces: Peacekeeping, Power and Performance in Haiti, Kosovo and Liberia* (Zed Press). His current research Fellowship funded by the Economic and Social Research Council and the Arts and Humanities Research Council is entitled: 'Mercenary Masculinities Imagine Security: The Case of the Private Military Contractor'.

The Pacification of Soldiering, and the Militarization of Development: Contradictions Inherent in Provincial Reconstruction in Afghanistan

RYERSON CHRISTIE

School of Sociology, Politics and International Studies, University of Bristol, Bristol BS8 1TY, UK

ABSTRACT *Provincial reconstruction teams (PRTs) are a natural outgrowth of the security/development nexus and serve as an institutional response to a perceived need to listen to the new subjects of Northern security: the helpless Southern villager who is suffering from underdevelopment and insecurity. This article, through an analysis of primary interviews, oral histories of PRT workers, and official documents undertakes an examination of the different portrayals of PRTs by contributing states, militaries, the Afghani government, and most importantly, local communities. By exploring the contradictory representations of these new teams and the civil-military cooperation (CIMIC) officers that are at their heart, the logic behind these teams can be explored. This article draws on literatures on militarized masculinities to highlight the contestations over PRT identities to reveal the tensions around the conflation of security and development. In so doing, this article challenges assumptions of local communities as passive subjects of security and development to be fought over, and it highlights the agency of Afghan communities that are too often rendered helpless recipients of aid.*

A new technology of the rescue industry emerged in 2002 with the establishment of military teams with the responsibility to engage in development and security work. These units rapidly evolved into the provincial reconstruction teams (PRTs), combining military and non-military personnel with the aim of providing a modicum of security and development in insecure regions of Afghanistan and Iraq. However, rather than being seen as a dramatic departure for

Western militaries, these teams are better understood as being the logical extension of the dominant patterns of liberal interventionism. Within this context PRTs should be viewed as the paradigmatic expression of the new security/development nexus that conflates insecurity and underdevelopment and understands modern interventions as being 'complex' and requiring the coordination of all elements of Northern intervention. The PRTs' mandate is premised on the belief that underdevelopment and insecurity are linked (Duffield, 2001, 2007), that modern humanitarian operations must work towards both goals simultaneously, and that military forces have a role to play in achieving these ends. At the same time, they are an institutional expression of the new rescue industry, and, while dominated (though not always led) by soldiers, they are supposed to be responding to local needs. As such, they provide an ideal site for the examination of modern international interventions and the ways in which these interventions are represented within the North as responding to Southern peoples' calls for assistance, and how they are perceived in the global South.

This article is primarily concerned with exploring the logic of the current forms of liberal intervention that warrant military interventions for the benefit of local peoples. Rather than engaging with technical debates (as important as they may be) about how to make these teams more effective (Bollen et al., 2006; Pruett, 2009) or with the intense disputes over whether these teams are a part of the process of the militarization of development (Pugh, 2001; Slim, 1996), this article uses the PRTs as a means of investigating how the interventions have been made possible. By focusing on the representational practices that surround the PRTs, this article will demonstrate how these teams are supposed to be listening to local communities, but that such claims are dependent on an institutionalized representation of locals as Orientalized and feminized, as either the passive recipient of aid or as the brutal and cowardly insurgent. This has informed how PRTs are perceived by contributing nations such as Canada, how their personnel are selected within the military, and how they in turn respond to local communities.

This article builds on the work of Anne Orford (1999) and Sharene Razack (2004) in its emphasis on the practices of representation surrounding the soldiers in the PRTs in order to shed light on the apparent disparity between the justification of missions for combat purposes (to search for, identify, and kill 'enemy combatants') and humanitarianism. To this end, this study draws upon literatures on militarized masculinities to frame the practices of representation in order to understand how the security/development nexus is being enacted, and how this is being done in a way that renders the local Afghan population passive targets (Tickner, 2002; Young, 2003), even though militaries claim that the PRT, and CIMIC officers that form their heart, are supposed to be attuned to local voices. These gendered representations are not politically neutral. Iris Young argues that

> . . . gendered meanings and images help organize the way people interpret events and circumstances, along with the positions and possibilities for action within them, and sometimes provide some rationale for action. (2003, p. 2)

By examining representations of PRT personnel and their activities, this article will show how the convergence of security and development is enacted and experienced, as well as how it relies on particular representations of the 'Other'. In so doing, this article is striving to engage more directly with Southern subaltern voices and to re-centre our analysis of the rescue industry on the local lived experiences.

The rescue industry is predicated on, and purports to listen to, a particular Southern voice. This means that structures of consultation are necessary for understanding local security and development concerns, yet because the voice of the South is interpreted through broader liberal narratives, the issues and concerns that are listened for are pre-structured. This has informed the representations of the PRTs and how the academic and policy literatures on these organizations have been able to avoid investigating locals' perceptions of PRT work. This is not to say that the locals are ignored, but rather that their voice is seen as irrelevant on the broader issues of how to pursue the aims of liberal pluralist society.

Critiquing these developments, including unsettling assumptions about the validity of 'humanitarian action', in order to open up space for local silenced voices demands a greater appreciation for the ways in which social practices determine what constitutes common sense and legitimate international behaviour. An examination of the representations of the PRTs (and in particular their core CIMIC officers) will reveal the tensions around the conflation of development and security under the leadership of the military. This will be done by concentrating on the narratives of identities that surround the PRTs, paying particular attention to how the CIMIC officers are represented in contributing nations, within militaries, and most importantly, within the recipient communities in Afghanistan. The study of PRTs is essential, precisely because they offer a microcosm wherein we can examine the impacts of the new security/development nexus.

The Evolution of the Provincial Reconstruction Teams

As archetypal expressions of the new international rescue industry, PRTs engage in both providing local security *and* development, which used to constitute two distinct forms of interaction between the North and South. However, the 1990s witnessed an emerging consensus that the New Wars in the global South were 'complex' and largely intractable, beyond the capacity of local communities to resolve on their own (Duffield, 2007; Weiss, 1999). This logic requires the coordination of the range of international actors, with the result that military operations, diplomatic activity, and development programs are now approached as an integrated whole (Paris, 2008; Pouligny, 2003, 2005; Pugh, 2001, 2004; Razack, 2004).

Within this context, the formation of the Joint Regional Teams (which evolved into the PRTs) by the US in November 2002 is hardly surprising; they were established precisely because of a perception that Northern militaries had a role to play, and thus required expertise, in development activities. The British Joint Doctrine on CIMIC makes this explicit: 'the PRT model is a logical . . . expression of the Comprehensive Approach' [the notion that security and development must be acted upon simultaneously] (United Kingdom Ministry of Defence, 2006). As such, the PRTs are mandated to '. . . assist The Islamic Republic of Afghanistan to extend its authority, in order to facilitate the development of a *stable and secure environment* . . ., and enable Security Sector Reform (SSR) and reconstruction efforts' (NATO, 2009, p. 3). According to the US government, PRTs are intended to:

> . . . help improve stability in Afghanistan and Iraq by increasing the host nation's capacity to govern; enhancing economic viability; and strengthening local governments' ability to deliver public services, such as security and health care. PRTs are a means of coordinating interagency diplomatic, economic, reconstruction, and counterinsurgency efforts among various U.S. agencies in Afghanistan and Iraq. (US Government Accountability Office, 2008)

To this end the PRTs are involved in a wide range of activities, many of which have traditionally been the responsibility of development and humanitarian organizations, including: humanitarian relief; the identification and implementation of Quick Impact Projects (QIPs); the construction of large infrastructure projects such as roads and schools; the training of police; and the coordination of state donor funds for projects in the communities where PRTs operate. Despite a complete lack of empirical evidence of their effectiveness, the teams have been embraced by NATO, and they have been rolled out across Afghanistan (there are currently 26 operational teams).[1]

Despite an overarching NATO mandate, there are a variety of forms of implementation, depending on the contributing states' priorities, resources, and the local provincial security situation.[2] The teams differ in terms of their integration of other government department (OGD) personnel (including development and diplomatic representatives), the extent to which they prioritize self-protection, and the types of activities that are favoured. A comparative analysis by the Woodrow Wilson School (Abbaszadeh et al., 2008, p. 5) identified three main forms:

- The US model, prioritizing QIPs and consisting of 80 personnel, of whom three to five are civilians;
- The German model, focusing on long-term development projects in relatively stable provinces with large teams of around 400 people. The teams can have around 20 civilians and have both a military *and* civilian leader; and
- The UK model, centred on local capacity building, often in conflict zones, consisting of around 100 personnel, of whom about 30 are civilians.

While these differences are important, they should not obscure the commonalities across the various models. Though there is significant variance of how well-funded the teams are, they all have economic assets at their disposal to directly, or indirectly, engage in development activities. American PRTs have access to US$100,000 per month under the Commanders Emergency Response Program (CERP) which is free of significant bureaucratic oversight. Larger projects are also possible, though these need to be approved by a higher Command. This does not include those funds that are distributed by various countries' donor agencies, which may be disbursed on the recommendations of PRTs, making them one of the largest sources of development funding in Afghanistan.[3]

Despite their clear importance, there has been little examination of the activities of PRTs, and the studies that have been conducted have tended to focus either on narrow technical analysis of their impacts (Abbaszadeh et al., 2008; Goodhand and Sedra, 2007; Jackson and Gordon, 2007; Malkasian and Meyerle, 2009; Piiparinen, 2007; Pruett, 2009) or broader assessments of the extent to which PRTs have led to the militarization of aid (Azarbaijani-Moghaddam et al., 2008; Save the Children, 2004; Wheeler and Harmer, 2006).[4] The first set of studies assess the usefulness of current practices in terms of measurable outcomes, summed up by one International NGO representative who argued that 'PRTs have never proven their worth and there have been no Impact Assessments done' (as is common practice in the aid community) (Interview, 2009b).

The second set of critiques focus on the basis on which PRTs make decisions about their activities and how they serve to militarize aid (Dziedzic and Seidl, 2005). Given their mandate, decisions about PRT activities and the projects that they contract out are not made on the basis of need, which is a central tenet of traditional humanitarianism. Rather, projects are selected and implemented on the basis of whether they will help in the fight to win 'hearts and minds', to combat the insurgency and to protect ISAF forces. In this way, development has become a weapon system to achieve the military aims of local security and to control territory and people (Wheeler and Harmer, 2006, p. 9). This is particularly evident in the role of the PRTs in intelligence gathering for ISAF, where there have been allegations that humanitarian aid is contingent on the exchange of intelligence (Braem, 2004, p. 44; Interview, 2010b). Other PRT projects have been selected to help secure infrastructure vital to ISAF military operations.[5] Even authors writing for a US military policy community argue that

> PRTs do not conduct development for development's sake. For the PRTs, development is a means of turning Afghans away from the insurgency and thereby creating a stable environment in which the Afghan government can exert its authority. This mandate largely still stands today. (Malkasian and Meyerle, 2009, p. 6)

This is defended by arguing that only the PRTs are able to undertake these development tasks in many provinces, as it is too dangerous for the UN or major international NGOs to operate, a point with which many critics of PRTs agree (Interview, 2010a, 2010b).

Unfortunately, by largely ignoring the logic that has given rise to these teams, these forms of critiques can at best result in a rejection of the PRT model, and in seeking to correct the operation of the international interventions they may serve to reinforce narratives of the security/development nexus. This extends to the militarization of aid debate, which generally fails to challenge the conjoining of security and development, presuming that humanitarian interventions are valid but that there should be a clear separation of roles between the military and the rest of the rescue industry.

Finally, and most importantly for this article, these forms of critiques occlude local communities. Afghan villagers are present either as victims or insurgents, as a social body to be fought over (Orford, 1999; Razack, 2004; Young, 2003). Their perceptions and interactions with PRTs are largely assumed to flow from their particular subject position, and locals are expected to either resist (if an insurgent) or welcome (if a victim) NATO forces. The possibility of far more complex perceptions of the PRTs, and of varying reasons for opting to cooperate with PRTs (and indeed with the broader rescue industry), is ignored.

The ways in which these teams, and their members, are represented reveal the competing visions of security and development; they also show how the PRTs work to justify the mission in contributing states yet subsume development to the requirements of military security. The voice of Afghans is not absent from the work on PRTs. Indeed the need for the PRTs, and for specialists able to interact with local communities, is indicative of this. At the same time, the militaries have sought personnel to work in these teams who demonstrate personality traits that are in some ways closer to those of NGO workers than of soldiers. This further highlights the tensions in the PRT mandates and provides a point of analysis.

Military Masculinity

Soldiers have historically denigrated development workers (Duncanson, 2009; Higate, 2007; Pruett, 2009; Stankovic, 2000), yet the new CIMIC officers are expected to be able to identify and interact effectively with this sector. Focusing on militarized masculinities sheds light on the nature of racialized and gendered relations and their interpenetration with practices of power. The representations are all the more acute as they are combined with the legitimate (or illegitimate) use of violence, a point that has been argued by Arkin and Dobrofsky (1978); Morgan (1994); Barrett (1996); Higate and Henry (2004); and Higate (2003; 2007). As a result, a detailed analysis of the interplay of masculinities in and around the teams is essential for understanding the emergence of the new rescue industry and its practices and how it impacts local communities in the South.

To date, the studies of gender and peacebuilding within military missions have focused on the dynamics inherent in having soldiers encultured into institutions that promote and harness hyper-masculinity (Cockburn and Zarkov, 2002; Higate, 2003; Higate and Henry 2004; Sasson-Levy, 2003; Whitworth, 2004) on the broader masculine protection narrative (Duncanson, 2009; Orford, 1999; Razack, 2004; Young, 2003), or on the ways militarization has made many people less secure, even when the nominal role of peacekeeping is to protect locals (Enloe, 2000; Whitworth, 2004). According to Bethan Benwell (2003, p. 8), there are two main approaches to understanding militarized masculinity as discourse: one that sees masculinity as a power project (Connell, 1995; Strathern, 1997); and another that sees it as an identity construct (MacInnes, 1998). My own approach draws heavily on Raewyn Connell's work, but read through the work of Paul Higate (2007) and Stephen Whitehead (2006), who avoid a more structural reading of masculinity in favour of one that recognizes alternative expressions of masculinity within militaries (both from within and from outside). This is crucial given the ways in which PRTs have provided a space where different forms of masculinity are not just tolerated, but are actively encouraged.

While the broader literature on masculinities recognizes this last point (Beynon, 2002; Carver, 2002; Connell, 1995; Zalewski, 1996), the *military* masculinity literature has, unfortunately, tended to ignore identities that do not accord with the hegemonic form. This arises, as Sandra Whitworth argues, from the observation that 'militaries replace uncertainty with a hegemonic representation of idealized norms of masculinity which privilege the tough, stoic warrior who is capable of and willing to employ violence to achieve whatever ends into which he may be ordered' (2008, pp. 121–2). This oversimplifies the nature of military activity and blinds us to the more pervasive means by which the military is involved in broader practices of Northern intervention, particularly, given the focus of this article, on humanitarian operations. It also occludes how new articulations of masculinity are constituted by, and reinforce, the rescue industry more broadly. These identities are constituted against a feminized Other that requires protection and development assistance. Militaries are now deliberately pursuing alternative masculinities, for at least some of its soldiers, that appear to be at odds with nominal hegemonic military masculinities. Rather than a hyper kinetic masculine ethos, armed services are seeking out individuals able to engage with local communities by listening to the concerns of villagers and cooperating with the broader development community to implement local aid projects. These characteristics of helping, listening, caring, supporting, and cooperating contrast with the aggressive physical masculinity of combat units (Duncanson, 2009). Appreciating the different representations of the CIMIC officers provides a window into the contextual structure of militaries engaging in 'complex operations' that combine humanitarian and combat operations.

Building on the literatures on militarized masculinity, the idea of the PRTs and the soldiers that work within them are constituted on a number of different levels. While these are not independent of one another, they can be analysed in different ways. To address these issues there are three areas of analysis for the tension between 'traditional' soldiering and the PRT activities and their intersection with the representations of the Afghan civilian:

- Northern public representations of the differences between PRT activities and the regular roles of armies;
- Internal military representations of these differences (how does the military itself represent the necessary skills and behaviour for a successful PRT, and in particular, its leadership); and

- How members of PRTs, local NGOs (by which I mean both International and Local NGOs working in the communities that the PRTs are affecting), Afghan government representatives, and local communities represent one another.

The First Analytic Focus: Public Narratives of the Work of CIMIC Officers

The first set of narratives about the identities and roles of the PRTs emanate from national media of the contributing states. These reflect and construct public perceptions of the teams and the people who work within them and are necessary because of Orientalist narratives of the foreign villager in need of assistance. The differentiation between the PRTs and the broader military missions disaggregate development and combat roles (while continuing to do both) in a manner that serves to legitimize the entire intervention. This is best illustrated through the stories that have been told in Canada's media about two officers who were trained and employed to liaise between the military and civilian agencies, government representatives, and local communities.

In March and April 2006, two Canadian officers serving in Afghanistan were attacked by locals. Lieutenant Trevor Greene was hit in the head with an axe while he was sitting talking with village elders. He had apparently taken off his helmet and laid down his weapon to demonstrate trust. While the injury was grave and debilitating, he did survive. The assailant, Abdul Kareem—a 16-year-old—did not; Trevor's colleagues shot him 14 times. Barely one month later Lieutenant Bill Turner, Greene's replacement, was killed when a roadside bomb detonated near his armoured vehicle. The reporting of these two attacks was distinct from stories of other Canadian casualties. Much more attention was paid to Turner's and Greene's back-stories, why they apparently were doing their work, and how working with the PRTs resonated with them, which reflected how the reporters perceived the work of the CIMIC officers in comparison to the broader combat mission. Greene, for example, was described by the *Toronto Star* as 'the one man in the platoon whose sole purpose in this country was to help Afghan villagers' (2006). He was lauded for the type of work he was doing, not just for showing bravery in the face of dangerous and difficult circumstances.

The reporting on Bill Turner continued this pattern. The *Ottawa Citizen* (2006) wrote the following account:

> Unlike the hard-core Canadian warriors he joined on patrol, Lieut. Turner did not go to Asia to hunt the Taliban or impose security in the lawless desert wastes around Kandahar.
>
> He carried weapons. He wore body armour. And as yesterday's tragedy makes brutally clear, he endured the same deadly risks as any Canadian soldier working 'outside the wire' of the main, well-defended base at Kandahar Airfield.
>
> Yet Lieut. Turner went to Afghanistan not to fight, but to carry on that quintessentially modern, Canadian military tradition—to help ordinary people, beleaguered by decades of war, rebuild their communities with aid and encouragement from Canadian soldiers.
>
> It was Lieut. Turner's job to accompany combat officers into a village or a district, and sit down with local elders, sometimes over tea or even a plate of rice and lamb, and figure out what the village needed—a water well, a school, a visit from a nurse or doctor—and take those needs back to headquarters.

The Canadian Forces and the two officers' families related how the men were motivated by a desire to help the local communities, that they were worldly, good listeners, and interested in continuing their work after they finished their military service. These characteristics are not normally associated with hegemonic expressions of soldierly behaviour. By focusing on their choices to undergo CIMIC training, these news reports contrast with the stories of other soldiers' deaths in Afghanistan, which typically describe personal courage, commitment to the military and the country, and the soldiers' support of the mission.

These narratives are not politically neutral; they ascribe the PRTs as a form of 'development' activity that is beneficial to the target society and separate from the broader combat roles. The PRTs, like much of the rescue industry, are then disaggregated from acts of violence, obscuring how the combat and development roles are aspects of the same intervention. This also echoes, and perhaps validates, a sense that there is a new masculine ethos of 'protection' that, unlike what Iris Young (2003) argues, extends beyond state borders and brings in foreign locals under the protective embrace of these PRT workers. As Razack, building on Edward Said, has argued, this is entirely consistent with long colonial traditions of seeing interventions as being '. . . *for their own good,* others who are expected to be grateful' (Razack, 2004, p. 10, emphasis in original).

Finally, media and government reports of PRTs in contributing nations lack any coverage of Afghan perspectives. This is not to say that they were absent, rather that they existed as the appreciative Southern subject for whom the officers were willing to sacrifice themselves. The Afghan local exists as the appreciative civilian or the illogical insurgent, whose voice the PRTs are responding to.

The Second Analytic Focus: Military Narratives of CIMIC Officers

While the first analysis provides insight into public perceptions of the activities of PRTs and their target communities, revealing a discourse about their activities that is consistent with the broader integration of security and development, it does not offer significant insight into the institutional narratives of such work. To be able to understand how militaries perceive, describe, and then recruit and train PRT personnel, a more detailed description of their roles is necessary. With the steady growth in military operations of both counterinsurgency and reconstruction efforts, soldiers on the ground in Afghanistan and Iraq are being asked to fulfil a range of tasks that seem to contradict the traditional concept of soldiering. The analysis of the selection of CIMIC officers and their training allows us to understand how militaries perceive the roles of the PRTs and the extent to which these roles are seen as being compatible with the hegemonic expressions of military identity.

Prior to 9/11, there was a general view that military activities engaged in by Northern forces were shifting away from war-fighting to non-traditional military 'humanitarianism' (Moskos et al., 2000). We now see new doctrines (such as the American Counter-Insurgency doctrine FM-324) that treat the two roles as co-dependent, with development activities becoming a component of the overall mission. However, this has occurred at the same time as many Northern militaries have refocused on war-fighting. This leads to an internal contradiction where there is, at least within the Canadian Forces, a return to a combat culture where soldierly behaviour is elevated, concurrent with a belief that the military needs to become more involved in development work. This is not to assert that all of these roles are equally valued by the military, just that they are called upon to participate in all of these functions. Victoria Wheeler and Adele Harmer (2006) argue that militaries see humanitarian activities as a distraction, focusing instead on their core competencies of war-fighting. Northern militaries have been called upon to engage in such activities and have sought the expertise to do so. The tension between traditional military action and peacekeeping (described as effeminate) has been explored by several scholars (Harris and Segal, 1985; Higate and Henry, 2004; Miller and Moskos, 1995; Sion, 2006; Whitworth, 2004). These same scholars have also shown how the combat arms have resisted these new roles, which are seen as diluting their core missions and making armies weaker and more 'civilian'. This has left the institutions with a struggle over how to engage in activities they deem necessary, while not eroding core institutionalized identities. The solution has tended to be to recruit and/or select individuals who would be capable of doing this development work and employ them in a sub-specialization.

In 2007 I was asked by a Canadian colonel to consider taking CIMIC training and deploying to a PRT. He stated that I was ideally suited for such a role as I 'knew the NGO community' through my academic work and my apparent political leanings, and that my experience in field work would help me listen to local communities. In short, I was sufficiently removed from normal military behaviour to be of use in this role. The Canadian military took the decision to select CIMIC officers on the basis of their capacity to relate to and interact effectively with civilian agencies. While I declined the offer (a luxury afforded to Reservists) this led me to investigate the logic behind the Canadian policies for CIMIC training. The CIMIC officers are nominally the individuals tasked with the responsibility of interacting with civilians, and while they may or may not be in charge of the PRTs, they are often responsible for running development projects and 'harmonizing' PRT and military operations (NATO, 2009, p. 28). These tasks are seen as incompatible with the broader kinetic masculinity of soldiers; Canadian and American militaries select CIMIC officers from the reserves, which are seen as less militarized and thus more 'civilian'. This was echoed by an American PRT commander who praised 'the civilian experience Guardsmen [who were deployed to the Qalat PRT] bring to the table, in addition to their military skills' (United States Army, 2007, p. 2). The point being made here is that soldiers from the National Guard have both technical *and* personal skills that arise from not being subsumed within the broader military.

In Canada the officers who are selected for CIMIC training receive a two-week course where they are trained to interact with governmental, non-governmental, and local society representatives. They are taught the basics of development work, cultural sensitivity, and other 'skills' seen as a necessary to their role as an interlocutor between the military and local communities. The work is described in ways that value characteristics that are quite different from the typical forms of behaviour valued within the combat arms. As the logic for military action increasingly incorporates humanitarianism, this has led to greater overlap between the identities of the humanitarian worker, which in the past have been described by soldiers as having feminine physical appearances with their 'scrawny beards, check shirts and hill-walking trousers' (Woolley, 2004, p. 124), and as having feminine behaviour characteristics and being naive 'do-gooders' (Duncanson, 2009, pp. 72–3; Stankovic, 2000, p. 64). Yet we find that some of these characteristics now resonate with the masculinities adopted by the CIMIC officers.

This examination of the formal institutional representation of the CIMIC officers and their PRTs provides a partial picture of the ways in which gendered identities affect the structure and behaviour of such teams. While there has been no systematic survey of how rank-and-file soldiers perceive PRTs and their CIMIC officers, there is evidence that in some instances their roles, and advice, can be dismissed (United States Institute of Peace, 2005, Interview 1, p. 15 and Interview 33, p. 17). One PRT representative related a US commander telling a PRT commander, 'I don't need your guys, I've got real soldiers' (USIP, 2005, Interview 36, p. 8). At the same time, numerous other United States Institute of Peace (USIP) oral histories relate how CIMIC officers were able to 'win over' senior military commanders, though such statements also indicate that some military elites are sceptical of the PRT input, at least until they can see the impact on the broader combat mission. The degree to which the CIMIC officers are able to secure the trust of their superiors would then appear to relate in part to the extent to which they are perceived to behave as a soldier. Regardless, an analysis of institutional discourse about the similarities and differences of PRT activities and the more traditional military activities illustrates that the rescue industry, of which militaries are one component, is seeking to graft together very different types of institutional cultures.

Additionally, the attempt to redraw the boundaries of what constitutes 'manly' behaviour, of re/ascribing at least a subset of military masculinity, along the lines that have traditionally been associated with development workers, shows the potential malleability of masculinities but also illustrates the resilience of the dominant hegemonic forms within armed forces. The fact that a new set of behaviours is being promoted for CIMIC officers also illustrates the military's own sense of unease with the new tasking of development that they have embraced. However, this also reveals a belief within the military that a different form of behaviour is necessary to interact with local communities, but that if conducted well, the PRTs will, in a contradictory sense, be perceived as separate from the broader combat mission (which is the basis of the dismissal of the NGOs' concerns of the militarization of aid). A simultaneous result of this different behaviour would facilitate the combat mission by winning hearts and minds. This all presumes a coherent local population that can be known and heard, a passive and needful population against which humanitarian workers, including CIMIC officers, partially construct identities as protector and helper.

Third Analytic Focus

The final frame of analysis, and arguably the one that is most glaring in its absence, is the mutual representational practices of the CIMIC officers (and their PRTs) and the local government, NGO representatives, and, most importantly, local communities. The PRTs are designed to respond to local needs, as is the entire rescue industry. Yet institutional narratives throughout the humanitarian sector are clearly gendered and racialized (Orford 1999; Razack, 2004; Young, 2003). The belief that local communities are calling to be 'saved from the Taliban' is in keeping with a paternal order that not only describes the South as requiring assistance, but that also defends, and indeed demands, interventionism. Local villages, with internal power dynamics and differing perspectives on politics and development, are reduced to one of two conditions: either helpless and generally passive recipients of aid; or brutal, cowardly, insurgents. Interestingly, this is not far removed from the discourse of many NGO workers or from the official narratives of development, which tend to tell similar stories of the communities they work in. The focus of the PRTs on providing local security reinforces such gendered and racialized interactions.

While NGO representatives may deride PRTs as a form of 'public relations team' that is ineffectual at best (Interview, 2010e) and quite possibly endangering NGO workers' lives, the broader rescue narrative is not actually placed under scrutiny. As such, it is imperative that a study of all three narratives be undertaken to gain an understanding of the complexities of the impacts of PRTs. Only examining military representations of local communities further obscures the agency of Afghan local communities.

The representations of local communities and the NGO sector by military personnel are consistent with descriptions of peacekeepers' discourses (Higate, 2007; Whitworth, 2004), as portrayed in academic and policy literatures, and as both my informal discussions with soldiers who have returned from Afghanistan have shown. In a recurring theme, Afghanistan is seen as incapable of overcoming its past without outside assistance: if the North withdraws the state would slip back into anarchy. At the same time, military personnel regularly describe the broader rescue industry, in particular NGO workers, as unorganized, unrealistic, and unable to work in the most dangerous and (by definition) the most needy of communities. According to a US liaison officer assigned to the UN Assistance Mission to Afghanistan (UNAMA):

> They [NGOs] just don't get it here in Afghanistan. I think there was a time and it was a long time where if you wore a UN badge or you wore an NGO emblem or a Red Cross emblem, you were protected; however, with the situation in the world now and with terrorism, with the attitude those folks have of making a quick impact by going after the soft targets, because they can't go against military forces, the humanitarian UN/NGO people are now at risk. . . . [T]hat's typically what happens in a counter insurgency type of war . . . . (USIP, 2005, Interview 10, p. 9)

Ironically, NGO representatives' critiques of PRTs are remarkably similar, attacking the military in part for its inefficiencies and lack of expertise in development (Interview, 2009a, 2009b; USIP, 2005, Interview 13, p. 13). The commonality is that both sectors purport to be more effective in listening to local needs and to be better placed to render assistance. This all presumes that the locals need and want foreign assistance.

In an environment where the population has become the problem, and its loyalty—or at least its acquiescence—is at the core of the militaries' campaigns for 'hearts and minds', local perceptions of PRTs, and how locals opt to interact with them, are of central importance. It may thus be surprising that so little work has been done on this topic, either from within academic or policy circles. Particularly telling is the way in which local views of PRTs are almost entirely absent from the 52 oral histories of PRT workers (exceptions include USIP, 2005, Interviews 26 and 33). There are only two other significant exceptions to this: Antonio Donini's (2007) analysis of Afghan perceptions of NGOs, which excludes PRTs; and Sippi Azarbaijani-Moghaddam et al. (2008). The majority of the work on PRTs either ignores local opinion or assumes local opinion is dependent strictly on PRT effectiveness.[6] The point here is that rather than being uninterested in local perceptions, the rescue industry is in fact tuned to hear local voices; from the participatory workshops of NGOs, human terrain mapping teams, through to the very formation of PRTs, there is abiding desire to hear locals. That they are not actually heard does not invalidate this. Indeed, the point is that the complexities and nuances are ignored in preference for the presumed authentic calls for assistance. Absent is any sense of agency on the part of local communities, or that the communities themselves are not coherent and closed social units.[7]

To examine local perceptions of PRTs we can disaggregate between three levels of Afghan society that are directly engaged with these teams: government representatives; local civil society; and local communities. Commencing with the government in Kabul, it is not surprising that at least some of its representatives are supportive of PRTs (USIP, 2005, Interview 13). After all, the teams' mandates are largely oriented towards protecting and extending the central government's authority into the provinces. In fact, when the PRTs were first deployed outside of Kabul, the Karzai government dictated where the teams should be located. Politicians and other government representatives have also been willing to show up to project launch events to attach their names to new initiatives. At the same time, it was related that government officials are wary to attach their name to projects that are not likely to be sustainable (Interview, 2010a) or that take place in insecure provinces (Interview, 2010e). There has also been a growing concern over the extent to which the PRTs actually serve to support the state: President Karzai has been critical of the ways that PRTs can undermine state authority, publicly declaring that

> . . . [T]he presence of the international community has created a parallel government to those such as of the Afghan government that are functioning. The PRTs in certain parts of the country have become a parallel structure to the governor of the province. (AP, 2008)

At the same time, it was related that the support of local and provincial governments by PRTs is ineffectual. According to one Afghan journalist,

> local people never consider the PRTs as a body to be supporting the local government. They think this it is a body representative of the foreign troops in Kabul. In practical to, as far as I know and I have seen the operations, they are not cooperating the way that they have written in their strategy papers and online, their websites and whatever you find. In practical they have their own projects, their own purposes, and they very little consider the suggestions of the provincial government. (Interview, 2010e)

The interaction between local civil society and PRTs is equally complex. There are numerous organizations that have decried much of the development work that PRTs have undertaken. These positions are represented by the Agency Coordinating Body for Afghan Relief (ACBAR), which has been a forceful critic of the expansion of the PRTs' roles and of the militarization of aid. These voices are in unison with much of the humanitarian industry in its opposition to the expansion of militaries into development work. At the same time, there are also numerous smaller Afghan NGOs who are willing to work with the PRTs. This has been described as resulting from a confluence of both pragmatism (the groups are desperate for funding and do not have a long cultural history embedded in the neutral and impartial tradition) and the ways in which some groups are thinly veiled money-making ventures in the shape of NGOs (Interview, 2010a, 2010b). These groups, though, are cautious about being affiliated with the international forces. According to Frekes et al., one LNGO representative stated, 'We are happy with their funding but don't want to be seen with them' (2006, p. 59).

Rather than institutional positions on PRTs, it is the question of how local communities perceive and opt to interact with PRTs that needs to be addressed. The interactions between local communities and PRTs are complex, informed by widely different contexts that vary from province to province, between ethnic groups, across the urban/rural divide, and according to the security situation in the region. In some parts of the north and east which are relatively stable, the PRTs operate quite freely and appear to be generally accepted by local communities. However, the situation is markedly different in the south-west. In these spaces, where communities are confronted with competing visions of Afghanistan, both of which are spearheaded by military force, villagers need to decide how to deal with the PRTs, while recognizing that overt support of such units can result in reprisals from the Taliban:

> There are different views about the PRTs. Sometimes communities ask for PRTs to go to their provinces and believe that it will bring funding and projects. This happens particularly in the provinces of the north while in the south people want them to leave. (Civil Society Representative, Kabul, cited in Azarbaijani-Moghaddam et al., 2008, p. 51)

As such, it should not be surprising that the teams are regarded with suspicion. One local NGO representative, in discussing local perceptions of PRTs, related this perspective:

> Okay, I'll tell you the PRTs belong to the army, belong to the military, and the people of Afghanistan, they are fed up with the military, they have suffered from war for many years. So since they are military people, they don't like PRTs, particularly in the areas where there are conflict. They do not see them as appropriate people. They don't look at them as providers of services, but they look at them as helping the military, for spying, for providing reports to the military, and all these things. (Interview, 2010b)

This individual also indicated that local communities will work with PRTs, but they do so for a variety of reasons. These reasons are tied up in the security and development activities of the PRTs, as well as with the identities that are simultaneously enacted by the PRTs and inscribed by local communities.

More interestingly, though, one NGO representative stated that local communities saw no difference between the broader combat missions that destroyed their homes and fields and killed their relatives, and the soldiers that came to 'secure' their communities (Interview, 2009a). As this individual stated, it is ludicrous to think that a community could differentiate between two identically dressed units, driving the same type of vehicle, based entirely on a shoulder patch. This is notable, as the Afghan bloggers who write about the military presence do not differentiate between various components of the military. Take, for example, Abbas Daiyar who writes: 'If the foreign troops in Afghanistan will not be serious about avoiding civilian casualties and making all-out efforts to avoid any innocent lives, they would never win the hearts and minds of people' (Daiyar, 2010). Another blogger, Waheed, argues:

> It's hard to believe for many villagers that coalition forces aren't deliberately killing them because a few times villages came mistakenly under attack and there is a lack of education. They just don't like anyone who kills their family members or relatives, regardless of whether they are Afghan forces, Taliban or coalition forces. (Waheed, 2007)

I would go further and assert that as the PRTs are reporting to the broader military Command, the arguments that they should be differentiated from combat missions only serve to obscure how military and PRT roles *are* intertwined *and* that the core combat mission is given priority.

The military strives to portray the PRTs as distinct from the broader combat operations, as having a more humanitarian drive. This extended in some instances to pushing suggestions to 'wear different hats or grow a beard or not be clean shaven . . . Just to try and make them [Afghans] see that you're trying to be more like them, maybe a little more familiar, more comfortable' (USIP, 2005, Interview 33, p. 6). Despite the ways in which the CIMIC officers have been selected on the basis of how they are 'less military', and despite the efforts that have been taken to disassociate the PRTs' activities from the combat missions, for most Afghans there is little if any discernable difference between the CIMIC officers and the security personnel (deployed together in the PRT sorties), let alone between PRTs and the broader military presence; they all look alike, do similar jobs, and use the same types of vehicles (Save the Children, 2004, p. 27). A Shura member went further and argued, 'The government, PRT, NGOs, they all look exactly the same—they are foreigners to us, even if there are local staff among them' (Shura member, Uruzgan, cited in Azarbaijani-Moghaddam et al., 2008, p. 37). Abbas Daiyar stated:

> in provincial areas, in areas where there are PRT presence. People see the PRTs as a part of the military. It is a common perception amongst people that foreign forces have come into their country, they are fighting the Taleban, and they have kind of captured their countries. So they see the PRTs as representing these troops. The PRTs are doing the same job, they are doing reconstruction efforts in an attempt to build a kind of public relations with the common people. (Interview, 2010e)

This extends, without any surprise, to the inability to distinguish between soldiers and civilians who work for the PRTs when they are all in uniforms. As one Afghan observer noted (Interview, 2010b), locals see uniforms, and what is under them is largely irrelevant:

> There are several civilians, civilian engineers, civilian doctors, they are wearing uniforms so they are not seen as civilian doctors, civilian engineers, agriculturalists. When they wear uniforms they are seen as military, not as civilians. They are seen to be completely as military. (Interview, 2010b)

This perspective, in fact, extended as far as erasing gender, in a narrowly constrained context: 'You see that there are women in uniforms, but to . . . these communities, these women are not seen as women, to them, they are seen as men' (Interview, 2010b). The crudest arguments that posit that all uniforms are perceived in the same way echoes some of the militarized masculinity literature, which does not leave room for different articulations of masculinity within armies. However, not all of the evidence supports the assertion that all uniforms are perceived in the same way; statements from Afghans demonstrate that the various countries' forces are perceived differently.

As one interviewee indicated, 'There is a myth that locals see generic uniforms and do not know the difference between them. But, US uniforms are US uniforms' (Interview, 2010a). Another observer commented that there is a hierarchy in how the various states' militaries are perceived—that the Americans are seen as the most violent, followed by British and Canadian troops (of course, it needs to be noted that this also reflects how these countries' forces have been involved in combat since the invasion of Afghanistan, where they continue to operate in the most hotly contested provinces) (Interview, 2010b). While locals may see the difference between uniforms, and thus distinguish American from British troops, distinguishing between elements of the British forces would be highly unlikely.

Indeed, among the local civilian populations in Afghanistan, the actions of the PRTs are rendered intelligible against the backdrop of the broader military campaigns in the country, of the history of ethnic violence, and of the violence perpetrated by the Taliban. This runs counter to Northern narratives speaking of a separation between the humanitarian element of the intervention and the sharp end of the Global War on Terror. This is evident from the words of an Afghan journalist in Kabul: 'I do not believe [PRTs] are very successful with winning hearts and minds. People still see them as invaders in the south and sometimes stop using the infrastructure they build' (Azarbaijani-Moghaddam et al., 2008, p. 38). Abbas Daiyar argued that in the south, 'Whenever they see a person in uniform [including PRTs] they think of an Operation, of a fire-fight with insurgents, that another operation is coming into our community' (Interview, 2010e). While PRTs are clearly seen as a part of the broader military engagement in Afghanistan, the next question is how their activities are perceived.

First, there is no indication that there is a sense of local ownership of the various PRT projects. Indeed, it was related that the PRT consultations with the local communities are, at best, superficial (Interview 2010a, 2010b). The teams rarely spend significant time in a village, favouring quick consultations with the village elders, obscuring local power dynamics. Daiyar stated:

> They do a formality, they call a meeting once a month, with local representatives, even if they do it once a month, or twice a month, or I don't know, once in 6 months. . . . . Even if they do it is a formality. Most of their projects are suggested from Kabul. (Interview, 2010e)

This stands in opposition to the orientation of development agencies that focus on community-centred development. At the same time, as a report by Save the Children indicates, communities *do* associate the projects with the broader military missions. After American rockets hit Peetai, PRTs visited the town weeks later with an offer to build a well, a village elder reportedly stated: 'We want them to leave—we don't want their help . . . let them keep their well' (Save the Children, 2004, p. 24). Such comments demonstrate that the Afghans perceive that the PRTs are undertaking projects for their own interests, not those of the communities (though obviously there can be overlap between the two). 'Afghan populations are sceptical about military intentions, and are not fooled by simplistic material incentives designed to "win hearts and minds"' (Azarbaijani-Moghaddam et al., 2008, p. 8). There is evidence that accepting PRT projects can result in violence from elements of the Taliban (Frekes et al., 2006, p. 59), a point acknowledged in the USIP oral histories of PRT workers (USIP, 2005, Interview 9 and Interview 31, p. 9). According to Save the Children, '. . . local residents do not want the military to undertake work in their villages; they fear them' (2004, p. 28). Yet some villages in Kandahar and Helmat do accept PRT projects. As Azarbijani-Moghaddam et al. argue: '. . . communities are desperate for assistance from whichever quarter; however they are also sensitive to the political and consequent security implications of accepting aid associated with contested military, international, or government agendas' (2008, p. 38). The point here is that the community members are cognizant of the implications of accepting, or not accepting, PRT assistance. They are not passive recipients of aid. This also means that their acceptance of projects cannot be treated as support for the broader international mission in Afghanistan.

Conclusions

The ongoing military operation in Afghanistan is dominating current conversations about the roles of militaries in humanitarian activities, about the ethics of peacebuilding, and the nature of international interventions. However, the study of the nominally least 'offensive' (both meanings of the word are intended) part of the military roles in these states, the PRTs, has been lagging. This is not surprising given the way in which this particular task is meant to address humanitarian needs, and is apparently concerned foremost with the human security of local populations. While these teams are widely seen as fitting within the broader mission of the military, they have remained in the background of analysis. The PRTs are indicative of the integration of security and development, and reflect the change of international interventions, with increasing roles for military action in what was previously reserved for humanitarian organizations. Thus while critical security studies has focused on the development-security nexus, and on the militarization of humanitarianism, the specific unit (and the men and women who populate it) has not received significant attention. It is this aporia of critical scholarship that must be filled in order to appreciate the broader logic of current international interventionism, limitations to its implementation (assuming one agrees with its guiding principles), and to identify points of resistance to what is presented as an inherently positive and beneficial activity.

At the same time, the PRTs have been the subject of a great deal of controversy within policy communities, with a number of international NGOs, including CARE Canada, Save the Children, and ACBAR, questioning the appropriateness of military-led humanitarian programs. Such initiatives are argued to be ineffective, as they are not commanded by individuals with professional training or extensive experience in humanitarian relief or development. Beyond this, the more profound critique is that the PRTs are contributing to an environment where the humanitarian and development missions are becoming militarized as underdevelopment has come to be seen as a source of insecurity. This is consistent with what Alice Hills (2003, p. 48) describes as the conflation of security and development which has validated a single operation that combines both air strikes and air drops.

I have argued here for a focus on PRTs as a means of exploring crucial themes around the rescue industry, and have presented one way that this could be done. While I have taken the first steps along such analysis, there is much that remains. In particular, there are a number of specific questions that arise from this initial examination of militarized masculinity within the context of integrated peacebuilding missions:

1. What are the technologies that make provincial reconstruction teams subordinate to military practice, and simultaneously draw on the results of PRT work to justify and legitimate the combat act?

2. What are the differences between the narratives of assistance that are deployed by CIMIC officers and those used by NGO workers?
3. How are CIMIC officers described by members from the combat trades, and in turn how do CIMIC officers describe the infantry and their representations of locals?

While the focus has been on the narratives *about* PRTs and CIMIC officers, with a particular emphasis on their accordance with norms of hegemonic militarized masculinity, this is only a partial picture. This also suggests another avenue of research: if the new rescue industry requires changes in some aspects of institutional identity within the military, what does this mean for the humanitarian community? Should we not be exploring the same questions through a focus on gender and identity within the aid sector?

In the conclusion of her text on militarism and masculinity, *Maneuvers*, Cynthia Enloe writes:

> More and more frequently, according to staff people working for agencies such as the International Red Cross and UNICEF, aid workers are having to request NATO military convoys and to make difficult deals with local commanders in order to ensure that their relief supplies reach those people displaced by acts of war. These staff people worry that their aid operations, maybe even their institutional cultures, are becoming militarized. They feel they are sacrificing demilitarization and, thereby, the very integrity of their professions and thus the trust of those people victimized by violent conflict. (2000, p. 292)

I feel that such a division between military and humanitarian activity can no longer be sustained, if it was ever appropriate to do so. We are now in the ironic position of witnessing militaries, reorganizing, and refocusing on war-fighting, albeit in low-intensity combat. This is happening at the same time as the military is being forced to embrace a greater role in development activities. PRTs are the physical expression of this new mandate; they represent perhaps the clearest example of the new security architecture around the rescue industry. Focusing on the narratives that surround the PRTs provides a means of critically exploring this industry.

The notion then that the logic of humanitarianism is distinct from broader military engagements has been significantly eroded. The ways in which new masculinities associated with an ethos of protection are being promoted is illustrative of how militaries have embraced—and largely come to lead—the new complex operations. This protective masculinity serves to both bolster public support for some elements of the missions and, in turn, to justify current and future interventions.

But these institutions, and the interventions of which they are a part, ultimately are responding to a broader Northern narrative about the people who are being helped. The PRTs, and indeed the entire rescue industry, are supposed to be assisting the calls for help emanating from the global South. The Southern victim of underdevelopment is becoming a new subject of security for Northern militaries, as the new feminized Other that must be protected. The irony is that while great effort is being put into creating mechanisms within the rescue industry to listen to people of the South, their voices are subsumed by expectations of what they want. However, as has been shown here, an examination of Afghan voices reveals a complexity of views and opinions about the development being imposed on the country. Individuals and communities cannot be reduced to a simplistic narrative of victim or insurgent. Finally, perhaps the most important challenge to the way the rescue industry is being enacted is that the narrative of PRTs being engaged in humanitarian work, promoted by ISAF and its contributing governments, does not resonate with local communities. They are not agentless recipients of aid; instead they opt to cooperate—or not—with the PRTs for complex reasons. However, they do not see the

PRTs as removed from the broader military roles in the country; they view the development projects as a part of the campaign to win their 'hearts and minds,' as well as to facilitate the campaign against the insurgents. For the recipient populations the uniform is what is important, connected as it is with the use of deadly force.

Notes

1 For a current list of teams, refer to http://www.nato.int/isaf/topics/prt/index.html.
2 For a discussion of the various models, and their respective strengths and weaknesses, refer to Abbaszadeh et al. (2008); Pearson Peacekeeping Centre Backgrounder (http://operationsdepaix.org/en/ci/ci_afghanistan_background.asp); Rubin (2006); and McNerney (2005–06).
3 For overviews of the amount of funding flowing through the PRTs, and how this affects issues of accountability, refer to Roberts (2009) and Waldman (2008).
4 This study has relied heavily both on interviews that I have conducted, but also on the transcripts of the oral histories of the Afghanistan Reconstruction Teams by the United States Institute for Peace (USIP) in 2005. These are available online at http://www.usip.org/resources/oral-histories-afghanistan-provincial-reconstruction-teams.
5 Communities that are situated at bridge sites in Helmand have received a disproportionate amount of PRT attention (personal communication with a British officer formerly deployed with a PRT, 16 March 2010).
6 For examples of such opinions, refer to USIP (2005), Interview 10, p. 9, Interview 11, p. 13, Interview 12, p. 18.
7 The apparent danger of doing fieldwork to hear the locals only exacerbates these dynamics.

References

Abbaszadeh, N. et al. (2008) *Provincial Reconstruction Teams: Lessons and Recommendations* (Princeton: Woodrow Wilson).

AP (2008) Karzai slams 'parallel government' set-up. Reported at Mail & Guardian online, 26 November, http://mg.co.za/article/2008-11-26-karzai-slams-parallel-government-setup.

Arkin, W. & Dobrofsky, L. (1978) Military socialization and masculinity, *Journal of Social Issues*, 34(1), pp. 151–168.

Azarbaijani-Moghaddam, S. et al. (2008) *Afghan Hearts, Afghan Minds: Exploring Afghan Perceptions of Civil-Military Relations* (Kabul: British Agencies Afghanistan Group).

Barrett, F. (1996) Hegemonic masculinity: the case of the US Navy, *Gender, Work and Organization*, 3(3), pp. 129–142.

Beynon, J. (2002) *Masculinities and Culture* (Buckingham: Open University).

Bollen, M., Linssen, E. & Rietjens, J. (2006) Are PRTs supposed to compete with terrorists? *Small Wars and Insurgencies*, 12(4), pp. 437–449.

Carver, T. (2002) Men and IR/men in IR, L. Odysseos, H. Seckinelgin (eds.), *Gendering the International* (Houndmills: Palgrave) pp. 86–105.

Cockburn, C. & Zarkov, D. (eds.) (2002) *The Postwar Moment: Militaries, Masculinities and International Peacekeeping* (London: Lawrence & Wishart).

Connell, R. W. (1995) *Masculinities* (Cambridge: Polity Press).

Daiyar, A. (2010) Civilian casualties: US troops not serious to avoid and Taliban cause larger, *Kabul Perspective*, Weblog 13 April, http://kabulperspective.wordpress.com/2010/04/13/civilian-casualties-us-troops-not-serious-to-avoid-and-taliban-cause-larger/.

Donini, A. (2007) Local perceptions of assistance to Afghanistan, *International Peacekeeping*, 14(1), pp. 158–172.

Duffield, M. (2001) *Global Governance and the New Wars: the Merging of Development and Security* (London: Zed).

Duffield, M. (2007) *Development, Security and Unending War: Governing the World of Peoples* (Cambridge: Polity Press).

Duncanson, C. (2009) Forces for good? Narratives of military masculinity in peacekeeping operations, *International Feminist Journal of Politics*, 11(1), pp. 63–80.

Dziedzic, M. & Seidl, M. (2005) Provincial reconstruction teams and military relations with international and nongovernmental organizations in Afghanistan, *USIP Special Report*, no. 147 (Washington, DC: USIP).

Enloe, C. (2000) *Maneuvers: the International Politics of Militarizing Women's Lives* (Berkeley & London: University of California Press).

Frekes, G., Klem, B. et al. (2006) *Principles and Pragmatism: Civil-Military Action in Afghanistan and Liberia* (Den Haag: Cordaid).

Goodhand, J. & Sedra, M. (2007) Bribes or bargains? Peace conditionalities and 'post-conflict' reconstruction in Afghanistan, *International Peacekeeping*, 14(1), pp. 41–61.

Harris, J. & Segal, D. (1985) Observations from the Sinai: the boredom factor, *Armed Forces & Society*, 11(2), pp. 235–248.

Higate, P. (ed) (2003) *Military Masculinities: Identity and the State* (Westport CT: Praeger).

Higate, P. (2007) Peacekeepers, masculinities, and sexual exploitation, *Men and Masculinities*, 10(1), pp. 99–119.

Higate, P. & Henry, M. (2004) Engendering (in)security in peace support operations, *Security Dialogue*, 35(4), pp. 481–499.

Higate, P. & Henry, M. (2009) *Insecure Spaces: Peacekeeping, Power and Performance in Kosovo, Haiti and Liberia* (London: Zed Press).

Hills, A. (2003) Basra and the referent points of twofold war, *Small Wars & Insurgencies*, 14(3), pp. 23–44.

Interview (2009a) International NGO worker (with experience in Afghanistan), Phnom Penh, 3 August.

Interview (2009b) International NGO worker (with experience in Afghanistan), Phnom Penh, 11 August.

Interview (2010a) Phone Interview with International (non Afghani) Local NGO worker, 15 March.

Interview (2010b) Phone Interview with Afghan Local NGO Deputy Director, Kabul, 19 March.

Interview (2010c) Phone Interview with International NGO worker, Kandahar, 26 April.

Interview (2010d) Phone Interview with Margaret Mills, 28 May.

Interview (2010e) Skype Interview with Abbas Daiyar, Kabul, 18 August.

Jackson, M. & Gordon, S. (2007) Rewiring interventions? UK provincial reconstruction teams and 'stabilization', *International Peacekeeping*, 14(5), pp. 647–661.

MacInnes, J. (1998) *The End of Masculinity: The Confusion of Sexual Genesis and Sexual Difference in Modern Society* (Buckingham: Open University Press).

Malkasian, C. & Meyerle, G. (2009) *Provincial Reconstruction Teams: How do we Know they Work?* Strategic Studies Institute, http://www.strategicstudiesinstitute.army.mil/pdffiles/PUB911.pdf.

McNerney, M. (2005–2006) Stabilization and Reconstruction in Afghanistan: are PRTs a model or a muddle? *Parameters*, 35(4), pp. 32–46.

Miller, L. & Moskos, C. (1995) Humanitarians or warriors? Race, gender and combat status in Operation Restore Hope, *Armed Forces & Society*, 21(4), pp. 615–637.

Moskos, C. et al. (2000) *The Postmodern Military: Armed Forces After the Cold War* (Oxford: Oxford University Press).

NATO (2009) *PRT Handbook*, 4th ed. (Brussels: NATO Headquarters).

Orford, A. (1999) Muscular humanitarianism: reading the narratives of the new interventionism, *European Journal of International Law*, 10(4), pp. 679–711.

Ottawa Citizen (2006) Slain soldier's goal was to improve life for Afghanis, 23 April, www.canada.com/story_print.html?id=9d1b1b35-9efe-47e5-bbb7-83a76baf2036&sponsor=.

Paris, R. (2008) *At War's End: Building Peace after Civil Conflict* (Cambridge: Cambridge University Press).

Piiparinen, T. (2007) A clash of mindsets? An insider's account of provincial reconstruction teams, *International Peacekeeping*, 14(1), pp. 143–157.

Pouligny, B. (2003) UN Peace Operations, INGOs, NGOs, and Promoting the Rule of Law: Exploring the Intersection of International and Local Nomms in Differnet Postwar Contexts, *Journal of Human Rights*, 2(3), pp. 359–377.

Pouligny, B. (2005) Civil society and post-conflict peacebuilding: ambiguities of international programmes aimed at building 'new' societies, *Security Dialogue*, 36(4), pp. 495–510.

Pruett, J. (2009) The interagency future: embedded provincial reconstruction teams in Task Force Marne, *Military Review*, September–October, pp. 54–63.

Pugh, M. (2001) The challenge of civil-military relations in international peace operations, *Disasters*, 25(4), pp. 345–357.

Pugh, M. (2004) Peacekeeping and critical theory, *International Peacekeeping*, 11(1), pp. 39–58.

Rubin, B. (2006) *The Political Context of Public Administration Reform* (Washington, DC: The World Bank).

Razack, S. (2004) *Dark Threats and White Knights: The Somalia Affair, Peacekeeping and the New Imperialism* (Toronto: University of Toronto Press).

Roberts, R. (2009) Improving mutual accountability for aid effectiveness, *Afghanistan Research and Evaluation Unit (AREU) Policy Note Series* (Kabul: AREU).

Strathern, M. (1997) Gender: Division or comparison, K. Hetherington & R. Munro (eds), *Ideas of Difference: Social Spaces and the Labour of Division, Sociological Review Monograph* (Oxford: Blackwell Publishers), pp. 42–63.

Sasson-Levy, O. (2003) Military, masculinity, and citizenship: tensions and contradictions in the experience of blue-collar soldiers, *Identities*, 10(3), pp. 319–336.

Save the Children (2004) *Provincial Reconstruction Teams and Humanitarian—Military Relations in Afghanistan* (London: Save the Children).
Sion, L. (2006) Too sweet and innocent for war? Dutch peacekeepers and the use of violence, *Armed Forces & Society*, 32(3), pp. 454–474.
Slim, H. (1996) The stretcher and the drum: civil-military relations in peace support operations, *International Peacekeeping*, 3(2), pp. 123–141.
Woolley, M. (2004) *Cleanse Their Souls: Peacekeeping in Bosnia's Civil War 1992–1993* (Barnsley: Pen and Sword Military).
Stankovic, M. (2000) *Trustéd Mole: A Soldier's Journey into Bosnia's Heart of Darkness* (London: Harper Collins).
Tickner, J. (2002) *Gendering World Politics: Issues and Approaches in the Post-Cold War Era* (New York: Columbia University Press).
Toronto Star (2006) Axe attack, 12 March, http://www.thestar.com/Unassigned/article/128769.
United Kingdom Ministry of Defence (2006) *JDP 3-90 Civil-Military Co-operation (CIMIC)* (Swindon: MOD).
United States Army (2007) 1st Battalion, 158th Infantry Regiment (May), *Cuidado* 1(2).
United States Government Accountability Office (2008) *GAO-09-86R Provincial Reconstruction Teams* (Washington, DC: USGAO).
United States Institute of Peace (USIP) (2005) *Oral Histories: Afghanistan Provincial Reconstruction Teams*, http://www.usip.org/resources/oral-histories-afghanistan-provincial-reconstruction-teams.
Waheed (2007) Civilian casualties, *Aghan Warrior*, Weblog 8 September, http://afghanwarrior.blogspot.com.
Waldman, M. (2008) *Falling Short: Aid Effectiveness in Afghanistan*, ACBAR Advocacy Series (Kabul: ACBAR).
Weiss, T. (1999) Sanctions as a foreign policy tool: weighing humanitarian impulses, *Journal of Peace Research*, 36(5), pp. 499–509.
Wheeler, V. & Harmer, A. (eds) (2006) *HPG Report 21: Resetting the Rules of Engagement: Trends and Issues in Military–Humanitarian Relations* (London: Overseas Development Institute).
Whitehead, S. (2006) *Men and Masculinities* (Cambridge: Polity Press).
Whitworth, S. (2004) *Men, Militarism, and UN Peacekeeping:a gendered analysis* (Boulder, CO: Lynne Rienner).
Woolley, M. (2004) *Cleanse Their Souls: Peacekeeping in Bosnia's Civil War 1992–1993* (Barnsley: Pen and Sword Military).
Young, I. (2003) The logic of masculinist protection: reflections on the current security state, *Signs: Journal of Women in Culture and Society*, 29(1), pp. 1–25.
Zalewski, M. (1995) Well, what is the feminist perspective on Bosnia? *International Affairs*, 71(2), pp. 339–356.

Ryerson Christie is a former Canadian Consortium for Human Security Doctoral Fellow and has worked extensively on issues of post-conflict peacebuilding, and state-civil society interaction. His work applies critical approaches to explore the ways in which security practices can disempower marginalized communities.

Turkey: An Emerging Hub of Globalization and Internationalist Humanitarian Actor?

REŞAT BAYER* & E. FUAT KEYMAN**

**Department of International Relations, Koç University, Sarıyer 34450, İstanbul, Turkey*
***Istanbul Policy Center, Sabancı University, Orhanlı Tuzla 34956, İstanbul, Turkey*

ABSTRACT *In an era of global turmoil generating significant challenges to global security and requiring global solutions, humanitarian intervention, and assistance become central concerns at the intersection of globalization studies and international relations. In this context, Turkey is emerging as a more proactive and autonomous actor in foreign policy and as a regional and global force in peacekeeping and humanitarian operations, making the country one of the key actors of world politics. In this article, we demonstrate Turkey's contributions to global security through its increasing involvement in humanitarian assistance in different regions of the world, and suggest that in doing so Turkey is not only contributing to global security but also creating new norms of democratic global governance that bridge several seemingly contradictory formations: European integration and Islamic solidarity; global South ascendance and NATO stabilization; Ottoman nostalgia and internationalist modernism. But the primary focus will be Turkish protagonism in peacekeeping interventions in Afghanistan to demonstrate the multilateral manner through which humanitarian assistance norms are implemented.*

May 2010 saw Turkey appear in the international peace and humanitarian spotlight in two different situations. First, Brazil and Turkey, with encouragement from the then International Atomic Energy Agency (IAEA) Director General Dr Mohamed ElBaradei, attempted to facilitate the attainment of an agreement, which would have acted as a confidence-building measure in regards to Iran's nuclear program. While Iran maintained that its nuclear program was peaceful, United States and some of other permanent members of the UN Security Council (UNSC) argued that Iran's nuclear program was moving towards the creation of nuclear weapons (Hafezi and Exman, 2010). On 17 May 2010, Iran agreed to a series of concessions whereby it would receive fuel-rods for use at Tehran Research Reactor within a year in return for transferring 1,200 kg of its low-enriched uranium (LEU) to Turkey within a month for safeguarding under IAEA auspices. However, the confidence-building measures were not seen as sufficient by the UNSC members who argued that Iran was not sufficiently transparent and that the concessions were not enough. The Turkish Prime Minister Recep Tayyip Erdoğan's view was that 'My expectation is that after this declaration there will not be a need for sanctions' (Hafezi and Exman, 2010). Brazil and Turkey found themselves soon afterwards to be the only two countries voting against a UNSC resolution (besides Lebanon, which abstained) imposing further sanctions against Iran.

Second, a Turkish NGO, Foundation for Human Rights and Freedom and Humanitarian Relief (İHH), organized the Gaza Freedom Flotilla along with the Free Gaza Movement. The ships were carrying humanitarian aid and construction materials to Hamas-controlled Gaza Strip and their main goal was to challenge the Israeli naval blockade of Gaza.[1] Israel indicated that the flotilla would be stopped beforehand. On 27 May, the then Turkish Foreign Ministry spokesman Burak Özügergin maintained that this was an international civil society endeavor and said, 'We do not look at the Middle East . . . only through security and stability prisms but also through human rights. . . . Problems can be avoided if this aid package is seen as humanitarian aid' (Republic of Turkey Ministry of Foreign Affairs, 2010a). On 31 May, eight Turkish civilians and one American civilian of Turkish origins onboard died during an Israeli military operation on to the main ship of the flotilla, while it was still in international waters. Israel maintained that İHH had close ties to Hamas and that its soldiers were attacked first (although this was after they had assaulted the ship) (Radikal, 2010). In June 2010, following widespread international outcry, both Egypt and Israel eased the blockade of Gaza but did not end it.[2]

In this study, we focus on Turkey's contribution to peace-building, which is broadly defined here to include activities such as mediation, peacekeeping, humanitarian activities, and other attempts with the goal of decreasing the chances of violence onset or resumption. We suggest that focusing on Turkey can help to understand how developing countries, which have capability and willingness, can contribute to international security. Turkey was in the past not considered a primary international actor (although its regional NATO role was well established), and understanding its behavior is partly important because it helps to understand the foreign policy of a country that is of interest due to its rapidly ascendant profile, as a agent of commercial and economic globalization, and as a new model for development and modernity. Moreover, Turkish foreign policy has received increasing attention recently as it has been described as simultaneously as a regional power, a middle power, and a pivot for globalization and geopolitical innovation (see Brzezinski, 1997). With its increasing economic prowess and military expertise, Turkey might possess the necessary capabilities to play a bigger role in global issues, and the country is willing to do so. Turkish academic, and foreign affairs minister since May 2009, Ahmet Davutoğlu has maintained in his book *Stratejik Derinlik* (2001) that his country's identity is the product of its distinctive history and regional specificities, and that these contexts provide it with unique assets. And it is maintained that, due to its presence in several geocultural spheres (including the Balkans, the Middle East, and Europe), Turkey has no choice but to be innovative and active as a policy leader and globalization visionary. At the same time, it is not just the state apparatus but also Turkish civil society that is increasingly overtly demonstrating its willingness to become involved in international security matters, as shown in the Gaza Flotilla case. It has to be noted that, as with the Turkish state, Turkish civil society's interest and involvement in such matters did not appear overnight. For example, an İHH representative says that it was the massacre of Bosnian Muslims during the Bosnian War that propelled them to institutionalize (ORSAM, 2011). However, as this study shows below this willingness to become involved has become much more apparent in the recent past.

Global Turmoil and Democratic Governance

Realist discussions of security in the field of international relations focus on national security, which require defense of territory and state interests, where key actors are defined as states and the military profile of others is consistently measured as the barometer of security threat. On the other hand, human security discussions refer to the 'welfare of ordinary citizens' (Paris, 2001, p. 87) broadening the notion of security threats beyond the parameters of military might and strategic threat. In fact, international organizations such as the United Nations Development Programme's 1994 Human Development Report and the Millennium Goals draw our attention to human security in the areas of poverty, food, water, and health security, which is akin to European Union (EU) and North Atlantic Treaty Organization's (NATO) 'comprehensive approach' to security. Turkey has been a leader, of late, in articulating together both notions of security while considering its placement at the intersection of various patterns of globalization.

As has been suggested by many, globalization is in turmoil, generating unprecedented challenges varying in a large horizon from security risk zones to human disparity to economic crisis to global climate change (Brzezinski, 2004; Brzezinski and Snowcroft, 2008; Falk 1995, 1999, 2010). At the very general level, addressing and responding effectively to these global challenges constitute the main foreign policy objective of the actors of the international system. The aforementioned challenges, whether of a more economic, security, or environmental nature, have the potential to affect all societies and, thus, individual and multilateral efforts are needed (Paris, 2001). Globalization of humanitarian aid is one of the ways to achieve this objective, and Turkey is no different in this regard. Indeed, both Turkey's recent proactive foreign policy regarding humanitarian aid and the fact that Turkey is becoming one of the significant global humanitarian states can and should be seen as a response to massive shifts in the balance of North and South, East and West. Moreover, the existing nature of globalization has been dominated by free market rationality, top-down decision making, and privileging state-centric security concerns over social justice and human development (Falk, 1999). In responding to shifting hegemonies, the improvement of the human condition and welfare, as well as the construction of norms to institutionalize democratic human governance, should be the central concern of the global community. As a globalization-conscious, internationalist state, Turkey's efforts in humanitarian aid respond to immediate crises while also claiming to pursue the long-term goal of contributing to the creation of a better human and stable global order. In this context, Turkey tends toward a preference for multilateralism over unilateralism in its peace-building policies. This means that new Turkish globalism is not simply an act of augmenting its power and influence or of revitalizing its Ottoman past to extend the sphere of its regional influence; on the contrary, it demonstrates its deep commitment to multilateralism and to enhanced cooperation as a way of making our world stable and peaceful.

Turkey's Non-Military Contributions

Turkey has often engaged in conflict management. One aspect where this is particularly seen in the recent past is with mediation. For example, Turkey offered to mediate between Iran and Iraq during their long war in the 1980s; and Armenia and Azerbaijan were willing to use Turkey as a facilitator and perhaps even a mediator in 1991 (Oran, 2001, pp. 154, 402) when Turkey was giving much more attention to that conflict than did the rest of the international community. Foreign Minister İsmail Cem was involved in shuttle diplomacy between Israel, Palestine, and Egypt in the beginning of the Second Intifada in 2000. Moreover, İsmail Cem believed that Turkey could play a role as a facilitator in conflicts within the Caucasus (Oran, 2001). Turkey's interest in mediation increased in the 2000s. Turkey has put itself forward as a mediator several times particularly in cases involving Israel. These included mediation attempts between Israel and Syria (several times after 2003), as well as between Israel and Lebanon after 2006, Pakistan after 2005, the Palestinian Authority after 2005, and with Hamas over a kidnapped Israeli soldier after 2006. In fact, Turkey had demonstrated an interest in contributing to Arab–Israeli peace even before March 1991 when President Turgut Özal offered to hold peace talks in Turkey (Gruen, 1995). The anger expressed by Prime Minister Recep Tayyip Erdoğan towards Israel after 2008 also needs to be seen within this prism, as Israel's 2008 Gaza operation began shortly after Israeli Prime Minister Olmert had been invited to Erdoğan's house to talk about advancing peace and reconciliation (Akyel, 2010). Thus the prime minister felt his personal efforts had been betrayed and that he had been humiliated, a feeling evidenced in Erdoğan's statement that Israel's attack on Gaza was 'also a sign of disrespect to us' (*Hürriyet*, 2008). In an attempt to diffuse the situation, the Israeli minister of social affairs, Isaac Hertzog, had a teleconference with Turkish journalists when he said that the decision for the operation was not taken until after Olmert had left Turkey, and he maintained that 'We had no intention to embarrass the Turkish Prime Minister or the Turkish people' (Gürcanlı, 2008). Syrian President Bashir al-Asad pointed out that if Syria and Israel could have found a better mediator than Turkey they would have accepted its mediation but that they had not found a better alternative, as Turkey understood the region better than others (Karan, 2010). Turkey has also offered to assist in various internal crises such as among Palestinian groups, as well as among conflicting parties in Lebanon (RTMFA, 2010b). It has also been active in the Caucasus, including Georgia. Moreover, in the case of Iraq, Turkey ensured that the legislative elections of 15 December 2005 took place by helping to convince Iraqi Sunnis to participate in the general elections, which is in contrast to the 30 January 2005 elections when only 0.1% of Sunnis participated (Binyon, 2010).

Turkey indicated that it would be happy to contribute to the main negotiations between Iran and permanent UNSC member countries even after the Iran–Brazil–Turkey declaration did not receive approval by the permanent UNSC members along with Germany, who did not find that Iran was being sufficiently transparent. Iran is not the only country with which Turkey assumed the position of the interlocutor in issues involving Western and non-Western countries. Turkey took the lead with Spain in co-sponsoring the United Nations Alliance of Civilizations. This initiative was launched in 2005 under the auspices of the United Nations and strives to promote global dialogue and particularly to decrease tensions between Islam and the West (UNAOC, 2011). Moreover, in 2006 Turkey was asked to assist during the Austrian presidency of the EU in Denmark's cartoon crisis over the depiction of Islam and the prophet in a Danish newspaper, which resulted in global fury (Kirk, 2006).

Turkey has been successful in being accepted as a mediator, such as between Israel and Syria; but at other times some of its offers to mediate, such as between Armenia and Azerbaijan in May 2004, fell on deaf ears. A more successful, but less heard, case is the trilateral commission established between Bosnia and Herzegovina, Serbia, and Turkey in fall 2009. This emerged from Turkey's concern about the rising separatist inclinations and general deterioration of relations within Bosnia (Yinanç, 2010). The goals included helping the various sides within Bosnia to reconcile, encouraging Serbia to use its ties to the Bosnian Serbs to help with internal stability in Bosnia, and improving Serbia's relations with Turkey. This commission helped to reestablish relations at ambassadorial levels between Bosnia and Serbia in addition to setting up regular monthly meetings. Through this process, Serbia made the important symbolic move of apologizing for its role in the 1995 Srebrenica massacre in which 8,000 Bosnian Muslim men were rounded up and executed. It has to be borne in mind that the International Court of Justice ruled in 2007 that Serbia had not done enough to prevent genocide from occurring at Srebrenica. The Turkish 'success' in contributing to Serbia's decision to apologize when the EU and the US had failed resulted in some soul-searching among EU officials (Vogel, 2010).

Turkey has also coordinated with others in conflict management and has acted within a multilateral setting. What is particularly underappreciated in the post Cold War era is the role that Turkey played in preventing conflicts from becoming forgotten by the international community. Crocker et al. (2004) maintain that forgotten conflicts can result in failed states (Bøås and Jennings, 2007; Ukeje, 2008). In the early 1990s, Foreign Minister Hikmet Çetin tried to bring the attention of Western leaders to the situation between Azerbaijan and Armenia, and his efforts contributed to the Organization for Security and Cooperation in Europe (OSCE) adding this matter to its agenda. Similarly, Turkey again was involved in assisting newly independent Central Asian republics to develop their influence and relationships at multilateral organizations such as OSCE, NATO, the Organization for Economic Cooperation and Development (OECD), and the Council of Europe (COE). In terms of conflict in Bosnia and Herzegovina, Turkey brought the issue to the forefront of all major organizations, such as OSCE, COE, Organization of the Islamic Conference, UN Security Council, and NATO, as it wanted the territorial integrity of Bosnia and Herzegovina to be preserved. It questioned the justice of an embargo on arms sales where everybody but the Bosnians had arms. Moreover, it played a role along with the US in the creation of the Bosnian–Croatian Federation in March 1994, even though there were times when Turkey and the US did not see eye to eye. For example, Turkey did not see the Vance–Owen plan as satisfactory (Oran, 2001, pp. 497, 501).

Moreover, Turkey has been engaging in activities in the developing world; these efforts can be seen as attempting to contribute to the economic development and, subsequently, to human security, as empirical studies demonstrate that per capita income, secondary education, and growth rate reduce internal violence (Collier and Hoeffler, 2004). Turkey's economic development activities are compatible with its main foreign policy objectives, which see economy, security, and human betterment as intertwined aspects of regional and global stability and peace. And of course, these activities would help build markets for Turkey's rapidly growing and globalizing commercial interests. In this regard, Turkey has been engaging in providing humanitarian assistance and education. The Turkish Ministry of Foreign Affairs calculates Turkey's value of in-cash and in-kind humanitarian assistance as having exceeded US$250 million in 2005 and 2006 (RTMFA, 2010c). The UN World Food Programme has listed Turkey as a major donor in addressing the food crisis in Africa. Turkey's voluntary contributions to the UN have reached almost US$12 million in 2005 and 2006 (RTMFA, 2010c). It has also spearheaded donor conferences. For example, Turkey along with Egypt co-chaired a donor conference organized by the Organization of the Islamic Conference to rebuild Darfur in March 2010. Turkey's own pledges amounted to US$60–75 million earmarked for water, education, and agricultural projects until 2015 (Arısoy, 2010). Turkey also has made several grants in the Balkans. For example, in 2010, it made a grant of US$200,000 to the International Commission on Missing People in its work in Bosnia and Herzegovina (ICMP, 2010). The Turkish International Cooperation and Development Agency (TİKA) has undertaken many projects in Central Asia and also in other parts of the world, including Africa, the Middle East, and Europe (Özkan, 2008). In the Balkans, for example, it has added and refurbished school buildings in Kosovo.

TİKA does not have a religious focus, and a major part of its African operations in 2005 took place in Ethiopia. The head of TIKA, Musa Kulaklıkaya, maintained that TİKA's international contribution has averaged US$700 million between 2006 and 2009, whereas it ranged from US$40 million to US$80 million between 2004 and 2006. He argued that this international assistance will contribute to Turkey's 'soft power' (*Hürriyet Daily News*, 2010).

Turkish non-governmental organizations have also been providing assistance in locations around the world. The Turkish Red Crescent is the largest humanitarian organization in Turkey. It has been active in hot spots such as in Gaza and Darfur (where it runs a hospital). It has been credited with creating the 'first humanitarian "decongestion" in Haiti' following the 2010 earthquake by setting up a small tented encampment for about 200 families in a relatively safer region (Wynter, 2010). More recently, other non-governmental organizations have become active, particularly in issues affecting Muslims, as shown in the Gaza Flotilla case.

Turkey also gives many grants for students from around the world to come and study in Turkish universities. While many other developing countries have similar programs, an interesting phenomenon is the opening of educational institutions (including universities) around the world, including in the United States, by the followers of a Turkish religious movement led by Fetullah Gülen (Tavernise, 2008). The opening of Turkish primary and secondary schools associated with this movement, with their focus on science and languages, can contribute to the education of these societies, which might than have a positive influence on their development. For example, a Turkish school opened at Yolunda, Cameroon in 2003 despite the fact that Turkish trade was limited with Cameroon and there was no embassy at the time. These schools have the stated goal of creating a dialogue of civilizations, which is reminiscent of Prime Minister Erdoğan's Alliance of Civilizations initiative with Spain (UNAOC, 2011).

Despite Turkey's impressive economic growth and increasing private wealth (Turkey is an upper middle-income country according to World Bank data with a 2009 GDP per capita of US$8,554) (Kirişci, 2009; World Bank, 2011), it is limited in how much development assistance it can provide compared to developed countries. However, more importantly from the point of development than public aid, Turkish private-sector companies have been trading at high levels in various parts of Africa and the Middle East. A recent Chatham House report (Cargill, 2010) maintains that trade rather than aid is what African countries need for their development; it points to Turkey as one of the countries whose firms are actively engaging in trade with African countries. In fact, Turkey's total imports (US$7,040 billion) from Africa, excluding the Republic of South Africa (RSA), were greater than the imports of RSA from the rest of Africa in 2008 (US$6,268 billion). Moreover, Turkey's exports to Africa have doubled from 2006 to 2008, going from US$4,465 billion to US$9,058 billion (Cargill 2010, p. 41).

Turkish business associations are active abroad with Turkish Industrialists' and Businessmen's Association (TÜSİAD), working particularly hard in Turkish–EU relations. TÜSİAD was called upon in June 2010 first by Iraqi Kurds to invest in Northern Iraq, and then by the Iraqi government to invest in the whole country and to contribute to the development of the country (Özdabak, 2010). The Union of Chambers and Commodity Exchanges of Turkey (TOBB) have to be highlighted for their Industry for Peace project. In 2005 TOBB agreed to develop and manage an industrial park in Palestine (with the endorsement of Israeli, Palestinian, Turkish, and US leadership) along with over US$50 million planned investment with the goals of decreasing unemployment and increasing interaction between Israeli and Palestinian businesspeople. This project was described as contributing to structural prevention of violence and nonviolent conflict resolution (Gürkaynak, 2007). However, the downturn in relations between Turkey and Israel, as well as the deteriorating security situation, has prevented the project from developing. Nonetheless, this reflects a growing interest among Turkish civil society in security matters.

Thus, Turkey has engaged in a considerable form of activities that had a non-military nature in various parts of the world. While Turkish attempts at mediation have received considerable attention, it is clear that while important, they by no means constitute the sole form of activity in which Turkey engages in peace-building. We next examine this nation's military contributions to peace-building efforts.

Turkey's Military Contributions

Turkey has contributed to global security efforts, particularly in regard to terrorism and weapons of mass destruction (WMD). But here we will focus on Turkey's explicitly internationalist peacekeeping operations. In order to better understand the Turkish military contribution in the 2000s, it is important to consider its past major contributions to multilateral missions. Turkish involvement in the Korean War between 1950 and 1953 was militarily very significant (only three countries contributed more troops to the United Nations mission in support of South Korea); over 15,000 Turkish personnel were involved during the conflict (Türk Silahlı Kuvvetleri, 2010). Turkish participation in UN peacekeeping missions, like that of many other countries, was limited during the Cold War. Turkey participated in the UN observer mission between 1988 and 1991 following the Iran–Iraq war (Türk Silahlı Kuvvetleri, 2010).

With the end of the Cold War, Turkey found greater space in which to raise its profile in peacekeeping. The UN Operation in Somalia was important for Turkey, as the first force commander of UNOSOM II was a Turkish Lieutenant-General. The total contribution between 1993 and 1994 was 300 personnel, which was considerable within UNOSOM (Türk Silahlı Kuvvetleri, 2010). Subsequently, Turkey's main contributions were in the former Yugoslavia where it participated in several multilateral operations. Over 18,000 displaced people from Kosovo were based in Turkey at one point. This is not the first time that Turkey has to deal with displaced people in the last couple of decades, as it is estimated that 400,000 displaced people came to Turkey after the first Gulf War, and Iranians had come to Turkey in the aftermath of the Iranian Islamic Revolution. It participated in the United Nations Protection Force (UNPROFOR) in Bosnia with over 1,000 troops in 1995, followed by participation in the Implementation Force (IFOR) and the Stabilization Force (SFOR) (Türk Silahlı Kuvvetleri, 2010). Turkey has, moreover, participated in various UN sanction monitoring missions with its air force and navy. Bosnia was also the first time that Turkish policemen participated in a multilateral mission. Turkey contributed actively to military training of Bosnians in the post-Dayton agreement situation with UN International Police Task Force (IPTF). There were 536 Turkish soldiers at KFOR, including 12 military advisors to Kosovo (RTMFA, 2010d). Turkish military involvement in Kosovo started in 1999 with its air force.

Turkey's current position in the European security architecture is affected by the fact that it is a central member of NATO but not of the EU. This has led at times to friction with some EU member countries who would like to see EU security apparatus grow by using NATO resources, without taking into account the considerations and positions of non-EU members. Nonetheless, Turkey has contributed to discussions on European security. It should be noted that no other non-EU member country participates as actively in EU missions, as demonstrated in the following three examples of current missions: the EU military operation in Bosnia and Herzegovina (EUFOR ALTHEA); the European Union Police Mission in Bosnia and Herzegovina (EUPM); and the European Union Rule of Law mission in Kosovo (EULEX). Turkey's

EUFOR ALTHEA contribution consisted of 213 military personnel and another 56 personnel from the Turkish gendarmerie, of whom a majority were part of the Integrated Police Unit (RTMFA, 2010d). Turkey's contribution made up about 10% of the entire mission. EUPM and EULEX are smaller missions with mainly police officers and also one judge. In the past, it has also participated in NATO and EU missions in Macedonia.

Turkey is an active participant within the Organization for Security and Cooperation in Europe (OSCE). The Adapted Treaty on Conventional Armed Forces in Europe (CFE) was signed in 1999 in Istanbul. Turkey considers the CFE Treaty, including its Flank Regime, as the cornerstone of European security and is supportive of the early entry into force of the Adapted Treaty once the Istanbul Commitments (relating to Russian presence in Moldavia and Georgia) are met. Turkey also participates in several OSCE missions including, as of 1 January 2010, the missions in Kosovo, Bosnia and Herzegovina, Montenegro, Serbia, the Spil-lover Monitor Mission to Skopje, the Center in Bishkek, the Office in Baku, and High Level Planning Group (HLPG) (RTMFA, 2010e). Turkey also participated in a multilateral military operation to create stability in Albania in 1997.

Turkey continues to participate in peacekeeping operations around the world. In February 2010 it was participating in the UN missions in Lebanon, Sudan, the Democratic Republic of Congo, Kosovo, Timor-Leste, Burundi, Cote d'Ivoire, Liberia, Haiti, Sudan, the Central African Republic, Chad, and the African Union (AU)-UN Hybrid operation in Darfur, with a total of 380 military personnel, 141 police, and 1 observer (RTMFA, 2010f). Most of the military personnel (376) were located in the Lebanon mission. The Turkish military has also engaged in other tasks such as assisting Pakistan following the earthquake there in 2005. And Turkey was one of the first nations to contribute ships to the international campaign to tackle piracy off the coast of Somalia (Türk Silahlı Kuvvetleri, 2010). Turkey has also provided support, in the form of a plane, for AU peacekeepers in their mission in Darfur in conjunction with NATO's decision to give support to the AU mission. Moreover, the Turkish gendarmerie has been providing training in Gambia for over two decades (*Jandarma Genel Komutanlığı*, 2011).

Turkey has been particularly proactive in the post Cold War era within the Balkans, the Black Sea region, and the Middle East. Turkey participates actively in NATO's Partnership for Peace program, which aims to increase cooperation in Eurasia. It has continued its attempts at contributing to peace and security in the Balkans by spearheading the creation of the South-Eastern Europe brigade (SEEBRIG), which is made up of NATO and Partnership for Peace countries with its headquarters based in Istanbul between 2007 and 2011 (Koçer, 2006). In the Black Sea region, it spearheaded multilateral, regional initiatives, starting with the Organization for Black Sea Economic Cooperation (BSEC) in 1992. More recently, Turkey has spearheaded the Black Sea Naval Cooperation Task Force (BLACKSEAFOR) (2001), which engages in search and rescue operations, environmental protection, and mine-clearing, as well as participating in Black Sea Harmony (2004) to deter terrorism and the spread of weapons of mass destruction. In the Caucasus, following the Georgia–Russia war of 2008, Turkey pushed for the formation of a Caucasus Solidarity and Cooperation Platform (Önis and Yılmaz, 2009) in 2009.

Turkey has called for a nuclear weapons-free Middle East and is against the proliferation of WMD and their means of delivery, as can be seen in President Gul's 2009 speech to the Bahraini Parliament where he clearly indicates Turkey's view that there is no need for nuclear weapons (Radikal, 2009). Prime Minister Erdoğan, despite his extensive support for Iran on several fronts, has also indicated that Iran's nuclear program can be civilian but not military: 'I told him I don't want to see nuclear weapons in the region, and Mr Ahmadinejad told me that they do not have an intention to produce nuclear weapons' (BBC News, 2010). Thus, Turkey shares other countries' concerns about Iran but believes that a diplomatic settlement is possible. More broadly, Turkey defends the right of all signatories, not just Iran, of the Non-Proliferation Treaty (NPT) who are fulfilling the responsibilities of the NPT, to make use of nuclear energy for peaceful purposes. It is within this light that Turkey is nudging Iran to increase cooperation and transparency with IAEA. Turkey is a party to all international treaties, agreements, organizations, or arrangements in the field of non-proliferation disarmament, arms control, and export control of dual-use material. In fact, 'Turkey's strong track record on nonproliferation issues was in a sense rewarded when Turkish ambassador Ahmet Üzümcü was elected last year as the new ... [Director General] of the Organization for the Prohibition of Chemical Weapons' (Ülgen, 2010, p. 17). Turkey has signed many international agreements on conventional weapons and weapons of mass destruction. For example, it is a founding member of the Wassenar Arrangement, which deals with controlling conventional and dual-use material that could be used to build weapons of mass destruction. Turkey has also supported the US and Russia in their initiative to combat nuclear terrorism and had hosted a global meeting in 2007 (RTMFA, 2010h). A further demonstration of Turkey's attention to weapons of mass destruction from a multilateral perspective is that Turkey is one of the 10 participating states in the Non-Proliferation and Disarmament Initiative, a cross-regional group that 'seek the total elimination of nuclear weapons from our world' (*The National*, 2011).

Afghanistan

We next turn to the factors of globalization and internationalism and their role in driving Turkey's contributions to security in Afghanistan. Afghanistan and the Afghanistan–Pakistan axis constitute one of the significant security zones in our globalizing world in turmoil (Gills, 2009). Indeed, responding effectively to the needs of Afghanistan is of paramount importance, and Turkey's involvement in Afghanistan should be seen in this context. Moreover, in line with its proactive foreign policy, Turkey's contribution is based on multilateralism and multidimensionality. Turkey's involvement in Afghanistan has both military as well as non-military features. While there is a considerable amount of military role, Turkey's non-military engagements are becoming more important and transformative. Turkey has, for example, spent over US$ 200 million on reconstruction in Afghanistan (Dymond, 2009). There are historical and religious ties between Afghanistan and Turkey, with Afghanistan being the first country to officially recognize the Ankara government in 1921, and with Turkey providing development assistance to Afghanistan from the very beginning of the republic; such ties contributed to the NATO senior civilian representative in Afghanistan being the former Turkish foreign minister, Hikmet Çetin, between January 2004 and August 2006.

Turkey has contributed troops to NATO's International Security Assistance Force (ISAF) in Afghanistan since the establishment of ISAF. It has been called upon to contribute more combat troops at various times (Dymond, 2009). For example, in March 2010, Turkey's military contribution to ISAF was 1,796 personnel and three utility helicopters (RTMFA, 2010g). Moreover, Turkey has assumed command of ISAF twice and the command of Regional Command Capital twice. It also contributes to the building of Afghan National Army. Turkish soldiers are embedded in Afghan battalions through the Operational Mentor and Liaison Teams (Yinanç, 2010). Turkey is a major sponsor of several military institutions in Afghanistan and has been providing financial support and advisors to the National Military Academy of Afghanistan, some of whose graduates receive additional training in Turkey. Turkey is also sponsoring the Kabul Military High School with advisors, educational material, and construction assistance (through TIKA). The Afghan

Defense University and the Ghazi and Kabul Military Training Centers have received financial and advisor support. As a result of the need for Afghan officers, Turkey now will now focus on training noncommissioned officers (Özerkan, 2010), and its training of Afghan officers was praised considerably by the Commander of US and NATO troops in Afghanistan (NTV, 2010). Moreover, Afghans, including women, are receiving training as medical doctors at the Turkish Gülhane Military Medical Academy (Kayaoğlu, 2010). Given Turkey's experiences with internal security matters, Turkish governors of southeastern provinces were called to mentor the Afghan governors in how to deal with multiple concentrations of regional power (Gürcanlı, 2008).

Turkey has hosted several summits involving the presidents of Afghanistan and Pakistan, who have had a variety of problems between them. It is noteworthy that Turkey was asked to become involved by the Afghan president himself (RTMFA, 2010g). In 30 April 2007, after the first meeting involving the presidents of all three countries, the countries signed the Ankara Declaration whereby they agreed to collaborate on fighting terrorism and sharing more information with each other. They have continued to meet on a yearly basis since then. Within summit meetings among the same nations, TOBB has had a series of meetings with counterparts from Afghanistan and Pakistan to discuss creating industrial zones. At the same time, the Turkish Foreign Minister Davutoğlu has claimed that Turkey could help to reach a settlement with the Taliban and in fact underscored the need to bring in all sides: 'We must persuade all to take part, including the Taleban' (Binyon, 2010).Turkey has been critical of the Taliban for its practices, including support of Al Qaeda and its treatment of people, but the Taliban appears to respect Turks and has allowed Turkish representatives to move freely and perform humanitarian work throughout Afghanistan (Erman, 2010).

Turkey has engaged in a series of development programs in 24 out of 27 provinces of Afghanistan. These include pledges of US$100 million at the London Donor's Conference in January 2006 and another US$100 million in Paris in 2008 (*Yeni Şafak*, 2008). Turkey transferred money to help with Afghan elections (*Yeni Şafak*, 2008), and Afghan political parties attend training sessions in Turkey. It is estimated that Turkey has been providing 250 tons material humanitarian assistance yearly throughout Afghanistan. Moreover, 13 hospitals and health clinics have been built or repaired, with a Turkish Ministry of Foreign Affairs estimate that that one million Afghans have benefited from these facilities (RTMFA, 2010g). Two of the hospitals and two clinics are operated by Turkey; and Afghan military personnel and civilians have received health treatment in Turkey. Turkey has made a clear effort to create better relationships with local communities. For example, local children are allowed to walk around a camp where a Turkish staffed hospital is located; this differs from the practice of other countries that see this as a security threat (Kayaoğlu, 2010). It has to be borne in mind that actual trade between Afghanistan and Turkey is relatively small, with total trade being US$121 million in 2007 with few direct commercial or institutional interests between the two nations (RTMFA, 2010i). Rather, much of Turkey's interest has to be seen as the continuation of Turkey's longstanding support to Afghanistan since the beginning of the Turkish republic.

Turkey is also involved in improving Afghan education and has contributed to the building or repairing of 68 elementary and secondary schools (with an estimate of 56,000 students benefiting from these facilities) (RTMFA, 2010g). Nine more schools are planned. A girls' school with teachers from Turkey and Afghanistan has provided education for 460 girls, and Turkey has provided the funding for the establishment and maintenance of a midwife education center. Turkey has given over 1,211 higher education scholarships as well providing training for over 500 civil servants (RTMFA, 2010g). Afghan police cadets have been attending the Turkish Political Academy since 2007, while Afghan police officers have been receiving training in various fields in Turkey, particularly counter-narcotics.

Turkey also has led a provincial reconstruction team (PRT) in the Afghani province of Wardak since November 2006 and a PRT has started in Shirbirghan in 2010 (RTMFA, 2010g). The governor of Wardak province has praised the Turkish contribution by indicating that 'The Turkish programs are very much receptive and acceptable to Afghans because they work within the Afghan culture. They are sensitive to Afghan values' (Cihan Medya Services, 2009). This discussion of sensitivity dovetails with findings from a study on Dutch and Turkish peacekeepers where Turkish soldiers were described as showing more empathy towards civilians in missions in Kosovo and Afghanistan than those from other European countries, by being more mindful of local religious and cultural sensitivities and needs. There is considerable amount of effort by Turkish military to reach out to civilians. Soeters et al. (2006, p. 92) point out that the Zorlu Doctrine (so named after the first Turkish commander, then Major General Akın Zorlui, in charge of ISAF) focused on attempts at developing good relations with local populace, including providing medical facilities for the circumcision of Muslim boys, which generated considerable local goodwill. Moreover, former President Demirel and former Prime Minister Ecevit were perceived as attempting to communicate far more with local populations and authorities in their respective visits in Kosovo and Afghanistan than European counterparts (Soeters et al., 2006).

The Turkish PRT is civilian-led in Wardak (RTMFA, 2010g). Over 33,000 families and 12,000 children received 222 tons of food, clothing, and school material (RTMFA, 2010g). Security problems continue in Wardak as in the rest of Afghanistan, but Turkey has not given up on a civilian-led PRT unlike other countries because, as the Turkish chief pointed out, 'PRTs exist to do reconstruction projects' (Lobjakas, 2009). Turkey is engaged in development projects throughout the districts of the province despite continuing insecurity, which has resulted in other foreign representations leaving the province (Sert, 2009). Completed and functioning projects developed by the civilian-led PRT include a variety of projects: an agricultural vocational high school with dormitory; a water storage facility; cold storage units for agricultural productions; the restoration of a mosque; two elementary schools and two girls' high schools; dried-fruit processing facilities; computer training centers; a radio station; and police checks points. The Turkish money being spent on the mosque has also contributed to the mullah being supportive of education for girls (Lobjakas, 2009). Turkey has also been providing a variety of training programs such as training of judges and prosecutors, agricultural training courses, carpet weaving courses, and various courses for women, including literacy courses. Ten Turkish police officers were involved in police training at Wardak PRT in a Police Training and Education Center constructed there. The Center's costs are covered by Turkey (RTMFA, 2010g). Also, Turkish agricultural programs have resulted in the cultivation of potatoes, apples, and other vegetables and fruits, which are stored in the cold storage unit that Turkey has built, before being sent to the rest of the country (Cihan Medya Services, 2009). Moreover, Afghan officials in Wardak claim that Turkish programs in agriculture have resulted in the termination of opium cultivation (*Milliyet*, 2007).

Assessing Turkey's Global Humanitarianism

It is clear that starting with the early 1990s Turkey has embarked upon peace-building activities. The main reason for this has to do with global and regional changes brought by the end of the Cold War, which has opened up additional space for Turkey to move. Moreover, Turkey found itself also surrounded by regional conflicts, about which it felt it must develop the capacity for acting effectively. Turkey has throughout this period preferred multilateral approaches. This can be seen with its activities in former Yugoslavia as well as its attempts in the Black Sea to form regional organizations.

It has to be recognized that the increase in Turkish economic and military strength has become more apparent over the years. As globalization has intensified interconnectedness in the world, which has involved both risks and uncertainties, Turkey's foreign policy is also becoming more and more embedded in globalization, aiming to respond to the challenges more effectively. As noted here, in this process Turkey has the advantage of increasing its capacity to carry out its goals. The economic reforms that Turkey embarked upon starting in the 1980s have allowed Turkey's economy to benefit increasingly from the global economy. Not only does the state draw upon the tax basis and commercial leverage of a much bigger GDP, which it can use abroad in various peaceful-building tasks, but at the same time, Turkish civil society has (slowly) grown, including organizations interested in humanitarian assistance internationally. On top of these developments, the Turkish military and diplomatic apparatus, such as the Foreign Ministry, has drawn upon a wealth of experience. For example, Turkey's long struggle against separatist terrorism, as well as its own experience with fighting drug production, has also given it lessons on how to approach situations as in Afghanistan where it has engaged in services such as building a cold storage facility. Building such a facility might at first be dismissed as a marginal contribution; but given the role that agriculture plays in the Afghan economy and the international community's interest in crops other than those that can be used for drugs—some of which are more resilient to extreme weather conditions—the importance of such a facility becomes clear.

Yet, changes in the international order and power dynamics only explain part of the story. Changes within Turkish society and among leaders are also important here. As mentioned previously, Turkish civil society is more active in global matters than in past eras as shown throughout this study. Its growth and interest in foreign policy along with changes in Turkish economy and democracy have been discussed elsewhere (see Mazlum and Doğan, 2006). Moreover, the Justice and Development Party (AKP) sees itself as reform- oriented and proactive both domestically and globally (Keyman and Öniş, 2007). This is also reflected in foreign policy with the opening of many new embassies and a record number of foreign visits by the president and foreign minister. Yet, there has been criticism that AKP interests in EU negotiations declined in the second half of the 2000s (Öniş and Yılmaz, 2009), and there might be a concern about whether this focus on peace-building will continue. As the evidence above has shown, Turkey was activist in global security matters in the 1990s as well. While there might be a decrease in interest, it is unlikely to decline.

Turkish foreign policy has been discussed as proactive and constructive in the post Cold War era (see Martin and Keridis, 2004). Proactive foreign policy has been increasingly institutionalized, as demonstrated in Turkey's regional engagements in the Middle East, the Balkans, and the Caucasus, aimed at creating peaceful and stable relations with its neighbors and providing with them economic and cultural cooperation. Turkey has played the role of a regional power focusing more and more on humanitarian aid and assistance as a way of contributing to making globalization more stable, humane, and just. Of course, Turkish foreign policy has also been active in the past,[3] but in the recent past the activism has been crystallized and developed its own unique 'brand' of internationalism.

Davutoğlu (2010) has maintained that Turkey is engaged in a 'proactive peace diplomacy' in the 2007–2010 period. This is separate from its 'zero-conflicts and problems with neighbors policy', which purports to eliminate Turkey's problems with all of its neighbors as it aims to contribute to regional peace in the Middle East as well as the Balkans and Caucasus regions. Turkey's activism has been controversial at times. For example, Prime Minister Erdoğan's speech to his political party, AKP, on 1 June 2010, stated that Turkey would not turn its back on the Palestinians (TRT, 2010). This stand can be interpreted in a benign way, as reflecting a concern for injustice and a commitment to peace, but it can also be viewed as menacing towards those who are perceived as committing injustice.

Ethical foreign policy is important to Foreign Minister Davutoğlu (Council on Foreign Relations, 2010) and the humanitarian activism of Turkey partly reflects a concern for justice. In this regard, Turkey is in many ways a middle power. Middle powers have been defined in many ways in terms of capability (less than that of great powers) and in terms of foreign policy strategy (preferring multilateral cooperation for global issues) (Müftüler-Baç and Yüksel, 1997). The fact that these operations rarely offer any immediate payoff or short-term national glory results in active middle powers earning reputations as good international citizens (Joordan, 2003). During the period under discussion in this study—the post Cold War era, particularly the 2000s—Turkey fits the label of a middle power as well as a regional power. Middle powers are also seen as not challenging the global balance (Joordan, 2003), and there is skepticism in the West about Turkey suggesting that the label of middle power might be insufficient to describe its status. Yet, as can be seen from the material presented above regarding Turkey's contributions, there is also the view that 'Turkey's proactive and multidimensional foreign policy ... symbolizes Turkey's expected role in the new global imagination that it is only through multilateralism activated on the basis of enhanced strategic partnerships, and by forging a more just, humane and interdependent world vision that the challenge of global turmoil can be addressed' (Keyman 2009b, p. 10; see also Aras and Fidan, 2009).

Conclusions: Limits and Prospects

Concerns about Turkish foreign policy since 2008 have taken several forms. One form of criticism is 'thick skepticism with a strong ideological take' (Keyman, 2009b, p. 6). From this perspective, Turkish peace activism can be seen as a continuation of an ideological Islamist foreign policy. The increasing tensions between Israel and Turkey, the support of Turkey to Iran at UNSC, and some of the supportive statements regarding Sudan's leadership might be put forward as substantiating this view. Yet, as the evidence presented above demonstrates, Turkey's peace activism predates AKP, and Turkish activism is certainly not limited to Islamic societies or Islamist regimes. This skepticism appears to be particularly related to Prime Minister Erdoğan's behavior and stance regarding Israel in the recent past. However, given that Erdoğan and AKP were heading the country only a couple of years ago when Turkey was the first Muslim-majority country to host an Israeli president in its legislature in 2007, this skepticism is unwarranted.

A second related skepticism is 'thin skepticism,' which Keyman (2009b) suggests might be more warranted as it suggests that the West believes that Turkey's activism constitutes 'neo-Ottomanism'. Here again there is the focus on religious-based cultural affinities. Both Erdoğan and Davutoğlu reject the Ottoman label as well as the argument that Turkey is turning eastward. However, both of them believe that the Ottoman past is central for Turkey's history and identity. Davutoğlu (2001, 2010) highlights the importance of geography and history. Geopolitics has been a matter of considerable concern for Turkish academics and policymakers for over five decades (Bilgin, 2007) as can be seen in Davutoğlu's emphasis on the Balkans, Caucasus, and Middle Eastern regions (2001). It is the Ottoman past—embedded in its physical, cultural, and diplomatic geography—that makes Turkey a center of gravity. Thus, Turkey's soft power is seen as partly emerging from its past history and its location.

It is not surprising that Turkey would be more engaged in the conflicts of its regional neighbors, most of which were former Ottoman territories, or that years of living within the same empire might have resulted in areas where Turkey and the countries in which it is engaged find areas of commonality. Similar descriptions are not used to describe countries that are active in their former colonies, such as Spain or Portugal. And the 'neo-Ottoman' label is something that Turkish foreign policy has to be wary of because the Ottoman era is not remembered as fondly throughout the former Ottoman territories; and Ottoman references might hamper Turkey's overtures. At the same time, countries are willing to receive assistance despite such historical issues: one of Turkey's successes has been with Bosnia and Herzegovina and Serbia, despite Ottoman history not being joyously remembered in Serbia, to say the least.

In fact, the question that has to be posed about Turkey's role in human-security globalization and humanitarian internationalism should be concerned with its realism and sustainability (Keyman, 2009a, 2009b). In the era of global turmoil, Turkey is expected to play a more active and constructive role both regionally and globally. This role needs to be played effectively and in a manner that can become sustainable. It is here that humanitarian aid and assistance is of significance, as part of Turkish foreign policy and response to global challenges. Here the question is whether Turkey's peaceful overtures reach their goals and whether they can be sustained over time. The demise of Turkey's formerly positive relations with Israel, let alone its attempts at conflict management there, demonstrates that there is a limitation to what Turkey can achieve. Turkey has been described as being addicted to offering mediation (Koç, 2010). Similarly, Turkey did not receive endorsement from the West or much of the Persian Gulf states for its attempts, along with Brazil, to convince Iran to agree to an aforementioned confidence-building measure relating to its nuclear program. Having said that, it has to be acknowledged that Turkey has been involved in Afghanistan for several years; since its efforts in the Balkans and the Black Sea have lasted for such a long time, it appears that there is continued interest.

There are, of course, other issues that Turkey has to address. Turkey's continuing internal challenges, including internal security, can limit the extent to which others take its efforts seriously. While Turkey's internal problems have given it unique experience, continuing internal problems can lead to questions about its know-how. Moreover, Turkey continues to have problematic relations with neighbors, a number of whom have their own internal or external problems. While Turkey has offered to mediate in many cases, this is partly because the neighborhood offers considerable opportunities for mediation. Two internal matters have to do with civil society and institutional preparedness. As mentioned above, Turkish civil society, including non-governmental organizations, has become increasingly relevant in these matters. Most of its work is praiseworthy. Yet, a non-governmental organization has contributed to the further deterioration of Turkey's relations with Israel. Moreover, the Ministry of Foreign Affairs is being called upon to engage in many new countries and to also address problems of the global community, and this requires even more support and training being given to this institution to carry out its tasks. Furthermore, Prime Minister's Erdoğan's populist criticism of Turkish diplomats is unlikely to have generated positive sentiment within the Foreign Ministry (Sevimay, 2010).

It is clear that the EU remains of importance. In fact, Davutoğlu maintains that Turkey's chances with the EU are affected by its position in Asia. The EU progress report (Commission of the European Communities, 2009) maintains that Turkish foreign policy is broadly aligned with the EU's common foreign and security policy (Müftüler-Baç, 2008). Its contributions in Afghanistan are praised. Moreover, the progress report also indicates that Turkey's official development aid of €557 million in 2008, constituting 0.1% of GDP, is satisfactory (Commission of the European Communities 2009, p. 85). The EU and the Europeanization process have been of considerable importance to Turkey in the 2000s (Öniş and Yılmaz, 2009) and, while it would be hard to argue that Turkey engages in global humanitarian activities due to the EU, it is clear that such activities have left a positive impression.

As pointed out above, in matters of European security, some EU countries want to benefit from NATO assets without taking into consideration the views of non-EU members like Turkey. This approach is rather problematic and causes resentment. Ill-feeling also came about in other areas. Turkish soldiers have reported that during peacekeeping missions, their experience is ignored by some Western European soldiers even though they have had much more combat and terrorism experience than the Europeans as well as, depending on the location, greater understanding of the local culture (Soeters et al., 2006, pp. 87–8). It is beyond the scope of this article to discuss why this occurs, but it can clearly hurt the success of a mission.

As the analysis section showed, there are several forms of skepticism about Turkey's foreign policy. Other developing countries might also face similar or other forms of skepticism. It has to be said that the forms of skepticisms also might be reflecting deeper, underlying tensions on whether developing countries are becoming too assertive and independent. There is merit to some of these concerns. Turkey cannot expect to be successful in all of its mediations. A country can, of course, offer to mediate in as many instances as it wishes, but in that case it is important to have institutions prepared to undertake mediation even when relations are not going well. It is here that we see the significance of multilateralism and enhanced dialogue and cooperation among actors, including non-state and state actors in our globalizing world. It is only through considering how to solve global challenges differently from existing neoliberal and state-centric norms of globalization that democratic and humane governance would be made possible. Turkey's efforts within the realm of humanitarian assistance should be seen in this context. The Turkish experience has not been based purely on an attempt to augment power and influence but, more importantly, on attempts to contribute to the creation and advancement of a human-focused norm for a better and more stable world.

Acknowledgements

The authors would like to thank Aybüke Aksoy, Bengü Ezgi Aydin, Ece Melike Çavdar, Gizem Sözündeduran, Şermin Tekin, and Muhammed Haşim Tekineş for their able assistance.

Notes

1 The blockade had been in place since 2007 following the breakdown of the Palestinian unity government and Hamas ousting Fatah officials from Gaza. Israel and Egypt severely curtailed the movement of goods and people into Gaza. Israel also maintained that the blockade was necessary to prevent attacks from Palestinian groups on to their settlements as well as a response to the capture of an Israeli soldier. This blockade received considerable criticism as it had considerable ramifications on Palestinian civilians and was seen as collective punishment. For example, a report by the World Food Programme and the UN's Food and Agriculture Organization (2009, p. 6) maintained that 'Over three quarters of the population is food insecure or vulnerable to food insecurity which means the large majority of the population is widening its consumption gap, over-stretching its coping mechanisms and relies heavily on aid subsidies to sustain its level of food security.'

2 Israeli–Turkish relations were negatively affected. Turkish Foreign Minister Ahmet Davutoğlu demanded that Israel issue an apology or accept an international inquiry. Israel rejected the international inquiry and set up its own inquiry. A UN Human Rights Council Report (2010), concluded that Israel's military response 'betrayed an unacceptable level of brutality' and that it violated human rights law and international humanitarian law (UNHRC Report, 2010); the more recent Palmer Report published in September 2011 while critical of Israeli boarding also questioned the motives of the Flottila organizers.

3 For example, Bağcı (1990) and Oran (2001) describe the Democrat Party's foreign policy as activist in 1950s. Oran (2001, p. 33) referred to the activism in Turkish foreign policy in the second half of the 1980s but also questioned the wisdom of a foreign policy focused on trade where the Ministry of Foreign Affairs was at times past over (see also Makovsy, 1999).

References

Akyel, D. (2010) What is Turkey doing in the Middle East, *International Crisis Group*, 13 July, http://www.crisisgroup.org/en/regions/europe/turkecyprus/turkey/akyel-what-is-turkey-doing-in-the-middle-east.aspx.

Arısoy, C. (2010) What is happening between Turkey and Darfur? *BİLGESAM*, 26 March, http://www.bilgesam.org/en/index.php?option=com_content&view=article&id=256:what-is-happening-between-turkey-and-darfur&catid=80:analizler-afrika&Itemid=138.

Bağcı, H. (1990) *Demokrat Parti Dönemi Dis Politikasi 1950–1960* (Ankara: İmge).

BBC News (2010) Iran nuclear programme 'solely civilian'—Turkish PM, 16 March, http://news.bbc.co.uk/2/hi/middle_east/8570842.stm.

Bilgin, P. (2007) Only strong states can survive in Turkey's geography: the uses of 'geographical truths' in Turkey, *Political Geography*, 56(4), pp. 740–756.

Binyon, M. (2010) We can broker peace with the Taleban, says Turkey, *The Times*, 13 January, http://www.timesonline.co.uk/tol/news/world/afghanistan/article6985590.ece.

Bøås, M. & Jennings, K. (2007) 'Failed states' and 'state failure': threats or opportunities?, *Globalizations*, 4(4), pp. 475–485.

Brzezinski, Z. (1997) *The Grand Chessboard: American Primacy and its Geostrategic Imperatives* (New York: Basic Books).

Brzezinski, Z. (2004) *The Choice: Global Domination or Global Leadership* (Cambridge, MA: Basic).

Brzezienski, Z. & Snowcroft, B. (2008) *America and the World: Conversations on the Future of American Foreign Policy* (Cambridge, MA: Basic Books).

Cargill, T. (2010) *Our Common Strategic Interests: Africa's Role in the Post G-8 World*, Royal Institute of International Affairs: Chatham House Report, http://www.chathamhouse.org.uk/publications/papers/view/-/id/888/.

Cihan Medya Services (2009) Turkey finds civilian solution in Afghanistan, 14 December, http://www.cihanmedya.com/media_services/product.do?productType=video&categoryId=3670029&langType=en.

Collier, P. & Hoeffler, A. (2004) Greed and grievance in civil war, *Oxford Economic Papers*, 56(4), pp. 563–595.

Commission of the European Communities (2009) *Turkey Progress Report 2009*, Brussels, 14 October 2009, http://ec.europa.eu/enlargement/pdf/key_documents/2009/tr_rapport_2009_en.pdf.

Council On Foreign Relations (2010) A Conversation with Ahmet Davutoglu, 14 April, http://www.cfr.org/turkey/conversation-ahmet-davutoglu/p21916.

Crocker, C. A., Hampson, F. O. & Aall, P. R. (2004) *Taming Intractable Conflicts: Mediation in the Hardest Cases* (Washington, DC: United States Institute of Peace Press).

Dymond, J. (2009) Turkey FM Davutoglu embraces mediation role, BBC News, 3 December, http://news.bbc.co.uk/2/hi/europe/8393516.stm.

Davutoglu, A. (2001) *Stratejik Derinlik*, 1st ed. (İstanbul: Küre Yayınları).

Davutoğlu, A. (2010) Turkey's zero problems foreign policy, *World Bulletin*, 26 May, http://www.worldbulletin.net/author_article_detail.php?id=2181.

Erman, A. (2010) How Turkey can help NATO in Afghanistan, *The Christian Science Monitor*, 9 February, http://www.csmonitor.com/Commentary/Opinion/2010/0209/How-Turkey-can-help-NATO-in-Afghanistan.

Falk, R. (1995) *On Humane Governance: Towards a New Global Politics* (University Park, PA: Pennsylvania State University Press).

Falk, R. (1999) *Predatory Globalization: A Critique* (Cambridge: Polity Press).

Falk, R. (2010) A radical world order challenge: addressing global climate change and the threat of nuclear weapons, *Globalizations*, 7(1), pp. 137–155.

Gruen, G. E. (1995) Turkey's emerging regional role, *American Foreign Policy Interests*, 17(2), pp. 13–24.

Gills, R. (2009) The end of the War on Terror, *Globalizations*, 6(1), pp. 157–162.

Gurkaynak, Ç. E. (2007) Turkey as a third party in Israeli-Palestinian conflict: assessment and reflections, *Perceptions*, 12, pp. 89–108.

Gürcanlı, Z. (2008) İsrail'den Erdoğan'a özür gibi yanıt, *Hürriyet*, 30 December, http://hurarsiv.hurriyet.com.tr/goster/ShowNew.aspx?id=10672518.

Hafezi, P. & Exman, F. (2010) Iran makes nuclear offer, but West unconvinced, *Reuters*, 17 May, http://www.reuters.com/article/idUSTRE64G18A20100517.

Hürriyet (2008) Bize karşı saygısızlık, 28 December, http://www.hurriyet.com.tr/dunya/10656187.asp.

Hürriyet Daily News (2010) Turkey unlike former colonizers in giving aid, TİKA head says, 2 November, http://www.hurriyetdailynews.com/n.php?n=turkeys-approach-to-international-aid-differs-from-that-of-china-or-former-colonists-2010-10-31.

International Commission on Missing Persons (ICMP) (2010) Turkey becomes new donor to ICMP, 22 February, http://www.ic-mp.org/press-releases/turkey-becomes-new-icmp-donor/.

Jandarma Genel Komutanlığı (2011) Dış İlişkiler, http://www.jandarma.gov.tr/diger/dis_iliskiler.htm.

Joordan, E. (2003) The concept of a middle power in international relations: distinguishing between emerging and traditional middle powers, *Politikon: South African Journal of Political Studies*, 30(2), pp. 165–181.

Karan, C. (2010) Türkiye'den daha iyi arabulucu bulamadık, *Radikal*, 17 July, http://www.radikal.com.tr/Default.aspx?aType=RadikalYazarYazisi&ArticleID=1008501&Yazar=CEYDA%20KARAN&Date=17.07.2010&CategoryID=100.

Kayaoğlu, B. (2010) Türkish military operations in Afghanistan: a continuation of peace by other means, *Turkish Weekly*, 22 March, http://www.turkishweekly.net/columnist/3312/turkish-military-operations-in-afghanistan-a-continuation-of-peace-by-other-means.html.

Keyman, E. F. (2009a) Globalization, modernity and democracy: in search of a viable domestic polity for a sustainable Turkish foreign policy, *New Perspectives on Turkey*, 40, pp. 7–27.

Keyman, E. F. (2009b) Turkish foreign policy in the era of global turmoil, *SETA Policy Brief*, 39, pp. 1–16.

Kirişci, K. (2009) The transformation of Turkish foreign policy: the rise of the trading state, *New Perspectives on Turkey*, 40, pp. 29–57.

Keyman, E. F. & Öniş, Z. (2007) *Turkish Politics in a Changing World* (Istanbul: Istanbul Bilgi University Press).

Kirk, L. (2006) EU hopes for Turkey to build bridges in cartoon conflict, *EU Observer*, 21 February, http://euobserver.com/9/20948.

Koç, Ş. B. (2010) Stratejik Dehlizlerde Derinlik Sarhoşluğu: Bir AKP Dış Politikası Eleştirisi, *21. yüzyıl*, 12, http://www.21yyte.org/tr/rapor5Stratejik_Dehlizlerde_Derinlik_Sarhoslugu_Bir_AKP_Dis_Politikasi_Elestirisi.html.

Koçer, G. (2006) Türkiye'nin Barış Destekleme Harekatlarına Katkısı, *Uluslararası İlişkiler Dergisi*, 3(11), pp. 47–71.

Lobjakas, A. (2009) Wardak, where nothing is what it seems, *Radio Free Europe Radio Liberty*, 16 January, http://www.rferl.org/content/Wardak_Where_Nothing_Is_What_It_Seems/1371007.html.

Makovsky, A. (1999) The new activism in Turkish foreign policy, *SAIS Review*, 19(1), pp. 92–113.

Martin, L. G. & Keridis, L. (2003) *The Future of Turkish Foreign Policy* (Cambridge, MA: MIT Press).

Mazlum, S. C. & Doğan, E. D. (2006) *Sivil Toplum ve Dış Politika: Yeni Sorunlar, Yeni Aktörler* (İstanbul: Baglam Yayıncılık).

Milliyet (2007) Türkiye, Afganistan'da Afyon Üretimini Bitirdi, 27 February, http://www.milliyet.com.tr/turkiye-afganistan-da-afyon-uretimini-bitirdi/siyaset/haberdetayarsiv/23.03.2010/190783/default.htm.

Müftüler-Baç, M. (2008) The European Union's accession negotiations with Turkey from a foreign policy perspective, *Journal of European Integration*, 30(1), pp. 63–78.

Müftüler-Baç, M. & Yüksel, M. (1997) Turkey: a middle power in the new order, in A. Cooper (ed.) *Niche Diplomacy, Middle Powers after the Cold War* (New York: Macmillan Press), pp. 184–197.

NTV (2010) *Çuvalcı Generalden Türk Ordusuna Övgü*, 16 July, http://www.ntvmsnbc.com/id/25115526/.

Oran, B. (2001) Türk Dış Politikası: Kurtuluş Savaşı'ndan bugüne olgular, belgeler, yorumlar, (İstanbul: İletişim).

ORSAM (2011) İnsan Hak ve Hürriyetleri ve Insani Yardim Vakfi (İHH) Ankara Temsilcisi Hanefi Sinan Ile Röportaj, Center for Middle-Eastern Strategic Studies, 24 May, http://www.orsam.org.tr/tr/orsamkonukgoster.aspx?ID=324.

Öniş, Z. & Yılmaz, Ş. (2009) Between Europeanization and Euro-Asianism: foreign policy activism in Turkey during the AKP era, *Turkish Studies*, 10(1), pp. 7–24.

Özdabak, M. (2010) TÜSİAD'ı Kuzey Irak'a çağırdı aldığı yanıt 'Ya Güvenlik' oldu, *Hürriyet*, 6 June, http://www.hurriyet.com.tr/ekonomi/14944181.asp?gid=373.

Özerkan, F. (2010) Turkish Army begins training Afghan officers in Kabul, *Hürriyet Daily News*, 20 June, http://www.hurriyetdailynews.com/n.php?n=turkish-army-begins-training-afghan-leaders-senior-nato-commander-2010-06-19.

Özkan, M. (2008) Turkey discovers Africa: implications and prospects, *SETA Policy Brief*, 22 September, pp. 1–8.

Paris, R. (2001) Human security paradigm shift or hot air?, *International Security*, 26(2), pp. 87–102.

Radikal (2009) Gül Bahreyn'den seslendi: Nükleer silahlara ihtiyaç yok, 16 April, http://www.radikal.com.tr/Radikal.aspx?aType=RadikalHaberDetayV3&ArticleID=931409&Date=16.04.2009&CategoryID=100.

Radikal (2010) İsrail'in savunması: Şiddetin sorumlusu gemidekiler, 1 June, http://www.radikal.com.tr/Radikal.aspx?aType=RadikalHaberDetayV3&ArticleID=999930&Date=16.07.2011&CategoryID=97.

Republic of Turkey Ministry of Foreign Affairs (2010a) *Dışişleri Bakanlığı Sözcüsü Burak Özügergin'in Olağan Basın Toplantısı Metni*, http://www.mfa.gov.tr/disisleri-bakanligi-sozcusu-burak-ozugergin_in-olagan-basin-toplantisi-metni-_27-mayis-2010_.tr.mfa.

Republic of Turkey Ministry of Foreign Affairs (2010b) *Turkeýs Political Relations with Lebanon*, http://www.mfa.gov.tr/turkey_s-political-relations-with-lebanon.en.mfa.

Republic of Turkey Ministry of Foreign Affairs (2010c) *Humanitarian Assistance by Turkey*. Available from: http://www.mfa.gov.tr/humanitarian-assistance-by-turkey.en.mfa.

Republic of Turkey Ministry of Foreign Affairs (2010d) Ülkemizin NATO- AB Misyon ve Operasyonlarina Mevcut Katkilarina İlişkin Tablo. Ankara: Ministry of Foreign Affairs Publication.

Republic of Turkey Ministry of Foreign Affairs (2010e) 2004–2010 yılları arasında vatandaşlarımızın görev aldıkları AGİT Misyonları. Ankara: Ministry of Foreign Affairs Publication.

Republic of Turkey Ministry of Foreign Affairs (2010f) BM Bariş Operasyonlarina Yaklaşimimiz ve Katkilarimiz, (Ankara: Ministry of Foreign Affairs Publication).

Republic of Turkey Ministry of Foreign Affairs (2010g) Turkish contributions to security and development in Afghanistan, (Ankara: Ministry of Foreign Affairs Publication).

Republic of Turkey Ministry of Foreign Affairs (2010h) *Arms Control and Disarmament*, http://www.mfa.gov.tr/arms-control-and-disarmament.en.mfa.

Republic of Turkey Ministry of Foreign Affairs (2010i) *Türkiye-Afganistan Ekonomik İlişkileri*, http://www.mfa.gov.tr/turkiye-afganistan-ekonomik-iliskileri.tr.mfa.

Republic of Turkey Ministry of Foreign Affairs (2010j) *NATO*, http://www.mfa.gov.tr/nato.en.mfa.

Sert, O. (2009) Vardak'ta kalan tek ülke Türkiye, *CNNTurk.com*, 8 January, http://www.cnnturk.com/2009/dunya/01/08/vardakta.kalan.tek.ulke.turkiye/508033.0/index.html.

Sevimay, D. (2010) Onurlu dış politika AKP'yle başlamadı, *Milliyet*, 21 June, http://www.milliyet.com.tr/onurlu-dis-politika-akp-yle-baslamadi/devrim-sevimay/siyaset/yazardetay/21.06.2010/1253372/default.htm.

Soeters, J. et al. (2006) Barış Gücü Operasyonlarında Türkiye Hollanda Buluşması, *Uluslararası İlişkiler Dergisi*, 3(11), pp. 71–102.

Tavernise, S. (2008) Turkish schools offer Pakistan a gentler vision of Islam, *New York Times*, 4 May, http://www.nytimes.com/2008/05/04/world/asia/04islam.html.

The National (2011) A common purpose to rid the world of nuclear weapons, 4 May, http://www.thenational.ae/thenationalconversation/comment/a-common-purpose-to-rid-the-world-of-nuclear-weapons?pageCount=0.

TRT (2010) Erdoğan'dan Sert Açıklamalar', 1 June, http://www.trt.net.tr/Haber/HaberDetay.aspx?HaberKodu=f138030e-31cc-478d-b5fb-6adc4f62bee8.

Türk Silahlı Kuvvetleri (2010) *Türk Silahlı Kuvvetlerinin Barışı Destekleme Harekatına Katkıları*, http://www.tsk.tr/4_ULUSLARARASI_ILISKILER/4_6_Turkiyenin_Barisi_DesteklemeHarekatina_Katkilari/konular/Turk_Silahli_%20Kuvvetlerinin_Barisi_Destekleme_Harekatina_Katkilari.htm.

Ukeje, C. (2008) Globalization and conflict management: reflections on the security challenges facing West Africa, *Globalizations*, 5(1), pp. 35–48.

United Nations Alliances of Civilization (UNAOC) (2011) *History*, http://www.unaoc.org/about/history/.

United Nations Human Rights Council (2010) Report of the international fact-finding mission to investigate violations of international law, including international humanitarian and human rights law, resulting from the Israeli attacks on the flotilla of ships carrying humanitarian assistance, http://unispal.un.org/UNISPAL.NSF/5ba47a5c6cef541b802563e000493b8c/bffafa61f26ca7c0852577a8004b405b?OpenDocument.

Ülgen, S. (2010) Preventing the Proliferation of weapons of mass destruction: What role for Turkey?, *EDAM Discussion Paper Series*, http://edam.org.tr/document/gmf-ulgen-final.pdf.

Vogel, T. (2010) Turkey succeeds where the EU has consistently failed, Europeanvoice.com, 17 June, http://www.europeanvoice.com/article/imported/turkey-succeeds-where-the-eu-has-consistently-failed/68270.aspx.

World Bank (2011) GDP per capita (current US$), http://data.worldbank.org/indicator/NY.GDP.PCAP.CD.

World Food Programme & Food and Agriculture Organization of the United Nations (2009) *Socio-Economic and Food Security Survey Report 2—Gaza Strip*, November, http://www.reliefweb.int/rw/RWFiles2009.nsf/FilesByRWDocUnidFilename/HHVU-7XNEB3-full_report.pdf/$File/full_report.pdf.

Wynter, A. (2010) In Haiti quake response, east meets west, *International Federation of Red Cross and Red Crescent Societies*, 21 May, http://www.ifrc.org/docs/news/10/10052102/index.asp.

Yeni Şafak (2008) Türkiye'den Afganistan'a Destek, 12 June, http://yenisafak.com.tr/Politika/?t=12.06.2008&i=122873.

Yeni Şafak (2010) The Principles of Turkish Foreign Policy by Ahmet Davutoğlu, 18 January, http://yenisafak.com.tr/english/?t=18.01.2010&i=236159.

Yinanç, B. (2010) Excluded by US and EU, Turkey undertakes own mediation, *Hürriyet Daily News*, 15 January, http://www.hurriyetdailynews.com/n.php?n=excluded-by-us-and-eu-turkey-undertakes-its-onw-mediation-in-bosnia-2010-01-15.

Resat Bayer is Assistant Professor of International Relations at Koç University, İstanbul. His research focuses primarily on conflict and cooperation, particularly peace.

E. Fuat Keyman is Professor of International Relations at Sabancı University, İstanbul. He is also the director of the Istanbul Policy Center (IPC) at Sabancı University.

Globalising Security Culture and Knowledge in Practice: Nigeria's Hybrid Model

ALICE HILLS

University of Leeds, Leeds, UK

ABSTRACT *Public police around the world share certain occupational commonalities, but this does not represent a globalising security culture. Certain norms may appear to facilitate a less ambitious internationalist or transnational culture by modifying police behaviour through processes of socialisation and internalisation, but they do so for instrumental, rather than intrinsic reasons and are limited in their effects. The experience of the Nigeria Police (which is both the target of, and a contributor to, the transnational rescue industry) makes this explicit. This article emphasises the extent to which Nigeria's commitment to the UN policing operations commonly thought to encapsulate a globalising culture is outweighed by domestic concerns. More significantly, the Nigeria Police's distinction between domestic and international practice exemplifies the ways in which intermediary states in the South construct, exercise, and validate hybrid forms of security knowledge. Distinguishing between utilitarian and theoretical forms of knowledge provides an analytical tool for understanding the pragmatic and flexible practices that result.*

What do globalising security cultures and internationalist intervention practices look like from West Africa? How does Nigeria, the region's oil-rich hegemon, understand the interplay between international, regional, and sub-state security organisations and cultures? How does it reconcile being both a recipient and a member of the international rescue industry? Processes that bring local agents into relationships with globalised structures such as the United Nations Organisation (UN) need managing, so how does Nigeria (which first contributed to UN peace-keeping operations in 1960) accommodate or manipulate humanitarian internationalism to its advantage? How do its security agents articulate and supervise the interface between national and international levels of security? Who are the brokers and intermediaries involved when cultural or occupational identities clash? What might this mean for understanding security knowledge and practice in the global South?

This article addresses the ways in which elite decision makers in an intermediary state such as Nigeria construct, exercise, and validate adaptive forms of security knowledge that are best described as hybrid. It emphasises the pragmatic ways in which Nigerian politicians and security officers accommodate the Western reform projects associated with UN policing (UNPOL) operations—including the notion of a globalising, democratically oriented security culture—while shifting the terms of, and practices associated with, internationalism and humanitarian deployment to suit their own agenda. In particular, it addresses the knowledge and practice shaping the rescue missions mounted by Nigeria's often brutal and corrupt police. Although no one state provides definitive evidence for, or against, a globalising culture, and no one police force has a monopoly on brutality or corruption, Nigeria offers an appropriate case with which to explore these issues. For its police are the recipients of international reform projects even as they develop an internationalist profile and assert themselves as legitimate peacekeeping actors. (UNPOL is a discrete element in UN peacekeeping operations, but its officers and officials commonly refer to their operations as peacekeeping, so 'UNPOL' and 'peacekeeping' are used here interchangeably.) As a beneficiary and contributor, the Nigeria Police illustrate the accommodation and trade-offs that typically take place, while their intermediary role casts light on the meeting points between national and international levels of security from where a globalising security culture—and also the less ambitious internationalist culture UNPOL facilitates—must presumably emerge.

It is impossible to say what a globalising security culture looks like from Nigeria's presidential palace or federal police headquarters, but, judging from the record of former president Olusegun Obasanjo and his three inspector generals of police, it represents political, financial, and personal opportunities (Hills, 2008a). It is probably understood in terms of the opportunities associated with the Western-dominated, technologically based global community of political, security, and business elites that is the UN, the International Criminal Police Organisation (Interpol), and Internet management companies such as Cisco Systems, rather than norms or processes. This orientation forms a basis for the adaptive practice characterising Nigeria's approach to tensions that might otherwise seem irreconcilable. Nigeria's contribution to UNPOL is a case in point. That Nigeria is publicly committed to the peacekeeping culture that UNPOL is part of, even as it is the recipient of international rescue missions is of minor significance as far as most Nigerians are concerned. Indeed, such tensions are easily accommodated by not only Nigerians (and by their regional peers from Ghana, Mali, and Senegal), but also by the UN itself, for whom the recruitment and training of sufficient numbers of suitable police are more pressing problems.

Even so, Nigeria is proud of its contribution to the UN operations in which its contingents are sometimes more respected than their Asian colleagues. As the commander of the 163 Nigerian police and prisons officers serving in Monrovia in 2006 said, his officers were proud to be part of UN efforts 'to restore peace, maintain law and order and to support the elections that ushered in a democratically elected government' (UNMIL, 2006). Two years later, the UN appointed two Nigerians as deputy police commissioners in recognition of their performance during missions in Darfur and Timor Leste (*Daily Champion*, 2008). And in May 2009, Nigeria's Osun State commissioner of police used the return of three policemen from Sudan to explain why Nigerian police peacekeeping contingents excel during foreign operations in fragile environments. He attributed their success to the 'discipline, hard work, dedication, loyalty' that are 'the hallmarks' of Nigerian peacekeepers. He added that the 'strenuous work environment' of Nigeria prepared

Nigerian police for effective peacekeeping; peacekeepers work for eight hours a day, whereas police in Nigeria must work long hours and are used to difficult working conditions (*Punch*, 2009).

In order to explain such developments, and what they imply for the notion of a globalising security culture, I consider the ways in which Nigeria's decision-making elite cultivate and implement a particular form of security knowledge. Rather than developing a codified account of typical practices, or identifying metrics for assessing the resultant knowledge, I build on the premise that Nigeria, as an influential broker with its own concerns, employs a security wisdom that engages with, but is separate from, the UN-style internationalist police culture influencing the notion of a globalising security culture. And these findings require us to think differently about how a globalising security culture is modelled. That is, I note the ways in which Nigeria's political and security elite accommodates what are essentially Western reform projects while shifting the terms of internationalism and international humanitarian deployment to suit its own agenda. Admittedly, focusing on the manipulation of international norms by an elite for its own advantage presents a partial picture. It is true, too, that such manipulation is disconnected from the discretion permitted to low-ranking officers as they go about their everyday business. Yet the difference may not be fundamental. For both levels illustrate Nigerians' pragmatic assessment of their working environment; one casts light on the ways in which politicians and senior officers manage the interface between international, regional, and sub-state concerns, while the other illustrates the ways in which low-ranking officers deal with their superiors, peers, and immediate social environment.

Hard data is difficult to obtain in this area, and the evidence base for what follows relies on personal observations, semi-structured interviews, and informal discussions with senior Nigerian, Norwegian, and UN officers, advisers, and officials in Abuja, Leeds, and New York, 2007–2009. Comments are unattributed because those I spoke to were serving, or spoke at meetings observing 'the Chatham House rules'. Drawing on this (admittedly impressionistic) experience, I argue that there is no meaningful globalising security culture. Such a culture would need to incorporate not only occupational commonalities, but also knowledge production, whereas Nigerian experience suggests that internationalist moves to facilitate a globalising culture using, for example, UNPOL are offset by distinctions between international and sub-state policing practices, and, significantly, by the ad hoc and time-urgent nature of UNPOL calls for officers and other ranks (Hills, 2009). In other words, the culture of international policing operations is instrumental; it is a utilitarian and context-specific product that reflects immediate requirements, as well as the specific cultural and/or occupational background and agenda of the officers concerned. The recent introduction of a two-week UN pre-deployment course does not challenge this assessment; many would-be UNPOL know less than the police they propose to reform.

My discussion proceeds in four phases. I compare the liberal tendencies at the heart of the notion of a globalising culture to Nigeria's pragmatically adaptive approach to UNPOL operations. I then assess the contextual issues moulding Nigerian police culture, knowledge, and practice, and note the implications for a globalising culture. The broader points that arise from my discussion of knowledge as practice or utility vis-à-vis knowledge as an ideological or normative truth are identified. I conclude that although certain international norms appear to modify police behaviour through temporary and localised processes of socialisation, they do so for instrumental, rather than intrinsic reasons.

Accommodating Liberal Tendencies

The co-operative model of policing promoted by the advocates of an interdependent globalising security culture is overlaid with political assumptions about the right 'professional' trajectory. The US's understanding of such a culture and expertise may be framed in terms of a war against transnational crime or terrorism, but more typical is the UN's goal of restructuring and rebuilding indigenous police 'to an acceptable level of democratic policing' (UN Police Division, 2007, p. xi). Similarly, influential intergovernmental organisations such as the EU and OECD, and donors such as the UK and Norway, see democratic-style policing as a means to promote conflict resolution and to facilitate or manage a new order consistent with liberal principles; policing is typically assessed in terms of its alignment with Western notions of 'good' policing such as accountability, service, and transparency. The universalising tendencies associated with this trend—and, more importantly, the ease with which understanding of the practicalities of policing is subjugated to theoretical (or, more accurately, normative) conviction—are evident from recent developments in Nigeria.

Despite Nigeria's pride in its peacekeeping record, and despite the UN's public recognition of its valuable contribution, the Nigeria Police is internationally regarded as one of the most corrupt institutions in a society that is notorious for fraudulence, politicisation, and communal conflict. Since independence from the UK in 1960, the police have received the equivalent of millions of UK sterling in technical assistance, training programmes, and support in kind, all to little avail. The UK's recent seven-year sector-wide 'Access to Justice Programme' had a budget of £37 million, but has yet to show evidence of sustained, wide-scale, or fundamental reform; witness the incidence of extrajudicial killings by police in cities where community-policing projects have been initiated (Amnesty International, 2009). However, while Nigeria shows that international efforts cannot easily change police behaviour through externally funded projects, or, indeed, through externally driven processes of education and internalisation, it has benefited from being the rescue industry's target. Indeed, the reason why in 2003 Tafa Balogun, Obasanjo's most notorious inspector general of police (he was sacked in 2003 for stealing or laundering US$98 million), supported and expanded the British Council's community-policing project was the access to resources it gave him.

The Nigeria Police's record suggests that it is not committed to the liberal-style internationalist and development-oriented police culture promoted by IGOs and donors, but it is politically and pragmatically committed to accommodating many aspects of that culture (Hills, 2008a). It is able to do so because, despite its record (and despite the cultural differences between it and, say, the Bangladeshi and Filipino police it works alongside in Darfur), a degree of occupational commonality exists within the artificial policing environment of UN operations, just as it exists outside; UNPOL could not otherwise function. However, understanding is built on functional issues, technical jargon, and on accommodation, personal relationships, and networking between the police concerned, rather than on norms or values per se. One reason for this situation is the gulf that exists between internationalist (as in UNPOL) and sub-state norms and practices, especially as it relates to the meaning of effective policing and the part that physical force plays within it (Hills, 2009). Building on this interpretation makes it possible to identify and explore the hybrid knowledge that results.

Playing the System

Independent Nigeria quickly recognised the possibilities peacekeeping offered for good public relations and international recognition, and while police did not deploy alongside Nigerian military peacekeepers to the Congo in 1960, their presence in countries such as the Democratic Republic of Congo (DRC), Liberia, and Sudan has increased since 2003, together with the institution's stated commitment to UNPOL operations and regional peacekeeping. In June 2009, the Nigeria Police's peacekeeping website recorded 616 officers and men as performing peacekeeping duties (Nigeria Police, 2009). Two hundred and forty-five were members of formed police units (FPUs) in Haiti and Liberia, while 371 individual officers were police monitors in UN and African Union (AU) missions. They were deployed as follows: 129 in Haiti (MINUSTAH); 57 in Timor Leste (UNMIT); 20 in Kosovo (UNMIK); 142 in Liberia (UNMIL); 4 in Sierra Leone (UNAMSIL); 57 in Sudan (UNMIS); four in Cote D'Ivoire (UNOCI); one in Afghanistan; and one in Burundi. Additionally, 201 were deployed in Sudan (UNAMIDS) as police monitors. The formal status of the Nigeria Police's peacekeeping operations and training section is indicated by the rank of its commander, who is a deputy commissioner of police reporting directly to the deputy inspector general of police, 'B' (i.e. operational) Department. Its potential value for a force that otherwise receives uniformly bad publicity is suggested by the frequency with which international visits involving UN officials to the police's federal headquarters in Abuja include a visit to the suite of rooms dedicated to peacekeeping. When I visited in 2008, the rooms (which were otherwise locked) contained some photographic displays, several dozen pamphlets and books, and some tables.

At the same time, the public picture of the police's contribution to UNPOL and regional peacekeeping operations is misleading. In Nigeria, as in most African countries, the rhetoric and organograms associated with peacekeeping—and policing more generally—bear little relation to the political priorities, financial imperatives, and resources allocated to it. However, UNPOL operations undoubtedly offer opportunities to those who know how to play the system. Nigeria's hybrid model of knowledge may, or may not, be representative of subregional approaches, but the police's embrace of the opportunities offered by UNPOL is similar to that shown by officers from Ghana, Mali, Senegal, and, indeed, Zimbabwe. For example, the commissioner of the Zimbabwe Republic Police (ZRP), Augustine Chihuri, consistently describes ZRP UNPOL in terms comparable to those used by senior officers such as Osun State's commissioner (*Punch*, 2009). When in February 2005 (a month after the US categorised Zimbabwe as one of the world's six 'outposts of tyranny') seven Zimbabwean officers returned from a UN mission to Liberia, Chihuri said that the ZRP 'have always been a beacon of policing not only in Africa but also in the whole world' (*Herald*, 2005). Such statements are indicative of the recognition by police of the opportunities peacekeeping offers for international recognition—that is, for peer acknowledgement of the professional and technical concerns that police from around the world share.

Similar considerations apply to FPUs. The Security Council likes FPUs because they are cheaper than individual officers or military units; it costs some $5 million to set up an FPU, whereas a regular military unit can cost up $30 million (UN News Service, 2006, pp. 4–5). Chief police officers like FPUs because they, rather than UNPOL officers and other ranks who are deployed as individuals, receive payment from the UN, and individuals volunteer because they want the special allowances that enable them to build a house or educate their children. Indeed, there is strong anecdotal evidence that FPU payments are sometimes seen by chief officers as means to offset bank loans, and (less controversially) that individuals must pay in order to be selected in the first instance (Personal communications, 2009a).

But the picture is more nuanced than this suggests. For example, while Southern governments use peacekeeping operations as a way of maintaining the professionalism of their militaries, this is not the case with police. Some mid-ranking graduate officers may be attracted to UNPOL operations for the opportunities they offer of exposure to Western policing practices, which are widely regarded as modern, internationally acceptable, and technically desirable, but most volunteers focus on the money UNPOL duties offer (this probably holds for the North, too). Even when officers are exposed to examples of professional good practice or the influence of Western role models, their knowledge and awareness of the 'democratic' and internationalist standards promoted by UNPOL's advisers probably evaporates on their return home. This may be an inaccurate conclusion, but there are as yet no systematic assessments by the UN or the Nigeria Police of the effects of peacekeeping on officers' knowledge and skills. Nevertheless, senior Nigerian officers consider it probable that the knowledge gained during international deployment loses its efficacy as soon as the officers concerned return to their usual duties; they are dispersed across units and locations, and their experience is undervalued by their superiors (Personal communication, 2009b). But this, too, is usual, in Australia and the UK as in Nigeria. Western commentators may regard such trends as problematic and internally contradictory, but Nigerians evidently do not; judging from newspaper reports since 2007, there are few if any public debates discussing the seemingly inconsistent and potentially contradictory imperatives driving Nigerian involvement in UN operations. Hence my characterisation of Nigerian knowledge of what works in UNPOL as hybrid: international standards and practices are publicly acknowledged even as understanding and behaviour are guided by more personalised and utilitarian motives.

How is this situation best understood, and what are its implications for the globalising culture? The gulf between rhetoric and reality, and the ease with which Nigeria's decision makers pursue their own goals while accommodating the terminology of UNPOL policing, means that in order to understand Nigeria's intermediary role and hybrid knowledge, it is not enough to look at Nigerian operations in Liberia or Sudan, or at Nigerian UNPOL vis-à-vis Ghanaian UNPOL. It is more informative to focus on the nature of policing, for this is where the imperatives moulding policing knowledge (transformative or otherwise) and the obstacles in the way of an internationalist, let alone globalising, culture, are most evident. Consequently, the explanation offered here builds on the notion of pragmatic forms of knowledge capable of integrating a range of variables and experiences, rather than on the aspirational and culturally specific vision of a globalising development-oriented culture; it develops the notion of knowledge as practice, as well as knowledge in practice.

To understand Nigeria's mixed model and the imperatives that determine the way it works requires that the broader context in which it operates must now be outlined.

Contextual Issues

A system of global governance may, or may not, be emerging (Dubber and Valverde, 2006; Duffield, 2001), but the notion of a police culture transcending territorial boundaries is influential, especially in the rich liberal democracies of Australasia, Europe, and North America in the vanguard of 'professional' policing and police studies and the organisations of which they are members (see Goldsmith and Sheptycki, 2007). UN spokesmen speak of the international standards underpinning peacekeeping operations while governments—including that of Nigeria—emphasise the need for police to co-operate in the face of transnational security threats such as organised crime. So, too, does Interpol, which promotes apolitical technical support and professional services. There is thus an international consensus regarding the nature of the security culture influential IGOs and governments wish to see promoted, which is evident in UNPOL operations. Witness the mandates of 11 of the 12 UNPOL missions authorised since 1999. All refer to monitoring, reforming, and rebuilding local police, which the UN understands in terms of democratic-style policing and which it presents as international policing, as evidence of a globalising security culture. With an annual growth rate of 30% since 2006 and a current mandated strength of 16,900 officers (11,577 officers are currently serving, with 7,775 of them present as individuals, and 4,402 serving in 35 FPUs) (Personal communication, 2009c), UNPOL operations reflect changing expectations of internationalist policing. In other words, if a globalising culture does not exist in the occupationally synthetic context of UNPOL, then it is unlikely to exist elsewhere.

In practice, UNPOL operations emphasise the limits of what such a culture could achieve while illustrating the pragmatic forms of accommodation associated with contributing states such as Nigeria. There are two main reasons for this. First, the contribution made by UNPOL contingents is uneven and temporary: UNPOL are the equivalent of temporary, miscellaneous, civilian (though increasingly paramilitary in nature), and comparatively cheap firefighters, most of whom are unfamiliar with liberal policing standards. The major contributing countries in April 2008 were Jordan, Bangladesh, and Pakistan, whose police rely on high levels of force to achieve their domestic security objectives, whereas countries (such as Canada, Germany, and Norway) advocating the use of minimal force—and the routine application of force is a key indicator of policing knowledge and style—are in a minority. As this suggests, the variables affecting UNPOL assessments of what is, and what is not, appropriate behaviour vary greatly. UNPOL aspires to provide the equivalent of a consistent or coherent globalising culture, but its structure and resources means that it does not and cannot do so.

Second, any discussion of a globalising security culture needs to engage with the domestic or sub-state context of policing. For this is the primary concern of governments and police, and it is the source and site of the critical variables affecting police values and behaviour. The immediate reason for the lack of a globalising culture may be political and correlated with power, but the deeper reason is that sub-state policing realities invariably outweigh the objectives of organisations such as the UN: policing is too important to be delegated by politicians to capricious international bodies, and each country's elite—North and South—assumes that its own practices are appropriate. Internal and sub-state concerns are invariably more influential on police than globalising imperatives, so the critical factor limiting globalisation's impact on security cultures is sub-state norms, practices, and concerns; it cannot be otherwise when security challenges in the South are primarily internal in origin and nature. The resilience of 'deep' police cultures to technical or ad hoc reform projects reinforces the strength of obstacles in the way of a globalising (or even merely internationalist or transnational) culture.

The balance between the sub-state and international, and the accommodation techniques typically employed by senior officers and politicians is managing it, is particularly marked in the case of the Nigeria Police. This is not to suggest that Nigeria's case can be used to make a broad generalisation about police in the 47 countries of sub-Saharan Africa, each of which has some form of regular and/or paramilitary police. Rather, it is to observe that Nigeria's police is representative of many forces in that it is under-funded, under-resourced, untrained, politicised, and parasitical, and its policing style is often repressive and ineffective. Untrained and poorly paid Nigerian officers kill hundreds of 'armed robbers' each year, but robbers kill dozens of officers, and abuse and extrajudicial killings are often a response to this. The death in police custody in July 2009 of Mohammed Yusuf, the militant Islamist leader blamed for instigating fighting between his sect and police and military forces, is an example of this tendency. Some officers extract confessions through torture or kill suspects in their custody whom they believe to be guilty precisely because they lack the skills or resources to carry out effective investigation. Suspects held in the custody of agencies such as the Economic and Financial Crimes Commission (EFCC) receive similar treatment (Human Rights Watch, 2007, p. 3). In truth, the Nigeria Police's 325,000 officers are incapable of effectively policing a country as big, populous, and divided as Nigeria, let alone doing so in the humane fashion advocated by UNPOL advisers. Despite this, some experienced Nigerian UNPOL arguably possess a specialised form of knowledge, skill, and status underpinned by a specific cultural and/or regional intelligence, and their style may be more appropriate for a Monrovia or Darfur than that of officers on a short-term secondment from Dhaka, Ohio, or Oslo. (For a discussion of the stereotyping of Bangladeshi, Nigerian, and Swedish military peacekeepers in Liberia, see Higate and Henry, 2009, pp. 118–136.) The theoretical and empirical implications of this for a genuinely globalising culture have yet to be addressed.

Issues Affecting Knowledge and Practice

Contextual issues matter because they shape the ways in which policing knowledge is created, articulated, enacted, recognised, and understood. We may not know how ethnic, cultural, or religious conceptual frameworks and practices, or language communities, influence the categories or types of policing knowledge transmitted during policing missions; yet it seems reasonable to assume that there are major challenges to be overcome. At the same time, however, it seems reasonable to assume that educated officers with international experience are sufficiently aware of the distinctions—and of the practices of other countries—to compare knowledge and expertise even if the criteria they use for assessing and appreciating knowledge remains fundamental unchanged.

As far as the Nigeria Police are concerned, two main issues affect knowledge and practice as it relates to a globalising culture. The first is police reform, which shapes the police's stated domestic standards and terminology. The last 10 years have seen the police subject to several internally driven reform projects, including, most recently, President Yar'adua's Presidential Committee on Police Reform headed by Alhaji Yesufu, a retired inspector general of police. At the same time, donors support reform and/or improved policing. For example, the UK's Department for International Development (DFID) funds community-policing projects while Canada, France, North Korea, and the US provide equipment and/or training; in June 2009, for example, the French National Police organised a two-day cyber crime training course for 20 officers (two months later, hackers attacked the police website recording the course). Inevitably, reform has been the subject of political manipulation. Thus the Yesufu Committee is widely seen as an attempt by the Yar'adua administration to gain legitimacy following international condemnation of the police's role in the electoral fraud that characterised Yar'adua's own election. In turn, politicisation compounds problems such as Nigeria's high levels of violent crime, much of which expresses or exploits political, religious, ethnic, and societal tensions that are rooted in poverty, unemployment, and competition for land. Nigeria may be Africa's biggest oil producer, but a globalising or internationalist culture means little to officers (let alone to other ranks) when petrol is imported and more than half the population live on less than US$1 a day.

The second—and subsidiary—issue affecting the police's knowledge and practice of internationalist policing relates to its international record and the peacekeeping training officers and other ranks receive. The police have not had the presence of Nigeria's military peacekeepers, which first deployed 50 years ago, but their role has increased since 2002. Also, they have made a number of moves towards accommodating the UN standards associated with a globalising culture. In 2007, for example, President Obasanjo invited Norway to train 250 Nigerian police for UN deployment. Norwegian officers provided a course that, in addition to including an overview of the UN's history, organisation, and legal framework, introduced the elements commonly considered to facilitate a globalising culture. These included human rights law versus host nation law, standard operational procedures, cultural awareness, humanitarian assistance, negotiation and mediation, ethics, the UN's policing standards and code of conduct, and the consequences of their violation (*National Daily*, 2008; *Nigerian Tribune*, 2008).

The courses clearly represented 'learning activities' as a form of cultural transmission, and no doubt the officers' classroom experience influenced their occupational knowledge. Also, the preparation was sufficient to satisfy UNPOL's immediate requirements (Personal communications, 2009a). However, the learning was in all probability superficial, rather than deep, and is unlikely to have fundamentally affected officers' judgement or practice, especially once they returned to Nigeria. It is difficult to substantiate this judgement since neither Norway nor Nigeria conducted any form of follow-up assessment (Personal communications, 2009a), while UNPOL's overstretched officials were under too much pressure to even contemplate such an exercise. The assessment is, however, consistent with the literature analysing the formation of police attitudes and values in the West and the challenges of changing police behaviour, let alone embedding democratic practices and values (for an overview of relevant literature, see O'Neill et al., 2007).

Whether training projects represent the foundations for a globalising culture is as a result questionable. Anecdotal evidence suggests that Nigerian police appreciate Norwegian assistance, aspire to the international status it promotes and the expert performance it promises, and are aware of the occupational commonalities UNPOL share. Yet appreciation does not represent commitment to a common culture. Also, UN operations are an inherently artificial exercise divorced from the realities of everyday domestic policing, and while this may not be a significant factor for Norwegian police, whose standards are relatively consistent across a range of environments, it is significant for Nigerians, whose international and domestic practices diverge (contrast UNMIL, 2006 to Amnesty International, 2009). Hence, the significance of contextual issues in obstructing the development of an internationalist or globalising culture based on knowledge as practice.

Knowledge Versus Practice

How, then, can the Nigerian police's experience of the interface between international and substate policing be explained, and how can the nature of the resultant knowledge be characterised? How can Nigerian understanding be conceptualised when we do not know why certain police procedures and norms transfer between societies while others do not. I suggest that understanding of the cultural transmission underpinning UNPOL-related learning, and of the hybrid knowledge that commonly results, is enhanced if we distinguish between knowledge and practice while drawing on insights from the literature on police culture.

Liberal understandings of a globalising culture and internationalist intervention practices are based on a specific type of knowledge and practice. This is invariably presented as universally applicable even though it is primarily influenced by Western experience and Western policy requirements. Trends in scholarship and policymaking play a part, too, as the incorporation of police reform into the security-as-development discourse shows. Western debate typically universalises on the basis of specific cases while forgetting the social and political conditions that make them possible. Some scholars and policymakers promote an ethical universalism

(Donnelly, 2007) while others advocate procedural goals developed in, and for, specific cultural conditions, but most collapse practical reason into normative (in other words, theoretical) reason. These approaches result in the neglect of contextual realities and the logic of practice embedded within them. In contrast, the Nigerian police's approach is, like that of most security practitioners, best characterised as practice based on knowledge of the world; that is, it is based on practice that accommodates security and political realities—most notably on what is seen to achieve the desired results—as they are today, rather than as they might be.

Allied to this is the issue of knowledge production and practice; that is, of the ways in which knowledge is constructed and exercised. For practitioners share common problems, practices, and assumptions, and their knowledge appears to be constructed and practiced in certain occupational ways, with what the Beninese philosopher Paulin Hountondji calls 'endogenous knowledge' being particularly influential (Kresse and Marchand, 2009, p. 2). By this Hountondji means knowledge as 'an internal product drawn from a given cultural background'. Hountondji's approach is not without drawbacks, but extending his observation to a specific occupational and cultural background such as Nigerian policing makes sense because most police knowledge is learned on the job and is influenced by the social environment in which it takes place.

The distinction between knowledge and practice that underpins Nigeria's understanding of international security relates to the established literature as follows. The possibility of cultural transfer between different societies and their police supports the development of a research agenda associated with globalising security that shapes international theory and policy. Yet the possibility and/or plausibility of transferring democratic norms and procedures to societies shaped by illiberal cultural legacies has never been rigorously assessed. Despite the vogue for transnational policing, police reform, police keeping, and international co-operation (e.g. Andreas and Nadelmann, 2006; Donais, 2008; Goldsmith and Sheptycki, 2007), remarkably little is known about Southern police culture and its institutions. The literature on police studies develops a normative, ideological, and/or technical agenda based primarily on Anglo-American experience, which is assumed to apply to all police; yet we do not know 'how "natives" think' (Sahlins, 1995). Even so, the idea that officers from very different societies share a distinctive outlook on the world and their job is well established and enables me to consider the issue of knowledge versus practice—and the emergence of a globalising culture—from a unified perspective.

The idea of occupational commonalities is particularly useful because it offers a context in which to explore knowledge as the internal product of a specific cultural background and of the heterogeneous forms of knowledge that result when that culture operates in a different or alien environment. Ironically, the idea of occupational commonalities was originally formalised by Westley, who, from research conducted in a US city in the 1950s, argued that the key to understanding the police was to see them as a social and occupational group (Westley, 1953). A consensus has since emerged that, although there is no single culture in any one police organisation, police typically share a 'set of assumptions, values, modes of thinking, and acting' (Cancino, 2001; Chan, 2007, p. 148) that enable a degree of occupational understanding despite attitudinal differences to issues such as timekeeping, the use of physical force, human rights, women, and so forth. But whether this amounts to evidence of a globalising security culture is debatable. The case of Nigeria suggests that it does not. Rather, it indicates that Southern states (especially those acting as intermediaries) construct, exercise, and validate an adaptive form of knowledge that integrates multiple norms and practices while accommodating or managing unavoidable political pressures.

The ways in which officers learn about the forms of hybrid knowledge has yet to be explored, but content is probably more significant than the manner of transmission. For it is known that police typically learn on the basis of personal experience, or from incidents occurring in their occupational environment, rather than on courses or colleges (Wilson, 1968, p. 283) and that this can include storytelling as well as more direct imitative means. Indeed, in an influential article published in 1991, Shearing and Ericson argue that culture is a figurative resource made available to officers through stories that provide a worldview and a library of gambits and precedents (Shearing and Ericson, 1991, p. 491); stories offer analogous meanings that permit the transfer of knowledge from one situation to another. We do not know what Nigerian police stories comprise, but stories probably offer greater scope for transmission than formal procedural rules, which do not necessarily guide/dictate officers' behaviour, especially among officers with only a rudimentary education. Also, stories offer scope for incorporating the occupational subculture that guides behaviour at, for example, Nigeria's ubiquitous roadblocks.

Distinguishing knowledge as theory from knowledge as utility provides an analytical tool for understanding the nature of Nigerian knowledge production. The arguments adopted by UNPOL and certain Western governments are based on knowledge as theory in that they promote a specific vision of an internationalist culture on the premise that it expresses a normative truth; they control its tone and objectives for specific goals that range from a responsibility to protect and poverty alleviation to anti-terrorism. In effect, empirically based reason is conflated or collapsed into theoretical or normative reason. In contrast, the knowledge that the Nigeria Police and its political masters value is utilitarian in nature; it is concerned with the facts, techniques, and experiences that can be used to achieve specific functional (and often financial) ends. Liberal commentators are inclined to see knowledge (e.g. of 'good' policing) as a form of truth, whereas Nigerian police value knowledge as a means to achieve a specific result. An additional reason for this last trend is that senior officers and politicians must accommodate and manipulate not only the internationalist imperatives promoted by IGOs and donors, but also Nigeria's ethnic and religious divisions, as well as the politics and realities of its policing.

The practical implications of this assessment can be seen in two episodes. The first is indicative of the ways in which utilitarian knowledge accommodates knowledge as theory, while the second suggests the ways in which Nigeria acts as an intermediary or broker between the UN's security culture and sub-state practices during UNPOL operations.

The first instance concerns the Nigeria Police's response to the British Council's promotion of community policing since 2002, which British advisers have always claimed is a universally applicable philosophy of policing, rather than a specific technique. The community-policing programme's original stated goals still hold: to transform the police's culture and organisation using community-based policing and partnerships. A 'culture of excellence in service provision' is to be introduced, individual officers are to be held accountable for their performance, and 'ethical policing' is to be 'placed at the core of all personal and organisational development programmes'. 'Social problems' are to be jointly identified, prioritised, and resolved by the police and public (BC/DFID, 2005, p. 2). Given the policing realities of Nigeria, where an under-resourced police is expected to manage high levels of unpredictable violence, such phrases emphasise that the universalising of a particular case (in this instance democratic-style interaction between personally accountable police officers and a 'community') tends to be accompanied by forgetfulness of the social conditions that originally make it possible. Hence the British Council's neglect of the embedded logic of Nigerian practice that men like former inspector general Tafa Balogun are able to exploit. Balogun's case is perhaps extreme, but my point is that his practice was based on utilitarian knowledge, i.e. on a knowledge built on practices that accommodate environmental realities and have realistic objectives.

Since 2005 the British Council has completely revised its programme, while the Nigeria Police has had three new inspectors general, each of whom has for various reasons promoted community policing—though Balogun's successor, Sunday Ehindero, was reportedly caught leaving office with the N200 million he had received as payment for rigging the April 2007 elections. The various community-policing projects that resulted have met with some success, especially when the implementing officers are personally convinced of the need to improve police–public relations, but overall the improvements have, to date, been localised, superficial, and temporary (Hills, 2008a). Significantly, the paramilitary Mobile Police is not included in the British Council's project, even though its rapid response capabilities secure the orderly environment needed for community policing.

The second instance concerns Nigeria's role in regional peacekeeping, which illustrates its understanding of knowledge as practice, its role as an intermediary, and its general assessment of UN culture.

As with most Southern states, peacekeeping for Nigeria has always been a foreign policy tool to protect its interests, rather than a humanitarian mission as such. Thus, Nigeria drove the Organization for African Unity (OAU)'s first peacekeeping operation in Chad in 1981, because it wanted to remove French and Libyan soldiers from a weak state on its border (Mays, 2002). It could not perform the task alone, so it acted as an intermediary between the OAU and France and the US (both of which were concerned about Libyan motives in Chad) in order to involve them in the mandate and operation. In fact, intervention for regional hegemons such as Nigeria is always instrumental; it is a means for obtaining resources or goals. This has implications for both Nigeria's assessment of contemporary threats and the relevance of a globalising culture, because it suggests that threat perception is location specific.

It would, however, be wrong to regard Nigeria's intermediary role as an attempt to play big brother. Take the case of its contribution to UN operations in Liberia in 2003. Nigerian military peacekeepers in Liberia may have been regarded as arrogant, but when there was fighting to be done they were usually the ones who did it, even if they were not too fussy about the finer points of their mandate (BBC News, 2003), and many UN officials thought the same of Nigeria's police. But this approach was arguably appropriate. The peace agreement of 2003 left Liberians feeling vulnerable to street boys, ex-fighters, political militias, secret societies, and machete gangs, while the ineffectual Liberian police (who were disarmed for three years after the 2003 agreement) were dependent on UN forces. Unsurprisingly, many Liberians thought that the UN (though not Nigeria as such) was the only organisation in the country capable of providing security (Mehler and Smith-Höhn, 2007, p. 54).

As this implies, Nigeria's adaptation to UNPOL standards is uneven. Publicly, UNPOL ideals guide Nigerian behaviour. In Liberia in 2006, for example, UNMIL police commissioner Mohammed Alhassan said that the Nigerian contingent served in Liberia with 'dignity and professionalism . . . courage, tolerance, understanding and respect for others' (UNMIL, 2006). Elsewhere, complicity and sexual exploitation were more common. In September 2005, for instance, Nigeria withdrew its 120-strong police contingent from Kinshasa after the UN launched an investigation into sexual harassment by 10 members of the unit on the basis that its actions contaminated all Nigerians. A spokesman said: 'We have contingents in about 19 countries right now and we want to send a message to all other contingents that if one finger collects oil, the whole hand is stained' (*Daily Trust*, 2007). But corruption probably went right to the top. Some senior military officers were accused of dubious business dealings with Liberian leaders, and this was presumably true of police too. Also, it was alleged that senior officers (including the inspector general) extracted the UN duty allowances of officers and men in Liberia (*Daily Trust*, 2007). Some officers undoubtedly adhere to UN norms and procedures, but UNPOL deployments are temporary, and the norms and behaviour encouraged during them often bear little resemblance to those shaping the routine policing in Nigeria to which they will return; adaptation to UNPOL's stated standards is for most officers a temporary response.

One other point deserves note. While the UN may try to mould police behaviour and organisation in a number of countries, and South Africa (Africa's other dominant power) may, for legacy reasons, influence police across Southern Africa, few African police exert cross-border influence on their neighbours: Nigeria has little influence in Ghana, let alone in Benin. Similarly, Nigeria is a member of the West African Police Chiefs Committee (WAPCCO), which promotes co-operative approaches to regional policing problems, including the illegal drugs trade in which Nigerians are heavily implicated (Ellis, 2009), but this means little when WAPCCO is essentially a list of addresses. Nigeria may regard itself as a regional and/or internationalist big brother, but the notion lacks substance.

Conclusions

Ideally, culture integrates knowledge production and practice, which are located within a general state of relevant knowledge. But in practice the two usually diverge, especially when the activity concerned is international policing. For the notion of a globalising security culture reflects the liberal agenda of organisations such as the EU and UN, rather than the illiberal practices of most Southern police; it concerns knowledge as a normative or ideological truth, rather than knowledge as utility or function, and is a work in progress. It is not surprising that knowledge remains uneven regarding the dynamics affecting the international space of policing operations in which such a culture is to act.

One way to avoid the analytical danger of modelling a potentially globalising culture on specific—albeit theoretically shared—liberal ideals is to test its meaning in relation to a repressive or ineffective police from the global South. I use the role of the Nigeria Police to do this (though I could equally well use police from the UN's top contributing countries of Jordan, Bangladesh, and Pakistan). This is analytically legitimate because, despite marked differences in technical standards and organisational values, police from around the world share a remarkably uniform discourse and a marked degree of occupational commonality. In the case of Nigeria, this is reinforced by the last five inspector generals having been career policemen. Further, there is a general (albeit fragmented) field of knowledge—police studies—within which knowledge and practice can be situated.

The Nigeria Police is an ideal subject through which to explore the multi-rationality of the officers, officials, and institutions involved in international operations, and the pragmatic ways in which senior officers manipulate internationalism. It not only acts as a nexus of occupational skills, cultural and social knowledge, and habitual activity, but it is also the target of, and a contributor to, the transnational rescue industry; its sub-state policing practices are harsh and corrupt even as its UNPOL role requires it to support the reform and restructuring of police in fragile or post-conflict states such as Côte d'Ivoire, DRC, Haiti, Liberia, Sudan, and Timor Leste. Ironically, Nigeria has developed a strong internationalist peacekeeping reputation even as its police fail to manage Nigeria's own crime and sectarianism. But this is understandable because the Nigeria Police's informal operating standards depend on whether it is working in Nigeria or under the auspices of an international organisation such as the UN—and in this it is typical of Southern police, for most of whom there is a sharper distinction between international and sub-state policing practices than between indigenous policing's street-level practices and the elite level at which its senior officers manipulate international norms or practices to their own advantage. In other words, the Nigeria Police Force is a typically pragmatic and complex agent of reform, in which knowledge is adaptive and multilayered.

Even so, much remains unknown. We do not, for example, know how Nigeria's security elite assess and manage globalisation's broad manifestations when they lack the institutional capacity to impose their authority in much of Nigeria, let alone across West Africa. What is known is that senior officers, in Nigeria as in much of Africa, display an intensely personal or local response to the interactions between the global, the regional, and the national, which operates underneath more formal arrangements and pronouncements (Hills, 2008b). Accordingly, occupational and cultural coherence is to be found in legacy issues and personal relationships, rather than international goals, and personal relationships are important partly because there is no globalising culture. Hence my suggestion that the pragmatic form of knowledge that results is best described as a political and occupational amalgamation of practice (utilitarian or functional knowledge) and theory (as in norm building). The ratio between the two is probably in the order of 90:10.

To conclude: the main argument of this article is that there is no meaningful globalising security culture; the necessary integration of occupational commonalities, knowledge production, and knowledge in practice has not taken place in either the global South or the North, let alone in both, and the possibility of collective regulation, or orchestration, is minimal. This is not to pass judgement on police practices and values originating in either the South or the North, for policing is a more nuanced, complex, and context-specific activity than many liberal commentators would wish. The best approximation to such a transnational culture is to be found in UNPOL operations, but UNPOL's culture is a functional and context-specific product that reflects the knowledge required for the contingents involved (and the intermediaries they represent) to work together in challenging environments. It cannot be otherwise when, as in 2007, British, Iranian, South African, and North Korean police trained the Uganda police; Chinese riot police joined a Brazilian-led UN force in Haiti's Port-au-Prince; and Indonesian police were committed to joint AU/UN operations in Darfur. The utilitarian forms of knowledge on which such operations are predicated have more to do with occupational commonalities and specific political goals than with a globalising culture as such. Even so, the Southern states involved pursue their own concerns even as they appear to be unable or unwilling to challenge or fundamentally shift the terms of internationalism and international humanitarian deployment to suit their own agenda.

Ultimately, there are two main reasons for questioning the reality of a globalising security culture. First, the notion reflects political imperatives rather than empirical reality. Influential IGOs such as the UN and donor organisations such as DFID conflate practical and normative reason, whereas the democratic-style policing they wish to see at the heart of an internationalist culture is influential only where compelling political pressures are reinforced by cultural resonance. Second, the most vocal advocates of a globalising culture ignore the dominance of sub-state imperatives in the security calculations of the police and politicians whose accommodation and/or consent is required to make the notion meaningful—and most peacekeepers come from Africa and South Asia where an internationalist policing style is of instrumental, rather than intrinsic, value. Further, although many UNPOL contributors receive international police aid, this does not ensure their commitment to democratic-style policing: recipients always find offers of technical assistance and equipment more attractive than projects on community policing. Witness Nigeria's acceptance in 2009 of not only British support for community policing projects but also North Korean training in unarmed combat. Certain occupational commonalities may be globalising in their effects, but the knowledge produced is not transformative in the sense that the international rescue industry would wish.

Acknowledgements

I am grateful to the Centre for Research into the Arts, Humanities and Social Sciences (CRASSH), University of Cambridge, which supported the research on which this article draws, and to the University of Leeds, for enabling me to visit Nigeria in March 2009.

References

Amnesty International (2009) *Killing at Will: Extrajudicial Executions and Other Unlawful Killings by the Police in Nigeria* (London: Amnesty International).

Andreas, P. & Nadelmann, E. (2006) *Policing the Globe: Criminalization and Crime Control in International Relations* (Oxford: Oxford University Press).

BBC News (2003) The perils of Liberian peacekeeping, 4 August, http://news.bbc.co.uk/1/hi/world/africa/3113009.stm.

British Council (BC)/DFID (2005) *Security, Justice and Growth: Nigeria* (London: DFID).

Cancino, J. (2001) Walking among giants 50 years later: an exploratory analysis of patrol officer use of violence, *Policing: An International Journal of Police Strategies & Management*, 24(2), pp. 144–161.

Chan, J. (2007) Police stress and occupational culture, in M. O'Neill et al. (eds.) *Police Occupational Culture: New Debates and Directions* (Oxford: Elsevier), pp. 129–152.

Daily Champion (Abuja) (2008) UN appoints 2 Nigerians as deputy police commissioners, 8 September, http://www.champion-newspapers.com/news/article_030908.htm.

Daily Trust (Abuja) (2007) Corruption and the police, 27 June, http://allafrica.com/stories/200706270723.html.

Donais, T. (ed) (2008) *Local Ownership and Security Sector Reform* (Zurich: Lit Verlag).

Donnelly, J. (2007) The relative universality of human rights, *Human Rights Quarterly*, 29(2), pp. 281–306.

Dubber, M. & Valverde, M. (eds) (2006) *The New Police Science: The Police Power in Domestic and International Governance* (Palo Alto, CA: Stanford University Press).

Duffield, M. (2001) *Global Governance and the New Wars: The Merging of Development and Security* (London: Zed).

Ellis, S. (2009) West Africa's international drug trade, *African Affairs*, 108(431), pp. 171–196.

Goldsmith, A. & Sheptycki, J. (eds) (2007) *Crafting Transnational Policing Police Capacity-building and Global Policing Reform* (Oxford: Hart).

Herald (Harare) (2005) ZRP's professionalism pays off, says Chihuri, 14 September.

Higate, P. & Henry, M. (2009) *Insecure Spaces: Peacekeeping, power and performance in Haiti, Kosovo and Liberia* (London: Zed).

Hills, A. (2008a) The dialectics of police reform in Nigeria, *Journal of Modern African Studies*, 46(2), pp. 215–234.

Hills, A. (2008b) Managing the interface: regional security and substate politics in Africa, *African Security*, 1(2), pp. 92–114.

Hills, A. (2009) The possibility of transnational policing, *Policing and Society*, 19(3), pp. 1–14.

Human Rights Watch (2007) Nigeria: investigate widespread killings by police; police chief boasts of 785 killings in 90 days, 18 November, http://hrw.org/english/docs/2007/11/16/nigeri17361.htm.

Kresse, K. & Marchand, T. (2009) Introduction: knowledge in practice, *Africa*, 79(1), pp. 1–16.

Mays, T. (2002) *Africa's First Peacekeeping Operation: The OAU in Chad, 1981–1982* (Westport, CT: Greenwood).

Mehler, A. & Smith-Höhn, J. (2007) Security actors in Liberia and Sierra Leone: roles, interactions, and perceptions, in T. Debiel & D. Lambach (eds.) *State Failure Revisited II: Actors of Violence and Alternative Forms of Governance* (Duisberg: Institute for Development and Peace: University of Duisburg-Essen), pp. 50–64, http://inef.uni-due.de/page/documents/Report89.pdf.

National Daily (2008) Norwegian police varsity trains Nigerian officers, February, http://www.nationaldailyngr.com/1law11.htm.

Nigerian Tribune (Ibadan) (2008) Nigeria police excel in UN operations, 8 February, http://www.tribune.com.ng/08022008/news/news20.html.
Nigeria Police (2009) *Peacekeeping Section*, 21 June, http://www.nigeriapolice.org/peacekeeping/67-peacekeeping-section.html
O'Neill, M., Marks, M. & Singh, A. (eds) (2007) *Police Occupational Culture: New Debates and Directions* (Oxford: Elsevier).
Personal communications (2009a) Senior international police officers and officials, New York (February), Abuja (March), and Turin (November).
Personal communication (2009b) Commissioner of police, NPF Headquarters, Abuja (March).
Personal communication (2009c) UN official, Brisbane (July).
Punch (Lagos) (2009) Why Nigerian cops excel in peacekeeping—Commissioner, 6 May, Online at NBT Topics, http://www.nigerianbestforum.com/generaltopics/?p=3107.
Sahlins, M. (1995) *How "Natives" Think: About Captain Cook, for Example* (Chicago: University of Chicago Press).
Shearing, C. & Ericson, R. (1991) Culture as figurative action, *British Journal of Sociology*, 42(4), pp. 481–506.
UNMIL (2006) *UNMIL's Nigerian Police Contingent Decorated with UN Peacekeeping Medals.* UNMILPIOPR21, 16 February (Monrovia, Liberia: UN. Mission in Africa Public Information Office).
UN News Service (2006) India pledges to send 125 female police officers for UN peacekeeping, *UN Police Magazine*, 4 December, pp. 4–5.
UN Police Division (2007) *Portfolio of Police and Law Enforcement Projects 2007* (New York: UN DPKO).
Westley, W. (1953) Violence and the police, *American Journal of Sociology*, 59(1), pp. 34–41.
Wilson, J. (1968) *Varieties of Police Behavior: The Management of Law and Order in Eight Communities* (Cambridge, MA: Harvard University Press).

Alice Hills is Professor of conflict and security at the University of Leeds, UK where her specialist area is security governance in fragile states. Her research focuses on why public police evolve as they do, and what explains the interactions among the police, governments, militaries, and societies in sub-Saharan Africa.

Indonesia and the Liberal Peace: Recovering Southern Agency in Global Governance

JONATHAN AGENSKY* & JOSHUA BARKER**

**University of Cambridge, UK*
***University of Toronto, Canada*

ABSTRACT *It is necessary to move beyond the marginalization of the global South towards a perspective that takes it as a relational, generative, and agentive site within world politics. Indonesia is an instructive case in this regard: its participation in various multilateral peace projects constitutes a narrative of Southern agency that runs counter to dominant accounts of contemporary global governance. The dominant methodologies of peacekeeping, worked out through various iterations into a project of liberal governance, have been deeply implicated in many sets of illiberal relations. This illiberal side to the 'liberal peace' can be seen in the ways particular North–South relations have been structured into peace governance, as well as its instrumentalization by powerful domestic elements of Southern states. This is well exemplified by the Indonesian case, whose postcolonial transitions have been caught up in problematic civil–military relations, with both its governments and armed forces deriving various types of support from the international community at various times. Following the Cold War, and especially post-Suharto, these have intertwined with matters of ethno-religious violence, military authority, democratization, and the rise of political Islam. Indonesia's participation in global liberal governance interventions raises questions about peace operations as a world-ordering technology.*

Analyses of Southern states in global governance remain largely undeveloped, especially regarding their roles in security relations.[1] Dominant accounts treat the global North–South in binary rather than relational terms, obscuring the many complex agencies that underpin international frameworks. These say little of the contradictions between hegemonic governance practices and their constructions of the South as a categorical object of intervention, in need of management for the security of a global liberal order—or 'liberal peace'. While many streams of scholarship address the localities and subjectifications of the South, they have fallen short of channeling these into a substantive critique of contemporary governance relations. They have also failed to generate an analytical framework through which such relations might be treated. This article opens up new lines of analysis in the literatures of governance, peace, and international relations, by rethinking the interconnections between global governance, world order, and North–South relations.

We argue that the 'liberal peace' framework, with its multifold entanglements and new global security norms, is a particularly productive domain for the reconceptualization of global North–South governance relations. In order to move beyond the marginalization and homogenization of the global South—as a hollowed-out, thin, and essentialized target of intervention—we adopt a perspective that takes it as a relational, agentive, and heterogeneous site within world politics. Here, we treat Indonesia as an exemplary case and argue that its participation in various multilateral peace projects constitutes a unique counter-narrative of contemporary governance.

Liberal governance has come to be equated with contemporary definitions of peace. However, the 'liberal peace' is not an international peace, and international liberalism does not necessarily engender liberal conditions—often doing the opposite. Southern states are negatively predisposed to these configurations, which are often exploited by powerful domestic elements for prestige, legitimation, entrepreneurship, and political cover. This is the case for Indonesia, whose postcolonial history has been rife with problematic civil–military and state–citizen relations, and whose governments and military derived various types of international support at various times. Following the Cold War, and especially post-Suharto, this has intertwined with matters of ethno-religious violence, military authority, democratization, and the rise of political Islam. States such as Indonesia, which has demonstrated moments of highly illiberal domestic conditions, are problematically both agents as well as targets of contemporary peace operations. Indonesia's participation in liberal governance thus raises questions about peace operations as a world-ordering technology.

This article has four main sections. First, we provide an overview of contemporary peace governance: its paradigms, transformations, and dominant developments. Second, we describe the intertwining history of both Cold War peace governance and the postcolonial Indonesian state—as an agent of this governance. Third, we examine the post Cold War moment as a point of rupture in global governance relations as well as in domestic Indonesian politics. Fourth, we show how Indonesia has been resituated as a target of global governance through its domestic and regional relations and its encounters with the (neo)liberal order. The article concludes with a discussion of the need to reconceptualize the North–South analytical focus as a means to problematize global liberal governance.

Context: Shifting Paradigms of Peace and Emergent Governance Relations

Traditional peacekeeping maintained strong 'Westphalian' commitments, privileging principles of territorial sovereignty and treating war and peace as interstate relations. 'First generation' operations were thereby designed for 'states with Clausewitzian, hierarchical militaries that wish to end the conflict and welcome outside conflict resolution initiatives' (Bellamy and Williams, 2004, p. 3).[2] As such, these have functioned according to a triumvirate of minimum force, consent, and neutrality—demonstrated by operations in Kashmir, Palestine,

Suez, and Cyprus. These operations were welcome and agreed to by combatants (states) and composed of lightly armed troops with limited mandates, such as border and ceasefire observations. Importantly, this excluded intervention into the social or political domestic arrangements of belligerent states.

However, the post Cold War era has brought a new interplay of powerful interests and emergent global norms—many of which developed in close relation to revised notions of international peace and security. Interstate warfare, the predominant focus of traditional peacekeeping, has become displaced by violent conflict involving non-state actors. These 'New Wars' are networked, intrastate, transnational, and polyarchical—collapsing many of the dominant frames of international relations (cf. Duffield, 2001; Kaldor, 2007).

Shifting modes of contemporary globalization have engendered transnational contestations and networked forms of militancy and resistance. In response, peace operations have grown more complex, resulting in practical and ideological convergences between security and development sectors, accommodations between civil and military sectors, and new types of humanitarianism.[3] This has become amplified following '9/11' and the predominance of counterterrorism on the global security agenda, the 'War on Terror', and a sector-wide internalization of security logics. Indonesia factors into these developments along a number of lines, both as a participant and as a target of international peace operations. While the latter has received much attention in the literature, the same cannot be said of the former—something this article seeks to redress.

Peacekeeping, Human Security, and Liberal Governance

In terms of governance, the post Cold War moment has been one of profound unsettling. On the one hand, the end of bipolarity strengthened the institutionalization of the international community, facilitating a more concerted and monolithic mode of governance—especially in terms of 'global security'. In the absence of Cold War constraints, the UNSC has become more empowered and UN peace operations have dramatically increased. Many of these involve the continuing participation of Southern states, including Indonesia. On the other hand, the international community (and the UN especially), has been indicted for its failures amidst the devastating effects of conflicts in Rwanda and Srebrenica. Moreover, operations in Cambodia, Somalia, and Mozambique have confounded traditional approaches, spiraling into 'complex emergencies' requiring multidimensional peace operations.[4]

Growing complexity and demands of operations have led to methodological shifts in peacebuilding as well as new normative approaches to humanitarian and administrative assistance (cf. Bellamy, 2004; Richmond, 2004). Human security referents increasingly characterize peace operations—a key shift from state-centrism—emphasizing instead the security of 'individuals, societies and groups, and an expansion of the scope of security to reflect the chronic and complex insecurities commonly faced by people' (Caballero-Anthony, 2005, p. 2).[5] In light of this, many have observed the increasingly biopolitical dimensions of global security as operations by-pass the state and focus on securing populations and humans—as such.[6]

Operations are now multidimensional, focusing on long-term goals such as democratization, human rights protection, and market and labor reform—all definitive of the 'liberal peace' and subject to a mix of neoliberal economic and neoconservative security interests. In contrast to traditional models, new approaches deemphasize principles of sovereignty and non-intervention. The liberal peace moves from state-centrism and the protection of borders towards regional stability, surveillance, and intrastate or transnational threats.[7] Importantly, liberal governance now focuses on the transformation of societies (cf. Duffield, 2001; Pugh, 2004). In the most extreme cases, this has included reassigning territorial sovereignty to international administrations, as in Bosnia and Herzegovina, Kosovo, and East Timor—the latter having obvious impact on the perception of Indonesia in the context of peace-building.

It is also worth highlighting the elevation of the UN within the administration of international peace projects. The UN is increasingly legitimized as the primary arbiter of global security by many Southern actors—including Indonesia and others in the Southeast Asian region. This has raised challenges for regional organizations, especially those rooted in Cold War relations struggling for a footing in a post Cold War order. This includes the Association of South East Asian Nations (ASEAN), of which Indonesia is a part, and illustrates the hegemonic operations of the liberal peace.

For Southern states, the centralization of the liberal peace raises risks of reifying enduring and asymmetrical decision-making structures, now less restrained by principles of non-intervention and sovereignty (cf. Askandar, 2005). These principles maintain strong commitments from post-colonial states whose histories of foreign intervention have been deeply formative. This is the case for Indonesia, whose own problematic relations with resistance, nationalist, and separatist movements in Aceh, East Timor, and West Papua have not only strained its relations with citizens of these localities, but with the international community and domestic reformers as well. These issues are part of broader post Cold War developments, including the state's shifting favor with international supporters and the changing fortunes of its political and military elite.[8]

Unfolding Histories: Postcolonial Indonesia and Cold War Era International Peace

The history of UN peacekeeping has unfolded concurrently with that of the postcolonial Indonesian state, in ways often interconnected. Traditional approaches were caught up in Cold War politics and strategic interests, constrained by its logics and ideological conflicts. At this time, peacekeeping was not a priority for major political and security establishments, nor did P5 states[9] actively participate in peacekeeping missions. These states focused instead on military preparedness for conventional war with each other, as well as covert counterinsurgency operations in the global South.[10] As a result, it had been the smaller Western states and developing nations that mainly implemented peacekeeping missions (Pugh, 2004, pp. 43–5). Among these countries, as this article argues, Indonesia has been a frequent although neglected participant.

Peacekeeping became institutionalized in the UN framework following the creation of the UN Emergency Force (UNEF), established to supervise the withdrawal of British French and Israeli forces from Egypt—an operation for which Indonesia contributed forces. From this moment, peacekeeping became an 'extension of UN diplomacy' (Pugh, 2004, p. 42). This is significant, firstly, for highlighting Indonesia's history within institutionalized multilateral peace operations. Peacekeeping played a large role in the state's foreign policy and rhetoric of post-independence national identity. Indonesia went so far as to lay this out in its constitution alongside other founding principles, demonstrating the North–South relationality behind the modern peace project. Together with its regional neighbors such as India, Pakistan, and Bangladesh, Indonesia has been a part of peacekeeping projects since their early beginnings.

Secondly, this is significant for highlighting the importance of relations between target and agent states, especially in terms of North–South relations and South–South solidarities. Indonesia's role in UNEF was informed by its relations with Egypt, then largely defined by their shared Southern status and religious constituencies. Egypt, a co-member of the Non-Aligned Movement (NAM), was the first country to recognize Indonesian independence, acting as an ambassador on its behalf throughout the 'Arab world'.[11] Soekarno subsequently conducted official visits to Egypt and other Arab states such as Saudi Arabia (1956) and Iraq (1960). Indonesia's participation in UNEF can't be disentangled from these various relations. Peacekeeping, as a mechanism of governance, and the participation of Southern states—typically understood as objects of governance—highlight deeper relations of co-constitution.

Third World Solidarities and Indonesian Peacekeeping

'Third World' solidarity served a number of purposes for Indonesian society and politics, strengthening its international ties and uniting its population around alterative internationalisms. The 1955 Bandung conference, attended mostly by newly independent Asian and African states, launched the NAM and was a symbolic moment for the crystallization of Southern solidarity into a determinate political principle of 'Third Worldism'. This functioned both as a corrective and an alternative to dominant world orderings and the powerful interests of Western and Soviet blocs. The Movement fostered economic and cultural cooperation among its members, united in opposition to the neocolonialism of dominant powers.

Indonesia's 'Non-Aligned' status tied together many of its domestic, international and regional relations throughout the Cold War period. During the Soekarno administration, this was used domestically to resituate the state's national identity within a larger frame and subordinate competing local claims to a 'broader and higher anti-imperialist solidarity' (Barker, 2008, p. 525). This was shaped by Indonesia's postcolonial experience and the initial reluctance of Western powers to recognize Indonesian independence.

The early Indonesian government emphatically refused to support either Cold War bloc, making much of an independent and pragmatic foreign policy.[12] This coincided with other aspects of Indonesian statecraft, such as the formulation of its *Pancasila* philosophy outlining Indonesian national identity and culture, to which competing notions would be either subjugated or submerged.[13] Importantly, *Pancasila* took up themes of social justice, which in combination with calls made for 'maintaining world order' by the Indonesian constitution (UUD 1945), resulted in an integrated domestic–foreign policy. This policy focused on building internal strength in order to play a proactive role in international affairs. However, Indonesia's 'passive pragmatist' foreign policy gave way to an explicitly anti-Western stance amidst pervasive poverty and underdevelopment, which generated sympathy for Marxist aligned critiques.[14]

Distance from the West grew as Indonesia's liberal parliamentary democracy was replaced by Soekarno's interventionist 'guided democracy', following rebellions in the 1950s by ethno-religious, nationalist, and separatist movements (met with brutally repressive state measures).[15] Soekarno's radicalization through 'autarchic, anti-imperialist and Third Worldist economic policies' resulted in the alienation of Indonesia's middle classes and the disruption of the regime's political support base, including support within the military (Hadiz, 2004, p. 65). Soekarno's repressive social interventions embittered many popular, ethnic, and religious groups, not least among which were fractions of Indonesia's modernist Islamic grouping, whose major political party, *Masjumi*, was banned (Liddle, 1996, p. 617). These moves had enduring effects upon civil–military and state–Muslim relations, both key concerns of contemporary liberal governance.

The effects of these shifts extended regionally as well. Soekarno's highly interventionist 'revolutionary programme', continued to link the state's domestic and foreign policies.[16] This culminated in the 1962 invasion of West New Guinea, the object of dispute with the Netherlands, and the 1963 action to 'crush Malaysia'—seen as an instrument of British foreign policy. Despite these events, at odds with the norms of international peace, requests were made of Indonesia to contribute forces to operations in the Democratic Republic of Congo, whose sudden independence from Belgium in June 1960 had resulted in crisis.

Suharto's New Order Regime

Cold War geopolitics was a major factor in the regime's foreign policy. Soekarno's moves to create a 'Jakarta–Phnom Penh–Beijing–Pyongyang Axis' were followed by policies aimed at bringing the Indonesian state into closer orbits with the People's Republic of China, and currying favor with domestic communist groups like the Indonesian Communist Party (PKI). However, factions within Indonesia's military—the TNI—who were already alienated by Soekarno's 'guided democracy' program, positioned themselves against the regime, drawing US support (Hadiz, 2004, p. 65).[17] This enabled the TNI to strengthen itself as a political entity, aligned with its 'Dual Function' military doctrine, and to intervene more effectively into Indonesian society. Under the pretext of an attempted communist coup, the TNI took political power in 1966 and pursued a violent and brutal anti-communist purge.[18] This resulted in the mass murder of hundreds of thousands of Indonesians and the official resignation of Soekarno, who was replaced by General Suharto, the military leader.

Indonesia transitioned from Soekarno's autocratic and autarkic regime into Suharto's highly centralized, authoritarian, and technocratic 'New Order'. This regime pursued a radical economic development program and predatory form of state capitalism, supported in the 1970s and 1980s through its petroleum economy, Cold War dividends, and repressive domestic security programs. Throughout this period, Indonesia's foreign policy underwent a number of changes, increasingly focused on Southeast Asian, Asia Pacific, and global engagements. In all, this laid the ground for Indonesia's relations within global and regional security circles, while at the same time entrenching a bureaucratic–administrative elite.[19]

Although Suharto reversed many of Soekarno's policies, focusing instead on stability and development, a close linkage between the state's domestic and foreign policies remained. Importantly, these included the immediate de-escalation of relations with Malaysia as well as other moves towards regional cooperation, such as the establishment of ASEAN in 1967 with the Philippines, Malaysia, Singapore, and Thailand. Although retaining its 'Non-Aligned' status, Soekarno's closed economic policies were also reversed, strengthening ties with Western states and bringing with them aid, trade, and investment. Indonesia thus developed closer relations with the United States, especially in exchange for its Cold War cooperation. These developments allowed the state to maintain its Non-Aligned bona fides for activities in peace operations, while also deriving military support and concessions for its illiberal domestic politics and state–society relations.

New Order Indonesia and the Cold War Peace

In addition to activities in the framework of ASEAN, Indonesia contributed to a number of UN-mandated missions throughout Suharto's regime, including operations in Namibia, Cambodia, Somalia, and Bosnia-Herzegovina. The state provided forces, observers, and logistical and operational leadership. For the United Nations Transitional Authority in Cambodia (UNTAC), for example—one of the largest and most costly UN peacekeeping missions of its time—Indonesia supplied the largest contingent, including two generals who served as chiefs of staff. In 1993, Indonesia also deployed military observers to the UN Operation in Somalia (UNOSOM I), monitoring the ceasefire of the Somali Civil War and providing and securing humanitarian relief.

Both these instances highlight Indonesia's early participation in multidimensional peace operations.

Indonesia also contributed to a number of Middle East operations, including Iran–Iraq, Iraq–Kuwait, and Egypt. New Order era Middle East interventions are relevant not only in terms of Indonesia's Southern relations but also for its ties to the Islamic world, the future of state–Muslim relations, and the shape of its Islamization policies in the late 1980s.[20] Domestically, Suharto both co-opted as well as repressed Islam. Soekarno was ambivalent about aligning with Islamic countries and reluctant to pursue a foreign policy based on shared religious constituencies. However, at that time, Indonesia required the support of Middle East states for its early statehood. Suharto's government made more of this relationship through cautious policy planning regarding the Middle East and Islamic issues (Sukma, 2003, pp. 26–50).

The history of Indonesia's participation in multilateral peace operations highlights the Westphalian logics also operative in the assembly of peace forces. Principles of sovereignty and non-intervention kept the domestic and regional affairs of implementing states beyond sanction. Cold War bipolarity not only shaped the preoccupations of major Western states but also informed their partnerships and proxies in the global South, or 'Third World'. States such as Indonesia, for example, derived military and financial support from Western states in exchange for cooperation and anti-communist politics.[21] These arrangements enabled illiberal and antidemocratic state–society and civil–military affairs within these states, as was the case for Indonesia. Cold War and governance relations cross-cut each other in highly problematic ways. The purpose here has been to illustrate how these dimensions were structured into the international peace project.

Indonesia and the Post Cold War Liberal Peace

There have been several key moments in Indonesia's postcolonial politics: Soekarno's autocratic 'guided democracy' regime, Suharto's New Order and authoritarian regime, and post-Suharto. Each of these has been caught up in global developments. Most recently, the post-Suharto moment has been deeply informed by the end of the Cold War, the Asian financial crisis, neoliberal global governance, the War on Terror, and the rise of political Islam. These developments intersect Indonesia's foreign policy contexts and international relations, in turn working back onto the state's domestic politics. Each forms part of the overarching narrative within which Indonesia's international activities need to be situated.

Post Cold War Indonesia

Indonesia's post Cold War politics have experienced critical changes. In addition to the cessation of Cold War dispensations—a significant source of support—other key and interrelated events were the 1997 Asian financial crisis and the subsequent demise of Suharto's 'New Order' authoritarian regime.[22] These culminated in the transformation of government–military and civilian–military relations, as well as the mobilization of Muslim groups and rise of political Islam. They have also coincided with the War on Terror and the accommodations of neoliberal market globalization forces in their neoconservative and imperial variants (cf. Steger, 2005). Many of these developments have had regional and international effects, as well as impacting the state's participation in liberal peace-building projects.

Suharto's regime had a variety of sociopolitical effects. The New Order encompassed a highly interventionist civilian and military apparatus and centralized administration. Despite the many material benefits deriving from Suharto's rapid technocratic development program, many segments of Indonesia's population became marginalized, leading to social and political discontent (something that would be heightened by the 1997 Asian financial crisis).[23] The regime also deployed an oppressive demobilization campaign targeting anti status quo elements in the name of national interest (Porter, 2002, p. 204). These strategies continued throughout the 1970s and 1980s, during which Suharto showed less interest in international matters, effectively neglecting ASEAN and rebuffing suggestions by member states for functional enlargements.[24] This continued into the early 1990s, with the TNI showing 'little intention of becoming a crucial player in Southeast Asia's security cooperation' (Mietzner, 2002, pp. 73–4).

However, from the mid-1990s until the 1997 financial crisis, Indonesia again participated in multiple peacekeeping operations. In 1994 alone, amidst its economic boom and liberalization and changing relations with the newly inaugurated Clinton administration, the state sent contingents to Georgia, Mozambique, and the Philippines.[25] As a seasoned troop-contributing nation, Indonesia could take on a number of roles. The success of Indonesia's development program in the early 1990s underpinned its proactive role in global affairs, resulting in a more assertive foreign policy. A key dimension of this had been the state's increased involvement in UN peace operations, as well as its renewed attention to the NAM, which it led from 1992 to 1995. While doing so, the state attempted to strengthen the Movement by enhancing its post Cold War relevance while also emphasizing its own role as a charter member.[26]

Nevertheless, this posturing had to contend with domestic developments, most notably the growing political mobilization of some Indonesian Muslims. Indonesia's handling of the Yugoslavian wars (1991–1995), particularly in terms of Bosnia and Herzegovina, illustrates the effects of these developments on its foreign policy. While resisting calls in 1992 by NAM states—and Malaysia especially—to officially reprimand Serbia, Indonesia triangulated between domestic and regional pressures and its own historical desire to downplay its religious identity.[27] Following a 1994 visit by a Bosnian presidential delegation and pressure from its domestic Muslim community, Indonesia pledged US$5 million in support and sent personnel as part of the United Nations Protection Force (UNPROFOR). In this case, however, Indonesia ruled out sending combat forces, limiting its contribution to military observers and medical detachments.

Importantly, this episode demonstrates the intersections of late New Order foreign policy and its 'Islamization' programs.[28] These programs began in earnest in the 1990s amidst growing contestations within the elite, increasing mobilization of separatist movements and precarious relations between the regime and military. They were aimed at expanding the regime's support base through political accommodation of Muslim groups.[29] At least in symbolic terms, this meant the increasing inclusion of Islamic-oriented issues, such as the Bosnian intervention, into Indonesian foreign policy in the early to mid-1990s. Besides serving its domestic political interests, such actions also allowed the regime to cultivate closer relations with Arab–Islamic states. However, for the most part, the state maintained a non-religious identity in its involvement in world affairs and the Department of Foreign Affairs resisted attempts to Islamize its foreign policy to any significant degree.[30]

By the late 1990s, pressures on the regime were being amplified by the Asian financial crisis, which exposed the social and economic vulnerabilities of many Asian states. Indonesia felt these effects in terms of its currency and industrial output as well as its state–society relations. The crisis also subjected the state to the influence of the International Monetary Fund, which moved to end the state's economic interventions and 'correct' long-standing market distortions.[31] These developments culminated in a rise of inter-communal violence and social unrest, playing a determinative role in the regime-level crisis that ultimately concluded Suharto's New Order.[32]

Civil–Military Relations

Suharto's regime derived support from the military, an entrenched bureaucratic elite, and a pervasive patron–client structure. Cold War dividends provided much international cover for the Indonesian government and anti-communist military (whose domestic purchase was also strengthened) (Porter, 2002, p. 202). In the post Cold War period, there has been a push for military reform—especially post-Suharto and most especially following events in East Timor. However, even before the New Order's end, there was a growing estrangement between the core administration and military establishment.

By 1997, the number of military actors in the House of Representatives had decreased significantly. Immediately following Suharto's resignation this further reduced. However, according to Lee, the military was still over-represented in cabinet and maintained its control of rural development, intelligence, and sizeable business holdings. Nonetheless, there was a rapid delegitimation of the military and its role within the social and political affairs of Indonesian society. This raised new challenges of asserting civilian authority and primacy (Lee, 2000, pp. 701–5).[33] The military responded to these developments by withdrawing from daily politics and revising its military doctrine—although leaving much room for equivocation.

Nevertheless, the post-Suharto moment has seen a new paradigm of civil–military relations, including the separation of police from the military structure in 1999 and the promotion of weaker forces such as the navy. Rehabilitating the TNI has been in the interests of both domestic and international actors. However, this has been a challenge given the extent of national symbolism invested in the TNI—to say little about the state's lack of strong civil alternatives. The Wahid government (1999–2001), which consisted of a loose and ad hoc federation of parties, was often threatened by and susceptible to hostile reactions from military elements resentful over their loss of political privilege.

The TNI has not only historically developed outside the direct control of parliament and the political administration, but did so in such a way as to become a key political and economic actor in its own right. Throughout the Suharto and post-Suharto period, the TNI has been lobbied for support by a number of political and business entrepreneurs, growing accustomed to having influence. The military has been, and remains, deeply entangled in the economic infrastructure across the archipelago, from which it has traditionally derived political and, importantly, economic support.[34] Although the Wahid government attempted to depoliticize the military by assigning civil servants to posts typically held by senior military, it was largely unsuccessful.[35] This was reflected by Indonesia's participation in peace operations at the time, which waned considerably.

Post New Order Indonesia

The dissolution of Suharto's New Order both opened the domestic political milieu as well as escalated tensions across the archipelago in the forms of ethnic, religious, and regional conflict. Separatist movements became increasingly galvanized following East Timor's independence, leading to violent clashes in Kalimantan, Central Sulawesi, North Maluku, and Ambon (Mietzner, 2002, p. 76). Many of these developments had roots in the regime's authoritarian policies as well as the state's colonial and early postcolonial history.[36]

Following Suharto, several developments have transformed core–periphery relations throughout the archipelago—notably relating to processes of decentralization and democratization.[37] The end of the New Order saw a rise of domestic mobilizations, including Muslim groups, student protest movements, and separatist nationalists. However, except for Suharto, Indonesia has no history of military coups, and local resistances have never made designs on the political administration (Dibb, 2001, p. 839). Nevertheless, Indonesia's domestic context was for a time highly fluid and fears of instability preoccupied the Megawati government, which succeeded Wahid in 2001. Still, the Megawati government participated in peace operations, albeit at a lower level. During her term, this included UN missions in the Democratic Republic of the Congo and Liberia.

Concurrent with this general decline of participation in peace operations, Indonesia raised the idea of a Southeast Asian peacekeeping force in the framework of ASEAN. Indonesia places considerable political importance on its multilateral peace engagements and has gone to lengths to make these happen. In 2004 Jakarta produced the first draft of the ASEAN Security Community Plan of Action, which included a proposal for a regional peacekeeping force.[38] Although rejected by other ASEAN members, the proposal has laid the groundwork for a regional network of peacekeeping centers, primarily linking Indonesia, Malaysia, and Thailand. Indonesia also resumed its proactive role in peace governance as its economic and political conditions stabilized.[39]

Participation in international peace governance has been part of Indonesia's national project, strengthening ties to its founding principles and reinvigorating its national identity. Importantly, this identity elevates internationalism and has been constructed through a liberally informed constitutional discourse promoting 'freedom, eternal peace, and social justice'. In this context, Indonesia became a non-permanent member of the UN Security Council in 2007–2008, after which it sent peacekeeping contingents to numerous operations including Sudan (UNMIS and UNAMID), Nepal (UNMIN), and Lebanon (UNIFIL). As of 2011, Indonesia had 1,700 peacekeeping personnel deployed in six UN peacekeeping operations in five countries, as well as engaging in other post-conflict activities such as capacity-building (UN Peacekeeping, 2011).

Resituating Indonesia

Post-Suharto Indonesia has seen problematic domestic and regional developments, especially from the perspective of liberal peace governance. The rise and ebb of ethnic and separatist conflict and the growing importance of political and militant Islam raise questions as to whether the 'post-Suharto' frame has given way to a newly defined moment (cf. Webber, 2006). The War on Terror is a large factor in this, reordering global relations and imposing new security and institutional arrangements upon states of the global South. Many of these states, including Indonesia, have become subjected to external pressures for democratization and political openness. Indonesia has attempted to meet these pressures, but the ability of local constituencies to articulate political alternatives has remained illusive.

These new contexts have not only affected Indonesia's negotiations of the international institutional system, regional partners, and emergent norms, they have redefined the state within global security imaginaries. Indonesia has increasingly become the object of new security concerns focused on stability in the global South.[40] Early in its post-Suharto transition, this included concerns of Indonesia becoming a 'failed state' amidst the reinvigoration of separatist movements following the economic crisis and tensions within the post-Suharto state-building project. These concerns now turn on the state's role in the War on Terror and the growth of local, regional, and transnational Islamist organizations.

To some extent, many of these issues have roots in unresolved colonial legacies suppressed by Indonesia's Cold War authoritarianism. Unsurprisingly, colonial rule left many problematic territorial boundaries making for a potent and unstable mix. For post-Suharto Indonesia, these have reemerged to complicate its differing global, regional and domestic relations. At the same time, separatist and ethno-nationalist mobilizations throughout the archipelago, and most prominently in Aceh, East Timor and West Papua, may also be seen as a direct response to measures taken by both the Sukarno and Suharto nation-building regimes (Aspinall and Berger, 2001, p. 1004).

These issues were determinative of the Megawati government, which was largely preoccupied by the continuing separatist insurrection in the western province of Aceh and a rise in Islamic militancy. These issues also garnered highly repressive counterinsurgency measures and heavy-handed responses, respectively, raising considerable amounts of domestic and international scrutiny. Islamic militancy has been an enduring issue, especially given the broader frames of the War on Terror, and the Bali bomb blasts and attack at the JW Marriott hotel in Jakarta. Additionally, Megawati had to deal with the effects of the 2004 Tsunami, the rise of local and international NGOs, IMF loans, and endemic corruption.

Although much has been made of reform—or *reformasi*—in post-Suharto Indonesia, deeply corrupt and dysfunctional patterns remain.[41] Development of a multiparty system has been dominated by highly partisan politics. Despite improvements, there have been increases in 'bureaucratization, ethnocentrism, and nepotism' (Widianingsih and Morrell, 2007, p. 1). There are a number of political and scholarly debates about post-Suharto Indonesia and many questions about its emerging political trajectories. These focus on development planning, decentralization, democratization, the changing role of the TNI, and the strengthening of domestic civil society—amidst a problematic regional context.[42]

Indonesia in Flux

For several years following the end of Suharto's rule, deep domestic dissatisfaction tended to manifest in ethnic and religious violence rather than formal political participation. Although Megawati became a focal point for popular anti-Suharto dissent as the opposition leader in the mid to late 1990s, Indonesia's political opposition has tended to 'lack depth'. This has been accentuated by the continuing corruption and patrimonialism of the post-Suharto government (Dibb, 2001, p. 839). A growing exception to this has been the rise of political Islam which, given the prevalence of ethnic–religious configurations, has dominated political culture by offering a thought-out alternative for political participation.[43]

Indeed, according to Porter, Muslim groups are 'shaping Indonesia's political future and determining the forms of political participation' (Porter, 2002, p. 221). Many of these groups pay increasing attention to international affairs and are informed by the global War on Terror and the rise of more militant transnational forms of Islam. Groups have become more globally oriented. Radical Islamic forms such as *Jemaah Islamiyah* have also become regionally focused, with bases of material and ideological support in Malaysia, Thailand, and Indonesia—in addition to strengthening connections with Middle Eastern and African co-religionists.[44]

International, Regional, Multilateral, and Bilateral Relations

The complex appearances of Islam in Indonesia's public life are part of a fluid situation in which different political opportunities emerge in conjunction with translocal developments. These have had subsequent effects on Indonesia's international and regional relations—especially with its proximate neighbors, such as Singapore, Malaysia, and Thailand, with whom it shares security concerns about piracy and a common and growing transnational network of Islamic organizations. Indonesia and Malaysia, for example, have come together in support of the Philippine and Thai governments in their efforts to mitigate the effects of their own respective Islamic separatist movements (Desker, 2003, p. 419).

The increasingly networked dimensions of these organizations have also factored into renewed discussions about formalized regional multilateralism and collective security. At the global level, this conversation derives support from the liberal peace framework and its general move away from state-centric security. Regional integration is seen as a way to strike 'a new balance of responsibility for mitigating instabilities' (Pugh, 2004, p. 44). The Southeast Asian region as a whole has seen a number of highly problematic and complex disputes, conflicts, and national and international responses. There have been many intrastate conflicts in the region, many of which involve Indonesia. Regionally, conflicts have taken place in Cambodia, Myanmar, Philippines, and Thailand. In the Indonesian context, these have included Aceh, East Timor, and West Papua. East Timor has stood as an exemplary tale in discourses on emergent security norms and practices. Between 1999 and 2004, this was the site of one the UN's most intensive peace operations.[45]

At the same time, regional security has also had some attractions for Southeast Asian states as a preventive measure against Northern interventions into their domestic affairs—especially in light of liberal peace methodologies. Regional conversations have involved the negotiation of normative changes within peace-building, humanitarianism, and security as well as the attempt to localize these in line with (often problematic) regional norms and interests.[46] This has been well exemplified by Indonesia, which despite its participation in international peace operations, has historically been less receptive as a target of international intervention.[47] As such, Indonesia has expressed interest in strengthening ASEAN and developing it into a regional security community.

ASEAN is sometimes heralded as one of the more successful regional actors for maintaining interstate peace since the late 1960s.[48] Notwithstanding its difficulties, ASEAN has shown resiliency in the post Cold War period and remains the primary regional actor in Southeast Asia. ASEAN has been undergoing revision amidst the liberal peace hegemony, attempting to both adapt to cooperative security and multilateral frameworks as well as localize emergent norms. Fruits of this labor can be seen in the presence of Philippine and Thai observers in the Indonesian province of Aceh in 2002, as well as Malaysian peacekeepers in the Philippines in 2004 (Caballero-Anthony, 2005, p. 10). Notwithstanding this uneasy fit between liberal peace ideologies and their negotiations by Southern actors, the success of regional interventions as a question of principle remains unanswered.

The rise of political Islam has also impacted Indonesia's bilateral relations with Northern states. Unsurprisingly, this includes the US, whose relations with Indonesia have been mixed since the Cold War and East Timor, but have revitalized amidst the War on Terror.[49] Australia is another key example that maintains strategic interests in the region, as well as particular concerns about Indonesian stability, networked Islamic terrorism, and immigration and refugees.[50] Indonesia's bilateral relations tell a different story about the inner workings of the global liberal order than do its relations with multilateral groups such as the UN. This was particularly apparent in the case of East Timor, where in contrast to the international community, Indonesia received tacit support from both the US and Australia, with whom it continues to enjoy deepening relations.[51]

Nevertheless, East Timor represents a watershed moment not only for the success of international peacekeeping and humanitarianism, but for the changing nature of UN missions in Asia and elsewhere (cf. Wheeler and Dunne, 2001, p. 807). In terms of Indonesia and its relations to the liberal peace, however, East Timor has become the defining discourse.

'Neoliberalization' of the Global System: The 'Three Ps'

Post Cold War globalization has confronted Southeast Asian states with a number of 'non-traditional' challenges, as well as with international institutional changes. States of the region have deepened their dependency on financial and development institutions which have concurrently revised their polices to accommodate global security concerns—a process intimately connected to the liberal peace often described as the 'security–development' interface.[52] Indonesia has been hard hit in the face of these challenges, particularly following the Asian financial crisis, early post Cold War reconfigurations, and the effects of the Tsunami—all of which have been complicated by the rise of translocal security threats.

Indonesia's domestic affairs have become subject to new international influences as the target of liberal peace operations—and the social, political, and economic interventions accompanying them. This has led to an influx of NGOs and constellations of hitherto unconnected actors, inline with global neoliberal and 'post-Washington consensus' trends.[53] The 'three Ps' of the late 1990s—'public–private partnerships' driven by principles of governmentality, self-management, and coordination—have increasingly shaped the domestic contexts of Indonesia. Partnership is a key strategy of the liberal peace and other governance initiatives, and is part of an overall push by major Northern states to develop regional capacities in order to offset governance demands.[54]

Especially following the financial crisis, there has been a neoliberal ascendancy within the state itself over nationalist and populist development ideologies (Barker, 2008, pp. 523–33). On the one hand, this has strengthened the formation of Indonesia's civil society. Governance reform in Indonesia has been the preeminent concern of key multilateral and bilateral actors, whose agenda-setting influence might be seen in the establishment of the 'Partnership for Governance Reform in Indonesia', launched in 1999 by the United Nations Development Programme (UNDP), the World Bank, and the Asian Development Bank (ADB).[55]

Already beginning in the early 1990s, prior to the collapse of the New Order, Indonesia channeled international funds into strengthening its social institutions. This attempted to address the damaging effects of the regime on the institutional fabric of Indonesian society. Funds have since been applied towards more recent processes of democratization and decentralization. These have produced new possibilities to connect emergent and energized domestic constituencies, while also bringing them into dialogue with international and transnational groups. In addition to a growing diversity of actors, Indonesia's ideological landscape has opened up as well.

On the other hand, the entrenched elite and its surrounding culture have impeded the substantive involvement of citizens in decision-making processes. Oligarchic tendencies and pervasive corruption have hindered governmental reform. While decentralization has gone some way in disrupting these configurations, it has also facilitated the exportation of patrimonial tendencies, cronyism, and nepotism to local and municipal levels.[56] Nevertheless, the participatory planning underway has led to a number of improvements in state–society relations through planning committee and local strategic plans, budgetary reforms, and developmental transparency.

Conclusion

There has been growing attention to the new liberal peace orthodoxies of international peace governance (Bellamy, 2004; Duffield, 2001; Pugh, 2004). Thinking differently about international peace operations, this article has focused on the agentive roles of Southern states within such projects. Importantly, this has entailed rethinking the entities of global politics and taking seriously the relationality and mutual constitution of the global North–South. Much has been written about the new market and security conditions of the liberal peace, seen in Pakistan and Indonesia, as well as its imposition of various legal, institutional, and political frameworks onto contexts traditionally defined by alternative arrangements, as in East Timor.[57] These works highlight the global–local problematics that tend to form primarily along North–South lines. Here we have opened new pathways of critique by focusing on the specificities of Indonesia in the broader frames of global North–South and security relations.

Peace operations maintain specific world orders and are—in and of themselves—world-ordering technologies. From the perspective of North–South relations, there are problematic continuities behind the reconfigurations of the liberal peace and its tacit support of illiberal regimes. Southern voices have increasingly called for the inclusion of Southern states at the levels of policy-making.[58] This is particularly relevant for states such as Indonesia, who are seasoned agents of multilateral peace operations but who, in the post Cold War era, have become their targets. Hegemonic frameworks such as the liberal peace operate in ways that continually exclude alternative possibilities, while generating benign self-images often at odds with their practical realities.

Representation has always been an overarching dimension of North–South relations—invoking issues of legitimacy, authority, and voice (cf. Doty, 1996). The limited attention paid to Indonesia as an agent of multilateral governance projects attests to this, as has the appropriation of the South into hegemonic global frameworks. Indonesia's sustained role in peace projects since its UN membership challenges many perceptions of global multilateralism and peace operations, and it suggests that the liberal peace is anything but.

The disempowering effects of the liberal peace on the domestic conditions of its Southern partners have also yet to be fully interrogated. We have addressed this by focusing on the Indonesian state and its complex entanglements within international peace projects. The global South is not a categorical site simply acted upon, nor is it a site easily defined by such needs. Analyses of Southern states remain incomplete without attending to their agencies in contemporary governance: as participants and partners in the delivery of the 'liberal peace'.

Acknowledgements

We would like to thank Mateja Peter, Paul Amar, and the two anonymous reviewers for their helpful comments on earlier drafts of the article. We are also grateful to Irene Poetranto, who provided research assistance.

Notes

1 See Barkawi and Laffey (2006, p. 55).
2 See also Bellamy (2004).
3 See Duffield (2001), Richmond (2007), Dillon and Reid (2000), Barnett (2005), Adamson (2005, p. 557).
4 See the *Report of the Panel on UN Peace Operations* known as the *Brahimi Report* (2000). See Bellamy and Williams (2004), Caballero-Anthony (2005).

5 On human security, see Paris (2001), Bellamy and McDonald (2002). On global security, see Buzan et al. (1998, p. 35). On Asian regionalism, see Towet al. (2000).
6 See Dillon and Reid (2001), Selby (2007).
7 See Buzan et al. (1998), Krause and Williams (1996).
8 On post Cold War Indonesia, see Aspinall (2005), Barker (2008), Hasan (2006), Li (2007), Tsing (2005).
9 China, France, Russia, UK, and USA.
10 These include British operations in Ireland, France in Algeria, and the many American adventures in Southeast Asia, Latin America, Afghanistan, and Africa in the 1980s. The Soviet Union was also active in these areas in addition to Eastern Europe.
11 Including setting up an Arab League conference in November 1946 urging for the state's recognition.
12 See Sukma (1995, p. 306).
13 A set of philosophical principles articulated by Soekarno in a 1945 speech aimed at unifying the pre-independence state and breaking free of its feudal past (see Barker, 2008, p. 528).
14 See Hadiz (2004, p. 58).
15 See Aspinall and Berger (2001), Crouch (1988), Hadiz (2004).
16 See Sukma (1995) and Murphy (2005).
17 See also Kahinand Kahin (1997, pp. 112–15).
18 See Roosa (2006).
19 On this transition, see Aspinall and Berger (2001), Hadiz (2004, p. 65).
20 Indonesia has the world's largest population of Muslims. On state–Muslim relations, see Hasan (2009), Liddle (1996), Mietzner (2002), Sidel (2007).
21 Non-aligned states also derived assistance from the Soviet bloc and, indeed, many from both.
22 On the end of Suharto regime in the context of the end of the Cold War and the Asian financial crisis, see Anderson (1998).
23 See Aspinall and Berger (2001, p. 1007), Barker (2008).
24 At the same time, Russia was shifting its Southeast Asia foreign policy, attempting to deepen ties with ASEAN and move away from alliances with Vietnam, Laos, and Cambodia (see Williams, 1991).
25 In 1997 Indonesia also sent forces to Tajikistan.
26 See Sukma (1995, p. 313).
27 Perwita (2007, pp. 132–57) provides a detailed discussion of the domestic politics surrounding Indonesia's involvement in the Bosnian mission.
28 On Islamization of the late Suharto regime, see Liddle (1996), Mietzner (2002).
29 See Barker (2008), Liddle (1996), Porter (2002, p. 205).
30 See Perwita (2007, p. 151) and Sukma (2003, pp. 71–8).
31 See Robison and Rosser (1998, p. 1594).
32 See Caballero-Anthony (2005, p. 2), Wheeler and Dunne (2001, p. 811).
33 See also Crouch (1988).
34 On the Indonesian Armed Forces and their post-Suharto reforms, see Mietzner (2002, p. 72) and (2009, pp. 240–1).
35 Wahid was eventually impeached, and his successor, Megawati, aligned herself with military conservatives in order to shore up her authority in the context of a fragmented civilian elite. It was only under Yudhoyono, who became president in 2004, that obstacles to TNI reform were gradually removed (Mientzer, 2009, pp. 225–30, 291–2).
36 See Bertrand (2004).
37 See Aspinall and Berger (2001, p. 1003), Barker (2008), Widianingsih and Morrell (2007).
38 For a discussion of Indonesia's proposal and its reception by other ASEAN states, see Acharya (2009, pp. 262–7).
39 Under Yudhoyono, Indonesia contributed troops to the 2006 UN Interim Force in Lebanon (UNIFIL)—a contingent recently replenished and one of UNIFIL's largest, alongside France and Italy.
40 See Dibb (2001, pp. 839–42).
41 On *reformasi*, see Budiman et al. (1999), Hasan (2009), Loh and Öjendal (2005, pp. 223–5), Manning and van Diermen (2000), Mietzner (2009).
42 For a sample of this growing body of scholarship, see Aspinall (2005), Aspinall and Fealy (2003), Barker (2008), van Klinken and Barker (2009), Dibb (2001), Emmerson (1999), Hadiz (2010), Hasan (2009), Kahin (2003), van Klinken (2007), Mietzner (2002), Nordholt and van Klinken (2007).
43 See Porter (2002), Sidel (2007).
44 On 'radical Islam' and Indonesia, see Desker (2003), Hasan (2006).
45 See Chopra (2002).

46 On ASEAN and the localization of norms in the context of ASEAN, see Acharya (2004).
47 Since the end of the Suharto regime, Indonesia has become more receptive to international interventions (Acharya, 2009, pp. 254–5).
48 See Caballero-Anthony (2005, p. 7).
49 See Murphy (2010).
50 See Mackie (2006).
51 See Wheeler and Dunne (2001).
52 See Maxwell and Riddell (1998).
53 See Ganie-Rochman and Achwan (2005), Widianingsih and Morrell (2007).
54 See Crawford (2003, p. 139).
55 See Crawford (2003, pp. 140–5).
56 There are numerous works on this. See, for example, Widianingsih and Morrell (2007, pp. 9–10) and note 42 above.
57 See Chesterman (2005), Fearon and Laitin (2004), Krasner (2004), Paris (2004). There have also been recent works addressing the indigenization of peace operations and new hybrid forms (see MacGinty, 2008).
58 See Askandar (2005).

References

Acharya, A. (2004) How ideas spread: Whose norms matter? Norm localization and institutional change in Asian regionalism, *International Organization*, 58(2), pp. 239–275.

Acharya, A. (2009) *Constructing a Security Community in Southeast Asia: ASEAN and the Problem of Regional Order*, 2nd ed. (New York: Routledge).

Adamson, F. B. (2005) Global liberalism versus political Islam: competing ideological frameworks in international politics 1, *International Studies Review*, 7(4), pp. 547–569.

Anderson, B. (1998) Sauve qui peut, in B. Anderson, *Spectre of Comparisons: Nationalism, Southeast Asia, and the World* (London: Verso), pp. 299–317.

Askandar, K. (2005) A regional perspective of UN peace operations in Southeast Asia, *International Peacekeeping*, 12(1), pp. 34–48.

Aspinall, E. (2005) *Opposing Suharto: Compromise, Resistance, and Regime Change in Indonesia* (Palo Alto, CA: Stanford University Press).

Aspinall, E. & Berger, M. T. (2001) The break-up of Indonesia? Nationalisms after decolonisation and the limits of the nation-state in post-Cold War Southeast Asia, *Third World Quarterly*, 22(6), pp. 1003–1024.

Aspinall, E. & Fealy, G. (2003) *Local Power and Politics in Indonesia: Decentralisation & Democratisation* (Institute of Southeast Asian Studies).

Barkawi, T. & Laffey, M. (2006) The postcolonial moment in security studies, *Review of International Studies*, 32(2), pp. 329–352.

Barker, J. (2008) Beyond Bandung: developmental nationalism and (multi) cultural nationalism in Indonesia, *Third World Quarterly*, 29(3), pp. 521–540.

Barnett, M. (2005) Humanitarianism transformed, *Perspectives on Politics*, 3(4), pp. 723–740.

Bellamy, A. J. (2004) The 'next stage' in peace operations theory? *International Peacekeeping*, 11(1), pp. 17–38.

Bellamy, A. J. & McDonald, M. (2002) The utility of human security: Which humans? What security? A reply to Thomas & Tow, *Security Dialogue*, 33(3), pp. 373–377.

Bellamy, A. J. & Williams, P. (2004) Introduction: thinking anew about peace operations, *International Peacekeeping*, 11(1), pp. 1–15.

Bertrand, J. (2004) *Nationalism and Ethnic Conflict in Indonesia* (New York: Cambridge University Press).

Buzan, B., Wæver, O. & De Wilde, J. (1998) *Security: A New Framework for Analysis* (Boulder, CO: Lynne Rienner Publishers).

Caballero-Anthony, M. (2005) Introduction: UN peace operations and Asian security, *International Peacekeeping*, 12(1), pp. 1–17.

Chesterman, S. (2005) *You, the People: The United Nations, Transitional Administration, and State-Building* (New York: Oxford University Press).

Chopra, J. (2002) Building state failure in East Timor, *Development and Change*, 33(5), pp. 979–1000.

Crawford, G. (2003) Partnership or power? Deconstructing the partnership for governance reform in Indonesia, *Third World Quarterly*, 24(1), pp. 139–159.

Crouch, H. (1988) Military-civilian relations in Indonesia in the late Soeharto era, *The Pacific Review*, 1(4), pp. 353–362.

Desker, B. (2003) Islam in Southeast Asia: the challenge of radical interpretations, *Cambridge Review of International Affairs*, 16(3), pp. 415–428.

Dibb, P. (2001) Indonesia: the key to South-East Asia's security, *International Affairs*, 77(4), pp. 829–842.

Dillon, M. & Reid, J. (2000) Global governance, liberal peace, and complex emergency, *Alternatives*, 25(1), pp. 117–143.

Dillon, M. & Reid, J. (2001) Global liberal governance: biopolitics, security and war, *Millennium: Journal of International Studies*, 30(1), pp. 41–66.

Doty, R. L. (1996) *Imperial Encounters: The Politics of Representation in North-South Relations* (Minneapolis: University of Minnesota Press).

Duffield, M. R. (2001) *Global Governance and the New Wars* (London: Zed books).

Emmerson, D. K. (1999) *Indonesia Beyond Suharto: Polity, Economy, Society, Transition* (East Gate Books).

Fearon, J. D. & Laitin, D. D. (2004) Neotrusteeship and the problem of weak states, *International Security*, 28(4), pp. 5–43.

Ganie-Rochman, M. & Achwan, R. (2005) Inclusion and exclusion, NGOs and critical social knowledge, in V. Hadiz & D. Dhakidae (eds.) *Social Science and Power in Indonesia* (Singapore: Equinox Publishing), pp. 197–221.

Hadiz, V. R. (2004) The rise of neo-Third worldism? The Indonesian trajectory and the consolidation of illiberal democracy, *Third World Quarterly*, 25(1), pp. 55–71.

Hasan, N. (2006) *Laskar Jihad: Islam, Militancy, and the Quest for Identity in Post-New Order Indonesia* (Ithaca, NY: Cornell Southeast Asia Program Publications).

Hasan, N. (2009) Reformasi, religious diversity, and Islamic radicalism after Suharto, *Journal of Indonesian Social Sciences and Humanities*, 1, p. 23.

Kahin, A. R. & Kahin, G. M. T. (1997) *Subversion as Foreign Policy: The Secret Eisenhower and Dulles Debacle in Indonesia* (Seattle: University of Washington Press).

Kahin, G. M. T. (2003) *Nationalism and Revolution in Indonesia* (Ithaca, NY: Cornell University Press).

Kaldor, M. (2007) *New & Old Wars* (Palo Alto, CA: Stanford University Press).

Krasner, S. D. (2004) Sharing sovereignty: new institutions for collapsed and failing states, *International Security*, 29(2), pp. 85–120.

Krause, K. & Williams, M. C. (1996) Broadening the agenda of security studies: politics and methods, *Mershon International Studies Review* , pp. 229–254.

Lee, T. (2000) The nature and future of civil-military relations in Indonesia, *Asian Survey*, 40(4), pp. 692–706.

Li, T. M. (2007) *The Will to Improve: Governmentality, Development, and the Practice of Politics* (Durham, NC: Duke University Press).

Liddle, R. W. (1996) The Islamic turn in Indonesia: a political explanation, *Journal of Asian Studies*, 55(3), pp. 613–634.

Loh, F. K. W. & Öjendal, J. (eds) (2005) *Southeast Asian Responses to Globalization: Restructuring Governance and Deepening Democracy* (Copenhagen: Nordic Insitute of Asian Studies).

MacGinty, R. (2008) Indigenous peace-making versus the liberal peace, *Cooperation and Conflict*, 43(2), p. 139.

Mackie, J. (2006) Reflections on the bilateral relationship – and beyond. In J. Monfries (ed.) *Different Societies, Shared Futures: Australia, Indonesia and the Region* (Institute of Southeast Asian Studies), pp. 171–183.

Manning, C. & Van Diermen, P. (2000) *Indonesia in Transition: Social Aspects of Reformasi and Crisis* (Institute of Southeast Asian Studies).

Maxwell, S. & Riddell, R. (1998) Conditionality or contract: perspectives on partnership for development, *Journal of International Development*, 10(2), pp. 257–268.

Mietzner, M. (2002) Politics of engagement: the Indonesian armed forces, Islamic extremism, and the War on Terror, *The Brown Journal of World Affairs*, 9(1), pp. 71–84.

Mietzner, M. (2009) *Military Politics, Islam, and the State in Indonesia: From Turbulent Transition to Democratic Con-Solidation* (Institute of Southeast Asian Studies).

Murphy, A. M. (2005) US rapprochement with Indonesia: from problem state to partner, *Contemporary Southeast Asia: A Journal of International and Strategic Affairs*, 32(3), pp. 362–387.

Murphy, A. M. (2010) US rapprochement with Indonesia: from problem state to partner, *Contemporary Southeast Asia: A Journal of International and Strategic Affairs*, 32(3), pp. 362–387.

Nordholt, H. S. & van Klinken, G. (2007) *Renegotiating Boundaries: Local Politics in Post-Suharto Indonesia* (Koninklyk Instituut Voor Taal Land).

Paris, R. (2001) Human security: paradigm shift or hot air? *International Security*, 26(2), pp. 87–102.

Paris, R. (2004) *At War's End: Building Peace After Civil Conflict* (Cambridge: Cambridge University Press).

Perwita, A. A. B. (2007) *Indonesia and the Muslim World: Islam and Secularism in the Foreign Policy of Soeharto and Beyond* (Copenhagen: NIAS).

Porter, D. J. (2002) Citizen participation through mobilization and the rise of political Islam in Indonesia, *The Pacific Review*, 15(2), pp. 201–224.
Pugh, M. (2004) Peacekeeping and critical theory, *International Peacekeeping*, 11(1), pp. 39–58.
Report of the Panel on United Nations Peace Operations (2000) Brahimi Report (A/55/305-S/2000/809).
Richmond, O. P. (2004) UN peace operations and the dilemmas of the peacebuilding consensus, *International Peacekeeping*, 11(1), pp. 83–101.
Richmond, O. P. (2007) Critical research agendas for peace: the missing link in the study of international relations, *Alternatives*, 32(2), pp. 247–274.
Robison, R. & Rosser, A. (1998) Contesting reform: Indonesia's New Order and the IMF, *World Development*, 26(8), pp. 1593–1609.
Roosa, J. (2006) *Pretext for Mass Murder: The September 30th Movement and Suharto's Coup D'état in Indonesia* (Madison: University of Wisconsin Press).
Selby, J. (2007) Engaging Foucault: discourse, liberal governance and the limits of Foucauldian IR, *International Relations*, 21(3), p. 324.
Sidel, J. T. (2007) *Riots, Pogroms, Jihad: Religious Violence in Indonesia* (Singapore: National Univeristy of Singapore Press).
Steger, M. B. (2005) From market globalism to imperial globalism: ideology and American power after 9/11, *Globalizations*, 2(1), pp. 31–46.
Sukma, R. (1995) The evolution of Indonesia's foreign policy: An Indonesia view, *Asian Survey*, 35(3), pp. 304–315.
Sukma, R. (2003) *Islam in Indonesian Foreign Policy* (London & New York: Routledge).
Tow, W. T., Thakur, R. C. & Hyun, I. T (2000) *Asia's Emerging Regional Order: Reconciling Traditional and Human Security* (New York: United Nations University Press).
Tsing, A. L. (2005) *Friction: An Ethnography of Global Connection* (Princeton, NJ: Princeton University Press).
UN Peacekeeping (2011) *Troops and Police Contributions*, http://www.un.org/en/peacekeeping/resources/statistics/contributors.shtml.
van Klinken, G. A. (2007) *Communal Violence and Democratization in Indonesia: Small Town Wars*, Volume 15 (Taylor & Francis).
van Klinken, G. A. & Barker, J. (2009) *State of Authority: The State in Society in Indonesia* (Cornell University Southeast Asia).
Webber, D. (2006) A consolidated patrimonial democracy? Democratization in post-Suharto Indonesia, *Democratization*, 13(3), pp. 396–420.
Wheeler, N. J. & Dunne, T. (2001) East Timor and the new humanitarian interventionism, *International Affairs*, 77(4), pp. 805–827.
Widianingsih, I. & Morrell, E. (2007) Participatory planning in Indonesia, *Policy Studies*, 28(1), pp. 1–15.
Williams, M. C. (1991) New Soviet policy toward Southeast Asia: reorientation and change, *Asian Survey*, 31(4), pp. 364–377.

Jonathan Agensky is a Ph.D. candidate in international relations at the University of Cambridge. His interests include faith-based humanitarianism, political advocacy and the global North–South. His dissertation examines the political subject formation of global Evangelicals targeting emergency in Sudan.

Joshua Barker is an Associate Professor of Anthropology at the University of Toronto. His research interests include political anthropology and the anthropology of policing. He is a contributing editor of the journal *Indonesia* and co-edited *State of Authority: State in Society in Indonesia* (Cornell Southeast Asia Program, 2009).

Kenya and International Security: Enabling Globalisation, Stabilising 'Stateness', and Deploying Enforcement

JAN BACHMANN

Gothenburg Centre of Globalization and Development, Sweden
School of Global Studies, University of Gothenburg, 405 30 Gothenburg, Sweden

ABSTRACT *On the international stage Kenya promotes itself as a regional peacemaker. The country is an important contributor to UN missions, has had an important role in mediating regional conflicts, and is a driving force in the implementation of Africa's peace and security architecture. However, there is another picture of Kenya's engagement in regional conflicts which, at first glance, seems to contradict international perception of the country. By discussing Kenya's historical and current practices in regional security, this article analyses how the Kenyan government balances what seem to be multiple security agendas, ranging from following a responsibility to protect, to pursuing economic self-interest, to executing international counterterrorism agendas. Rather than being a shift in the country's foreign policy, it will be argued that Kenya's involvement in rights and norm-violating practices—more specifically in arms deliveries to Southern Sudan and the illegal military training of youths in defence of the Somali transitional government, as well as repressive 'counterterrorism' practices against its own population—illustrates how the conditions of globalisation not only limit but also enable new opportunities for the positioning of postcolonial states in the international arena. It confirms patterns in Kenya's political history in which the politics of attracting, sustaining, and diversifying international partners and external revenue is part of the regime's continuing efforts at consolidating 'stateness'. Actively engaging with international norms to make them comply with one's own perceptions of security demonstrates how actors in the South shape the terms of reference in regional security.*

> I have requested the US government to support Kenya, to strengthen its security as an essential element in the fight against terrorism. This assistance will also enhance Kenya's role as a peacemaker in the Horn of Africa.
>
> (Kenyan President Mwai Kibaki at a White House press briefing with George W. Bush, Washington, 6 October 2003)

Introduction

On the international stage Kenya promotes itself as a regional peacemaker that is worth investing in. It has much to offer: the country has a long history of reliable partnership with the West in matters of security. It has been, at least until the post-election violence in 2007/2008, a strategically important guarantor of stability in a troubled region and a hub for international humanitarian missions in the Horn of Africa. The country is understood to share Western humanitarian and security concerns. For a considerable time the Kenyan government has successfully nourished this geopolitical imaginary: it continues to be one of the largest African recipients of Western security assistance. In addition, Kenya[1] has for a long time spearheaded a multilateral approach towards the mediation and resolution of the continent's conflicts. The country has accentuated its responsiveness to human security, which centres on the protection of the individual rather than the state, by being a central contributor to UN missions and a driving force in the implementation of the African Union's architecture on peace and security.

Since the end of the Cold War, African countries have increasingly taken on the responsibility to prevent and manage threats and crises on their continent through regional mechanisms on peace and security. These mechanisms are based on liberal norms that are linked to human security. This commitment and the steps taken within the African Peace and Security Architecture (APSA) have been welcomed by donors who, by providing the main share of funding, retain a certain level of political control. Yet how African countries creatively appropriate international expectations to make them work with their own economic and political agendas, and how these performances shape the terms of reference in international security, has gained less attention in studies of African security policies.

Discussing Kenya's historical and current debates and practices in regional security, this article analyses how the Kenyan government balances what seem at first glance contradictory security agendas, ranging from following a responsibility to protect, to exercising economic self-interest, to executing international counterterrorism interests. It will be argued, however, that the country's involvement in rights and norm-violating practices—more specifically in arms deliveries to Southern Sudan and the illegal military training of youths for the Somali transitional government, as well as repressive 'counterterrorist' actions against its own population—in fact does not constitute a contradiction to what is otherwise perceived as a moderate and multilaterally oriented foreign policy. These activities are rather to be seen as state formation practices in response to tensions in globalisation and securitisation. Processes of globalisation are assumed to significantly limit the autonomy of the state, as they compel it to negotiate sovereignty with sub-national, regional, or international authorities and to comply with international norms. In contrast, the securitisation of social spaces around the world since the 1990s, and particularly since 9/11, reasserted the notion of a state capable of executing authority over its territory and population (Wiener and Young, 2006). It will be shown how both processes have provided the Kenyan political executive with new opportunities for state-consolidating practices in which attracting, sustaining, and diversifying international partners and external revenue have been central features. While confronted with contested and unstable domestic authority, successive Kenyan governments have furthered the country's position as a reputable and stable partner in the international sphere, characterised by security alliances with the West, compliance with international norms, and a moderate role in regional security. Kenya's role in the international counterterrorism regime, as well as its recent more active economic and security engagement in Southern Sudan and Somalia, is the result of the country's positioning in the international system but also reflects its efforts to appropriate pressures of globalisation and its current security rationales which require to cede as well as to expand state sovereignty.

However, excessive and illegal security practices may nevertheless undermine this position when they contribute to a culture of impunity in the security sector which, in turn, further erodes the legitimacy of the political system. This also has implications for practices of global security governance, since much of the recent international effort in the post-9/11 context has focused on modernising state enforcement agencies through the training, equipping, and capacity-building of peacekeepers and national militaries, as well as counterterrorism institutions. The article begins with a brief review of the post Cold War problematisation of the global South and the mobilisation of African actors to confront new security challenges perceived to be emerging from fragile statehood. It then discusses African agency and ownership within the African Union's peace and security architecture, and in particular Kenya's contribution. The second part contrasts Kenya's position as a promoter of multilateral conflict mediation and its history of quiet diplomacy with its recent controversial role in the conflicts in Sudan and Somalia as well as in international counterterrorism.

Mobilising African Agency . . . and Responsibility

It has long been demonstrated that (neo-)realist foundations and assumptions cannot account for the realities of how authority is exercised in many postcolonial spaces (Ayoob, 1995; Brown, 2006; Dunn and Shaw, 2001; Thomas, 1987). Moreover, in largely Eurocentric security studies, agents in the global South are regarded 'as marginal or derivative elements of world politics, as at best the site of liberal good intentions or at worst a potential source of threats' (Barkawi and Laffey, 2006, p. 332). In such a view, the interdependencies between Western and non-Western concepts in global politics too often remain out of the picture (Bilgin, 2008). In globalisation theory it is now accepted that the diversification and 'proliferation of authorities' (Rosenau, 2009, p. 2) has not led to a general retreat of state authority, but rather to its manifold reconfiguration (Held and McGrew, 2007; Scholte, 2005). Critical social theory conceptualises the state not as a given entity, but rather as a series of practices in which 'stateness' has to be permanently performed. These practices then 'call into being the abstract concept of the state' (Dunn, 2010, p. 88; see also Mitchell, 1991; Weber, 1995). Sociologically informed studies on state authority in postcolonial contexts have additionally demonstrated the fragility of these state-formation and consolidation processes, both historically and in relation to globalisation (Gupta and Sharma, 2006; Hansen and Stepputat, 2001; Migdal and Schlichte, 2005). Yet pressures arising from increasing economic interconnectedness and changing international security interventions do not simply restrain local elites' scope for action but, to the contrary, 'often have a strong dynamising effect on local power constellations' (Bliesemann de Guevara, 2010, p. 115; see also Brydon, 2009). A focus on how external security interventions are appropriated helps us in coming to terms with practices that seem at first glance contradictory. Excessive security practices on the one hand, and a commitment to multinational norms on the other, are then inseparable parts of the struggle to consolidate (notions of) 'stateness'. Seen through this lens '. . . purposeful attempts at establishing state institutions are always "bent" by the complex social processes they provoke and the compromises they require . . .' (Bliesemann de Guevara, 2010, p. 116). Under the conditions of globalisation, postcolonial states are caught between the expectation of ceding sovereignty (and implementing international norms such as human security) on the one hand, and the pressure of the international system to extend their 'stateness' (i.e. to actualise their authority over their territory) on the other. Ong has argued that globalisation forces governments to find 'new ways of governing' and to let private or external entities regulate domestic domains. Such dynamics have resulted in forms of 'graduated sovereignty' in which external resources both govern and invigorate the state's authority (Ong, 2003, pp. 42–3; Harrison, 2004).

With regard to state formation processes in Africa, it is no longer disputed that African states have barely matched the Weberian ideal-type of a legal-rational authority. In African political settings, authority is carried out by different actors among which 'state authority' is only one (Engel and Olsen, 2010). Rather than reading this constellation as a dilemma for Africa in the international system, Jean-François Bayart has shown how African actors throughout history have not only actively engaged with the outside world, but also how this outward orientation has served as a key strategy for mobilising resources (Bayart, 2000). Analysing the multiple ways in which actors make sense of insecurities and security interventions and negotiate and appropriate authoritative security agendas would sharpen our understanding of how these actors influence global politics.

Despite the strong emphasis on 'African solutions' by the pan-African movement after independence, efforts to 'africanise' security issues only re-emerged after the stabilising (and paralysing) effects of the bloc confrontation ceased. Africa lost most of its strategic importance to the West, symbolised by the US withdrawal from Somalia and the international community's apathy towards the genocide in Rwanda. In policy circles, an emphasis on political chaos, famine, and—after 9/11—violent extremism in the global South established popular geopolitical demarcations between the 'premodern' African world and its implications for the 'postmodern' West (Cooper, 2001).

Despite the hope for a post Cold War 'liberal peace', the prevalence of violent conflict in some African regions set in motion a search among Western policymakers and scholars for symptoms and therapies for what were now perceived to be new security challenges (Kaldor, 1999; Krasner, 2004; Rotberg, 2004; critically: Bilgin and Morton, 2002; Milliken and Krause, 2002) The problematisation of 'new wars' and 'fragile states' resulted in a series of remedies—namely conflict prevention, and human security—all of which have made the assumption of a mutual dependence between security and development indisputable for Western policymakers (Duffield, 2001, 2007). Although these remedies lack clear policy guidance, they are supposed to convince through their normative appeal. By stating the importance of overcoming the priority for state sovereignty in order to protect insecure populations on the one hand, and by maintaining that the state is the most effective provider of protection on the other, it can be argued that human security has deepened the notion of an international division between responsible states and states that fail to protect their citizens, which then requires action by the former on behalf of the insecure populations of the latter (Pupavac, 2005). Yet the normative linking of security and development with the vision of a global enactment of human security has not only broadened the liberal responsibility to intervene on behalf of insecure populations, but works through the participation, activation, and empowerment of the targets to be reformed.

This rationality places the primary responsibility to resolve conflicts upon African actors. This axiom of 'Africa first' has been embraced by African governments. The most comprehensive action taken by African states in the formation of a continental security model is the creation of the APSA (Engel and Gomes Porto, 2010; Franke, 2009; Williams, 2007). Turning away from the reluctance of the Organisation of African Unity (OAU) to end conflict, one of the guiding principles of its successor, the African Union (AU), is the 'right of the Union to intervene in a Member State pursuant to a decision of the Assembly in respect of grave circumstances, namely: war crimes, genocide and crimes against humanity' (African Union, 2000, article 4 h). The AU adheres to the principles of preserving existing borders and non-interference in domestic affairs, but at the same time reserves the right to restore peace and security and take a stand of 'non-indifference' towards internal conflict. The step of graduating national sovereignty has been read as the development of a new security culture, in which widely accepted liberal norms (e.g. a responsibility to protect being prioritised over non-interference) are negotiated and institutionalised on a continental level, and may be guiding the AU's practices (Williams, 2007). The APSA's institutional fundament is the AU's Peace and Security Council as a 'standing decision-making organ' aiming at establishing a 'collective security and early warning arrangement' (African Union, 2002, Article 2). Other main institutional components are a continent-wide conflict early warning system, the Panel of the Wise, the setting up of a peace fund and, finally, the creation of the Africa Standby Force in order to maintain stability and resolve conflict (Engel and Gomes Porto, 2010, pp. 5–12; Franke, 2009, pp. 139–49).

The autonomy of African actors in establishing a progressive continental framework for preventing conflict and restoring peace has been met with enthusiasm among Western countries. The African commitment is seen as convenient for many Western states, who perceive their primary role as providing expertise and funding rather than having to send their own troops into African conflicts. Since Bill Clinton issued his Presidential Decision Directive 25 in 1994 that aimed at limiting US contributions to UN peacekeeping missions, US assistance has mainly been channelled through the funding and training of African peacekeeping forces and through conflict prevention programmes (White House, 1994). By 2009, more than 45,000 African soldiers from 22 countries had been trained for UN and AU peacekeeping missions under the US African Contingency Operations and Training Assistance programme (AFRICOM, 2009). While the institutionalisation of the AU's mechanisms for peace and security is a manifestation of the ambition of African governments to be in control of preventing future crises, it has also provided the West with new steering powers exercised at a distance. Franke asserts that 'through the selective, conditional and purpose-bound provision of financial and technical assistance under the pretext of "enabling Africans to help themselves", states like the US, the UK and France thus continue to maintain full control of the African security agenda with the added benefit of having outsourced the actual work to the Africans' (Franke, 2009, p. 29). Klingebiel et al. (2008, p. 82) have argued that the establishment of the regional brigades of the African Standby Forces has become the 'donors' darling'. It is estimated that 90% of the donor contributions towards the AU Commission are provided to the AU's peace and security directorate rather than to other directorates. Given the donors' overwhelming support for military components at the cost of civilian capacities, Klingebiel et al. assert that the aim of peace support is 'still primarily equated with military missions', a policy that may negatively affect the AU's role in areas other than security (Klingebiel et al., 2008, pp. 31, 82).

Given this dependence on donor funding, the question of who sets the agenda in this peace and security initiative is crucial. External parties portray themselves as partners, as neutral providers of expertise and funding, emphasising the African partners' ownership in these security arrangements. However, perceptions of what constitutes a security threat to whom differ between the donors and the African governments. While the West reminds the African governments about their responsibility to protect their citizens, 'new security challenges' for the West, perceived to be emerging in 'undergoverned' spaces, have an equally important role. On the other hand, as will be shown, the aim of African elites for reconciling liberal principles of civilian protection and human security with the need for regime stabilisation produces ambiguous effects.

Spearheading International Peacekeeping

Kenya is a driving force behind regionalisation processes, both in economic and in security terms. It is a key proponent of the East African Community (EAC), as well as the Intergovernmental Authority on Development (IGAD). Since the end of the Cold War, Kenya has been one of the most important contributors to UN peacekeeping missions. Until the mid-2000s, Kenya belonged to the top 10 troop-contributing countries for UN peace missions, providing up to 2,000 troops, civilian police, and military observers annually to missions worldwide. For example, in the UN Operation in Burundi (2004–2006), Kenya was the second largest contributor, with more than 1,000 personnel (Center on International Cooperation, 2006, p. 184). Since 2005, however, there has been a steady decline in Kenya's contributions.[2] This decline correlates with Kenya's increasingly important role within APSA and may hint to shifting priorities with regard to contributing to the regional standby force rather than UN missions. Together with Nigeria, South Africa, and Ethiopia, Kenya is driving this regionalisation process forward. It also hosts the Coordination Mechanism of the Eastern Brigade (Easbricom) as part of the proposed African Standby Force and is home to the International Peace Support Training Centre, the regional training centre for peacekeeping forces in Eastern Africa.[3]

Kenya's proactive engagement within the regional security mechanisms of IGAD and APSA underline the country's role as an advocate of a multilateral approach towards conflict prevention and resolution in the region. Historically this policy feeds into the country's strategic positioning as a reliable and responsible player in the East African sub-region. Despite the country's alliance with the West during the Cold War, for a long time Kenya was considered to be pursuing a moderate and low key foreign policy.

Kenya's Historical Positioning in International Security

During the Cold War, Kenya's security interests were closely tied to external security interests and geopolitical considerations. Yet, rather than portraying this relationship as one of pure dependence, the focus here is on how Kenyan governments mobilised Cold War tensions and managed to establish a regime that Lancaster has called 'balanced benefaction', in which recipient countries gained assistance from a diversity of donors without becoming too reliant on a single one (Lancaster, 2000, p. 233). This holds true for development (which will not be addressed here) as well as for security cooperation. At the dawn of independence, 60,000 Europeans, who dominated the Kenyan economy, lived in the country (*Time*, 1959). It was thus in the interests of the former colonial power to build a relationship that guaranteed a politically as well as economically stable independent state. Shortly after independence, Kenya and Britain signed several defence agreements, and until the 1970s the UK remained the largest provider of arms and training for the Kenyan military (Cumming, 2001, pp. 242–3; Makinda, 1983, p. 302).

Despite the fact that the Cold War was ravaging the African continent, the Kenyatta government promoted a foreign policy based on the principles of 'positive non-alignment', African unity, anti-colonialism, and UN multilateralism (Howell, 1968, pp. 34–5). For example, it took a radical stand against US involvement in the Congo Crisis but also prevented the socialist wing's attempts to ally the country with the Soviet Union. Consequently, in 1964 Kenyatta stopped Vice President Oginga Odinga, who had secured a promise of $45 million in Soviet military and development assistance (Laïdi, 1990, p. 9). The country positioned itself as an independent and strong voice for 'what is right and just in international affairs' (Manifesto of the Kenya African National Union, quoted in Howell, 1968, p. 35). Due to the country's strong commitment to African nationalism, Kenya was regarded as a neutral yet prestigious force on the continent throughout the 1960 and early 1970s.

Following the OAU's Cairo declaration in 1964 to leave the colonial borders untouched, most African postcolonial governments faced challenges to their sovereignty from within their territories. However, in the first years of its independence, the main threat to Kenya's territorial integrity had an international dimension related to Somali nationalism. When British and Italian Somaliland became the independent Somali Republic, the status of the Somali-populated Northern Frontier District (NFD)—what is now Kenya's North Eastern Province—remained unresolved. Even though a survey, commissioned by the British, found an overwhelming majority of the population in the NFD favouring unification with Somalia, in 1963 the British granted the Kenyan nationalists of the Kenya African National Union the administration of the NFD (Kromm, 1967, pp. 362–3). This decision triggered a Somali insurgency in this province, which lasted until 1967. Kenya's government declared a state of emergency and sent the military and paramilitary police units (the latter founded by the British for fighting the Mau Mau during the colonial state of emergency) against Somali secessionists in the North Eastern Province. The state of emergency in North Eastern Province, which granted extensive powers to the security forces, was in place until 1991.[4]

Except for Kenya's strained relationship with Somalia, its foreign policy remained moderate in the first decade of independence. Scholars of Kenyan foreign policy agree that there is a close relationship between the consolidation of a balanced and responsible foreign policy and Kenya's pursuit of foreign investments (Howell, 1968, pp. 44–5; Makinda, 1983, p. 303; Okumu, 1977, p. 136). Foreign capital has been an important factor in the country's industrialisation policy. Kenya's subsequent economic hegemony in East Africa (such as its attempt to disproportionately increase its gains from the EAC) stirred up conflicts with Uganda and Tanzania, who perceived Kenya's policy as acting on behalf of Western interests (Musambayi, 1995). As a result, Kenya's relations with its neighbours deteriorated from the mid 1970s: Somalia and Idi Amin's Uganda threatened to attack Kenya, and Tanzania closed the border following the collapse of the EAC in 1977 (Makinda, 1983, pp. 307–10).

Additionally, the geopolitical climate was heating up. Following the increased interest of the US in the Horn of Africa after the Ogaden War, in 1980 the US and Kenya signed a (still existing) agreement which allowed the US to use the airports of Nairobi and Mombasa, as well as Mombasa's seaport, for its own purposes (Carson, 2005, pp. 178–9). The US invested heavily in the modernisation of Kenyan military infrastructure and became the biggest donor of military and development assistance to Kenya (Musambayi, 1995, pp. 44–5). While this might seem like a deeper engagement in Cold War politics, Kenya managed to keep its interests in regional security in balance with global security interests, and so even maintained close security cooperation with Ethiopia after the country became a client of the Soviet Union (Musambayi, 1995, p. 28). Rather than seeing Kenya as a mere passive object in the Cold War games, Makinda reads this as another step in the government's emancipation from the former colonial power and the effort to diversify its sources of external support (Makinda, 1983, pp. 312–18). However, the ambition of a proactive foreign policy, particularly under Daniel Arap Moi, who succeeded Kenyatta as president in 1978, was quickly to be determined by the deteriorating economic situation in the course of structural adjustment programmes and the superpowers' decreasing strategic interest in the Horn of Africa towards the end of the 1980s.

State-Making Performances: Kenya's Engagement in Sudan and Somalia

From the mid-1990s, Kenya attained an important role in mediating the conflicts in Sudan and Somalia under the aegis of the Intergovernmental Authority for Development (IGAD). Kenya hosted negotiations between the Sudanese government and the Sudanese People's Liberation Movement (SPLM) of the South, which in the end led to the Comprehensive Peace Agreement signed in 2005 in Naivasha (Murithi, 2009). In order to resolve the conflict in Somalia, Kenya additionally hosted a two-year reconciliation conference that resulted in the formation of the Somali Transitional Federal Government in 2004. With its mediating role within IGAD, and record contributions of Kenyan peacekeepers to UN missions, Kenya once more strengthened its position as a prudent yet engaged driver for multilateral action on peace and security.

However, the examples of Kenya's controversial and less well documented engagement in the conflicts in Southern Sudan and Somalia, as well as within the international counterterrorism regime, expose state practices that differ highly from the country's international reputation as spearheading a multilateral approach towards conflict resolution. It will be argued that these at first glance conflicting practices are inseparable and seem to validate a historical configuration in Kenya's relation to the world. The practice of appropriating international norms on peace and security while pursuing its own economic and security agendas is part of the performativity of state-making efforts, in which the constant diversification of revenue is a key strategy.

Kenya as an Emerging Donor? The Relationship to South Sudan

Kenya's facilitating role in mediating peace between the Sudanese government and the SPLA/M recently became compromised after the Kenyan government was suspected of arming the government of South Sudan. A more proactive Kenyan engagement came at a time of growing tension between the North and the South ahead of the referendum on latter's independence in January 2011. One of the most prominent events is the hijacking of the Ukrainian cargo ship MV *Faina* on its way to Kenya by Somali pirates in September 2008. The ship carried 33 T-72 tanks, along with rocket launchers, anti-aircraft guns, ammunition, and spare parts for the tanks (Small Arms Survey, 2009). The hijacking of MV *Faina* caused public furore when it emerged that these tanks were not destined for the Kenyan but for the Southern Sudanese government. The Kenyan government insisted that the tanks were for its own use. However, the diplomatic cables of the US State Department, published by Wikileaks in late 2010 exposed this statement to be a lie. The documents furthermore demonstrate that the Bush administration was not only aware of this arms deal between Kenya and South Sudan but had also tolerated previous shipments of more than 60 similar tanks to South Sudan during 2007 and 2008. It was only the Obama administration that changed course and called upon the Kenyan government not to ship the tanks to Southern Sudan (*New York Times*, 2010).[5] The shipment of heavy weaponry to Southern Sudan would be in breach of the Comprehensive Peace Agreement and would increase worries about an arms race between the newly independent South Sudan and Khartoum.

Relations between Kenya and the SPLA/M have traditionally been close, but at the same time Kenya also managed to keep a good relationship with Khartoum. Since 1991 the SPLA's headquarters were based in Nairobi, and Kenya allowed entry to tens of thousands of Southern Sudanese refugees. Since the Comprehensive Peace Agreement, Kenya has applied an unusually proactive foreign policy towards Southern Sudan. Kenya has become somewhat of a donor country. The Kenyan government has pledged to assist Southern Sudan with $4.5 million in order to establish a civil service (*Daily Nation*, 2010; *SudanTribune.com*, 2011). It has additionally bilaterally dispatched up to 300 military staff to train SPLA forces in their effort to transform the former rebel group into a regular army (*SudanTribune.com*, 2009; *Voice of America*, 2010).

However, the most important aspect of Kenya's support for South Sudan's security agencies might be the economic gains the Kenyan government expects from a self-determined Southern Sudan. Kenyan companies have been the biggest investors there, mainly in banking, construction, infrastructure, and air transport, but also in the small trading sector. Additionally, an independent South Sudan is likely to trigger a dynamic favourable to Kenya's own national development. Kenya hopes to attract millions of dollars of external investment, as it will be at the centre of the extension of the wider East African infrastructure, including new highways and railway networks that integrate Southern Sudan. Yet the main benefit will come from a planned new pipeline from Juba in Southern Sudan to a new port and refinery in the Kenyan archipelago of Lamu. The export of Southern Sudan's oil through Lamu would, according to these plans, boost the economic development of Kenya's neglected North (*Business Daily*, 2010; International Crisis Group, 2010b, pp. 2–3). However, the influx of Kenyan workers and investors into Southern Sudan has raised suspicion that it is Kenya that benefits from the exploitation of the South's resources, rather than the people of South Sudan themselves. Critical South Sudanese voices warn that every product is imported from Kenya and Uganda and that moves to increase tax collection or to diversify the Southern Sudanese economy are insufficient (JohnAkecSouthSudan blog, 2010). These opportunities for Kenyan businesses in Southern Sudan have also opened a window on the transnationalisation of governance arrangements, as the Kenyan state, through its investments and capacity-building programmes, tries to extend its authority to external spaces that are not (yet) regulated by a state authority. This not only consolidates Kenya's strong position vis-à-vis South Sudan, but also demonstrates its deep involvement in this not yet resolved conflict.

Kenya and Somalia: Where External and Internal Security Become One

The West's multiple problematisations of Somalia—as providing the open door for recruitment of Al Qaeda-style militias in Africa, as a humanitarian disaster zone, as a potential future target for international state-building operations—have increased Kenya's strategic relevance for Western countries engaged in the region. As shown above, the situation in Somalia has historically been closely linked to Kenya's security interests. After the Ethiopian invasion of Somalia in 2006, Kenya closed its border to Somalia and stepped up border patrols, with international counterterrorism assistance. In 2009 and 2010 the Somali al-Shabaab militia repeatedly threatened to launch attacks on Kenyan territory, and minor incursions into Kenya by Somali militias have become more regular (*The Standard*, 2010a). Therefore, Kenya is at the centre-stage when it comes to supporting international efforts to stabilise Somalia, or at least to contain the spread of instability. Surprisingly, for many years Kenya was not a frontline actor when it comes to official engagement in the current Somali crisis (*Christian Science Monitor*, 2009; *Daily Nation*,

2009c). Kenya had an important mediating role in the formation of the Transitional Federal Government (TFG) in 2004, but recently Kenya's Somalia policy has become a somewhat quieter affair (International Crisis Group, 2010a, p. 12). Until the military invasion in Somalia in October 2011 it was official government line that Kenya will not interfere with Somalia's internal affairs (*The Standard*, 2010b). Even though Kenya has been involved in police training for the AU mission to Somalia (AMISOM), the country does not provide troops to AMISOM.

There have been ongoing discussions as to what could explain Kenya's long silence with regard to Somalia, given that Kenya's security is directly affected. One reason might be that the Kenyan economy benefits from the disorder in Somalia in several ways. It has been speculated that shares of Somali piracy ransoms are invested in the real estate market in Nairobi, which drives up prices (Odula, 2010). Yet this popular explanation overlooks that Somalis have long been important investors in diverse sectors in Kenya, including construction and transport, as well as the wholesale and retail industry. In fact, the Somali and the Kenyan economies have become increasingly entangled, and the activities of Somali business networks have become an important pillar of the Kenyan economy. It has been argued that the reason why Somalis have invested so heavily in Kenya is because the country has 'over time evolved a more adaptive and mutually beneficial strategy for domesticating the threat of Somali irredentism' (*The East African*, 2010). Apart from allowing networks of Somali investment and trade to flourish in Nairobi's Eastleigh estate, which arguably contributes to a growing and consuming middle class, Kenya also gains from the ongoing Western engagement in the wider region, as the international community, including humanitarian NGOs, manage (not only) the Somali crises from their headquarters and hotels in Nairobi.

Nevertheless, Kenya's embroilment in Somalia can hardly be reduced to economic aspects. Quite to the contrary, Somalia's political crisis materialises in Kenya on an everyday basis as, according to UN reports, almost half of the foreign fighters of the Islamist militia al-Shabaab are Kenyans. Around particular Nairobi mosques, networks exist that engage in recruitment and funding for Somali Islamist groups (UN Monitoring Group on Somalia, 2010, pp. 25–7). Yet the Kenyan government also seems to have shifted its policy behind the scenes. The UN Monitoring Group on Somalia has recently accused the Kenyan government of having recruited and trained 2,500 youths from Somalia and North Eastern Kenya to establish a military force for Somalia's TFG and to create a buffer zone along the border. Since these activities are not approved by the UN Security Council, this constitutes a breach of UNSC resolution 1772 (2007) (UN Monitoring Group on Somalia, 2010, pp. 53–6). The Kenyan government has denied the existence of this training programme. Observers interpret this new focus on military training as a change in Kenya's Somalia policy towards one which is more confrontational (International Crisis Group, 2010a, p. 12).

In the last 15 years, Kenya has had an important function in multilateral efforts to resolve the conflicts in Somalia and Sudan. However the country's unilateral security practices in both countries, which breached international embargos, could in fact contribute to growing instability in the region. It remains to be seen if Kenya's military adventure in Somalia, which was uninvited but supposedly backed by the US and France (New York Times, 2011) will undermine the government's self-portrayal as a regional peacemaker or if it will be seen as proof of Kenya's willingness and capability to engage coercively in regional conflicts. However, taken together these operations shed light on the government's multiple balancing acts, in which rights violations may be accepted for benefits including international security assistance as the following discussion of Kenya's role in international counterterrorism agendas demonstrates.

Enforcement Practices: Kenya and International Counterterrorism

The internationalised character of Kenyan security issues has become most visible in relation to counterterrorism practices. The discourse of the 'global war on terror' has provided the Kenyan government with a new source of revenue. Kenya has not only become a core country Western counterterrorism and counter-radicalisation programmes but also one of the biggest recipients of 'hard' security assistance (Bachmann and Hönke, 2010). The main share of the funding, largely provided by the US, was used in the modernisation and extension of security institutions. This enforcement-centred infrastructure was then used for a series of rights-violating practices against parts of the Kenyan population.

More than 200 people died in the attacks against the US embassy in Nairobi in 1998 and against a hotel in Kikambala near Mombasa in 2002. In the dominant geopolitical imaginary—fed by Kenya's experience of being a target for terrorist attacks, the porous borders to Somalia, the existence of large areas in which state authority is patchy at best, as well as the existence of a large Muslim minority and its perception of being both economically and politically marginalised by the Kenyan government—the country is perceived to be a fertile ground for terrorist activities (Combating Terrorism Centre, 2007, p. 63). In response to the securitising gaze of the 'war on terror', the Kenyan government once more presented itself as a credible partner, as sharing the same security concerns and interests as its Western counterparts. Since 2003, units of the US-led antiterrorism programme Combined Joint Task Force-Horn of Africa (CJTF-HoA) have patrolled the Kenyan border region to Somalia to capture suspected terrorists. During the crackdown on the 'Union of Islamic Courts' in early 2007, special counterterrorism operations into Somalia were launched from the US military base in the archipelago of Lamu (*Business Daily*, 2007a, 2007b; *New York Times*, 2007).

Kenya does not only serve as a base for international counterterrorism operations, but has also received the main share of some of the US's largest counterterrorism programmes, including the East African Counterterrorism Initiative (EACTI) and the Antiterrorism Assistance Programme (ATA). For years Kenya has been among the top six ATA recipients worldwide, alongside Pakistan, Indonesia, Afghanistan, Jordan, and Iraq (USAID/US Department of State 2009, pp. 63–4).[6] The massive international resources for the fight against terrorism enabled the Kenyan government to expand and upgrade the infrastructure of its security sector. Using EACTI and ATA funding, the Kenyan government established the Antiterrorism Police Unit, the National Counterterrorism Centre (NCTC), the Joint Terrorism Task Force (JTTF), and the National Security Advisory Committee in 2003 and 2004 (Hanneke, 2007, p. 29; Volman, 2008). These external counterterrorism measures, which strengthen the enforcement capacities of the state's security apparatus, have directly and indirectly made possible several controversial security practices that have come under severe national and international criticism.

One of the most controversial issues has been the introduction of the Suppression of Terrorism Bill in the spring of 2003 without consultation with the public, only months after the historic victory of Mwai Kibaki's Rainbow coalition over KANU (*Kenya Gazette*, 2003). Since several of the provisions in the bill would have violated basic civil rights as guaranteed in the Kenyan Constitution, the human rights community and Muslim groups in particular organised a massive protest against the passage of the bill, which forced the government to withdraw it (Amnesty International, 2004; ICJ, 2006). The Kenyan government was under increasing pressure from the international community to introduce antiterrorism legislation.[7] Widespread rumours about US involvement in this matter fuelled the resistance of civil society and of an increasing number of MPs. A more balanced second draft was circulated among parliamentarians and the human rights community in 2006, but it had to be withdrawn before its introduction to the parliament. The government recognised that it would not be able to win a majority in parliament on this contested issue.[8]

Even without the law being enacted, some of its discriminatory provisions were nevertheless carried out in practice by the security forces. After the terrorist attacks in Kikambala, raids and mass arrests of suspected terrorists were carried out in the Somali quarters of Nairobi, and particularly in Kenya's Coast Province, causing widespread fear among Muslim communities.[9] Hundreds of people were detained, many of them held incommunicado, with access to legal counsel denied. Witnesses reported that they were being tortured (Amnesty International, 2005; Bachmann and Hönke, 2010; ICJ, 2006).

The willingness of the Kenyan government to act as an auxiliary for external counterterrorism agendas was met with protest within the Muslim minority. Particular anger was raised by the 'extraordinary renditions' of almost 90 suspected terrorists to Somalia and Ethiopia in 2007, where they were interrogated by Ethiopian and US officials. Some of the detained reported having been tortured (Human Rights Watch, 2008; Muslim Human Rights Forum, 2008; Redress and Reprieve, 2009). With regards to the role of the Antiterrorism Police Unit in these detentions and deportations, a Muslim human rights group asserts that '. . . the US-funded unit has continued to push the impunity by the Kenya Police to higher levels' (Muslim Human Rights Forum, 2008, p. 37). Despite the government's constant denial, it emerged that almost 20 of the deported were Kenyan citizens. One of them, Mohammed Abdulmalik, was sent to Guantanamo Bay and remains there to date (*New York Times/NPR*, 2011). The Kenyan government breached several international conventions—including the UN Convention Against Torture and rights against arbitrary detention, arbitrary detention, and enforced deportation—provided under the International Covenant on Civil and Political Rights (see Human Rights Watch, 2008, pp. 40–1; Muslim Human Rights, Forum 2008). In the eyes of the affected, as well as the critical public, the government has eagerly ceded its duty to protect its citizens in return for a closer security partnership with the US. For the Kenyan human rights community and representatives of the Muslim community, the step to violate international law in order to attract more external assistance is additional proof of the government's opportunism, which further erodes its legitimacy.[10]

While this episode might be read as a governmental strategy to gain resources from abroad, it additionally illustrates the importance of domestic pressures. Standing accused of disregarding newly won civil rights, the government found itself confronted with a coordinated protest against the antiterrorism legislation and the looming loss of electoral support. As a consequence, the government had to constantly rebalance its stand on this topic, answering to both external and domestic expectations and pressure. Whitaker has described the relationship between the Kenyan and US governments on counterterrorism as a 'reluctant partnership' characterised by public contention and behind-the-scenes cooperation (Whitaker, 2008).

Indicative for the reading that the role of the Kenyan political elite cannot be reduced to one of subservience is the Kenyan government's refusal to sign a bilateral immunity agreement with the US, which would exempt Americans suspected of being involved in genocide, crimes against humanity, or war crimes from being extradited to the International Criminal Court (CICC, 2006a). As a consequence, Kenya was excluded from several security-related funding programmes and lost $13 million in 2005 alone (*New York Times*, 2006). However, after warnings that the cuts undermined the US's counterterrorism efforts in strategically important countries, in October 2006 the US Congress and later President Bush waived several restrictions on IMET (International Military Education and Training) and ESF (Economic Support Funds) in the 'national interest of the US', and security assistance to Kenya resumed (CICC, 2006b; White House, 2006). By refusing to enter the bilateral agreement with the US, Kenya publicly presented itself once more as a champion of human security over national sovereignty. While the government risked losing US security assistance (a tactical loss), it was aware of the geopolitics of the 'war on terror' and Kenya's importance as a regional hub for the US counterterrorism agenda and industry. In the end it was a strategic win by gaining international credibility and resuming US counterterrorism assistance.

Another, more recent, example in relation to Kenya's strategic handling of international norms and domestic expectations is the government's refusal to arrest persons who are subject to an arrest warrant by the International Criminal Court, even though the country is obliged to do so as a party to the Rome Statute. On the one hand, the Kenyan government has promised full support to the ICC's investigation of crimes against humanity committed during the Kenyan post-election violence in 2007/2008, recognising that the idea of having an international body investigating the violence is favoured by many Kenyans (Musila, 2009). On the other hand, in August 2010 the government invited the Sudanese President Omar al-Bashir, who is wanted by the ICC for counts of crimes against humanity, war crimes, and genocide, to Kenya in order to celebrate the adoption of the new Kenyan Constitution. Even though the Kenyan government came under domestic and international fire for undermining international law, it can legitimise its actions as being in accordance with multilateral decisions. In July 2010 the AU decided not to cooperate with the ICC in its request to arrest al-Bashir (African Union, 2010).

Concluding Remarks: The State and Global Security Governance

The previous section has illustrated some of the ambiguous implications of international assistance to Kenyan enforcement agencies, in which external counterterrorism support has made possible a series of rights-violating practices against suspect sections of the population. This concluding section relates Kenya's autonomy in globalised issues of security to the general debate on Western security governance in the global South and its imaginations of the postcolonial state.

Globalisation debate has drawn attention to the pluralisation of authorities for the provision of security, as well as to the existence of processes and regimes of security beyond the state (Abrahamsen and Williams, 2010; Johnston and Shearing, 2003; Shearing and Wood, 2007). In particular, the literature on nodal security governance has contested that the postcolonial state is capable of providing security and justice for its population. The permanent struggle of the postcolonial political elite over gaining authority over its population usually unleashes its authoritarian tendencies (for a critique, see Loader and Walker, 2006). At the same time, these approaches concede the state to constitute a 'meta-authority' for establishing guiding principles for security provision (Johnston 2006, pp. 47–9).

Both dynamics—scepticism towards the state and reliance on the state—are reflected on the policy level with regard to security sector reform. On the one hand, it has become established in policymaking circles that any transformation of security institutions must be case sensitive and include wider areas of governance, such as justice sectors, parliaments, traditional authorities, the media, and nongovernmental organisations (Caparini, 2004; OECD/DAC, 2008). On the other hand, the mixed record of security sector reforms in the global South has shown that there is a substantial 'resilience of police institutions' (Hills, 2008, p. 221). What makes these enforcement agents resilient is that security, both as concept and practice, is still commonly understood to be at the core of state sovereignty (Albrecht and Buur, 2009, pp. 392–5). Any security sector reform is potentially tied into the process of state transformation and thus subject to close scrutiny by the targets of reform.

The dilemma of postcolonial state security institutions becomes apparent in relation to security assistance to Kenya. As demonstrated above, the global counterterrorism regime has strengthened state authority, in so far as the vast resources it made available for the Kenyan government overwhelmingly benefited its security apparatus. It aimed at extending the policing capacities of intelligence services, the military, and various police units in a country where the structure of the security institutions is still hallmarked by colonial policing, i.e. where paramilitary police units were central for political purposes (for the debate on colonial policing with regard to Africa and Kenya, see Clayton and Killingray, 1989; Sinclair, 2006; Throup, 1992). The colonial system of dual policing, where a decentralised force dealt with customary law in the villages and a central force dealt with civil law, is still in place. The mandates of the Administration Police (formerly the 'tribal police') and the Kenya Police are blurred, and this has caused competition and some deadly skirmishes between the two forces (*The Standard*, 2009; *Daily Nation*, 2009a). Constitutional provisions to transform the police into a neutral force with civilian oversight, discussed immediately after independence, were never implemented (CHRI/KHRC, 2006, p. 6; Ruteere and Pommerolle, 2003).

The history of extrajudicial killings, the use of excessive force, and its use for political purposes in Kenya was most recently once more confirmed by the Commission of Inquiry into Post-Election Violence. It estimates that during the violence that erupted after the general elections in 2007, more than one third of the more than 1,100 dead might have been shot by police (Commission of Inquiry into Post-Election Violence, 2008, pp. 384–5, 418; *The Economist*, 2008). In an additional UN inquiry into unlawful killings by the Kenyan police, the UN rapporteur, Philip Alston, confirmed 'the existence of systematic, widespread and carefully planned extrajudicial executions undertaken on a regular basis by the Kenyan police and 'that the police are free to kill at will' (UN High Commissioner for Human Rights, 2009). However, the post-election violence once more pointed to the urgency of the transformation of the security sector. With a new constitution adopted in the summer of 2010, Kenya's crisis may provide a window of opportunity for wholesale reform of the security apparatus. Some important structural changes have been included in the new constitution, yet for many it is not the radical break the country perceived itself to be in dire need of immediately after the crisis (Kenya National Task Force on Police Reform, 2009).

The international focus on military capacity at the cost of civil–military expertise in the APSA and the renewed emphasis on the modernisation of the state security apparatus, with its devastating effects in the context of counterterrorism in Kenya, once more confirm the central position of traditional state security institutions in the imagination of global security governance. Yet this article has defied the notion that actors in the South are merely on the receiving end of international security interventions where governments simply jump on the bandwagon of Western agendas. Kenya's juggling of international norms on the one hand and its own security and economic logics on the other have evolved historically and illustrate how the social capital emerging from Kenya's adherence to international norms or from bilateral alliances is used to sustain and diversify external support as an important part of the regime's effort of stabilising (the perception) of statehood. However, these processes are inherently unstable, as the particular history of postcolonial state transformation and global pressure on economic and security governance in many countries in the global South require a re-evaluation of practices in which (multinational) expectations are met and (state) sovereignty is demonstrated and reaffirmed. Yet what is even more important is that even though the performance of negotiating and appropriating international security agendas, as a struggle for positioning, is an endeavour with contingent outcomes, this process highlights how emerging actors in the South not only claim a 'normalised' role of pursuing their own economic and political agendas, but also redefine the terms of reference in entangled regional and global issues of security.

Notes

1 When Kenyan political agency ('Kenya', 'the government', 'security institutions') is addressed in this article, I refer broadly to the executive. This somewhat simplifying conceptualisation serves the analytical purpose of the article which focuses on the elites' *practices* of positioning the 'state' in the international arena.

2 In 2009 the number of Kenyan personnel in UN missions had fallen to 900. Currently Kenya contributes to the UN mission in Sudan (UNMIS, military and police), the AU-UN Hybrid Mission to Darfur (UNAMID, military), the UN Mission in the Central African Republic and Chad (MINURCAT, military), the UN Mission in Liberia (UNMIL, police), and the UN Mission in the DRC (MONUC, military) (UN Peacekeeping website).

3 Its predecessor organisation was initially established as part of the Kenyan Defence College in order to live up to Kenya's increasing role in multilateral peace operations. The donors had greater ambitions and—after some years of struggle over its ownership and funding—the centre is now independent from the Kenyan Ministry of Defence and has been transformed—with the help of more than $3.5 million from Japan—into a regional training school as part of APSA (UNDP, 2009).

4 Local pastoralists in this border region, in which state authority is fragmentary at best, have since regularly attacked state institutions. The attacks were answered with excessive force by the Kenyan security state. The massacre of up to several hundred people by the Kenyan military near Wagalla in 1984 became an infamous example (Human Rights Watch, 2009a, pp. 12–16). Government distrust of ethnic Somali Kenyans prevails until today. Somali Kenyans encounter systematic difficulties when it comes to citizenship rights. Since the 1960s, Kenyan Somalis not only have a special identity card, they must also report if they wish to move into another district. Additionally, in 1989 the 'pink card' was introduced, which is evidence that the bearer had been 'screened' and his or her lineage had been confirmed (Africa Watch, 1990). This card has acquired a bitter smack as it revived memories of the *kipande*, a special ID card which every male from the age of 15 had to wear to allow British control over the 'native's' movements. In the course of the screening process in 1989, more than 2,000 people who claimed to be Kenyans were deported to Somalia and hundreds fled Kenya to neighbouring countries or Europe and Canada (Africa Watch, 1990).

5 While the list of parties that carry the mischief of this embarrassing affair is quite short (the Kenyan government), the list of beneficiaries is longer and involves international actors, including the governments of Ukraine and Southern Sudan, as well as companies and private individuals from Ukraine, the UK, Germany, and Kenya (Small Arms Survey, 2009, p. 44).

6 Additionally, Kenya regularly received support from the IMET, foreign military financing (FMF), and ESF. More specifically, in 2007 the US announced a package worth $14 million for antiterrorism assistance. This included $5.5 million for the 'training and equipment of various Kenyan law enforcement and security programs', $3 million for the 'construction of Coastal Maritime Training Facility on Camp Manda' in the Lamu archipelago, over $2 million for the installation of a 'secure IT network and case management project for the Antiterrorism Police Unit (ATPU)', $400,000 for a security system at the port of Mombasa, $1.2 million for a cyber forensic laboratory, and $200,000 for a border control management course. The antiterrorism training facility was opened in February 2009 and provides training to military and ATPU officers (US Embassy in Nairobi, 2007).

7 Author interview Paul Muite, former MP and between 2002 and 2007 chair of the Committee of the Administration of Justice and Constitutional Affairs, Nairobi, 11 September 2008.

8 Author interview Muite.

9 Mass arrests and abuse of suspected illegal migrants, refugees, or suspected terrorists from Somalia by Kenyan authorities continue to occur regularly (Africa Watch, 1990; *Daily Nation*, 1999; Human Rights Watch, 2009b; *The Standard*, 2002). In one of the most recent swoops, 1,000 migrants were detained (*The Standard*, 2010c).

10 Author interview, Muslim human rights organisations, Nairobi, 4 September 2008.

References

Abrahamsen, R. & Williams, M. C. (2010) *Security Beyond the State: Security Privatization and International Politics* (Cambridge: Cambridge University Press).

Africa Watch (1990) *Kenya: Screening of Ethnic Somalis, The Cruel Consequences of Kenya's Passbook System* (New York: Africa Watch).

African Union (2000) *The Constitutive Act of the African Union*, http://www.africa-union.org/root/au/AboutAu/Constitutive_Act_en.htm.

African Union (2002) *Protocol relating to the establishment of the Peace and Security Council of the African Union* (Durban: Ordinary Session of the Assembly of the African Union).

African Union (2010) *Decisions, Declarations, Resolution* (Kampala: General Assembly of the African Union, 25 July).

AFRICOM (2009) Africa Contingency Operations Assistance and Training: Fact Sheet (Stuttgart: US Africa Command), http://www.africom.mil/getArticle.asp?art=3585.

Albrecht, P. & Buur, L. (2009) An uneasy marriage: non-state actors and police reform, *Policing and Society: An International Journal of Research and Policy*, 19(4), pp. 390–405.

Amnesty International (2004) *Memorandum to the Kenyan Government on the Suppression of Terrorism Bill 2003* (London: Amnesty International).

Amnesty International (2005) *Kenya: The Impact of 'Anti-Terrorism' Operations on Human Rights* (London: Amnesty International).

Ayoob, M. (1995) *The Third World Security Predicament: Statemaking, Regional Conflict, and the International System* (Boulder, CO: Lynne Rienner).

Bachmann, J. & Hönke, J. (2010) Peace and security as counterterrorism? The political effects of liberal interventions in Kenya, *African Affairs*, 109(434), pp. 97–114.

Barkawi, T. & Laffey, M. (2006) The postcolonial moment in security studies, *Review of International Studies*, 32(2), pp. 329–352.

Bayart, J. (2000) Africa in the world: a history of extraversion, *African Affairs*, 99(395), pp. 217–267.

Bilgin, P. (2008) Thinking past 'Western' IR?, *Third World Quarterly*, 29(1), pp. 5–23.

Bilgin, P. & Morton, A. D. (2002) Historicising representations of 'failed states': beyond the Cold War annexation of the social sciences?, *Third World Quarterly*, 23(1), pp. 55–80.

Bliesemann de Guevara, B. (2010) Introduction: the limits of statebuilding and the analysis of state-formation, *Journal of Intervention and Statebuilding*, 4(2), pp. 111–128.

Brown, W. (2006) Africa and international relations: a comment on IR theory, anarchy and statehood, *Review of International Studies*, 32(1), pp. 119–143.

Brydon, D. (2009) Competing autonomy claims and the changing grammar of global politics, *Globalizations*, 6(3), pp. 339–352.

Business Daily (Nairobi) (2007a) African Command: American Military's New Frontier, 23 July.

Business Daily (Nairobi) (2007b) The Americans Have Landed, 20 July.

Business Daily (Nairobi) (2010) Kenya reaps billions from Sudanese separation plan, 1 June.

Caparini, M. (2004) A response to Herbert Wulf's paper, in Berghof Research Centre for Constructive Conflict Management (ed.) *Berghof Handbook For Conflict Transformation*, Dialogue Series 2 (Berlin: Berghof Research Centre for Constructive Conflict Management), pp. 1–10.

Carson, J. (2005) Kenya: the struggle against terrorism, in R. Rotberg (ed.) *Battling Terrorism in the Horn of Africa* (Washington, DC: Brookings Institution), pp. 173–192.

Center on International Cooperation (2006) *Annual Rreview of Global Peace Operations* (Boulder, CO: Lynne Rienner).

CHRI/KHRC (2006) *The Police, the People the Politics: Police Accountability in Kenya* (London/Nairobi: Commonwealth Human Rights Initiative/Kenyan Human Rights Commission).

Christian Science Monitor (2009) Kenya poised to intervene in Somalia, 25 June.

CICC (2006a) *Countries Opposed to Signing a US Bilateral Immunity Agreement (BIA)* (The Hague: Coalition for the International Criminal Court).

CICC (2006b) *Comments by US Officials on the Negative Impact of Bilateral Immunity Agreements (BIAs) and the American Servicemembers' Protection Act (Aspa)* (The Hague: Coalition for the International Criminal Court).

Clayton, A. & Killingray, D. (1989) *Khaki and Blue: Military and Police in British Colonial Africa* (Athens, OH: Ohio University Center for International Studies).

Combating Terrorism Centre (2007) *Al-Qaeda's (Mis-)Adventures in the Horn of Africa* (West Point, NY: US Military Academy).

Commission of Inquiry into Post-Election Violence (2008) *Report of the Commission of Inquiry into Post-Election Violence* (Nairobi: Commission of Inquiry into Post-Election Violence).

Cooper, R. (2001) The post-modern state, in M. Leonard (ed.) *Re-Ordering the World: the Long-Term Implications of September 11th* (London: Foreign Policy Centre), pp. 11–20.

Cumming, G. (2001) *Aid to Africa: French and British Policies from the Cold War to the New Millennium* (Aldershot: Ashgate).

Daily Nation (Nairobi) (1999) 600 illegal aliens arrested in police raids, 3 September.

Daily Nation (Nairobi) (2009a), Alerts as APs threaten protest, 29 June.

Daily Nation (Nairobi) (2009b) Kenya: Police to return police funds, 10 October.

Daily Nation (Nairobi) (2009c) Somalia: PM hints at military option for crisis, 22 June.

Daily Nation (Nairobi) (2010) Kenyan donor money and firms helping build Southern Sudan, 5 June.

Duffield, M. (2001) *Global Governance and the New Wars* (London: Zed Books).

Duffield, M. (2007) *Development, Security and Unending War: Governing the World of Peoples* (Cambridge: Polity).

Dunn, K. C. (2010) There is no such thing as the state: discourse, effect and performativity, *Forum for Development Studies*, 37(1), pp. 79–92.

Dunn, K. C. & Shaw, T. (eds) (2001) *Africa's Challenge to International Relations Theory* (Basingstoke: Palgrave Macmillan).

The East African (Nairobi) (2010) Forget piracy—Somalia's whole 'global' economy is booming—to Kenya's benefit, 10 May.

The Economist (2008) Kenya: spread the blame, 23 October.

Engel, U. & Gomes Porto, J. (eds) (2010) *Africa's New Peace and Security Architecture: Promoting Norms and Institutionalising Solutions* (Farnham: Ashgate).

Engel, U. & Olsen, G. R. (2010) *Authority, Sovereignty and Africa's Changing Regime of Territorialisation* (Leipzig: Research Academy Leipzig Working Papers 7).

Franke, B. (2009) *Security Cooperation in Africa: A Reappraisal* (Boulder, CO: First Forum Press).

The Guardian (London) (2008), Trained in terror, 30 July.

Gupta, A. & Sharma, A. (eds) (2006) Introduction: rethinking theories of the state in an age of globalization, *Anthropology of the State: A Reader* (Malden/Oxford: Blackwell), pp. 1–41.

Hanneke, J. (2007) *In What Ways Have US Security Cooperation Programs Been Effective in Helping Kenya to Build Partnership Capacity to Counter Transnational Terrorism?* (Fort Leavenworth: School of Advanced Military Studies. United States Army Command and General Staff College).

Hansen, T. B. & Stepputat, F. (2001) Introduction: states of imagination, in T.B. Hansen & F. Stepputat (eds.) *States of Imagination: Ethnographic Explorations of the Postcolonial State* (Durham, NC and London: Duke University Press), pp. 1–38.

Harrison, G. (2004) *The World Bank and Africa: The Construction of Governance States* (London: Routledge).

Held, D. & McGrew, A. (2007) *Globalization/Anti-Globalization: Beyond the Great Divide* (Cambridge: Polity).

Hills, A. (2008) The dialectic of police reform in Nigeria, *Journal of Modern African Studies*, 46(2), pp. 215–234.

Howell, J. (1968) An analysis of Kenyan foreign policy, *The Journal of Modern African Studies*, 6(1), pp. 29–48.

Human Rights Watch (2008) *'Why am I still here?' The 2007 Horn of Africa Renditions and the Fate of Those Still Missing* (New York: Human Rights Watch).

Human Rights Watch (2009a) *'Bring the Gun or You'll Die': Torture, Rape and Other Serious Human Rights Violations by Kenyan Security Forces in the Mandera Triangle* (New York: Human Rights Watch).

Human Rights Watch (2009b) *From Horror to Hopelessness: Kenya's Forgotten Somali Refugee Crisis* (New York: Human Rights Watch), http://www.hrw.org/en/reports/2009/03/29/horror-hopelessness.

ICJ (2006) *International Commission of Jurists—Kenya Chapter Eminent Jurist Panel on Terrorism, Counter-Terrorism and Human Rights. East African Regional Hearings* (Nairobi, 27 February 2006).

International Crisis Group (2010a) *Somalia's Divided Islamists* (Nairobi: International Crisis Group).

International Crisis Group (2010b) *Sudan: Regional perspectives on the prospect of Southern independence* (Brussels: International Crisis Group).

JohnAkecSouthSudan blog (2010) Circumventing the curse of petro-wealth (Part 1), 24 May, http://johnakecsouthsudan.blogspot.com/.

Johnston, L. (2006) Transnational security governance, in J. Wood & B. Dupont (eds.) *Democracy, Society and the Governance of Security* (Cambridge: Cambridge University Press), pp. 33–51.

Johnston, L. & Shearing, C. (2003) *Governing Security: Explorations in Policing and Justice* (London: Routledge).

Kaldor, M. (1999) *New and Old Wars* (Cambridge: Polity).

Kenya Gazette (2003) *The Suppression of Terrorism Bill*, Supplement 38 (Nairobi: Government of Kenya).

Kenya National Task Force on Police Reform (2009) *Some Key Recommendations Summarised* (Nairobi: Kenya National Task Force on Police Reform).

Klingebiel, S. et al. (2008) *Donor Contributions to the Strengthening of the African Peace and Security Architecture* (Bonn: German Development Institute).

Krasner, S. D. (2004) Sharing sovereignty: new institutions for collapsed and failing states, *International Security*, 29(2), pp. 85–120.

Kromm, D. E. (1967) Irredentism in Africa: the Somali-Kenya boundary dispute, *Transactions of the Kansas Academy of Science*, 70(3), pp. 359–365.
Laïdi, Z. (1990) *The Superpowers and Africa: The Constraints of a Rivalry, 1960–1990* (Chicago: University of Chicago Press).
Lancaster, C. (2000) Africa in world affairs, in J. W. Harbeson & D. Rothchild (eds.) *Africa in World Politics: The African state system in flux* (Boulder, CO: Westview), pp. 208–234.
Loader, I. & Walker, N. (2006) Necessary virtues: the legitimate place of the state in the production of security, in J. Wood & B. Dupont (eds.) *Democracy, Society and the Governance of Security* (Cambridge: Cambridge University Press), pp. 165–195.
Makinda, S. M. (1983) From quiet diplomacy to Cold War politics: Kenya's foreign policy, *Third World Quarterly*, 5(2), pp. 300–319.
Migdal, J. S. & Schlichte, K. (2005) Rethinking the state, in J.S. Migdal & K. Schlichte (eds.) *The Dynamics of States: The Formation and Crises of State Domination* (Aldershot: Ashgate), pp. 1–40.
Milliken, J. & Krause, K. (2002) State failure, state collapse, and state reconstruction: concepts, lessons, strategies, *Development and Change*, 33(5), pp. 753–774.
Mitchell, T. (1991) The limits of the state: beyond statist approaches and their critics, *American Political Science Review*, 85(1), pp. 77–96.
Murithi, T. (2009) Inter-governmental authority on development on the ground: comparing interventions in Sudan and Somalia, *African Security*, 2(2–3), pp. 136–157.
Musambayi, C. I. (1995) The politics of regime consolidation and entrenchment: Moi's foreign policy, 1978–1994, *French Institute for Research in Africa Working Paper 23.*
Musila, G. M. (2009) Options for transitional justice in Kenya: autonomy and the challenge of external prescriptions, *International Journal of Transitional Justice*, 3(3), pp. 445–464.
Muslim Human Rights Forum (2008) *Horn of Terror: Report of US-Led Mass Extra-ordinary Renditions from Kenya to Somalia, Ethiopia and Guantanamo Bay, January–June 2007*, revised edition (Nairobi: Muslim Human Rights Forum).
New York Times (2006) U.S. cuts in Africa aid hurt War on Terror and increase China's influence, officials say, 23 July.
New York Times (2007) U.S. used base in Ethiopia to hunt Al Qaeda, 23 February.
New York Times (2010) Pirates' catch exposed route of arms in Sudan, 8 December.
New York Times (2011) Kenya says Western nations join fight in Somalia, as US denies role, 23 October.
New York Times/National Public Radio (2011) The Guantanamo Docket, http://projects.nytimes.com/guantanamo.
OECD/DAC (2008) *Concepts and Dilemmas of Statebuilding in Fragile Situations: From Fragility to Resilience* (Paris: Organisation for Economic Cooperation and Development/Development Assistance Committee).
Odula, T. (2010) Pirate cash suspected cause of Kenya property boom, Breitbart online, 1 January, http://www.breitbart.com/article.php?id=D9CV5UUO0&show_article=1.
Okumu, J. (1977) Kenya's foreign policy, in O. Aluko (ed.) *The Foreign Policies of African States* (London: Hodder and Stoughton), pp. 136–162.
Ong, A. (2003) Zones of new sovereignty in Southeast Asia, in R. Perry & B. Maurer (eds.) *Globalization Under Construction: Governmentality, Law, Identity* (Minneapolis: University of Minnesota Press), pp. 39–69.
Pupavac, V. (2005) Human security and the rise of therapeutic governance, *Conflict, Development and Security*, 5(2), pp. 161–182.
Redress & Reprieve (2009) *Kenya and Counterterrorism: A time for Change* (London: Redress/Reprieve).
Rosenau, J. N. (2009) Global governance or global governances? in J. Whitman (ed.) *Global Governance* (Basingstoke: Palgrave), pp. 1–6.
Rotberg, R. I. (ed.) (2004) *When States Fail: Causes and Consequences* (Princeton: Princeton University Press).
Ruteere, M. & Pommerolle, M. (2003) Democratizing security or decentralizing repression? The ambiguities of community policing in Kenya, *African Affairs*, 102(409), pp. 587–604.
Scholte, J. A. (2005) *Globalization: A Critical Introduction* (Basingstoke: Palgrave Macmillan).
Shearing, C. & Wood, J. (2007) *Imagining Security* (Uffculme: Willan Publishing).
Sinclair, G. (2006) *At the End of the Line: Colonial Policing and the Imperial Endgame 1945–1980* (Manchester: Manchester University Press).
Small Arms Survey (2009) *Skirting the Law: Sudan's Post-CPA Arms Flow* (Geneva: Graduate Institute of International and Development Studies).
The Standard (Nairobi) (2002) 840 foreigners arrested in Nairobi, 31 May.
The Standard (Nairobi) (2009) Hidden war at the office of the president, 28 June.
The Standard (Nairobi) (2010a) Somali militia overrun village in Kenyan soil, 28 May.

The Standard (Nairobi) (2010b) Why Kenya won't help troubled Somalia, 23 May.

The Standard (Nairobi) (2010c) You are safe here, Raila assures Somalis, 27 January.

SudanTribune.com (2009) Kenya dispatches military experts to train South Sudan army, 31 August, http://www.sudantribune.com/Kenya-dispatches-military-experts,32298.

SudanTribune.com (2011) Relations between South Sudan and Kenya vital—Kiir, 20 February, http://allafrica.com/stories/201102210838.html.

Thomas, C. (1987) *In Search of Security: The Third World in International Relations* (Brighton: Wheatsheaf).

Throup, D. (1992) Crime, politics and the police in Colonial Kenya, 1939–1963, in D. Anderson & D. Killingray (eds.) *Policing and Decolonisation: Politics, Nationalism and the Police 1917–65* (Manchester: Manchester University Press), pp. 127–157.

Time (1959) Kenya: opening the Highlands, 26 October.

UN High Commissioner for Human Rights (2009) *UN Special Rapporteur on Extrajudicial, Arbitrary or Summary Executions Mission to Kenya* (New York: United Nations), http://www.unhchr.ch/huricane/huricane.nsf/view01/52DF4BE7194A7598C125756800539D79?opendocument.

UN Monitoring Group on Somalia (2010) *Report of the Monitoring Group on Somalia Pursuant to Security Council Resolution 1853 (2008)* (New York: UN Monitoring Group on Somalia).

UN Peacekeeping, http://www.un.org/en/peacekeeping/resources/statistics/contributors.shtml

UNDP (2009) *Launch of IPSTC* (video), http://www.youtube.com/watch?v=4Z2iG-qc_FA.

US Embassy in Nairobi (2007) *Joint U.S.-Kenya Statement Regarding the Official Visit of the Minister of State for Provincial Administration and Internal Security to the United States* (Nairobi: US Embassy, 4 March 2007).

USAID/US Department of State (2009) *Foreign Operations Congressional Budget Justification Fiscal Year 2010* (Washington, DC: US Agency for International Development/Department of State).

Voice of America (2010) Kenya denies helping arm Southern Sudan, 1 February.

Volman, D. (2008) *U.S. Military Activities in Kenya* (Washington, DC: Association of Concerned Africa Scholars), http://concernedafricascholars.org/us-military-activities-in-kenya/.

Weber, C. (1995) *Simulating Sovereignty: Intervention, the State and Symbolic Exchange* (Cambridge: Cambridge University Press).

Whitaker, B. E. (2008) Reluctant partners: fighting terrorism and promoting democracy, *Kenya International Studies Perspectives*, 10(3), pp. 254–271.

White House (1994) *President Clinton Signs New Peacekeeping Policy*, Press Statement, Washington, DC: White House, 5 May 1994, http://www.fas.org/irp/offdocs/pdd25.htm.

White House (2006) *Memorandum for the Secretary of State: Waiving the Prohibition on the Use of Fiscal Year 2006 Economic Support Funds with Respect to Various Parties to the Rome Statute Establishing the International Criminal Court*, (Washington, DC: White House, November 28), http://www.gpo.gov/fdsys/pkg/FR-2006-12-12/pdf/06-9665.pdf).

Wiener, J. & Young, J. (2006) Globalisation and after? Continuity and change in the politics of securitization and responsibility, in S. Dasgupta & R. Kiely (eds.) *Globalization and After?* (London: Sage), pp. 265–292.

Williams, P. D. (2007) From non-intervention to non-indifference: the origins and development of the African Union's security culture, *African Affairs*, 106(423), pp. 253–279.

Jan Bachmann is a postdoctoral research fellow at the Gothenburg Centre of Globalization and Development and the School of Global Studies, University of Gothenburg, Sweden. He holds a Ph.D. from the University of Bristol, UK. He is working on critical security studies, the security–development nexus, and international relations with a focus on Africa.

Bolivarian Globalization? The New Left's Struggle in Latin America and the Caribbean to Negotiate a Revolutionary Approach to Humanitarian Militarism and International Intervention

THOMAS MUHR

Centre for Globalisation, Education and Societies, University of Bristol, UK

ABSTRACT *Within a critical globalization theory framework, this article analyses the military dimension of the Bolivarian Alliance for the Peoples of Our America–Peoples' Trade Agreement (ALBA-TCP) and its agenda of 'peacekeeping' and 'humanitarian intervention' in Haiti. Since its launch in 2004, the ALBA-TCP has established itself as an increasingly institutionalized, multidimensional, and pluriscalar counter-hegemonic Latin American and Caribbean (LAC) regionalism and globalization project. Integral to the pursued transformation of world order is the launching of a counter-hegemonic military agenda. Grounded in the Bolivarian philosophy of regional union, the article explores the ALBA-TCP collective defence policies, institutionalized in the Permanent Committee of Sovereignty and Defence, and the ALBA-TCP-Haiti cooperation before and after the earthquake of January 2010. By interrogating the nature of the military alliance and its humanitarian agenda, I propose that the ALBA-TCP's revolutionary approach to internationalism, peacekeeping, and intervention may be understood as employing an 'enlarged conception' of humanitarianism that means neither militarized humanitarianism nor humanitarian assistance as isolated, short-term technical disaster relief, but as long-term emancipatory structural transformation. Military alliance, however, is necessary to defend the project against imperialist aggression.*

Introduction

In recent years, the Bolivarian Alliance for the Peoples of Our America–Peoples' Trade Agreement (*Alianza Bolivariana para los Pueblos de Nuestra América–Tratado de Comercio de los Pueblos*, ALBA-TCP) has established itself as an increasingly institutionalized, multidimensional, and pluriscalar Latin American and Caribbean (LAC) regionalist project jointly driven by inter- and transnational state and non-state forces across the de jure (formal ALBA-TCP-members) and the de facto regions (the entire LAC) (Muhr, 2008a, 2008b; 2010a, 2010b, 2010c).[1] Analyzed through a neo-Gramscian, critical globalization theory approach (Cox, 1981; Gill, 2008), which generates insights into how institutions and their practices translate the ALBA-TCP ideological framework that is antagonistic to the capitalist imperialist and neo-imperialist logic, the ALBA-TCP can be understood as a counter-hegemonic globalization project.[2] Within this framework, this article focuses on the military dimension of the ALBA-TCP to explore the possibility of a new, revolutionary approach to internationalism, intervention, and peacekeeping. While notions of 'revolution' are contested, it is here conceptualized as a combination of structural theories of revolution, with their emphasis on outcome as the seizure of state power, with actor-centred theories and their view of revolution as a mass-based, open-ended 'fundamental transformation of the state and social structure' (Stahler-Sholk, 2001) that implies a 'significant restructuring of the social configuration of power' (Walker, 1985, p. 27).

The ALBA-TCP revolutionary approach to internationalism, peacekeeping, and intervention departs from both the Cuban 'export of revolution' to Latin America, Africa, and the Middle East—i.e. Cuba's military support to guerrillas during the 1960s and to 'progressive' governments in the 1970s (Klepak, 2005; LeoGrande, 1982)—as well as from the contemporary form of humanitarian intervention as exercised by the United Nations Stabilization Mission in Haiti (MINUSTAH). As an integral, explicitly anti- and de-colonialist development and international cooperation paradigm, the ALBA-TCP can be understood as employing an 'enlarged conception' (Newman, 2009) of humanitarianism that neither means militarized humanitarianism, nor humanitarian assistance as isolated, short-term technical relief of suffering in emergency situations, but long-term, emancipatory structural transformation.

I will first introduce aspects of the ALBA-TCP that are of direct relevance to the issues under discussion. This means concentrating on the ALBA-TCP as an inter-state project, to the detriment of the 'organized society' institutionalized as the ALBA-TCP Council of Social Movements, which complements the state as the second pillar of the emergent ALBA-TCP governance regime (see Muhr, 2010c). The case of the ALBA-TCP–Haiti cooperation before and after the earthquake of January 2010 is of particular analytical and theoretical interest, as it illustrates the ALBA-TCP's rising political and economic profile within the context of global financial and aid crises and shows how countries that are not members of the formal regionalism are integrated in the regionalist project. This provides a basis for understanding the revolutionary character of the counter-hegemonic form of internationalism, peacekeeping, and intervention that seeks the long-term reconfiguration (i.e. democratization) of the existing power asymmetries and state and social structures in the social, economic, political, and cultural spheres. Military alliance, however, is necessary to protect the project against imperialist aggression.

The ALBA-TCP

The eight-member ALBA-TCP (Antigua and Barbuda, Cuba, Bolivia, Dominica, Ecuador, Nicaragua, St Vincent and the Grenadines, and Venezuela)[3] is a geostrategic project governed by the principles of solidarity, cooperation, complementarity, reciprocity, and sustainability (Muhr, 2010c)—principles that economic theory regards as distinctly different from market exchange (Gibson-Graham, 2006; Polanyi, 2001 [1944]). To some observers, the ALBA-TCP puts forward a cohesive, human rights-based counter-vision of international trade law, thus pushing for an emancipatory transformation of the international legal regime (Al Attar and Miller, 2010). This should not suggest that power asymmetries among the range of actors involved would disappear. After all, political projects are advanced by those social forces with the material capability and discursive power to propose, mobilize, institutionalize, and govern territorial, political, and market-making claims that are able to secure new regional frontiers (Robertson, 2010). While Venezuela, due to its material capabilities, is a more powerful actor than other members within the ALBA-TCP, the aim of progressive politics, however, consists in the recognition of the existence and significance of unequal power-geometries as a precondition for emancipatory political action (Massey, 2009). The significance of this to peace-building and humanitarian intervention, for the purposes of this article, does not consist in attempting to resolve the (inevitable) limitations in the practice of the mobilization of the concept of power-geometries, but to recognize that the ALBA-TCP politics of solidarity are foundational of a new, counter-hegemonic framework for action.

Key actors in the transformatory processes are the bi-/multi-state-owned *grand-national projects* (GNPs), *grand-national enterprises* (GNEs), and *grand-national institutes* (GNIs). By drawing on Simón Bolívar's vision of a 'Grand Homeland' [*Patria Grande*], i.e. *Our America*, they are the counter-hegemonic responses to capitalist multi- and transnational corporations (MNCs/TNCs) in the creation of a regional economy, which also integrates private (e.g. cooperatives) and social (e.g. community-owned) forms of organization (small- and medium-sized enterprises) within and beyond the de jure region. At this moment, the effort of constructing an alternative political economy thus concentrates on targeting the power of global capital, rather than limiting private property per se.

As Table 1 shows, the *Permanent Committee for Sovereignty and Defence* institutionalizes the ALBA-TCP military security policies. The outlined ALBA-TCP development and cooperation dimensions, however, operate in a complementary and holistic fashion. This is perhaps most clearly manifest in the interrelatedness of the social–humanitarian and energy security dimensions, which is of particular relevance to the proposed revolutionary notion of peace-building and humanitarian intervention. They are closely intertwined through the PETROAMERICA regional energy integration initiative (oil, gas, renewable energies), through which the social–humanitarian is largely funded.

Here, with respect to Haiti, the 18-member PETROCARIBE, which is one of the three sub-regionalist blocs that compose PETROAMERICA besides PETROANDINA and PETROSUR, is of particular interest. Founded in 2005 within the ALBA rationale, PETROCARIBE is one mechanism that puts the ALBA-TCP principles into practice by use of Venezuela's material capabilities derived from its oil resources, through: the elimination of intermediaries along the value chain; a long-term, low interest financing scheme; payment in kind and services; and bi- and multilateral strategic development funds, such as the *ALBA Caribe Fund* (see Muhr, 2010a, 2010b). Similar to European Union (EU) structural convergence funds, such funds serve the purpose of levelling out the geographies of uneven development across the region, upon which successful integration hinges (cf. Hettne, 2003, p. 361).

In addition to the institutionalization, Table 1 also draws attention to the historical, ideological, and legal as key coordinates of the ALBA-TCP, in which the initiative's ethos is rooted. In the effort of constructing an ideology counter to the predominant liberal-bourgeois values and

Table 1. ALBA-TCP dimensions and institutionalization

Dimension	Institutions
Cultural	TeleSur. ALBA Houses. RADIOSUR. Bookshops of the South. Sports Tournaments. ALBA Shops. GNP ALBA Cultural
Education and Knowledge	GNP ALBA-Education. GNP Literacy and Post-Literacy. GNI Geology, Mining and Metallurgy. GNE ALBATEL; GNE ALBA-SATELLITE; UNIALBA and other higher education institutions. ALBA-TCP Publishing Fund.
Energy	Petroamérica (Petroandina, Petrosur, Petrocaribe). OPPEGASUR. GNE-PETROALBA, GNE-PETROSURAMERICA, GNE-Energy.
Environmental	Mission Energy Revolution International. GNE ALBA-Timber. Environment GNPs.
Financial	ALBA Bank. SUCRE Common Monetary Unit (Unitary System of Regional Payment Compensation): Regional Monetary Council; Common Unit of Account SUCRE; Central Chamber of Payment Compensation; Regional Reserves and Trade Convergence Fund.
Industry and Trade	Mixed Enterprises. GNE Aluminium. GNE Iron and Steel. GNE ALBATEL. GNE ALBA-Timber. GNE Export and Import (ALBAEXIM). GNE-Mineralba. GNE-PESCALBA. Recuperated Factories. ALBA Shops.
Legal	An international juridical and regulatory framework (GNE jurisdiction, SUCRE, recognition of diplomas and titles, democratic norms).
Military	Permanent Committee for Sovereignty and Defense.
Politico–ideological	ALBA Houses. TeleSur. RADIOSUR. GNE ALBA-Culture. GNP ALBA Cultural.
Social– humanitarian	Health, food, and housing missions (e.g. Misión/Operación Milagro). GNE ALBA-Foods. GNE-Soya. GNE ALBAMED; GNP ALBAPROR; GNP ALBA-Health. GNE ALBAFARMA. Petroamérica (social and humanitarian funds, e.g. ALBA Caribe Fund).

Note: Reproduced from Muhr (2011, p. 187). Based on ALBA-TCP-related integration documents. Listed institutions are exemplary rather than exhaustive.

norms, the ALBA-TCP discourse (selectively) integrates virtually all regional, national, and local anti-colonialist/imperialist indigenous resistance and nationalist liberation fighters and *guerrilleros* of the past 500 years. This strongly points to the construction of a distinct identity, a set of common values—in this case a collective popular-revolutionary consciousness or a culture of resistance—mobilized around the Bolivarian 'Grand Homeland' in the discourses and legal and normative frameworks of the ALBA-TCP countries, most comprehensively perhaps in Venezuela, but also in Cuba, Bolivia, Ecuador, and Nicaragua, in the latter case already in the 1987 constitution. Accordingly, Venezuela's constitutional mandates include 'Latin American and Caribbean integration' and a common LAC foreign policy—the 'democratisation of the international society'—and the promotion of 'peaceful cooperation' under the principles of 'non-intervention and self-determination of the peoples', guided by the international human rights norms and the 'solidarity between the peoples' (RBV, 2000, Preamble, Articles 152–5). Venezuela's national development plans thus express the objectives of a multipolar world order, 'equitable interaction in global decision-making' (especially in the UN Security Council), a common Latin American security and defence policy, and the 'construction of a new matrix of global power in the financial, media, military and political fields', within the maxim of a 'New International Geopolitics' (RBV, 2001, pp. 155–62; 2007a, p. 46).

Venezuela's *Law of International Cooperation*, awaiting ratification at the time of writing, adds to the agenda of Bolivarian internationalism to '*prevent* and attend' emergency situations via 'humanitarian aid' (RBV, 2005a, Article 5, my italics). *Prevention* in humanitarian aid goes beyond the traditional understanding of humanitarianism, as it conceptually relates to development and geopolitics (Newman, 2009, p. 5). Subsequently, the *Exposition of the Motives* that accompanies the Law states that unlike the traditional, so-called 'development cooperation' by the world powers through their global governance regime, the ALBA-TCP seeks to develop an 'innovative conception of international cooperation' in the 'social, economic, political, cultural, and regional defense and security', with the 'principal objective of preserving Latin American autonomy and identity' (RBV, 2005a). Therefore, as the following sections will show, by recognizing the existing power asymmetries and by conscious application of the ALBA-TCP principles, 'humanitarian intervention' in the Bolivarian, revolutionary sense is conceived of as long-term structural transformation both in terms of social, human, and economic development (reduction of poverty, inequality, and injustice) and of counter-hegemonic geopolitics, rather than as (direct) political and/or military intervention in foreign territories.[4]

ALBA-TCP Military Cooperation

With Venezuela in many respects being the 'hub' of the ALBA-TCP (especially in economic and institutional terms), military integration has been a priority of the presidential diplomacy agenda. Between 1999 and 2005, several attempts were made to promote a regional 'security, sovereignty and defense strategy', a 'South American Defence Council', and the 'fusion of the armed forces' in the conventional sub-regional fora, such as MERCOSUR (Otálvora, 2006). However, President Chávez has also recognized that both the historical role of the military on the continent and distrust and interests-related resistance at the commanding heights makes the issue not only a sensitive one, but a taboo to civil and military sectors alike. Therefore, Chávez early on identified two prerequisites for military integration: as outlined, political integration rooted in a Bolivarian philosophy, conceptualized broadly in order to increase its integrationist potential; and a redefinition of the role of the military through civic–military integration as done in Venezuela under Plan Bolívar 2000 (using the army for public works) and, as will be further detailed below, through the creation of the *International Civic–Military Rescue and Humanitarian Assistance Brigade 'Simón Bolívar'* and the *Humanitarian Task Force 'Simón Bolívar'* (Chávez, 2004, 2009).

The dynamics of military cooperation, however, only proliferated with Bolivia's adherence to the ALBA-TCP in March 2006. Two months later, a Bolivia–Venezuela technical cooperation agreement included the areas of military legislation, defence, and humanitarian operations, as well as plans for the construction of civil and military installations in Bolivia and logistical support by Venezuela through donation and credit (e.g. asphalt processing plants) (ALBA, 2006). Within this framework, Venezuelan military equipment and personnel have been sent to Bolivia, including two helicopters for presidential use (ILSED, 2006). Similar technical–military agreements have been signed between Bolivia and Ecuador in 2008 (RESDAL, 2008, p. 82; *Ecuador Inmediato*, 2008), and between Ecuador and Venezuela in 2009, covering, inter alia, military intelligence, peace operations, technology transfer, and defence industry development (ALBA, 2009e). Publicly available documentation of such bilateral cooperation, however, is scarce. One would expect similar agreements between Venezuela, Cuba, and Nicaragua, due to the stronger ideological affinities between the armed forces of these countries. Indicative of this is, for instance, Chávez's proposal on 27 January 2008 of Venezuela supporting the Nicaraguan army through maintenance assistance of Nicaragua's helicopters of Russian make, within the general discussion with Nicaraguan President Ortega of a 'united army', a 'joint defence strategy' and an 'ALBA Defence Council' (*Aló Presidente*, 2008)—a proposal that also found Bolivian President Morales' support (*Aporrea*, 2008).[5]

In the aftermath of the coup d'état against Honduran President Zelaya in June 2009, calls for an ALBA-TCP 'security council' (*Aporrea*, 2009b) and a 'regional military school with our own doctrine' (VTV, 2009; *El 19 Digital*, 2009) increased. Moreover, in September 2009, the 2nd Political Council of the ALBA-TCP warned of

> . . . the danger of concepts such as the responsibility to protect, responsible sovereignty, humanitarian intervention, preemptive wars, human security, amongst others, that can be manipulated by the great powers to assault countries of the South, violating their sovereignty, independence, self-determination and territorial integrity. (ALBA, 2009d)

At the ALBA-TCP summits of October and December 2009, the Permanent Committee of Sovereignty and Defence, integral to a declared 'counter-offensive' to the increased militarization of the region by the United States of America (USA), was created, and the objectives of a 'Joint Strategy of Popular Integral Defense' and a 'School of Dignity and Sovereignty of the Armed Forces of the ALBA-TCP countries' were defined (ALBA-TCP, 2009a, 2009b). A civil–military 'ALBA-TCP Defence School', announced in 2010, was opened in the Bolivian city of Sucre in 2011 (ANEB, 2010; ALBA-TCP, 2011).

At this moment, however, only Cuba, Bolivia, Ecuador, Nicaragua, and Venezuela integrate the Permanent Committee for Sovereignty and Defence, as Antigua and Barbuda, Dominica, and St Vincent and the Grenadines expressed their reservations due to their membership in the Regional Security System of the Eastern Caribbean States (ALBA-TCP, 2009a). In this respect it is useful to draw attention to the fact that the military expenditure as percentage of gross domestic product of the relevant ALBA-TCP countries (Bolivia, Ecuador, Nicaragua, Venezuela) has not significantly increased since Chávez's first election in 1998, averaging 1.8% in 1998 and 1.9% in 2009. This is within, or well below the trends in LAC, as in 2009 Brazil allocated 1.6%, Chile 3.5%, and Colombia 3.7% of their gross domestic products to the defence sector (SIPRI, 2011).[6] In absolute terms, in 2010, the military expenditure of ALBA-TCP members Bolivia, Cuba, Ecuador, Nicaragua, and Venezuela totalled US$7,829 million, as compared to US$6,198 million (Chile), US$9,191 million (Colombia), and US$28,096 million (Brazil).[7] For comparison, the USA's arms spending almost doubled between 1998 and 2010, rising from US$360,995 million to 687,105 million (SIPRI, 2011).

These data are important in two respects: first, they contradict the USA government-driven propaganda of a supposed destabilization of the region because of Venezuela's upgrading of its military equipment with purchases from Russia after the USA's arms embargo against Venezuela in May 2006; second, the relatively low military budget of the ALBA-TCP members underscores the defensive character of their armies as part of the strategy of asymmetrical warfare, i.e. the use of non-conventional means (including a civilian militia for guerrilla warfare) against traditional armies.[8]

ALBA-TCP Internationalism and Peacekeeping in Haiti

Since 2004, Venezuela has created two humanitarian intervention forces for both national and international (on diplomatic request) deployment. The first force, the *International Civic–Military Rescue and Humanitarian Assistance Brigade 'Simón Bolívar'* (henceforth, International Brigade) was legally constituted in November 2004. The Brigade is composed of civil and military professionals (emergency medicine, nursing, firefighting, rescue, engineering, architecture, and paramedics) (RBV, 2004a). It has gradually extended its field of operations in geographical and functional terms: from emergency assistance principally in Central America and the Caribbean, such as reconstruction work in Cuba, Grenada, Haiti, and Jamaica in the aftermath of Hurricanes Ivan and Jeanne (RBV, 2004b), to deployment in Guyana, Ecuador, Suriname, Chile, Bolivia, Peru, and Lebanon, as well as involvement in preventative measures, such as a housing project in Mali (Fundación Misión Hábitat, 2009). The second force, the *Humanitarian Task Force 'Simón Bolívar'* (henceforth, Task Force), formalized in June 2005, explicitly recognizes international cooperation as a 'foreign policy tool' designed 'to coordinate and execute operations of prevention and attention of natural and man-made disasters' (RBV, 2005b). While it is not clear from the statutes why two different intervention forces have been created, both the International Brigade and the Task Force echo Venezuela's *Law of International Cooperation* in emphasizing the need for prevention in addition to rescue and emergency. Although originally both intervention forces were staffed by Venezuelans exclusively, a military cooperation memorandum between Bolivia and Venezuela of May 2008 points to internationalization within the ALBA-TCP, in this case through the participation of Bolivian navy personnel in operations of Venezuela's International Brigade (*Aporrea*, 2008; *Prensa Presidential*, 2008). Subsequently, a regional 'ALBA international brigade of humanitarian aid' has been proposed, as one component of a 'system of prevention and mitigation of risks' for the ALBA-TCP member countries (ALBA, 2009b; ALBA-TCP, 2011, Point 5).

ALBA-TCP–Haiti Cooperation

Haiti—the country with the lowest human development index in the area (UNDP, 2009)—is of particular social, geopolitical, and historico-ideological importance to the ALBA-TCP. The notion of a 'historical debt' that Venezuela has with Haiti due to the nation's support to Bolívar's liberation struggle (RBV, 2007b) was mobilized in the aftermath of the earthquake of 12 January 2010 when Chávez (2010, p. 16), by reference to Toussaint L'Ouverture and Alexandre Pétion, construed Haiti as the bedrock of 'South American revolution' since the country was the first in the region to gain independence through 'the world's only successful slave revolution' (Aristide, 2008, p. vii; also RBV, 2010c). Furthermore, the USA-led coup against Aristide on 29 February 2004, supported by Canada and France, was of the same pattern as those against Chávez (2002) and Zelaya (2009). In all three cases, destabilization (illegal external opposition funding through the 'development aid' apparatus, a discrediting corporate media campaign, etc.) preceded and accompanied the forceful removal of constitutional presidents who epitomize structural transformation in the interest of the masses, involving their kidnapping under the guise of supposed resignation, followed by the installation of dictatorships—'civilian' (elite-entrepreneurial) governments backed by the repressive military and security forces (e.g. Golinger, 2005; Gordon and Webber 2011; Pina, 2007; Rossier, 2006). In contrast to the post-coup scenarios in Venezuela (11–13 April 2002) and Honduras (since 28 June 2009), however, Haiti has been occupied on request by the 'Transitional Government' of Boniface Alexandre, initially as the USA-led UN Multinational Interim Force, replaced by the UN Stabilization Mission in Haiti (MINUSTAH) since June 2004. MINUSTAH is officially defined as 'humanitarian assistance', 'development', and 'peacekeeping' (UN, 2004a, 2004b).[9]

Of concern here are the liberal and neoliberal underpinnings of the MINUSTAH mandate. Underlying to the hegemonic notion of peacekeeping and humanitarian intervention is the ideology of 'liberal peace' as postulated by liberal constitutionalism and internationalism. Such an ideology contends that domestic and international peace evolves through the reproduction of (neo)liberal democracies, more appropriately, however, referred to as polyarchy or low intensity democracy, as the political complement to global neoliberal economics (Gills et al., 1993; Robinson, 1996): free market, sovereign state, and the liberal normative and institutional system of government and international/global governance, which fosters global trade, international cooperation, and respect for international law, combined with conflict resolution and societal reconstruction (Duffield, 2001; Lidén et al., 2009). This agenda has been incorporated in the 1992 UN *Agenda for Peace*, and the various MINUSTAH resolutions are replete with the neo-imperialist conditionalities of official (North–South) development cooperation, integral to what Stephen Gill (2008) has termed 'disciplinary neoliberalism': 'democracy', 'good governance', 'rule of law', 'institutional reform', 'human rights', and 'economic development' to 'combat poverty' (UN, 2004a, 2004b; see Richmond 2009, p. 559; Klein, 2005). The 'liberal peace' may thus represent another tool of the neoliberal project for global governance that often is at the root of conflict (Lidén et al., 2009; Pugh, 2005), as is the liberal project of 'development' by definition (Duffield, 2007). Especially when considering that Aristide had been removed from office with CIA backing before (Cavallaro, 2005), Haiti emerges as a particularly instructive case of the mobilization of humanitarian intervention for regime change (see Newman, 2009, pp. 84–7; also Damrosch, 1995).

Venezuela joined CARICOM in not recognizing the regime of Gerard Latortue (which followed Alexandre's interim government), installed by the USA from March 2004 to May 2006 (Pina, 2007). Only with René Preval as president-elect (late 2005), did a significant qualitative and strategic shift occur. On 15 May 2006, the Venezuela–Haiti PETROCARIBE Energy Agreement was signed, with a trade volume of 7.000 barrels per day (bpd) (PETROCARIBE, 2009), doubled to 14.000 bpd a year later by the *ALBA Energy Agreement*, that also established a mixed (Venezuela-Haiti) enterprise in charge of the operations (ALBA, 2007b). The *ALBA–Haiti Framework Cooperation Convention Bolívar, Petión, Martí* (Venezuela, Haiti, Cuba) ratified the participation of Venezuela's International Brigade in what has been defined as 'integral development' cooperation for the transformation of historical structural problematics (ALBA, 2007c). While the more specific *Haiti Cooperation Plan* was proposed in the areas of health and education, agriculture and fair trade (ALBA, 2007a), three energy GNPs (regasification, power plant, refinery) were approved for Haiti by Bolivia, Cuba, Nicaragua, and Venezuela as well as an ALBA House as part of the GNP ALBA-Culture and an ALBA air connection to link Puerto Príncipe with Caracas, La Habana, La Paz, Managua, and Quito (ALBA, 2007f).

In July 2007, the Haiti–Cuba–Venezuela intergovernmental Office of Tripartite Cooperation was set up in Haiti. Its executive organ (Directive Council) is in charge of the administration of resources and provision of technical assistance and training (ALBA, 2007d). The following August, at the 3rd Presidential Summit of PETROCARIBE, Haiti joined the sub-regional project as a full member (ALBA, 2007e), and signed up for the PETROCARIBE Energy Security Treaty (oil, gas, electricity, renewable energies) on 11 August 2007 (PETROCARIBE, 2007). The confluence of energy and social security in ALBA-TCP/PETROCARIBE has further meant Haiti's participation in the ALBA-TCP food sovereignty and security programme, which responds to the global food crisis through comprehensive and integral agricultural and environmental policies and projects, including the ALBA-Foods initiative and the creation of the GNE ALBA-Foods (PETROCARIBE, 2008; ALBA, 2008a, 2008b, 2009a). In April 2009, US$5.0 million were allocated to Haiti in support of the Cuba-led literacy campaign, as well as over US$9.3 million for agricultural development in the L'Artibonito region, including a rice cultivation project and processing plant (ALBA, 2009b, 2009c). At the 6th PETROCARIBE Summit in June 2009, Haiti was among those countries selected for pilot projects within the Master Plan for Gas Supply for the Caribbean (PETROCARIBE, 2009, RES05.14-06). Within the rationale of the GNP ALBA-Education (see Muhr, 2010a), Haiti has been offered participation in the Grandnational Programme of Formation in Integral Community Medicine (ALBA-TCP, 2009c).

Contested Terrain: The ALBA-TCP Offensive in Haiti in 2010

Between 2007 and early 2010, the ALBA-TCP–Haiti development cooperation administered by the Haiti–Cuba–Venezuela Tripartite Commission amounted to US$154 million (RBV, 2010b). This cooperation volume has been surpassed by the humanitarian aid and reconstruction and development cooperation funds released by the ALBA-TCP in response to the earthquake of 12 January 2010. In the days following the earthquake, ALBA-TCP governments, including Ecuador and Nicaragua (Ministerio de Relaciones Exteriores, 2010; Radio La Primerisima, 2010), reacted individually by sending military disaster relief personnel, and Venezuela's navy and air force established an air and sea 'corridor' with Russian participation to ensure aid supply, distributed in Haiti by both the International Brigade and the Task Force (RBV, 2010a, 2010b). However, by late January, a more concerted approach had been developed. At the Emergency Meeting of the ALBA-TCP Political Council and a delegation of the Embassy of Haiti in Caracas on 25 January, the 'ALBA National Coordination' was established to 'organise in a rotary fashion the joint tasks of the Alliance in Haiti' (ALBA-TCP, 2010). The specific tasks are outlined in the eight-point *Plan for the Solidarian Contribution of the ALBA Countries to the Effort of Reconstructing Haiti*, covering several areas: health (emergency, epidemiology, rehabilitation); financial aid via the ALBA Humanitarian Fund for Haiti, administered by the ALBA Bank; guaranteed free-of-charge energy supply; agriculture and food security within the ALBA-Foods initiative (supply and production; reforestation; water; seed, tool, and machinery donations; a school for agro-ecological education); migration amnesty (regulation of the status of Haitians in ALBA-TCP countries to facilitate family reunion and the formation of solidarity brigades); education (literacy, technical, infrastructure); reconstruction; and the coordination of transport and logistics to maximize the efficiency and security for the Haitian people (ALBA-TCP, 2010).

The eight-point plan of reconstruction reiterates the long-term, preventative character of the cooperation by emphasizing that the ALBA-TCP humanitarian aid provision is not an isolated act in response to the earthquake, but the short-term component of the larger, 'collective effort' of structural transformation that has been going on since 2006 (RBV, 2010b). That is, as earlier stated, the notion of humanitarian intervention as social, human, and economic development and counter-hegemonic geopolitics, rather than military intervention. This explains, as previously indicated, why the deployed ALBA-TCP military contingents are composed of professionals (technical personnel, etc.), rather than soldiers in battle gear (as the USA and MINUSTAH forces). It is noteworthy that Cuba and Venezuela present the intervention operation as a *collective* enterprise, considering that they are the only ALBA-TCP members that contribute in real material terms: Cuba via in-kind contribution to Haiti's national health system, valued at US$691 million in four years; and Venezuela with US$2.42 billion, which includes the cancellation of Haiti's total PETROCARIBE debt of US$395 million (RBV, 2010b). The ALBA-TCP contribution to the reconstruction and development of Haiti thus amounts to almost a quarter of the total of US$9.92 billion, as pledged by the UN members and international financial institutions (UN 2010b). In comparison, the USA and EU contributions are stated at US$1.15 and 1.67 billion, respectively. The ALBA-TCP share appears all the more impressive when considering the relatively small size of the ALBA-TCP economies. MINUSTAH, on its part, stepped its force levels up to 8,940 troops and 3,711 police (UN, 2010a), while the USA reportedly deployed more than 10,00 additional troops—an act the ALBA-TCP has criticized as the 'military occupation' of Haiti (RBV, 2010a, 2010d; ALBA-TCP, 2010).

Towards a Revolutionary Approach to Humanitarian Intervention

Bolivarian internationalism and its approach to peace-building and humanitarian intervention appears as contradictory, which is not surprising in periods of transformation. On the one hand, while the values of national and regional sovereignty are defended, ALBA-TCP members, Bolivia, and Ecuador participate in MINUSTAH as well as other UN missions.[10] Despite the participation of troops from countries of the South in such international missions, however, the normative and political demands remain being set by the liberal imperialist project (see Duffield, 2007). On the other hand, the ALBA-TCP refutes the neo-conservative humanitarian militarism, whether legitimized by the UN Security Council, as in the case of MINUSTAH, or unauthorized, as unilaterally enacted by the USA in Haiti in 2010, within the rationale of 'disaster capitalism' (Klein, 2005). Given that the UN Security Council is controlled by past colonial and present (neo-)imperialist powers, a revolutionary position from the periphery, which seeks the 'construction of a new matrix of global power' (RBV, 2007a, p. 46), legitimately warns of 'humanitarian intervention' and 'peacekeeping' as tools of a disciplinary framework (ALBA, 2009d). This is not to argue that the ALBA-TCP does, or should, categorically reject the use of warranted military power for human protection in the most exceptional circumstances, such as ethnic cleansing and genocide. However, as the liberal peace prescriptions avoid exploring the root causes of armed conflict, the 'crisis of legitimacy' of liberal peace-building manifests itself in questions of its efficiency, lack of international and local legitimacy, aggressiveness, coercion and militarism, individualism, and the social and environmental crises (Richmond, 2009).

I suggest here that the ALBA-TCP embodies and perhaps transcends what Oliver P. Richmond calls a 'post-liberal peace'—a form of peace that broadens its focus from the liberal elite and institution-centred international or regional peace to an 'ontological commitment to care for others in their everyday contexts, based upon empathy, respect, and the recognition of difference', thus allowing for 'genuine self-government, self-determination, democracy, and human rights' (Richmond, 2009, pp. 566, 568). Rather than seeking emancipation after providing security and building institutions, a preventative post-liberal peace recognizes that the 'responsibility to protect' encompasses non-military politics and action to address 'gross violations' of the human person arising from acute poverty (Richmond, 2009, p. 568). This requires abandoning the limited understanding of humanitarianism as supposedly apolitical disaster relief, as embodied in international law, and building on an 'enlarged conception of humanitarianism' that confronts and seeks to transform international and global power structures—that is, global capitalism—guided by the emancipatory Right to Development and the idea of a New International Economic Order, for which the ALBA-TCP stands, to transcend the victimizing notions of rescue and protection altogether (Hauge, 2009; Newman, 2009). Such 'sustainable peace' can hardly be brought from outside but will be an endogenous project, constructed from within—in this case by the Bolivarian, Our American philosophy and ideology of resistance and liberation. Looking at the world from this angle, the liberal ideology stands for elitism, tyranny, and totalitarianism through its construction of the 'illiberal other' that has to be fought by any means (cf. Duffield, 2007; Lidén, 2009).

Grounded in a politics of solidarity, Bolivarian internationalism, upon which the revolutionary conception of intervention and peace-building rests, does not mean militarized humanitarianism nor humanitarian assistance as isolated, short-term disaster relief, but long-term, emancipatory structural transformation. Despite limitations in its full realization due to structural and contextual constraints, as well as human shortcomings, the agenda stands as outlined in this article. The USA's re-militarization of the region and resuscitation of the coup-and-dictatorship policy of past decades speaks for itself and explains the defensive, rather than interventionist, ALBA-TCP military doctrine.

Notes

1 This article is grounded in an interdisciplinary doctoral and post-doctoral research programme made up of discrete projects, funded by the UK Economic and Social Research Council (ESRC, PTA-030-2003-00417; PTA-026-27-1902). Within a critical theory research approach (rather than problem-solving, Cox, 1981), I use Michael Burawoy's reflexive science research model and extended case method (Burawoy, 2009). A set of data gathering tools, including participant observation, were employed during a total of 16 months of fieldwork in Venezuela, Nicaragua, and El Salvador. Critical discourse analysis techniques (Fairclough, 2003) were used on policy strategy papers, 400+ ALBA-TCP-related cooperation and integration documents (2000–2010), and 67 semi-structured open-ended interviews with officials, coordinators, legal advisors, academics, and civil and organized society actors. In accordance with the objective of the extended case method, I seek theory reconstruction—extension of pre-existing theory, in this case (counter-)globalization theory—through multiple dialogues (intervention, process, structuration, reconstruction). Each study (ALBA-TCP country and policy cases) on its own only provides a 'slice' of the larger picture, and has to be linked with the other studies in search for common patterns in the region (around the world) and the forces that create them. Therefore, this article only gives partial answers to the many questions that arise from this complex and under-researched phenomenon. See Muhr (2008b; 2011) for the application of Burawoy's methodology to this research field and the attempt of extending the extended case method to global ethnography, and Muhr (2008a, 2010a, 2010b, 2010c) for other case studies. References and quotations from primary sources serve to underscore key analytical findings. They are carefully selected and should be understood as a counter-colonizing practice, rather than unreflective romanticization, to counter effects of power: domination, silencing, objectification, normalization. Translations from originals in Castilian are my own.

2 I follow Robert Cox's (1981) argumentation that hegemony is constructed and reconstructed through the dialectical interaction of forces—material capabilities, ideas, and institutions—that are both products and facilitators of a particular world order. Counter-hegemony involves offering a new commonsense, i.e. new understandings and practices capable of replacing the dominant ones (Santos and Rodríguez-Garavito, 2005). Traditional imperialism principally exercises direct control over foreign states through territorial conquest; the neo-imperialist global capitalist governance regime relies on Gramscian hegemony (rule by consent and only exceptionally by force) and seeks control over spaces, resources, and specified people through a dialectical relationship between territorial and capitalistic logics of power (Callinicos, 2009; Harvey, 2003).

3 'ALBA-TCP' (rather than 'ALBA') has been adopted in the official documentation especially since the 7th ALBA-TCP Summit in October 2009. Honduras joined ALBA in 2008, but was withdrawn in January 2010 by the unconstitutional regime following the military-entrepreneurial coup d'état against President Manuel Zelaya on 28 June 2009.

4 This article is not concerned with providing empirical evidence of the significant social, cultural, and economic democratization (necessary for the exercise of political democracy) of the societies within the ALBA-TCP space. For example, in 2009, Bolivia, Ecuador, and Nicaragua were declared illiteracy-free in accordance with United Nations standards (Muhr, 2010a).

5 Also see the announcement of joint Venezuelan–Nicaraguan military manoeuvres (*Aporrea*, 2009a).

6 Bolivian and Colombian 1998 values are SIPRI estimates. Cuban figures are not available. For comparison, the USA government allocates 4.7% of the gross domestic product to defence.

7 Figures are in constant 2009 United States dollars. Cuba is the 2009 value (2010 figure not available), and refers to Defence and Internal Order. The Venezuelan value is the adopted budget rather than the actual expenditure and may be higher due to extra-budgetary expenditure.

8 For this argument with respect to Cuba, see Klepak (2005).

9 In international law, 'humanitarian intervention' is associated with coercive force by a state or group of states without the consent of the state in question in order to prevent or end grave and widespread violations of fundamental human rights (Holzgrefe, 2003, p. 18; see Duffield, 2007, for a critique grounded in the liberal civilized/barbarian dichotomy and its contemporary effective/ineffective state variant). Coercion, obviously, was not necessary in the case of Haiti, where the coup installed an imperialist-friendly regime in the first place.

10 On 31 December 2009, contributions to MINUSTAH's force level were: Bolivia, 208 contingent troops; Ecuador, 67 contingent troops. Total troops and military experts in UN missions were 441 (Bolivia) and 82 (Ecuador) (UN Peacekeeping, n.d.). Both countries started participating in MINUSTAH prior to their membership in the ALBA-TCP. While the apparent contradiction is interesting, it has not been possible to investigate the issue within the scope of this article (Bolivia, Ecuador, Haiti).

References

Al Attar, M. & Miller, R. (2010) Towards an emancipatory international law: the Bolivarian reconstruction, *Third World Quarterly*, 31(3), pp. 347–363.

ALBA (2006) *Acuerdo Complementario al Convenio Basico de Cooperación Técnica entre la República de Bolivia y la República Bolivariana de Venezuela en Materia de Defensa*, La Paz, 26 May.

ALBA (2007a) *Declaración de Tintorero* (Encuentro de los Movimientos Sociales en el Marco de la V Cumbre de la Alternativa Bolivariana para los Pueblos de Nuestra América), Tintorero, 29 April.

ALBA (2007b) *Acuerdo Energético del ALBA*, Barquisimeto, 29 April.

ALBA (2007c) *Convenio Marco de Cooperación ALBA-TCP-Haiti Bolívar, Petión, Martí, entre la República Bolivariana de Venezuela, la República de Cuba y la República de Haití, en el Marco del Acuerdo para la Aplicación de la Alternativa Bolivariana para los Pueblos de Nuestra América*, Barquisimeto, 29 April.

ALBA (2007d) *Estatuto de la Oficina de Cooperación Tripartita entre la República de Haiti, la República de Cuba y la República Bolivariana de Venezuela*, Puerto Príncipe, 5 July.

ALBA (2007e) *Declaración de Adhesión de la República de Haití al Acuerdo de Cooperación Energética de Petrocaribe*, Caracas, 11 August.

ALBA (2007f) *V Cumbre del ALBA: Proyecto Grannacional*, Barquisimeto, 29 April.

ALBA (2008a) *Declaración Final Cumbre Presidential 'Soberanía y Seguridad Alimentaria: Alimentos para la Vida'*, Managua, 7 May.

ALBA (2008b) *Acuerdo de Seguridad y Soberanía Alimentaria de los Países Miembros de PETROCARIBE y el ALBA. ALBA ALIMENTOS*, Tegucigalpa, 25 August.

ALBA (2009a) *Acuerdo para la Constitución de una Empresa Grannacional de Alimentos en el Marco de PETROCARIBE y el ALBA*, Caracas, 2 February.

ALBA (2009b) *Declaración de la V Cumbre Extraordinaria del ALBA-TCP*, Cumaná, 16 April.

ALBA (2009c) *Declaración de la VI Cumbre Extraordinaria del ALBA-TCP*, Maracay, 24 June.

ALBA (2009d) *Declaración del II Consejo Político del ALBA-TCP*, New York, 24 September.

ALBA (2009e) *Acuerdo de Cooperación Técnico-Militar entre el Gobierno de la República Bolivariana de Venezuela y el Gobierno de la República del Ecuador*, Caracas, 7 October.

ALBA-TCP (2009a) *Declaración de la VII Cumbre del ALBA-TCP*, Cochabamba, Bolivia, 17 October.

ALBA-TCP (2009b) *Declaración Final*, on the Occasion of the 5th Anniversary of the Signing of the Joint Declaration of 14 December 2004, La Habana, 14 December.

ALBA-TCP (2009c) *Acta del Consejo Social ALBA-TCP*, La Habana, 14 December.

ALBA-TCP (2010) *Plan para la Contribución Solidaria de los Países de la Alianza Bolivariana Para los Pueblos de Nuestra América—Tratado de Comercio de los Pueblos (ALBA-TCP) al Esfuerzo de Reconstrucción de Haití*, Caracas, 25 January.

ALBA-TCP (2011) *ALBA defense school to be open this Tuesday*, 31 May, http://www.ALBA-TCP.org./en/contenido/alba-defense-school-be-open-tuesday-31-may-2011.

Aló Presidente (2008) Programme 302, 27 January. Caracas: MINCI.

ANEB (Agencia de Noticias del Ejército de Bolivia) (2010) *Ejército presenta proyecto de creación de la escuela de defensa y soberania de los ejércitos del ALBA-TCP*, 17 November, http://aneb.ejercito.mil.bo.

Aporrea (2008) Bolivia apoya fuerza armada del Alba, 29 January, http://www.aporrea.org/internacionales/n108285.html.

Aporrea (2009a) Ejercito de Nicaragua y Venezuela realizarán maniobras militares, 3 December.

Aporrea (2009b) Chávez propone creación de Consejo de Seguridad para países miembros del ALBA, 17 October, http://www.aporrea.org/tiburon/n144023.html.

Aristide, J.-B. (2008) Introduction, in N. Nesbitt (ed.) *Jean-Bertrand Aristide Presents Toussaint L'Ouverture: The Haitian Revolution* (London: Verso), pp. i–xxxiii.
Burawoy, M. (2009) *The Extended Case Method* (Berkeley: University of California Press).
Callinicos, A. (2009) *Imperialism and Global Political Economy* (Cambridge: Polity).
Cavallaro, J. (2005) *Keeping the Peace in Haiti?* (Cambridge MA/Rio de Janeiro/São Paulo: Harvard Law Student Advocates for Human Rights/Centro de Justiça Global).
Chávez, H. R. (2004) Condiciones Políticas de la Integración Militar Latinoamericana, in H. Dieterich (ed.) *La Integración Militar del Bloque Regional de Poder Latinoamericano* (Caracas: Instituto Municipal de Publicaciones), pp. 9–25.
Chávez, H. R. (2009) *La Fuerza Armada Nacional Bolivariana y la Batalla de las Ideas* (Caracas: MINCI).
Chávez, H. R. (2010) *Mensaje Anual 2010. Rumbo a la Independencia Plena* (Caracas: MINCI).
Cox, R. W. (1981) Social forces, states and world orders: beyond international relations theory, *Millennium: Journal of International Studies*, 10(2), pp. 126–155.
Damrosch, L. F. et al. (1995) Agora: the 1994 US action in Haiti, *The American Journal of International Law*, 89(1), pp. 58–84.
Duffield, M. (2001) *Global Governance and the New Wars* (London: Zed Books).
Duffield, M. (2007) Development, territories, and people: consolidating the external sovereign frontier, *Alternatives*, 32, pp. 225–246.
Ecuador Inmediato (2008) Ecuador y Bolivia se unen en cooperación para defensa nacional, 6 June, http://www.ecuadorinmediato.com/Noticias/news_user_view/ecuador_y_bolivia_se_unen_en_cooperacion_para_defensa_nacional–79797.
El Digital (2009) Evo Morales propone un colegio militar regional para el ALBA, 23 July, http://www.el19digital.com/index.php?option=com_content&view=article&id=5190:evo-morales-propone-un-colegio-militar-regional-para-evo-morales-propone-un-colegio-militar-regional-para-alba&catid=24:internacionales&Itemid=15.
Fairclough, N. (2003) *Analysing Discourse* (London: Routledge).
Fundación Misión Hábitat (2009) *Venezuela dignificó 100 familias en República de Malí en el marco del Proyecto África 2008*, 21 July, http://www.fmh.gob.ve/node/981.
Gibson-Graham, J. K. (2006) *A Postcapitalist Politics* (Minneapolis: University of Minnesota).
Gill, S. (2008) *Power and Resistance in the New World Order*, 2nd ed. (New York: Palgrave/Macmillan).
Gills, B., Rocamora, J. & Wilson, R. (1993) Low intensity democracy, in Rocamora Gills, Wilson (eds.) *Low Intensity Democracy: Political Power in the New World Order* (London: Pluto), pp. 3–32.
Golinger, E. (2005) *The Chávez Code: Cracking US Intervention in Venezuela* (La Habana: José Martí).
Gordon, T. & Webber, J. R. (2011) Canada and the Honduran Coup, *Bulletin of Latin American Research*, 30(3), pp. 328–343.
Harvey, D. (2003) *The New Imperialism* (Oxford: Oxford University Press).
Hauge, W. (2009) A Latin American agenda for peace, *International Peacekeeping*, 16(5), pp. 685–698.
Holzgrefe, J. L. (2003) The humanitarian intervention debate, in J. L. Holzgrefe, R. O. Koehane (eds.) *Humanitarian Intervention: Ethical, Legal and Political Dilemmas* (Cambridge: Cambridge University Press), pp. 15–52.
ILSED (Instituto Latinoamericano de Seguridad y Democracia) (2006) *Venezuela enviará militares a Bolivia*, 30 May, http://www.ilsed.org/index.php?option=com_content&task=view&id=139&Itemid=2.
Klein, N. (2005) The rise of disaster capitalism, *The Nation*, 2 May, http://www.thenation.com/article/rise-disaster-capitalism.
Klepak, H. (2005) *Cuba's Military 1990–2005* (New York: Palgrave/Macmillan).
LeoGrande, W. M. (1982) Cuban foreign policy in Africa, in C. Mesa-Lago, J. S. Belkin (eds.) *Cuba in Africa* (Pittsburgh: University of Pittsburgh), pp. 15–50.
Lidén, K. (2009) Building peace between global and local politics: the cosmopolitical ethics of liberal peacebuilding, *International Peacekeeping*, 16(5), pp. 616–634.
Lidén, K., Mac Ginty, R. & Richmond, O. P. (2009) Introduction: beyond Northern epistemologies of peace: peace-building reconstructed? *International Peacekeeping*, 16(5), pp. 587–598.
Massey, D. (2009) Concepts of space and power in theory and in political practice, *Documents d'Anàlisi Geogràfica*, 55, http://ddd.uab.cat/pub/dag/02121573n55p15.pdf.
Ministerio de Relaciones Exteriores (2010) *Tercer Vuelo de Ecuador a Haiti: Presidente Rafael Correa Viaja a Haiti*, 28 January, http://www.mmrree.gob.ec/2010/bol023.asp.
Muhr, T. (2008a) Nicaragua re-visited: from neoliberal 'ungovernability' to the Bolivarian alternative for the peoples of Our America, *Globalisation, Societies and Education*, 6(2), pp. 147–161.

Muhr, T. (2008b) Venezuela: Global Counter-Hegemony, Geographies of Regional Development, and Higher Education for All, PhD Thesis, University of Bristol, http://www.bris.ac.uk/education/research/centres/ges/post-doc-fellows/thomas-muhr/006.pdf.

Muhr, T. (2010a) Counter-hegemonic regionalism and higher education for all: Venezuela and the ALBA, *Globalisation, Societies and Education*, 8(1), pp. 39–57.

Muhr, T. (2010b) Nicaragua: constructing the Bolivarian alliance for the peoples of Our America (ALBA), in U. Schuerkens (ed.) *Globalization and Social Inequality* (New York: Routledge), pp. 115–134.

Muhr, T. (2010c) TINA go home! ALBA and re-theorising resistance to global capitalism, *Cosmos & History*, 6(2), pp. 27–54.

Muhr, T. (2011) *Venezuela and the ALBA: Counter-Hegemony, Geographies of Integration and Development, and Higher Education For All* (Saarbrücken: VDM).

Newman, M. (2009) *Humanitarian Intervention: Confronting the Contradictions* (New York: Cambridge University Press).

Otálvora, E. C. (2006) *Cooperación, Integración o Fusión Militar en Suramérica* (Caracas: ILDIS).

PETROCARIBE (2007) *Tratado de Seguridad Energética Petrocaribe (TSE)*, Caracas, 11 August.

PETROCARIBE (2008) Resoluciones No. 04.03–05, *Adoptadas por la 5ta Cumbre Extraordinaria de Jefes de Estado y de Gobierno de Petrocaribe*, Maracaibo, 13 July.

PETROCARIBE (2009) *Resoluciones Adoptadas por la 5ta Reunión del Consejo Ministerial de Petrocaribe*, Basseterre, 11 June, http://www.petrocaribe.org/index.php?tpl=interface.sp/design/union/readmenu_acerca2.tpl.html&newsid_obj_id=632&newsid_temas=4.

Pina, K. (2007) Haiti and America Latina: it is as it always was, *Race & Class*, 49(2), pp. 100–108.

Polanyi, K. (2001 1944) *The Great Transformation* (Boston: Beacon).

Prensa Presidential (2008) Venezuela y Bolivia firman Acuerdo de Cooperación Militar, 22 May, http://www.minci.gov.ve/noticias-prensa/28/178179/venezuela_y_boliviairman.html.

Pugh, M. (2005) The political economy of peacebuilding: a critical theory perspective, *International Journal of Peace Studies*, 1(2), pp. 23–42.

Radio La Primerisima (2010) *Unidad militar humanitaria viaja a Haití*, 14 January, http://www.radiolaprimerisima.com/noticias/general/68528.

RBV (República Bolivariana de Venezuela]) (2000) *Constitución de la República Bolivariana de Venezuela* (Caracas: RBV).

RBV (2001) *Líneas Generales del Plan de Desarrollo Económico y Social de la Nación 2001–2007* (Caracas: RBV).

RBV (2004a) Decreto No. 3.229, *Gaceta Oficial de la República Bolivariana de Venezuela*, 38.065, 15 November.

RBV (2004b) Resolución No. DG-029447, *Gaceta Oficial de la República Bolivariana de Venezuela*, 38.087, 15 December.

RBV (2005a) *Proyecto de Ley de Cooperación Internacional*, http://www.asambleanacional.gob.ve/index.php?option=com_dbquery&Itemid=182&task=ExecuteQuery&qid=7&leyes_id=20776.

RBV (2005b) Decreto No. 3.697, *Gaceta Oficial de la República Bolivariana de Venezuela*, 38201, 3 June.

RBV (2007a) *Líneas Generales del Plan de Desarrollo Económico y Social de la Nación 2007–2013* (Caracas: RBV).

RBV (2007b) *Intervención de Venezuela en la XXI Reunión Ministerial del Grupo de Rio-Unión Europea*, Santo Domingo, 20 April.

RBV (2010a) *Intervención del Representante Permanente de la República Bolivariana de Venezuela ante las Naciones Unidas, Embajador Jorge Valero, en ocasión de la aprobación del Proyecto de Resolución de la Asamblea General 'Asistencia Humanitaria, socorro de emergencia y rehabilitación en respuesta a los efectos devastadores del terremoto en Haití'*, New York, 22 January.

RBV (2010b) *Intervención del Viceministro para América Latina y el Caribe de la República Bolivariana de Venezuela, Francisco Arias Cárdenas, en ocasión de la Conferencia Internacional de Donantes para el Nueov Futuro de Haití*, New York, 31 March.

RBV (2010c) Acuerdo en Solidaridad con el Pueblo y el Gobierno de la República de Haití luego del Terremoto que Devastó a ese País, *Gaceta Oficial de la República Bolivariana de Venezuela*, 39.347, 15 January.

RBV (2010d) Acuerdo en Rechazo a la Intervención Militar que Estados Unidos Hace en Haití luego del Desastre Natural Ocurrido en la Isla Caribeña, *Gaceta Oficial de la República Bolivariana de Venezuela*, No. 39.350, 20 January 2010.

RESDAL (Red de Seguridad y Defensa de América Latina) (2008) *A Comparative Atlas of Defence in Latin America* (Buenos Aires: RESDAL).

Richmond, O. P. (2009) A post-liberal peace: eirenism and the everyday, *Review of International Studies*, 35, pp. 557–580.

Robertson, S. L. (2010) The EU, 'regulatory state regionalism' and new modes of higher education governance, *Globalisation, Societies and Education*, 8(1), pp. 23–37.
Robinson, W. I. (1996) *Promoting Polyarchy: Globalization, US Intervention, and Hegemony* (Cambridge: Cambridge University Press).
Rossier, N. (2006) *Aristide and the Endless Revolution*, Documentary, http://www.firstrunfeatures.com.
Santos, B. D. S. & Rodríguez-Garavito, C. A. (2005) B.D.S. Santos, C.A. Rodríguez-Garavito (eds.), *Law and Globalization from Below* (Cambridge: Cambridge University Press).
SIPRI (Stockholm International Peace Research Institute) (2011) *The SIPRI Military Expenditure Database*, 27 July, http://milexdata.sipri.org.
Stahler-Sholk, R. (2001) Revolution, in N. J. Smelser, P. B. Baltes (eds.) *International Encyclopedia of the Social and Behavioral Sciences* (New York: Elsevier), pp. 13299–13302, 20.
UN (2004a) Resolution 1529. Adopted by the Security Council at its 4919th meeting, 29 February.
UN (2004b) Resolution 1542. Adopted by the Security Council at its 4961st meeting, 30 April.
UN (2010a) Resolution 1908. Adopted by the Security Council at its 6261st meeting, 19 January.
UN (2010b) International Donors' Conference Towards a New Future for Haiti. Over USD 5 billion pledged for Haiti's recovery, 31 March, http://haiticonference.org.
UN Peacekeeping (n.d.) Peacekeeping Statistics, http://www.un.org/en/peacekeeping/contributors/.
UNDP (2009) *Human Development Report 2009* (New York: UNDP).
VTV (Venezolana de Televisi6n) (2009) *Países del ALBA aprobaron eleborar nueva doctrina militar*, 16 October. Reported at blog de T. Campos, 18 October, http://www.viejoblues.com/Bitacora/node/9914.
Walker, T. W. (1985) *Nicaragua: The First Five Years* (New York: Praeger).

Thomas Muhr is a research associate in global development, Centre for Globalisation, Education and Societies (GES), University of Bristol (UK). He works on globalization and regionalism, political economy and development, democracy, rights, security, and education, with a focus on Latin America and the Caribbean and its international and global relations.

Brazil's Grand Design for Combining Global South Solidarity and National Interests: A Discussion of Peacekeeping Operations in Haiti and Timor

W. ALEJANDRO SÁNCHEZ NIETO

Council on Hemispheric Affairs (COHA), 1250 Connecticut Avenue, NW, Suite 1000, Washington, DC, 20036, USA

ABSTRACT *This study analyzes how Brazil has assumed visible leadership of peacekeeping operations in order to increase its international status, with the ever-present goal of attaining a permanent seat in the UN Security Council, but also with the larger aim of cultivating forms of political-economic, cultural, and military globalization in which the Lusophone giant can articulate new forms of transnational influence. Brazil's role in MINUSTAH (the UN Stabilization Mission in Haiti) and in peacekeeping interventions in Timor have become cornerstones of Brazilian nationalism, which is evolving into a particular, global South framed 'Brazilian exceptionalism'. I will argue that these operations are seen by Brazilian policymakers as win–win scenarios: Brazil increases its international peacekeeping credentials while these fragile states obtain internal security, a first step towards development. But is this what is actually happening? I will conclude by addressing how peacekeeping in Haiti and Timor fit into Brazil's grand design for long-term global extension.*

Brazil has become Latin America's powerhouse, with its increasing influence and prestige reflected in the international extension of its security profile, as it entertains ambitious programs like developing a nuclear-powered submarine and obtaining a permanent seat on the UN Security Council.[1] Furthering its international visibility and influence, the Portuguese-speaking nation has volunteered to serve in a number of UN peacekeeping missions throughout the past decade. One mission in which Brasilia has taken a leadership role is the UN Stabilization Mission to Haiti (MINUSTAH), which was created by UN resolution 1542 (April 2004) to aid the transitional government that took control of Haiti after President Jean-Bertrand Aristide was deposed by a US-supported coup. The goal was to bring order to the country, in coordination with the Haitian police, and assist with a national reconciliation process. The mission originated in controversy, as Aristide's ouster was regarded as unconstitutional, as was the subsequent government of Prime Minister Gerard Latortue (2004–2006). Brazil provided the military commanders for MINUSTAH along with a significant portion of the troops. In view of the January 2010 earthquake that virtually destroyed much of the capital city's infrastructure, the UN mission is regarded by its supporters, and in the hopes of Brazilian diplomats, as the cornerstone for a stable and orderly reconstructed Haiti.

In addition to its role in Haiti, Brazil has also provided leadership for the UN peace mission efforts in East Timor, one of the world's newest independent nations having separated from Indonesia in 2002. Leading up to East Timor's independence, Brazilian diplomat Sérgio Vieira de Mello served as the special representative of the UN Secretary-General and as UN transitional administrator (a sort of de facto governor) from December 1999 to May 2002. More recently, since 2004, Brazilian military police have been stationed in the sovereign nation. It is asserted that some of Brazil's success in East Timor can be traced to common cultural and language links between both countries, both former Portuguese colonies, a topic that will be explored below.

But first let us examine how globalization analysts and geopolitical studies assess Brazil's new surge in UN participation. Is the Republic of Brazil, today, behaving as a continuation of either the Portuguese or Brazilian empire? Evidence presented here will indicate that the South American giant can be regarded more as an expansionist republic, not seeking to annex territory like it did in the nineteenth century, but seeking influence by targeting nations in peril to increase its bona fides, which arguably has the positive effect of Brazil being regarded as a benevolent Big Brother/Good Samaritan.

The South Rises

The rise of Brazil as a global power needs to be seen in the context of forms of political globalization, South–South solidarity, and expanding multipolarism through which India and South Africa, as well, have become regional—and increasingly global—powers. The push for changing the model of the United Nations Security Council is only the latest and most prominent expression of these types of countries demanding a larger role in global affairs. It should be stated that Third World countries have attempted to promote integration among themselves in the past such as with the establishment of organizations like the Non-Aligned Movement and the Group of 77. Dr Sally Morphet (2004, p. 525) argues that, when it comes to global South achievements in the UN, '[they] were most successful in the UN between the early 1960s and mid-1970s, when they managed to enlarge, to their advantage, the Security Council, the Economic and Social Council (ECOSOC), and the number of vice-presidents of the General Assembly. During this period, they also ensured the negotiation and entry into force of the Convention on the Elimination of Racial Discrimination. They were also able to set up an enlarged disarmament committee, a committee (of twenty-four) on decolonization, a special committee on apartheid, and UNCTAD.'

It is beyond the scope of this article to discuss how the UN was used in the Cold War by South nations as a tool to carry out their own goals (i.e. decolonization), though it can be argued that there is a strong organic link between the larger global South nations. Indeed, Richard Saull (2005, p. 257) explains that 'national liberation as social revolution locked revolutionary movements and states in the South into direct conflict with the postwar objectives of the USA.'

I would argue that the UN came to be not just the new tool of the great powers in the postwar world, but that the South learned how to utilize it as well, in order to come out ahead as part of the changing world order. From that point of view, how the South used the UN in the 1960s–1970s and how Brazil is utilizing it today shows that the UN can be a useful tool for both the North and for the South (whether it is a useful tool for the North and South at the same time is debatable).

In her 2004 study entitled 'Multilateralism and the Non Aligned Movement', Morphet explains how some scholars argue that 'the end of the Cold War weakened the collaborative dimension of Southern multilateral policies' (Morphet, 2004, p. 528). She quotes Braverboy-Wagner who states that 'there is no longer a coordinated foreign policy decision-making body, for multilateral or other purposes, for the global South' (Morphet, 2004, p. 528). Morphet looks at the NAM to argue the contrary. This author argues that, if anything, the plethora of global South/Third World organizations and summits exemplifies a willing desire for some kind of global South unity, which tends to generate the usual problems of some countries attempting to be leaders of such movements instead of followers. In addition, the increasing relations between Brazil, India, and South Africa (IBSA), in addition to the rise of other regional powerhouses like Mexico, Nigeria, Egypt, and Malaysia (which I will label as second-tier powerhouses), show that the global South is mutating into a different kind of entity. In addition, the global South appears to be utilizing the established international order, i.e. the UN and its peacekeeping missions, to have a greater independence from the Global North.

Writing in 1994, Baghat Korany explained how in the scholarly literature on international affairs, the Third World's role was morphing after the demise of the USSR. Indeed, an effect of the end of the Cold War was the widespread use of the term 'global South' as compared to 'Third World'. Korany added at the time of his writing that the collapse of the USSR brought about the 'Third Worldisation' of some former East-bloc members, while members of the South's Third World dropped down to the Fourth World (Korany, 1994, p. 11). Today scholarly literature has relabeled the regions in the developed world as the global South, within which there are rising powerhouses (i.e. Brazil), developing powers (i.e. Mexico), or failed states (i.e. Haiti). This author doesn't see the rise of the South as a new development but rather, as Morphet argues, as a process that dates back to the 1960s–1970s (speaking in terms of the post World War II era), at least vis-à-vis the UN.

Brazilian Exceptionalism: Histories of Conflict and Contradiction

While the emerging powers of the Third World morphed to keep pace with global changes (sometimes dictating them) throughout the Cold War and in the post Cold War era, Brazil has had a long interest in becoming a powerhouse, whether it is regional or global. Brazil's assertion of itself as a distinctive internationalist power began with the term (1902–1912) of Minister of Foreign Affairs Barão do Rio Branco (born José Maria da Silva Paranhos Júnior), in which values of an developmentalist republic began to be articulated with imperial ambitions.

During the period of Brazilian Imperialism (roughly mid-nineteenth century to early twentieth century), the country embarked on the expansion of its Amazonian borders, either via warfare or diplomatically. Events that are included in this period include the War of the Triple Alliance in which Brazil joined Uruguay and Argentina against Paraguay (1864–1870). In 1903, Foreign Minister Rio Branco negotiated the Treaty of Petropolis between Brazil and Bolivia, through which Brasilia annexed the Acre territory, coveted for being rich with rubber. Explicitly and officially speaking, Brazil called itself an empire from its independence in 1822 until 1889, when a federal republic was established. However, it is interesting that, like the US, certain actions of Brazil's imperialist period, like territorial annexations, occurred after the country became a republic.

Scholars have argued that one of Brazil's diplomatic particularities should be described as 'paradigmatic resilience', meaning foreign policy paradigms that were defined and first implemented in the past continue to influence the mindset and worldview of Brazilian decision makers in later periods.[2] When analyzing the country's foreign policy in 2003, a professor from the University of Brasilia, Amado Luiz Cervo, explained that 'Brazil's foreign policy has its origins in four paradigms: the Liberal-conservative State from the nineteenth century to 1930; a Developing State from 1930–1989; the Normal State; and the Logistical State, being that the last three coexist and integrate the Brazilian model of international affairs, from 1990 to today' (Cervo, 2003, p. 8; translation by the author).

An early example of this 'forward' vision by Brazilian policymakers was the deployment of 25,000 troops during World War II, called the Brazilian Expeditionary Force, which fought in Italy. No other Latin American country carried out such a deployment. It should be added that the leadership of troops sent to fight in World War II were the ones that ultimately constituted the military junta government of the 1960s. Indeed, the World War II deployment can be seen as a starting point for future Brazilian military operations abroad, now under the flag of the UN. One of the first Brazilian UN deployments occurred in 1956 when Brasilia sent peacekeepers to the Sinai, under President Juscelino Kubitschek. Brasilia also has served in the UN Observer Mission in El Salvador (ONUSAL) and the UN Mission in Angola (UNAVEM) to which it sent 1,300 troops. It is worthy to highlight that that Angola, Brazil, and East Timor are all Portuguese-speaking nations, all part of a Lusophone empire that disintegrated in the 1970s and into whose sphere Brazil's new power flows.

Under the military junta of 1964–1985, Brazil launched ambitious military projects including planning for the domestic construction of a nuclear submarine (RIA Novosti, 2009). Even though the project did not succeed, the idea was taken on again by the now former Lula administration. Nevertheless, the most optimistic estimates point out that, even with French help, the submarine would not be ready until 2021 (MercoPress, 2009), hence raising the question of the relevancy of a nuclear submarine at a time when interstate wars are generally scarce in the region. Needless to say, no other Latin American or Caribbean state is at a level to even discuss the idea of building such armaments.

If for no other reason, the submarine project helps support the prevalent idea of Brazilian exceptionalism, just like its still-infant but quickly evolving space program and the reemerging power of military–industrial companies, particularly Embraer (Sanchez, 2009). In addition to the 'military edge', the country's economy has made Brazil a coveted trading destination. In 2009, China surpassed the US as its major trading partner. Welber Barral, the Brazilian trade minister, was quoted in May 2009 as saying that total trade between Brazil and China had amounted to \$3.2 billion (£2.14 billion) in April 2009, representing a near twelvefold increase since 2001 (China Monitor, 2009, p. 11). The sum was greater than the \$2.8 billion of imports and exports to the US and represented the second consecutive month that China had topped the trade table. The country has also slowly pursued South–South coalitions by befriending South Africa and India (IBSA). Another example of Brazil being 'the country to befriend', occurred in 2005 when France declared that year the 'year of Brazil', with Jacques Chirac having Lula at his side during the Bastille military parade (BBC, 2005b; AREVA, 2005).

With discussions regarding the possibility of expanding the permanent members of the UN Security Council, many in Brazil hope that the Portuguese-speaking country, because of its successes, will stand out as the natural choice to represent not just Latin America but also the Portuguese-speaking world. In order to achieve this national goal, Brazil is utilizing the current multilateral international system, including, as previously mentioned, participation in a growing number of UN peacekeeping missions. Brazil has a history of participation in global organizations and the changing global order over the past century. Soares and Hirst highlight how Brazil 'was the only South American nation to take part in the First World War as a belligerent country, and this assured its presence at the Paris peace conference in 1919. Brazil sought to reform the incipient collective security system created by the League of Nations. ... Brazil also participated actively in the main conferences that led to the multilateral order created after 1945. The country was a founding member of the United Nations and one of the 23 founding fathers of GATT, as well as one of the 56 nations represented in the ITO (International Trade Organization) in Havana' (Soares and Hirst, 2006, pp. 25–6).

In June 2009 there was a public debate in the Brazilian Senate's Foreign Relations Committee regarding the country's role in Haiti. Among the speakers was Senator Geraldo Mesquita Júnior (Brazilian Democratic Movement Party, PMDB-Acre) who explained that in 2004 he was originally against sending Brazilian troops to Haiti, mindful of the UN's weakness at the time due to Washington's military intervention in Iraq. He changed his mind, however, after visiting the island, describing it as 'a country that was destroyed, but that supported Latin American troops' (BBC, 2009). This represented an extraordinarily rare case of a Latin American senate inviting the participation of foreign speakers (Haitians attended the debate) in order to comment on its long-term military role in another country.

Brazil's Global Policies

In its own self-understanding, Brazil stands out from other Latin American countries because of its melting-pot type of history, and also because it has developed particularly strong relations with a number of extra-hemispheric regions. Relations with the sub-Saharan Africa as well as fellow Portuguese-speaking countries stand as examples of the success of Brazil's expansive foreign policy achievements. When it comes to Africa, Brazil seems to be facing a steep learning curve. A 2000 article by Ambassador José Vicente de Sá Pimentel argued that there are two Brazilian schools of thought regarding how the country should behave towards Africa. The diplomat explained that 'the *nostalgicos*' who argue that Brazil has 'historical responsibilities' regarding Africa wish to see a role for Brazil in African affairs like in the 1970s (de Sá Pimentel, 2000, p. 5). Meanwhile, the '*catasfrofistas*' argue that Brazil has nothing else to do with Africa, in view of the numerous conflicts and human catastrophes that the continent experiences (de Sá Pimentel, 2000, p. 5). Taking into account Brazil's relationship with South Africa, as well as its cultural relationship with Angola and common oil interests with Algeria and Nigeria, one would think that the South American giant would have greater interests in the African continent. That being said, Pimentel explains that 'the insistence of an *African policy* is a curiosity, which would seem to suggest an equanimous division of Brazilian diplomatic resources between countries as different as Angola and Burkina Faso, South Africa and Rwanda, Nigeria and Djibouti'. Writing in 2002, Professor José Flávio Sombra Saravia (2002) acknowledged that during the Cardoso administration, Brazil lost interest in Africa, and even that Brazilian civil society has, in recent times, lost part of its '*encantamento*' (this author translates the word as 'fascination') with constructive opportunities vis-à-vis Africa. 'The silence regarding what happens in Africa in the national debate, universities and press are hints of a general disinterest about the other side of the Atlantic,' Sombra Sarabia argued at the beginning of the Lula administration (2002, p. 10). Brazil and sub-

Saharan Africa did have a number of initiatives to bring the two sides together over the past couple of years, but these appear to be targeted at a small number of particularly high profile countries rather than an overall Brazil–African initiative. The African countries that Brazil has recently approached include Nigeria, Angola (*Africa News*, 2008), and Mozambique (Xinhua, 2009a) though the agreements reached appear to be focused around commerce and/or tourism, except with regard to South Africa (for SA–Brazil relations see Penna Filho, 2001) with which there seems to be a special, more multidimensional relationship. It is beyond the scope of this article to compare Brazil's relations with Africa today as compared to the 1970s, though modern literature hints that in the 1970s, Brasilia paid the African continent more attention (for a review of Brazil–Africa trade relations, see de Santana, 2003).

Likewise, Brazil has taken steps to promote the Community of Portuguese Language Countries (*Comunidade dos Países de Língua Portuguesa*; CPLP), which was established on 17 July 1996 by Angola, Brazil, Cape Verde, Guinea Bissau, Mozambique, Portugal, and São Tomé and Príncipe. The CPLP summits and meetings have tackled issues including promoting the Portuguese language (Angola Press Agency, 2010), joint military exercises (*AllAfrica*, 2011) and even the circulation of citizens of CPLP countries within the community (*Africa News*, 2010). Of primary importance to Brazil may be the fact that the CPLP countries, including East Timor now as an independent state, have supported Brazil's candidacy for a UNSC permanent seat (for a review on Brazil–CPLP relations, see Miyamoto, 2009). Brazil's interim Foreign Minister Antonio Patriota said CPLP countries support each other in all their claims in international institutions like the United Nations, adding that 'The idea is that we mutually support our bids. When a country from our family is a candidate for a position in an international organ, it will have our support' (Xinhua, 2010a).

If anything, Brazil's attention is in high demand nowadays, not resented, and the country is having issues figuring out where to concentrate its diplomatic resources while formulating specific regional policies (i.e. Africa or the Portuguese-speaking world). Indeed, Brazil seems to be adopting the appearance of a global power; if 'American exceptionalism' is a valid phrase, so could be 'Brazilian exceptionalism'.

Why Help Others?

Brazil has become involved in peacekeeping operations for a variety of reasons besides the UN Security Council seat. The following five reasons have been articulated by analysts and policymakers:

1. *International Good Samaritan Syndrome*

Brazil, as a growing power, wants to aid other nations in distress. Vigevani and Cepaluni explain that 'The presence in Haiti, approved in 2003, is linked to the tradition of Brazilian diplomacy of co-operating in policies that seek to promote international (Sinai) or national (Angola) peace' (2007, p. 1318). The scholars have added that 'the Haitian case perfectly exemplifies the meaning of autonomy through diversification. Diversification not only means the search for broadening the range of relations with non-traditional partner states. It also implies the capacity for intervention in areas that are not of immediate interest and refer to internationally recognized public goods. Brazil chose to take on this responsibility, supported by other countries of the region, such as Chile and Argentina, because its objective strengthens the country's international status' (Vigevani and Cepaluni, 2007, p. 1319).

East Timor, like Brazil, is a member of the Community of Portuguese Language Speaking Countries; thus it can be argued that a major motive for Brazil's involvement in the East Timor mission is Brasilia's desire to approach non-traditional allies, particularly states that share cultural ties (i.e. Portuguese), especially if there is an opportunity to aid them (Leone and Kalil, 2006). In her 2008 work, Paulina Alberto argued that '[i]n their attempts to court African partners, the Quadros and Goulart governments made unprecedented assertions of Brazil's own Africanness' (2008, p. 80). It is debatable to what extent Brazil's African heritage has a role in taking over MINUSTAH, as Haiti also shares such a heritage. Since Brazil's African policy appears to have diminished when compared to the 1970s, a common ancestry may not have had as big an influence as expected.

In their 2004 review essay in the *Journal of Third World Studies*, de Arimateau de Cruz and Kohler de Cruz provide a 'peaceful Brazil' argument, stating that the government does have a worldview 'but it is non-threatening to the rest of the international community and its neighbors' (2004, p. 268). The authors certainly appear to be pro-Brazilian in their portrayal of the South American country today, distinct from sharply negative portrayals of Brazil during its expansionist period. That being said, it is this idealistic argument that suggests that Brazil considers it as its duty to help fellow nations in need, should they request for aid.

2. *National Interests-Driven Strategic Actor*

In this line of analysis, Brazil invests in peacekeeping as a strategy to increase its status and become a permanent member of the UN Security Council. In 2010, Latin American and Caribbean states held two seats among the non-permanent members of the UN Security Council. From 1946 to the present day, Brazil has held a seat an impressive 10 times. The way these periods are organized is interesting. Originally, Brasilia had a seat in 1946–1947, 1951–1953, 1954–1956, 1963–1965, and 1967–1968. The country had a military government from 1964 to 1985 during which time it was sometimes at odds with the US. The Portuguese-speaking country would not return to the UN Security Council until 1988–1989 (when the military government left power). Soares and Hirst agree with this assessment, explaining that 'The first date [1964] coincides with the Brazilian refusal to sign the NPT, the second [1988] with the re-establishment of democracy in Brazil in the form of a new constitution' (Soares and Hirst, 2006, p. 28). Since democratization, Brazil has had a seat almost non-stop: in 1993–1995; 1998–2000; 2004–2006; and currently in 2010 until the end of 2011. If anything, Brazil already appears to be a de facto semi-permanent member of the Council—but, crucially, without veto power.

The 'national interests' reason for aiding others can be also labeled as the 'pragmatic' reason. Brazil's aiding other countries will help promote its international status. While discussing Brazil's oil relations with the Middle East in the 1970s, Brazilian diplomat Carlos Ribeiro Santana explained that since the 1960s, Brazilian diplomacy has focused its international commerce wing in looking for markets that have products necessary for the nation, with a need for petroleum being the reason for the Brazilian–Middle Eastern rapprochement of the 1970s (during the Medici, Geisel, and Figuereido governments) (Ribeiro Santana, 2006, p. 169).

3. *Monetary Compensation from the UN*

The UN pays for the deployment of the troops and disburses a fee to the home nation that provides troops. Looking at the size of Brazil's defense budget, however—$27.1 billion in 2009, the biggest one in Latin America, followed by Colombia with $10.1 billion (Just the Facts, 2011; MercoPress,

2010)—it is unrealistic to think that whatever money Brasilia is obtaining from the UN is a major motive for deploying troops. Another way to look at things is that Brazil's entire defense budget of $27.1 billion in 2009 is significantly greater than the July 2010–June 2011 budget for MINUSTAH, which was of just over $853 million (Minustah Facts and Figures, 2011).

According to statements by Defense Minister Nelson Jobim, UN payments appear to be in deficit to what Brazil has spent on the Haitian mission. In December 2009, Minister Jobim declared that since 2004 the country has spent more than 703 million reais ($401 million) to keep its forces in Haiti; of this total, the UN has repaid around 290 million reais ($165 million) (Xinhua, 2009b).

4. *Live-Combat Training*

Another reason for Brazil's peacekeeping operations is that peace operations provide soldiers with something vital for their training: real combat situations. This is particularly interesting, as Brazil has not engaged in a war with another state since World War II. The Brazilian military, South America's largest, may be aching for a way to show what it's capable of doing. The country's last war with an immediate neighbor was the War of the Triple Alliance (1864–1870), in which Brazil joined Argentina and Uruguay against Paraguay. Hence, two issues arise: (a) Brazilian military leaders arguably lack an immediate external security threat. Brazil borders nine South American states and a French territory (French Guyana), and an interstate war with any of its neighbors remains unlikely (though Venezuela is sometimes discussed as a possible exception); and (b) training exercises, even those with live fire, cannot be compared to the experience that real-life operations bring (such as in Haiti and East Timor). While discussing China's role in peacekeeping operations, Drew Thompson of the Jamestown Foundation, a think tank in Washington DC, explains that 'deployment provides the opportunity to field-test equipment and methods, gain first-hand experience in the field and assess the capabilities of other nations deploying or supporting the mission.' He adds that 'Because of the short deployment cycles in the UN system, experienced personnel regularly return to their units with greater skills and experience which they disseminate to their colleagues' (Thompson, 2005). Similarly, Sergio Barrera, a Brazilian police captain and second generation UNPOL (United Nations Police) officer (his father reportedly served in Mozambique and he in East Timor) has been quoted as saying that 'As UNPOL we can act directly in police actions, just like in Brazil. We lead police operations and joint actions, we make arrests, are deployed during worker's strikes and are on the scene in confrontations ... You see things from a different perspective and an important part of what you see is that you learn to value your own experience and the role of the police officer in ways that escape you before being deployed overseas' (Moriconi, 2010).

Hence, it is possible to speculate that some Brazilian commanders may be lobbying for a continuous presence in peace operations like Haiti and Timor in order for officers and troops alike to gain combat experience (such as the Cité Soleil neighborhood battles). Thus, in the event that Brazil has a new interstate war, it would already have cadres of combat-experienced soldiers, and police offers, thanks to the UN missions.

5. *National Pride*

'I have been going to Haiti since 1995, and I have been living there for the past 20 months and not once have I worn a helmet or a bullet proof jacket. Haiti is today safer than the Dominican

Republic, and safer than Jamaica,' said the Brazilian Ambassador to Haiti, Igor Kipman, in late 2009 (Horta, 2009). Brazil takes great pride in the successes achieved in Haiti via MINUSTAH, as it is a Brazil-run operation. As Michael Snell, a retired Canadian colonel who now works with the Canadian Pearson Peacekeeping Centre, explained to the author, 'it seems clear that Haiti has become part of Brazilian nationalism; it is utilized, for lack of a better work, to showcase Brazil as a growing global power' (Sanchez, 2010).

An example of this can be found in the UN operations in Cité Soleil (the huge shantytown community of 400,000 residents in Port-au-Prince) in late 2005 against street gangs that controlled various neighborhoods. During a firefight, reports arose that criminals had actually managed to rout the UN blue helmets. Moroccan Colonel Elouafi Boulbars, a UN military spokesman, would then declare to the media 'How could thousands of well trained professional soldiers, well equipped, defending a noble cause, be put to rout by a group of badly armed bandits that have no legal or moral or even popular support? ... On the contrary, the Brazilian battalion gave the bandits a hard time today' (BBC, 2005a). The 'success' of the operation in Cité Soleil enhanced the image of MINUSTAH and the Brazilian troops that took part in the deployments.

Nevertheless, it should be stressed that even such victories brought about drama, as there were numerous accusations of the blue helmets abusing human rights, like shooting at civilians on purpose as well as committing extrajudicial killings. In December 2006, HIP videographers taped UN troops shooting at civilians from helicopters during an operation in Cité Soleil: '[d]ocumentary evidence finally forced the UN to admit that unarmed civilians had been killed by UN forces despite their attempts to cover it up' (Haiti Information Project, 2007). The Council on Hemispheric Affairs, a think tank that has been critical of MINUSTAH since its inception, has argued that 'yet as scores of attempts by U.N. missions sponsored by NGOs and foreign diplomats have come and gone, the human condition in Haiti has barely improved' (Rosenblum, 2009).The 2010 earthquake in the island arguably showed that, six years into the mission, the Haitian government is still unable to care for its own population and still has to rely on this international mission to impose some kind of order.

MINUSTAH Origins

In 2004, gangs of protesters, many of which were made up of former Haitian military and police members including notorious gang leader Guy Philippe (a former soldier and police captain), took to the streets to protest the rule of President Jean-Bertrand Aristide. Shockingly enough, instead of protecting the constitutional order, the international community (with the exception of the Caribbean Community; CARICOM) accepted and even tacitly supported the coup. It has been widely reported that US troops were sent to Port-au-Prince to physically remove Aristide from the palace of government instead of aiding his crumbling government.[3] The disgraced Haitian leader was taken to a plane that eventually ended up in South Africa. Gérard Latortue became the provisional prime minister, with elections in 2006 declaring Rene Préval as new head of state.

Meanwhile, the UN, which had been involved in Haitian affairs for years, took up a new role in the country. UN missions to Haiti throughout the 1990s include the United Nations Mission in Haiti (UNMIH), the United Nations Support Mission in Haiti (UNSMIH), the United Nations Transition Mission in Haiti (UNTMIH), and the United Nations Civilian Police Mission in Haiti (MIPONUH). And finally, the largest of all, the UN Stabilization Mission in Haiti, MINUSTAH, would be created as a way to restore order in Haitian streets, even though the constitutional order had been clearly violated and the legitimacy and sovereignty of an international occupation had no basis in Haitian law. MINUSTAH was a follow-on mission from the 3,000-strong 'multinational interim force' (MIF) originally sent to Haiti as Aristide was deposed. The MIF was made up of troops from Canada, Chile, France, and the US. The UN Security Council unanimously passed Resolution 1542 on 30 April 2004, authorizing the creation of MINUSTAH (UN S/RES/1542 - 2004). As a side note, it is important to highlight that Resolution 1542 recognizes the Transitional Government of Haiti, with Latortue as head, as the rulers of Haiti, not even mentioning Aristide as the constitutional head of state or asking for his return. Indeed, MINUSTAH came to be regarded as a sort of peace enforcer as well as tacit protector of the new, unconstitutional regime.

Brazil, MINUSTAH, and State Building in Haiti

According to Defense Minister Jobim, Brazil has deployed 1,266 soldiers, 223 vehicles, and other equipment in Haiti. After the January 2010 earthquake, the Brazilian congress passed a bill allowing for the dispatch of more troops to Haiti, raising the total to 2,200, to help with the relief and reconstruction operations; before the earthquake, MINUSTAH's total number of troops was of 9,000 troops (Xinhua, 2010c). A similar situation had occurred after Hurricane Noel struck the island in 2007, prompting Brazilian Defense Minister Nelson Jobim to state, 'My position is that the Brazilian personnel in Haiti has to be increased to work for reconstruction' (BBC, 2007). It is unclear if the increase of Brazilian troops will be permanent or if their presence will return to pre-earthquake levels. The leadership of the mission is generally Brazilian, including commanders like Brazilian General Heleno Ribeiro, General Jose Elito Carvalho, General Alberto dos Santos Cruz, Lieutenant General Urano Teixeira da Matta Bacellar who shot himself in the head on January 2006, and Major General Floriano Peizoto Viera Neto. During a ceremony in honor of the 22 Brazilian soldiers who died in the earthquake, President Lula stated that the military participated in the 'noblest humanitarian mission ever carried out by the Brazilian Armed Forces' (Xinhua, 2010b).

In addition to sending troops for the UN, Brasilia has carried out a number of development programs and supported long-term investments in the island. It would seem that Brasilia wants to be the cornerstone for not only peacekeeping in Haiti but also state building. Walter Dorn, regarded as the most influential scholar on intelligence operations in peacekeeping, explains that '[t]he United Nations, especially the Brazilian contingent, was quick to repair the damage done to the neighborhood during combat operations. "Immediate Impact Projects", even more ambitious than the UN's traditional "Quick Impact Projects", helped provide basic necessities to the locals at a time when they needed rapid assistance and reassurance' (Dorn, 2009, p. 819).

It should be stressed that Brazil has not only taken a leading role with MINUSTAH. The South American giant is also a member of the so-called 'Haiti core group', a group of nations that took the reins after the 2004 overthrow of Aristide to bring order and install a new government (BBC, 2006). The group's membership includes the US, France, Canada, Brazil, Argentina, and Chile. It is impossible not to note that the first three countries on the list are the same ones accused of fomenting the violent overthrow of President Aristide.

Considering Haiti's importance in Brazil's grand design, does this mean that Brasilia's commitment in the area is long term? Speaking in 2006, Lula declared, before Rene was elected to the presidency of Haiti, that 'if the new government tells Brazil, "it's time," we'll leave quietly, because I believe we will have fulfilled our mission' (Agènce France Presse, 2006a). He also explained that there is no deadline for Brazil to withdraw its troops from the island. Nevertheless, it is revealing that the Cité Soleil street wars, the accusations of human rights violations (Aldridge, 2005; Jacobs, 2007; Lindsay, 2005; Sequera, 2005), and the deaths of Brazilian peacekeepers caused by the 2010 earthquake have not caused any visible cracks in Brasilia's motivation to provide occupying military authority in the Caribbean country.

Timor Peacekeeping

Brazil also sent troops to the UN peacekeeping in Timor-Leste, one of the newest independent states in the world following its breaking away from Indonesia in 2002. As part of United Nations Integrated Mission in Timor-Leste (UNMIT), the Brazilian contingent has been awarded the Timor-Leste Solidarity Medal (*The Straits Times*, 2009). The Solidarity Medal of Timor-Leste was introduced by the President Ramos-Horta in 2008 to recognize contributions to peace and stability operations in East Timor. In addition, Sérgio Vieira de Mello, a former Brazilian diplomat, was a special representative of the UN Secretary-General to East Timor. In addressing the Timorese Parliament during a brief visit in 2008, President Lula stated that 'East Timor is a sovereign nation and worthy of our support ... Brazil will help East Timor as much as we can' (Sulekha.com, 2008). While Brazil has not taken the sole leadership position in UNMIT, Brasilia envoys to the mission have made sure their voices are heard. In 2006, during a meeting of the Fifth Committee (Administrative and Budgetary) regarding the proposed budget for UNMIT, the Brazilian envoy, Paulo Roberto Campos Tarrise, said that UNMIT must have all the resources it needed to help Timor-Leste strengthen its institutions and foster socio-economic development (M2 Presswire, 2008).

An issue that should be stressed is that Brazilian peacekeepers have been welcomed, in the broad sense of the word, in Timor-Leste, in part because Brazilian music is particularly popular in the country. Timor-Leste is a former colony of Portugal, but it is debatable to describe Portuguese as a widely spoken tongue there (though it is an official one), particularly after Indonesia invaded the island in 1975 and annexed it in 1976. A 2006 piece in the *Asashi Shimbun* explains that traditional Brazilian songs like Lambada are popular in the country. When peacekeepers from Brazil and Portugal came to the country, they brought along new music tapes, from which pirated copies were made and sold in Dili. The article explains that, in 2004, 'the Brazilian Embassy in East Timor arranged for 25 Brazilian student volunteers to teach Portuguese at a university in Dili using Brazilian music.' The article ends by quoting a local singer, Anito Matos, stating that 'in 10 years time ... we will be able to feel that the Brazilian songs are our own' (Fujitani, 2006). While the goal of this article is not to discuss music as cultural diplomacy and how it has been utilized by Brazilian peace missions abroad, it is something that should be considered.

It could be argued that Brazil's peacekeeping–musical diplomacy was the first step to create strong cultural relations between the two countries. In March 2009, the Brazilian media giant Globo TV International began transmitting Brazilian comedies to East Timor, via Radio and Television of East Timor (RTTL). Also in 2009, Brasilia sponsored a Brazilian cultural month in East Timor, which included concerts of Brazilian music (known to be popular) and workshops to promote the common culture between the two Portuguese-speaking states. In the case of East Timor, Brazil undoubtedly takes pride in aiding a fellow Portuguese-speaking country, particularly since there is a 'cultural addendum' to it. As a corollary of this section, it should be once again mentioned that East Timor is now a member of the Community of Portuguese-Speaking Nations and supports Brazil having a permanent seat in the UNSC.

Then again, the UN presence in East Timor has not been without some criticism, not so much because of UNMIT carrying out human rights violations but for its failure to 'reform, restructure and rebuild the country's national police force and to assist the government to review its security sector' (Murdoch, 2011). In addition, specialists like Gordon Peake, who worked on police reform in Timor-Leste from 2008 to 2011, have reported how the UN mission 'once lauded by Timorese for helping to usher in independence, seems to be held in ill-esteem and barely disguised contempt by many members of the political elite' (Peake, 2011). The newly independent country is scheduled to have national elections in 2012, which will determine the future of the UN mission there.

The Inevitable Backlash

Brazil's leadership role in Haiti caused as consequence the 'snubbing' of Brazil by Caribbean and African governments. At the time of the 2004 coup, CARICOM members had complained that the coup against Aristide was unconstitutional and demanded an inquiry, as they accused Canada, the US, and France of being behind the overthrow. Likewise, the African Union labeled Aristide's removal as 'unconstitutional' (Brath, 2004). These demands and protests generally fell on deaf ears, particularly at the UN as it organized MINUSTAH. As previously stated, MINUSTAH's mandate was to support the transitional government, not oversee the return of the constitutional president. CARICOM had demanded that the UN investigate Aristide's overthrow and suspended Haiti's membership in 2004 (when Latortue came to power) and only readmitted the state in 2006 (when Preval was elected). The fact that Brazil took command of MINUSTAH instead of siding with the Caribbean and African states can be regarded as an example of Brasilia putting its grand plan in front of the inclination of other states. Thus, one can say that Brazil put its pragmatic national interests ahead of its Good Samaritan role.

In addition, numerous Haitians have developed a clear theory for why Brazil is in their country to begin with. In March 2005, Leopold Berlanger (BBC, 2005a), director-general of the Haitian radio station Radio Vision 2000 stated to his listeners that 'I find that an attitude of politicking has developed among the MINUSTAH forces commanded by Brazil . . . Brazil's ambition is first to have a seat on the UN Security Council. Let us say that [pauses] at the same time they want to show that they have the capability to lead an international force, to deploy an international force, whereas they do not want to assume the responsibility, all the responsibilities implied by that. Therefore, I think that the commander of the force in particular has relayed this politicking attitude of Brazil on the ground, because we have found that there is a lack of serenity in MINUSTAH's statements.' Berlanger was referring to statements by then-head of MINUSTAH, Brazilian General Heleno Ribeiro Pereira. Other complaints coming from Haiti include the charge that the island has been controlled by MINUSTAH since its creation in 2004, and that the mission was used as a praetorian guard of sorts for the regime of interim Prime Minister Gérard Latortue and of current President René Préval. Such accusations became widespread particularly in 2005, when reports came out saying that MINUSTAH was complicit in numerous killings since 2004 either acting alone, or with the Haitian National Police (Buncombe, 2006). In the interest of fairness, Michael Dziedzic and Robert M. Perito report that a poll during the neighborhood wars says that despite the casualties, material losses, and delays in making repairs, 97% of respondents believed that the UN crackdown on the gangs was justified (Dziedzic and Perito, 2008, p. 5).

It should be noted that even though Brazil is the leader of MINUSTAH, with a Brazilian military officer as commander of the international contingent, Haitian critics declare that Brasilia is only following the orders of other countries. During a public debate in the Brazilian Senate, Carole Pierre Paul-Jacob, head of the Haitian Women's Solidarity NGO (Sofa, in French), declared that Brazil does not hold a true control of MINUSTAH, instead describing it instead as 'a false leadership, guided by the North Americans and the Canadians' (BBC, 2009). This Haitian national told the Brazilian *Correio* that 'the true objective of MINUSTAH corresponds in many ways to a system of supervision for the country, in a plan of economic dependence linked to multi-nationals and a global capitalist project' (BBC, 2009).

One can only wonder to what extent Brazilian policymakers listen to complaints by the Caribbean states and Haitian civil society. While one hears Haiti radio managers make such editorials to their listeners, Brazilian Ambassador in Haiti Igor Kipman stated in February 2010 that departing President Lula thinks MINUSTAH's role should expand from peacekeeping to boosting economic development. The diplomat explained that besides acting in MINUSTAH, Brazil maintained 31 projects of bilateral cooperation with Haiti dating from before the earthquake, mainly in agriculture, health, and education. In 2006, amid the death of Haitian civilians during firefights between UN troops and armed gangs, the Brazilian Ministry of Foreign Affairs defended such operations stating that '[t]he chaos in the country was contained and the activity of illegal armed groups is almost completely restricted to one neighborhood of Port-au-Prince: Cité Soleil' (Agènce France Presse, 2006b). Since then firefights in Cité Soleil itself have been contained.

Conclusions

> Why shouldn't we just imitate the behavior of the powerful? (Cervo, 2003, p. 20)

How does Brazil's behavior fit with the five possible reasons previously discussed? We can rule out monetary compensation by the UN, as Brazil's economy is particularly strong and not dependent on international funding for its military to operate (as is the case of some other military donors to the UN). Likewise, a need for live-combat training is probably part of the reason for Brazil's UN participation, but not a critical one. This article has not discussed in depth the influence of the Brazilian military on the government's decision-making process when it comes to UN missions, a topic worthy of further research. What is clear is that the Lula administration took care to keep the military happy, authorizing the nuclear submarine project as well as the purchase of other major weaponry, even though the country lacks a traditional external security threat. Thus, deploying Brazilian officials and regular troops may be also a way for Lula, like other civilian presidents since the dictatorship, to keep the armed forces occupied and happy. In this author's opinion, the 'live-combat training' theory for Brazilian participating in the UN is *a* reason, but not *the* principal reason.

The other three theories, namely the Good Samaritan theory, national interests, and national pride are generally mixed together and arguably provide the cornerstone for Brazilian participation in UN missions in recent years. The Good Samaritan theory can be successfully applied to both Haiti and East Timor. In the Caribbean state's case, Brazil wanted to aid a fellow hemispheric country, largely regarded as a failed state, to achieve internal order after the 2004 coup so it could finally prosper. In East Timor's case, Brasilia wanted to aid a fellow Portuguese-speaking state. Then again, from a more realist point of view, we can find more realpolitik reasoning for these interventions that go back to traditional national interests. Both interventions help Brazil achieve its national goals. First and foremost, taking the lead in MINUSTAH and playing a strong role in East Timor help Brazil's bona fides for achieving a UNSC permanent seat, something that Brazil covets. East Timor's and the CPLP's overall support for Brazil's UNSC membership suggests that this plan is working. Then again, realpolitik–national interest politics usually means that not everybody is a winner. While Brazil has arguably brought some internal order to Haiti, the very existence of MINUSTAH has been criticized as supporting an illegal change in the constitutional order of Haiti as Jean-Bertrand Aristide was illegally removed from the presidency. By taking the part of MINUSTAH right after the Haitian 2004 coup aftermath, Brazil put its national interests ahead of protests by Caribbean and African states.

Finally, national pride is a sentiment that touches on both the previously discussed theories. Indeed, Brazil is taking great pride in its role in Haiti and East Timor. In addition, if it attains a UNSC seat, it would be representative of both Latin America, the Caribbean (should they forget about Haiti), and the Portuguese-speaking world. In April 2010, at a graduation of new Brazilian diplomats, President Lula stated that 'when a country gets important, it stirs up jealousy. Those who were not capable of doing what you did get jealous' (Xinhua, 2010c). 'The Ministry of Defense and the Brazilian government insisted that we have to stay in Haiti,' said Minister Jobim, adding 'Brazil has an obligation to be there' (Xinhua, 2009b). For a 'middle power', the South American giant is certainly behaving like a major one. The phrase normally used to describe countries like Brazil and India are 'rising powers', not at the level of the US, the Russian Federation, the EU, or China, but more influential and with a growing global agenda (including particular policies regarding extra-hemispheric regions, as we have discussed), as compared to second-tier powerhouses like Nigeria, Egypt, or Mexico. It would appear that Brazil will continue participating in UN missions, maybe wanting to play a bigger role in others like it has done in MINUSTAH. In late 2009, the Brazilian Marine Corps, the *Corpo de Fuzileiros Navais*, CFN, concluded its first year of peacekeeping training at the recently inaugurated CFN School of Peacekeeping Operations.

The authors of the previously mentioned *Journal of Third World Studies* article (de Arimateau de Cruz and Kohler de Cruz) quote Helio Jaguaribe who, writing in 1958, summarized Brazil's nationalistic vision when he stated '[Brazil's] nationalism is not the imposition of our peculiarities, not even the expression of our national characteristics. It is, on the contrary, a means to an end to obtain a goal, namely, development' (de Arimateau de Cruz and Kohler de Cruz, 2004, p. 272). Indeed, Brazil hasn't sought to impose its culture in East Timor or Haiti; though it should be highlighted that East Timor has some cultural links (broadly speaking) with Brazil, and the civilian population apparently have welcomed Brazilian culture. One cannot help but notice how Brazil has been received in both countries, considering that in Haiti Brasilia has been accused of following Washington and Ottawa's orders, while in Timor the locals used the arrival of the blue helmets to dance to the latest hits of Brazilian music.

Regarding Jaguaraibe's half-century old statement, while it is true that domestically Brazil continues to suffer from traditional Third World problems including unemployment and major levels of poverty, at the international level, Brazil's foreign policy is not aimed only at national development but at international recognition as well. Participation in the UN missions in Haiti and East Timor has little to do with domestic Brazilian development; it is more motivated by global-power level goals. Scholars like de Arimateau de Cruz and Kohler de Cruz have argued that Brazil is a non-threatening power (2004, p. 268). I would agree with this, as I doubt that Brazil will today embark on a land expansionist scheme as it did during the nineteenth century. That said, by taking a leading role in MINUSTAH, Brazil has indirectly supported an unconstitutional coup against a democratically elected leader, a threat to the democratic order of similarly fragile states. Taking part in UN missions (the legitimate facility for the world's Good Samaritan) is a way for the South American state to achieve major goals, and Brasilia has taken this role seriously, though Haiti counts as at least one deployment in which Brazil's Good Samaritan wishes and pragmatic national interests clashed with MINUSTAH's controversial origins. In view of this, Brazil is behaving as a global power.

Notes

1 A discussion of Brazil's relationship with the UN can be found in Caixeta (2005).
2 The goal of this article is not to provide a comprehensive analysis of Brazilian foreign policy. Examples of such analyses that target the general topic include Alden and Vieira (2005), Burges (2006), Cervo (2003), and Vieira (2001).
3 Scholarly debates regarding Aristide's ouster include Dupuy (2006), Erickson (2005), and Robinson (2007).

References

Alberto, P. (2008) African-Bahian exchanges in the reinvention of Brazil's racial democracy, 1961–1963, *Luso-Brazilian Review*, 45(1), pp. 78–117.

Alden, C. & Vieira, M. A. (2005) The new diplomacy of the South: South Africa, Brazil and India and trilateralism, *Third World Quarterly*, 26(7), pp. 1077–1095.

Aldridge, L. (2005) Hundreds of UN peacekeepers storm pro-Aristide slum in Haiti, kill at least two men, *AP Worldstream*, 6 July.

Africa News (2008) Angola: Parliament Speaker and Brazilian Ambassador analyze cooperation, AllAfrica.com, 8 December, http://allafrica.com/stories/200812081405.html

Africa News (2010) Angola: Free circulation of CPLP must consider members' reality, AllAfrica.com, 8 March, http://allafrica.com/stories/201003081209.html

Agènce France Presse (2006a) No deadline for Brazilian peacekeepers in Haiti: Lula, 9 February. Reported in Caribbean NetNews, 10 February, http://www.caribbeannewsnow.com/caribnet/cgiscript/csArticles/articles/000004/000455.htm.

Agènce France Presse (2006b) Annan names Brazilian to head UN force in Haiti, 18 January. Reported in Caribbean NetNews, 19 January, http://www.caribbeannetnews.com/service/sitemap/

AllAfrica (2011) Angola: Army chief of staff opens feline, 15 March, http://allafrica.com/stories/201103160127.html

Angola Press Agency (Luanda) (2010) CPLP criticized for lack of Portuguese language policy, ANGOP online, 10 March, http://www.portalangop.co.ao/motix/en_us/noticias/politica/2010/2/10/CPLP-criticised-for-lack-Portuguese-language-policy,f09d09af-32e8-4c36-85f1-c499b5e47c9.

AREVA (2005) *Honoring Brazilian Culture*, http://www.areva.com/EN/group-919/areva-s-funding-for-year-of-brazil-in-france.html.

BBC (2005a) , Monitoring Latin America—Political: Haiti: Radio director criticizes MINUSTAH commander's statements, 5 March. Text of report from the *News Here and There* program broadcast by Haitian Radio Vision 2000, 7 March 2005. Reported at Access My Library: Asia Africa Intelligence Wire online, 8 March, http://www.accessmylibrary.com/coms2/summary_0286-19020041_ITM.

BBC (2005b) , Monitoring Latin America—Political: Brazilian politicians excluded from presidential party in France, 14 July. Text of report from Brazilian news agency Estado, 12 July.

BBC (2006) , Monitoring Latin America—Political: UN Core Group begins 'political mission' in Haiti, 18 January.

BBC (2007) , Monitoring Latin America—Political: UN troops, Haitian government join forces in hurricane relief, 2 November. Originally published by Caribbean Media Corporation News Agency website, 2 November.

BBC (2009) Monitoring Latin America—Political: Brazilian presence in Haiti discussed in senate, 24 June. Originally published in: V. Vaz (2009) Haiti: senate discusses Brazilian mission, *Correio Braziliense*, 18 June.

Brath, E. (2004) Aristide's ouster, African lessons, *New African*, April, pp. 13–17.

Buncombe, A. (2006) UN admits civilians may have died in Haiti peacekeeping raid, *The Independent*, Americas online, 10 January, http://www.independent.co.uk/news/world/americas/un-admits-civilians-may-have-died-in-haiti-peacekeeping-raid-522317.html.

Burges, S. W. (2006) Without sticks and carrots: Brazilian leadership in South America during the Cardoso era, 1992–2003, *Bulletin of Latin American Research*, 25(1), pp. 23–42.

Caixeta Arraes, V. (2005) O Brasil e o Conselho de Segurança da Organização das Nações Unidas: dos anos 90 a 2002, *Revista Brasileira de Política Internacional*, 48(2), pp. 152–168.

Cervo, A. L. (2003) Política exterior e relações internacionais do Brasil: enfoque paradigmático, *Revista Brasileira de Política Internacional*, 46(2), pp. 5–25.

China Monitor (2009) , Business Briefs, p. 11. Centre for Chinese Studies online, http://www.ccs.org.za/wp-content/uploads/2009/07/china-monitor-may-2009.pdf.

De Arimateau de Cruz, J. & Kohler de Cruz, B. (2004) Review essay: Brazil's foreign policy behaviour in the post-cold war international system, *Journal of Third World Studies*, 21(2), pp. 267–276.

De Sá Pimentel, J. V. (2000) Relacoes entre o Brasil e Africa subsaarica, *Revista Brasileira de Política Internacional*, 43(1), pp. 5–23.

De Santana, I. (2003) Notas e comentários sobre a dinâmica do comércio Brasil-África nas décadas de 1970 a 1990, *Revista Brasileira de Política Internacional*, 46(2), pp. 113–137.

Dorn, W. A. (2009) Intelligence-led peacekeeping: the United Nations Stabilization Mission in Haiti (MINUSTAH), 2006–07, *Intelligence and National Security*, 24(6), pp. 805–835.

Dupuy, A. (2006) *The Prophet and the Power: Jean-Bertrand Aristide, the International Community and Haiti* (New York: Rowman and Littlefield).

Dziedzic, M. & Perito, R. M. (2008) *Haiti: Confronting the Gangs of Port-Au-Prince*, United States Institute of Peace, Special Report, September. http://www.usip.org/files/resources/sr208.pdf.

Erikson, D. P. (2005) Haiti after Aristide: Still on the brink, *Current History*, February, pp. 83–90.

Fujitani, T. (2006) East Timor looks to Brazil for songs of freedom, *The Asahi Shimbun*, 23August 2006, http://www.etan.org/et2006/august/26/23etlook.htm.

Globo TV International (2009) , Brazilian comedies are broadcast in East Timor and South Korea, 25 March, http://www.globotvinternational.com/newsDet.asp?newsId=43.

Haiti Information Project (2007) , UN in Haiti accused of second massacre, 27 January, http://www.haitiaction.net/News/HIP/1_21_7/1_21_7.html.

Jacobs, T. (2007) Hundreds of UN peacekeepers raid Haitian slum in major operations against gangs, Associated Press Worldstream, 9 February [AP Television]. Reported at 7 News wsvn.com, http://www.wsvn.com/news/articles/world/MI39398/.

Jaguaribe, H. (1958) *O Nacionalismo na Atualidade Brasileira*, (Rio de Janeiro: Ministério da Educação e Cultura, Instituto Superior de Estudos Brasileiros).

Just the Facts (2011) Trends in Latin American military spending: a conversation with SIPRI's Carina Solmirano [podcast], Center for International Policy, Latin America Working Group and the Washington Office on Latin America, 10 June, http://justf.org/blog/2011/06/10/podcast-trends-latin-american-military-spending-conversation-sipris-carina-solmirano.

Korany, B. (1994) End of history, or its continuation and accentuation? The global South and the 'new transformation' literature, *Third World Quarterly*, 15(1), pp. 7–15.

Leone, L. P. & Kalil, S. M. (2006) O envolvimento do Brasil na questão timorense, *Revue Lusotopie*, 13(2), pp. 49–58, http://www.ingentaconnect.com/content/brill/luso/2006/00000013/00000002/art00002.

Lindsay, R. (2005) Civilians caught in crossfire of Haiti slum; UN peacekeepers confront gangs, but the violence continues, *South China Morning Post*, 6 May, p. 14.

M2 PressWIRE (2008) United Nations: speakers underscore value of quick-impact projects as fifth committee considers proposed budgets for peacekeeping missions in Timor-Leste, Liberia. Reported at HighBeam Research, 22 May, http://www.highbeam.com/doc/1P3-1482481021.html.

MINUSTAH Facts and Figures, http://www.un.org/en/peacekeeping/missions/minustah/facts.shtml.

MINUSTAH Mandate, http://www.un.org/en/peacekeeping/missions/minustah/mandate.shtml.

MercoPress (2009) Brazil's plans first nuclear powered submarine for 2021, 31 August, http://en.mercopress.com/2009/08/31/brazils-plans-first-nuclear-powered-submarine-for-2021.

MercoPress (2010), Brazil leads Latam in military spending; Colombia as percentage of GDP, 2 June, http://en.mercopress.com/2010/06/02/brazil-leads-latam-in-military-spending-colombia-as-percentage-of-gdp.

Miyamoto, S. (2009) O Brasil e a comunidade dos paises de lingua portuguesa (PCLP), *Revista Brasileira de Política Internacional*, 52(2), pp. 22–42.

Moore, M. (2009) China overtakes the US as Brazil's largest trading partner, Telegraph.co.uk, 9 May, http://www.telegraph.co.uk/finance/economics/5296515/China-overtakes-the-US-as-Brazils-largest-trading-partner.html.

Moriconi, L. H. (2010) Brazil sends record number of police officers in UN missions, *Comunidad Segura*, 5, November, http://www.comunidadesegura.org/en/STORY-Brazil-sends-record-number-of-police-officers-in-UN-peacekeeping-missions.

Morphet, S. (2004) Multilateralism and the Non Aligned Movement: what is the global South doing and where is it going? Review Essay, *Global Governance*, 10, pp. 517–537.

Murdoch, L. (2011) East Timor angered by UN report, *The Age*, (Australia), 3 January, http://www.theage.com.au/national/east-timor-angered-by-un-report-20110102-19d33.html.

Peake, G. (2011) , Timor-Leste declares open season on the UN, Lowy Institute for International Policy, The Interpreter, 7 June, http://www.lowyinterpreter.org/post/2011/06/07/Timor-Leste-declares-open-season-on-the-UN.aspx.

Penna Filho, P. (2001) Africa do Sul e Brasil: diplomacia e comercio (1918–2000), *Revista Brasileira de Política Internacional*, 44(1), pp. 69–93.

RIA Novosti (2009) Brazil aims to build first nuclear sub within 12 years—agency, 18 May, http://en.rian.ru/world/20090518/155036599.html.

Riberio Santana, C. (2006) O aprofundamento das relações do Brasil com os países do Oriente Médio durante os dois choques do petróleo da década de 1970: um exemplo de ação pragmática, *Revista Brasileira de Política Internacional*, 49(2), pp. 157–177.

Robinson, R. (2007) *An Unbroken agony: Haiti, from Revolution to the Kidnapping of a President* (New York: Basic Civitas).

Rosenblum, D. (2009) 'The rock in the sun': Haiti's Préval pleads for the U.S. and rest of the world to end global negligence towards Latin America's poorest country, Council on Hemispheric Affairs, 9 February, http://www.coha.org/%E2/%80/%9Cthe-rock-in-the-sun/%E2/%80/%9D-haiti/%E2/%80/%99s-preval-pleads-for-the-us-and-rest-of-the-world-to-end-the-world/%E2/%80/%99s-negligence-towards-latin-america/%E2/%80/%99s-poorest-country/.

Sanchez, A. (2009) Embraer: Brazilian military industry becoming a Global Arms Merchant? Council on Hemispheric Affairs, 1 September, http://www.coha.org/embraer-brazilian-military-industry-becoming-a-global-arms-merchant/.

Sanchez, A. (2010) *Peacekeeping and Military Operations by Latin American Militaries: Between Being a Good Samaritan and Servicing the National Interest*, Report [online], Council on Hemispheric Affairs, 22 January, http://www.coha.org/peacekeeping-and-military-operations.

Saull, R. (2005) Locating the global South in the theorization of the cold war: capitalist development, social revolution and geopolitical conflict, *Third World Quarterly*, 26(2), pp. 253–280.

Sequera, V. (2005) Brazilian general denies accusations of human rights violations in Haiti, AP Worldstream. Reported at HighBeam Research, 23 November, http://www.highbeam.com/doc/1P1-115586202.html.

Soares, M. R. & Hirst, M. (2006) Brazil as an Intermediate state and regional power: action, choice and responsibilities, *International Affairs*, 82(1), pp. 21–40.

Sombra Saravia, J. F. (2002) Politica exterior do Governo Lula: o desafio africano, *Revista Brasileira de Política Internacional*, 45(2), pp. 5–25.

The Straits Times (2009) Honored for Timor Leste mission, 10 November.

Sulekha.com (2008) , Brazil's president meets with East Timor leaders, 11 July, http://newshopper.sulekha.com/brazil-s-president-meets-with-east-timor leaders_news_930608.htm.

Thompson, D. (2005) Beijing's participation in UN peacekeeping missions, The Jamestown Foundation, *China Brief*, 5(11), http://www.jamestown.org/single/?no_cache=1&tx_ttnews%5Btt_news%5D=3860.

UN (2004) Security Council Resolution 1542, http://www.un.org/ga/search/view_doc.asp?symbol=S/RES/1542(2004).

Vieira, M. A. (2001) Ideas and institutions: a reflection on the Brazilian foreign policy in the early 1990s, *Contexto Internacional*, 23(2), pp. 245–293.

Vigevani, T. & Cepaluni, G. (2007) Lula's foreign policy and the quest for autonomy through diversification, *Third World Quarterly*, 28(7), pp. 1309–1326.

Xinhua News Agency (2009a) Mozambique, Brazil formalize cooperation in tourism. Reported at HighBeam Research, 18 June, http://www.highbeam.com/doc/1P2-20447792.html.

Xinhua News Agency (2009b) Brazil's expenses in Haiti far exceed payment refunded by UN, 9 December, http://news.xinhuanet.com/english/2009-12/10/content_12621934.htm.

Xinhua News Agency (2010a) Portuguese-speaking countries support Brazil's bid for UNSC permanent seat, 31 March. Reported at balita online, 1 April, http://balita.ph/2010/04/01/portuguese-speaking-countries-support-brazils-bid-for-unsc-permanent-seat/.

Xinhua News Agency (2010b) Brazilian president pays tribute to soldiers killed in Haiti quake. Reported at Global Times online, 22 January, http://world.globaltimes.cn/americas/2011-04/500435.html.

Xinhua News Agency (2010c) Brazil reaffirms support for expanded MINUSTAH role in Brazil. Reported at HighBeam Research online, 27 February, http://www.highbeam.com/doc/1P2-21341602.html.

W. Alejandro Sánchez Nieto is a research fellow at the Council on Hemispheric Affairs (COHA) where he focuses on geopolitics and security issues. He holds a Master's degree in international peace and conflict resolution from the School of International Service at American University. His analyses have appeared in numerous refereed journals including *Small Wars and Insurgencies*, *Defense Studies*, *The Journal of Slavic Military Studies*, *European Security*, *Studies in Conflict and Terrorism*, and *Cuban Affairs*.

Egypt as a Globalist Power: Mapping Military Participation in Decolonizing Internationalism, Repressive Entrepreneurialism, and Humanitarian Globalization Between the Revolutions of 1952 and 2011

PAUL AMAR

Global & International Studies Program, University of California, Santa Barbara, CA, USA

ABSTRACT *By intervening in the 2011 Revolution and moving to assert control over state and society during the subsequent transitional period, the Egyptian military became visible again not just as a defense institution and coercive apparatus operating in domestic space, but as a regional and international actor. Much recent scholarship on and press coverage of Egypt since the uprisings of 2011 have neglected the vibrant and contentious history of the country's participation in globalist politics and international interventions. In this light, this study reflects upon three types of globalism—decolonizing developmentalism, humanitarian militarism, and UN-centered internationalism—articulated by the state, political elites, and transnational social movements in Egypt since the 1950s. This piece describes globalization in Egypt from military and diplomatic history perspectives. Here I begin to develop a theoretical apparatus that aims to identify mechanisms that shape convergence and disjuncture between modes of* developmentalism *and* internationalism *in three periods: the Third Worldist (1956–1973), Neoliberal (1973–2000), and Human Security (2000–2011) epochs.*

In 2011 the Armed Forces of Egypt reentered the global history stage with a vengeance—as a collective agent of (counter) revolution and coercion; as conjurer of class, gender, and sectarian phobias; as an arbiter of global financial arrangements; and as an advocate of a revived 'Third Worldist' humanitarian internationalism. Egypt's Armed Forces during this period reflected—

and aggravated—the violent contradictions of a region experiencing social revolution and democratic transition. During the Arab Spring events, Egypt's military intrigues and convolutions served as supercharged feedback loops, amplifying the crises of dominant models of globalization, humanitarianism, neoliberalism, and militarism, emitting indiscriminate shockwaves of repressive gender, class, and sectarian violence. The military emitted mixed signals as it adapted past interventionist doctrines and military models to the twenty-first century momentum of an emergent Global South centered, multipolar world order, asserting itself as a collective economic agent intervening in patterns of globalization, a repressive political apparatus in the domestic context, an interventionist in the Middle East regional context, and an ardent internationalist in the global context.

This study reflects upon the past legacies and political conjunctures that allowed the Egyptian military in 2011 to return to or flirt with roles and agendas identified with the revolutionary decolonization era of the 1950s (Aclimandos, 2001, 2005; Frisch, 2001; Harb, 2003; Perlmutter, 1969; Vatikiotis, 1975), raising a new set of questions about military institutions, globalization dynamics, and internationalist discourses in Egypt today. And I examine in historical sequence three types of globalism —decolonizing developmentalism, humanitarian militarism, and UN-centered internationalism—articulated by the state, political elites, and transnational social movements in Egypt since the 1950s. Egypt's legacies of globalism have been neglected by recent scholarship on and press coverage of Egypt's military and diplomatic assertions since the uprisings of 2011. Here I begin to develop a theoretical apparatus that identifies mechanisms that shape convergence and disjuncture between modes of *developmentalism* and *internationalism* in three periods: the Third Worldist (1956–1973), Neoliberal (1973–2000), and Human Security (2000–2011) epochs. This study is still largely descriptive because my reflections represent a preliminary exercise, the initial 'ground clearing' stage of a larger research project on the current contradictions of militarism, sovereignty, and humanitarian intervention in the post-'Arab Spring' Middle East region.

Third Worldist Period

During a brief window of experimentation and opportunity that extended from the mid-1950s to the mid-1970s, Egyptian military actors and institutions emerged as central players and global innovators in a surprisingly radical combination of decolonizing developmentalism with internationalist peacekeeping practices. Not unified by any explicit anti-capitalist ideology (Cook, 2011; Aclimandos, 2008), Egyptian nationalists in and around the Armed Forces started focusing on megaprojects of infrastructure—the Aswan Dam, Lake Nasser, the Suez Canal, roads, airports, oil wells, and military bases—in what President Gamal Abdel Nasser described in his speeches (Nasser, 1962, 1966) as an effort to cement a new world system of independence for decolonized peoples. These grand projects would replace colonial patterns of commercial dependence and military submission with a new grid of circulations, protections, and alliances. I label this nationalistic, territorially focused politics of infrastructural interventions 'infranationalism' (Amar, 2012).

During the Third Worldist period, these infranationalist forms of decolonizing developmentalism melded with United Nations-deployed forms of peacekeeping interventionism. The mechanisms that enabled this fusion included (1) realignment in the postcolonial international system that facilitated the rise of Third Worldism and Non-Aligned Movement politics, (2) actions that triggered a brief but extraordinary breach in the logic of cold war bipolarism which temporarily repositioned US interests, and (3) the Egyptian military's assertion of decolonizing infranationalism on the world stage. All combined, these factors favored the United Nations' validation of Egypt's globalist vision.

In the years following Egypt's 1952 revolution, the Revolutionary Command Council of the Egyptian military launched waves of domestic repression (Abdel-Malek, 1968; Brownlee, 2007, pp. 52–53; Dekmejian, 1971; El Kosheri Mahfouz, 1972) that resembled somewhat their actions in the face-offs with protesters in 2011. However, on the international scale in the 1950s and 1960s they identified with anti-colonial state-building projects and with what we would call today an alternative globalization movement. Egypt's emergence from colonial dependency and onto the world stage of Third Worldism did not happen with the 1952 revolution that threw out the occupying British bankers and troops, but with the nationalization of the Suez Canal on 26 July 1956 (Hallberg, 1975, p. 375).

In an attempt to reduce its economic dependence and political vassal status, Egypt's military moved in early 1956 to strengthen ties with the Soviet Union and distance itself from the US and the UK (Shupe et al., 1980, p. 479). In early 1956, Egypt also recognized the People's Republic of China at a time when the US was still clinging to the nationalist KMT regime in Taiwan. In response, Britain and the US withdrew their offer to finance the Aswan Dam (Shupe et al., p. 480). For the Egyptian military, the Aswan Dam served as a monumental example that mega-infrastructure projects would concretize a new notion of sovereignty. The Egyptian military served as the central technical-organizational force of this Third Worldist notion of sovereignty. Infranationalism became a decolonizing agenda as Nasser took advantage of the Aswan Dam crisis, seizing this opportunity to 'delink' from patterns of Eurocentric power, as Egyptian dependency theorist Samir Amin called it (1990). This meant Egypt would sever colonial patterns of commercial domination, led by a military that shifted the attention of the nation and the world from one hydrological megaproject, the dam, to another, the canal.

From the perspective of Egyptian nationalists, the Suez Canal long stood as a monument that embodied the deceit and injustice of colonial-capitalist globalization. The canal had been built entirely by Egyptian corvée labor (forced, conscript labor) for the benefit of European merchants and investors (Mitchell, 1988, pp. 96–97). Thousands of Egyptian workers died during its 10-year (1859–1869) construction (Beinin, 2001). French engineer Ferdinand de Lesseps received all the credit for building the canal, while the Egyptian treasury received all the bills. In a further act of humiliation, in 1882 when Egypt was unable to meet the steep debt payments imposed by European Suez Canal shareholders, Britain used the default to justify the invasion of Egypt and the establishment of financial and political dominion over the country (Vatikiotis, 1991, pp. 154ff).

By the 1950s, the Suez Canal continued to serve, more than ever, as the lifeline that connected Britain and France to its colonial and postcolonial dominions in South and Southeast Asia and East Africa. The canal also enabled large-scale oil shipments whose military and industrial importance had become apparent during World War II. Suez also provided naval supremacy and troop-transport routes so that Britain could provide support to allies in the Baghdad Pact of 1955 (Britain, Turkey, Iraq, Iran, and Pakistan) (Shupe et al., 1980, p. 478) and the Manila Pact of 1954 (Thailand, Philippines, New Zealand, Australia, Pakistan, France, US, UK) (Southeast Asia Collective Defense Treaty, 1954). During a rousing public speech on 26 July 1956, Nasser carefully pronounced the name 'Ferdinand de Lesseps', a code-word that signaled to his troops to move in and occupy the canal. Britain, enraged over the loss of 'its' canal and at the threat to its Baghdad Pact, moved to invade Egypt, retake the canal, and depose Nasser (Goodman, 2006). France—which was furious with the Egyptian military for supporting freedom fighters in Algeria—joined Britain's plan. In Israel, David Ben Gurion and IDF Chief of Staff Moshe Dayan saw this crisis as a chance to end the Egyptian Revolution and to assert Israeli control of the Red Sea.

On 29 October 1956 the 'Tripartite Aggression' began with an Israeli assault within Israel on Arab villages suspected of serving as Nasser's 'fifth column'. Then the IDF began a push through the Sinai toward the canal. The French Air Force was then to launch bombing sorties and deploy parachutists, redeployed from the Indochinese and Algerian Wars. Their aim was to unleash an 'aero-psychological campaign' (a proto-'Shock and Awe' operation) to produce an 'ever increasing disruption of Egyptian economy, morale, administration and armed forces' (Kyle, 1991, p. 237). But the Egyptian Armed Forces scored early successes. The Egyptian Navy attacked Haifa; a popular uprising of Palestinians took Gaza; and Egyptian Army operations enjoyed moderate success in slowing the Israeli advance across the Sinai. Nevertheless, a rain of British paratroopers did succeed in taking the canal itself and the French shock-and-awe mission was averted.

UN Peacekeeping Mixes Decolonizing Internationalism and Egyptian Infranationalism

As the military invasion of the Sinai proceeded, in Hungary the Soviet Army was crushing independence uprisings and pro-democracy movements. Simultaneously, in Britain, huge mass protests among Labour Party and progressive activists demanded that both Soviet repressions in Hungary and British imperial aggressions in Egypt end and that the UN step forward to protect popular uprisings and self-determination campaigns worldwide (Newens, 2006). President Eisenhower's administration in the US worried that it could not continue to strongly denounce the Soviet action in Hungary while also championing the Anglo–French–Israeli aggression in Egypt. For an extraordinary but brief moment, the US joined with its fellow large postcolonial power as a UN Third Worldist. Republican President Eisenhower joined with Jawaharlal Nehru, the socialist prime minister of India, to draft and pass a UN General Assembly resolution demanding the end of British, French, and Israeli aggressions in Egypt, the withdrawal of all foreign troops, and the restoration of pre-invasion borders (Smolansky, 1965, pp. 588–589). Under US and UN pressure, Britain and France withdrew from Egypt and relinquished their claims to the canal, although it took another year to pressure Israel to withdraw.

During this extraordinary moment, the Egyptian military became partners and hosts of the first United Nations 'blue helmet' humanitarian peacekeeping operation, the United Nations Emergency Force (UNEF) (*BBC News*, 2000; Goulding, 1993). Embodying the UN mission for decolonization and against aggressive war, UNEF aimed to escort all foreign forces out of Egypt and to protect Egypt's borders and Nasser's government from threats, particularly from Israel. Egypt had also been central to the staffing and organization of the predecessor UN Truce Supervision Organization (UNTSO), established in (British controlled) Cairo after Israel's emergence in the 1948 war, to patrol the boundaries of the new state of Israel as well as to protect displaced Arab populations (UNTSO, n.d.). The UNTSO force—a transitional structure between the League of Nations notion of a protectorate and a modern UN operation—was not yet labeled either 'peacekeeping' or 'humanitarian'. In 1956, UNEF forces (building upon UNTSO) were stationed in the Sinai and Gaza (which was governed by Egypt until the Israeli invasion during the 1967 war). UNEF's headquarters was in Gaza. Canadian Army officials oversaw the first months of deployments, but after 1959 UNEF deployments began to reflect Third Worldist or Non-Aligned Movement internationalism and its increasing assertiveness at the UN (Mansour, 1977). From 1959 to 1967, UNEF operational leadership alternated regularly between generals from India and Brazil. In a parallel expression of UN humanitarianism in this early incarnation as a decolonization force, Egyptian paratroop battalions cooperated with Irish and Canadian forces in 1960 to launch the UN Operation in Congo (ONUC) to usher Belgian forces out of the country and assure its independence (UN ONUC, 2001).

President Eisenhower's flirtations with portraying the US as an ally of decolonization and UN-based Third Worldism were short-lived. As Arab nationalism and the Non-Aligned Movement gained momentum, the US turned its power against it. In 1958, the Free Officers in Iraq led a Nasser-like revolution against US/British ally King Faisal II; and then in the same year, the majority of Lebanese rose up to support joining Nasser's United Arab Republic (Cleveland, 2000, pp. 326–327) (the UAR united Egypt and Syria as the first stage of an anticipated pan-Arab political and economic union). Despite the fact that a UN Security Council investigation sent to Lebanon found no evidence of UAR or Egyptian military interference in Lebanon, Eisenhower launched 'Operation Blue Bat', the first expression of what was to be the Eisenhower Doctrine (Cleveland, 2000, p. 327; GlobalSecurity.org, n.d.). Blue Bat dropped 40,000 US troops into Beirut to support Maronite Christians and anti-Nasserists in the country. This invasion forced a reversal in Lebanon's drift toward Third Worldism and Arabism (and also sowed the seeds of decades of civil war to come).

In Cairo in June 1961, Indonesia's Sukarno, India's Nehru, and Egypt's Nasser drew up the principles of the Non-Aligned Movement (Morphet, 2004). The Non-Aligned Movement is often thought of as an economic and diplomatic grouping. But four of its five founding principles were military in nature. Documents from 1961 underlined that member countries must support movements for national independence, none should be a member of a multilateral military alliance 'concluded in the context of Great Power conflicts', and no member may shape bilateral military agreements or military base concessions in the interest of Great Power conflicts. During this period, the Egyptian military hosted and staged the founding of the United Nations peacekeeping operations (and the operationalization of the UN as a postcolonial force, in general). These meetings articulated the principles of the new Third World arc of agendas and aspirations that had begun to emerge in Bandung in 1955 but which gradually came to a close as Egyptian military and 'humanitarian intervention' in Yemen exhausted its promise.

From 1962 to 1970, the Egyptian military invested a third of its manpower and much of its technology and leadership in the North Yemen Civil War, which served as a 'proxy war' between the project of Third Worldist emancipation and Great Power imperialism. Arab socialist rebels and Yemeni pro-democracy social movements were on one side (supported by the Egyptian military) and right-wing tribal and Yemeni religious leaders were on the other (supported by Saudi Arabia, the US, Israel, and Britain) (Dawisha, 1975). Nasser aimed to extend the Egyptian military's successes in the Algerian theater, where they had assisted the FLN in securing the North African country's independence from France. Anwar Sadat led the Egyptian forces, while Israel sent Mossad forces and dropped supplies from the air to support the royalists (Jones, 2004, p. 136), with Golda Meir sending increasing support after 1969. At a huge cost, the Egyptian military succeeded in supporting the Yemeni Revolution and holding back the Saudis and allies. A republic was founded in North Yemen after 1967, although Egypt's conflicts with Israel during and after 1967 shifted attention from Yemen and allowed royalists and tribalists to trickle back into leadership positions in North Yemen over the next 20 years and gradually to regain much power.

In South Yemen, the British military withdrew and a Soviet-backed and Nasser-friendly socialist regime was founded in 1967 (Cleveland, 2000, p. 440). The military exhaustion of Yemen and the cost to Cairo's treasury weakened Egypt and probably caused its feeble military performance in the 1967 war with Israel (Barnett and Levy, 1991). But the Yemen conflict was a huge symbolic and strategic victory that nations on the Arabian Peninsula recall until today, positively or negatively. The Egyptian military had framed its Yemen intervention as a fraternal 'decolonizing humanitarian military intervention' along the same lines at the UNEF in Sinai (although Yemen operations were never endorsed or overseen by the UN). During the uprisings of 2011, protest groups in Yemen fondly remembered Egypt's military assistance in Yemen's struggle for democracy, socialism, and independence from Saudi Arabia and the British Empire in the 1960s (Robinson, 2011); they displayed pictures of Gamal Abdel Nasser and revived a nostalgic view intertwining Egyptian military heroism and pan-Arab populism that recall this pre-War on Terror, pre-neoliberal era.

The Neoliberal Period

During the neoliberal period in Egypt (roughly 1973 through the early 2000s) the two forms of Egyptian globalism—decolonizing internationalism and military-driven developmentalism—that had united during the Third Worldist period split apart. Findings presented below demonstrate that the mechanisms embedded in the Camp David Peace Accords as well as the IMF restructuring agreements, although they did not end the 'infranationalist' proclivities of the military, did reshape them radically. Military-associated developmentalism turned toward entrepreneurialism and investment-return maximization. They turned away from the aims of decolonization, delinking, or concretizing trade and defense patterns that favored the Third World. These same neoliberal mechanisms encouraged the Armed Forces to turn their attentions inward. The state began to outsource a broad swath of military and coercive practices to the 1.4 million officers of the Interior Ministry (police) and security services (Sayigh 2011, p. 403). Nevertheless, during this period the decolonizing legacies of Third Worldism and Egyptian internationalism did not vanish. In fact, they flourished in the realm of the UN system where these political projects and mobilizations had sought refuge from the neoliberal imperatives of military and financial spheres.

After the military defeat of the 1967 war and the exhaustion of the Egyptian Army in Yemen, Egypt turned inward, reflecting the 'Egypt First' policy of President Anwar Sadat, who became president upon Nasser's death in 1970 (Saliba, 1975). Sadat was one of the Free Officers who had led the revolution alongside Nasser and had commanded forces in Yemen. However, Sadat had fewer socialist and Third Worldist proclivities than his predecessor (Saliba, 1975). Turning away from socialism, Sadat was much more interested in remobilizing forms of moralism and Islamism in order to counter the protests of restive youth, workers, and other elements of the un-coopted left and pro-democracy movements (Harb, 2003, p. 288). Following the Camp David Accords of 1978, Sadat signed a controversial treaty with Israel in 1979, which bought the Egyptian military's compliance by explicitly redirecting their energies toward domestic infrastructure, tourism development, land development businesses (Springborg, 1989, p. 107; Gotowicki, 1997, p. 3). And the military continued its success in the arms manufacturing industry, producing artillery for regional armies, jets for China, helicopters for Britain, etc. (Sayigh, 1992, pp. 45–46; Vayrynen and Ohlson, 1986). Also during this period, a raft of free-trade-oriented Open Door policy and austere structural adjustment agreements were imposed at the IMF's behest which required the militarization of the police who repressed social resistance on the domestic front, particularly during the 'bread riots' in January 1977 (Harb, 2003, p. 288).

During the 1980s and 1990s, the Egyptian military was gradually ushered out of several Cabinet posts as the government was civilianized, but the Armed Forces continued to accumulate new kinds of power and influence, shielded from public scrutiny, as it avoided war (except in terms of its participation in covert rendition operations, US-partnered intelligence missions, and counterterrorism efforts) and focused on its projects. Most notably, Field Marshall Abd al-Halim Abu Ghazala (Defense Minister from 1981–89) built several major military owned and managed cities, such as Nasr City which provided "sumptuous flats" to military personnel at subsidized prices (Springborg, 1989), high-end shopping malls that sold a globalizing consumer lifestyle (Abaza, 2006, pp. 203–204) and "nurseries, schools, and military consumer 'cooperatives' which sell a range of domestic and imported products [to military men] at discount prices (Gotowicki, 1997, p. 10)." Its leadership became increasingly involved in profit-oriented tourism and canal, infrastructure, and settlement projects (Harb, 2003, p. 285), and in negotiating deals for arms and airplane contracts with Russia, China, and the US. Of course, the military in Egypt did not simply blend into society as just another group of private sector business interests. The military remained a patriotic organization staffed by universally conscripted male soldiers drawn from all classes and regions of the country. These soldiers had been trained in the revolutionary, anti-colonial discourse of the 1950s and taught to identify with the military's role as the protector of the people and of the Arab nation. Furthermore, the military leadership remained keenly aware of the fact that its control over crucial territories, resources, and economic development projects was not due to the market viability of these projects, nor to the military's technical or technological superiority (although the military does employ many of the country's top engineers and scientists). These activities of the 1980s and 1990s put the military into an intensely contradictory position as an economic actor in for-profit projects central to the neoliberal development model (tourism villages, elite housing settlements, oil/gas extraction facilities, free trade zone developments, etc.) and as a public sector sovereign whose role remains wholly dependent upon state authorization and national-security designation of these economic sovereignties.

Egypt Globalism Returns to the UN

In the 1990s, Egyptian globalism survived and prospered, particularly in and around the UN system, even as the military became increasingly parochial and internally focused. The survival or revival of these globalist (or, more properly, 'internationalist' as they became embedded in formal UN policy and legal-juridical frameworks) politics owe much to the unjustly slandered term of Egyptian Boutros Boutros-Ghali as Secretary General of the United Nations from 1992 to 1996. During his tenure in the 1970s as deputy foreign minister for Anwar Sadat, Western officials came to think of him as a mild-mannered, pro-Western official. He is a Coptic Christian, liberal, Paris-educated lawyer. By 1980, Boutros-Ghali had become identified with his work as a chief international law expert who drafted the Camp David Accords (Boutros-Ghali, 1999). He seemed a safe choice to be the first Secretary General from the Global South. But the US diplomats who had supported his nomination had not read his extensive writings in French and Arabic on international socialism, decolonization, and international law; African and Arab unification; and his detailed juridical and social arguments for strengthening forms of 'decolonized' and democratized cosmopolitan justice (Boutros-Ghali, 1963, 1968, 1971, 1993, 1995a, 1995b, 1996). Although he had been best known in the US for his work for Sadat and at Camp David (Boutros-Ghali, 1997), Boutros-Ghali's identity as an international jurist was shaped in the 1940s to 1960s, the age of decolonization, the Suez Crisis, the Bandung conference, and Third Worldism (Boutros-Ghali, 1969, 1972; Boutros-Ghali and Shallalah, 1958, p. iii; Prashad, 2008, p. 292). Many of his principles, and the force of his conviction, returned with surprising force when he assumed the title responsibilities of UN Secretary General.

Boutros-Ghali's boldest contribution as Secretary General was his articulation of the *Agenda for Peace* (1992) (Boutros-Ghali, 1995a), which laid out a military role for UN humanitarian intervention and peacekeeping activities. This role would be strictly based in a 'neutral' interpretation of international law rather than in response to the realpolitik of Security Council powers. Its application was to be guided by the Global South dominated General Assembly rather than manipulated by the Global North dominated Security Council. Taking advantage of the end of the cold war, and the possible emergence of a multipolar rather than superpower centered world order, Boutros-Ghali, inspired by the UNEF mission of 1956, declared that the UN would develop a humanitarian military arm for stopping gross violations of human rights and wars of aggression, and would follow consistent and neutral internationalist frameworks, blocking the tendency of superpowers to instrumentalize humanitarian and peacekeeping interventions to assert hegemony.

His *Agenda for Peace* was also aimed at arresting the trend in the 1980s of northern powers funding guerrilla and paramilitary operations in the Global South to undermine popular movements or national independence struggles there. Thus, the first actualization of the *Agenda for Peace* was in the El Salvador Reconciliation and Pacification agreement, which successfully demilitarized paramilitaries and ended international interference in conflict and insurgency in that country. Extending these principles, Boutros-Ghali subsequently launched an *Agenda for Development* (1995b), which included a strong critique of neoliberalism and put global redistribution and southern economic autonomy back on the UN agenda. Not stopping there, he launched a move to redemocratize the UN, aiming to move the center of decision-making back to the General Assembly and out of the hands of the Security Council powers (Carlsson, 1995). These moves, taken together, shocked and threatened the United States, which had wrongly thought they could manipulate Boutros-Ghali. When Boutros-Ghali challenged the legality of NATO's bombing of Yugoslavia and when he implied that the UN would need to deploy 'peace enforcement' activities in Israel and the Occupied Territories after the 1993 Oslo Accords, the US lashed out against him. US Secretary of State Madelaine Albright crafted the 'Operation Orient Express', which aimed to fire Boutros-Ghali and put him on the 'train' back to Cairo (Boutros-Ghali, 1999; Traub, 2006, p. 63). Thanks to US maneuvering in the Security Council, Boutros-Ghali became the only Secretary General not reappointed to his post.

Some of the same themes and dramatic conflicts unfolded when another prominent Egyptian lawyer ascended to a top position in the United Nations a few years later, bringing Egyptian internationalism to bear on the realm of arms-control and weapons-inspections regimes. Dr Mohammed ElBaradei, like Boutros-Ghali, is certainly not a military man, and was always a liberal internationalist who had challenged Nasser's authoritarian statism and militarized nationalism. Yet, in his youth, he served Nasser's government as a diplomat in Egypt's foreign ministry delegation to the United Nations, specializing in arms-control law (IAEA, n.d.). In 1997, the General Conference of the International Atomic Energy Agency appointed ElBaradei as Director General (IAEA, n.d.). In that same year the agency had adopted a new Model Additional Protocol that empowered it to engage in much more aggressive intervention to investigate and monitor violations of nonproliferation agreements. Like Boutros-Ghali, ElBaradei assumed leadership of a UN organization empowered to be more forceful and interventionist in the post-cold war era; and again like Boutros-Ghali, he refused to tailor this new power to the dictates of the United States. ElBaradei's earlier publications did not match the diversity and radical breadth of Boutros-Ghali's but did cover topics from disaster relief (ElBaradei, 1982), international law reform (ElBaradei et al., 1981), and global negotiations from a Global South perspective (ElBaradei and Gavin, 1981). In the lead-up to the US invasion of Iraq in 2003, ElBaradei insisted that the UN weapons inspections and IAEA investigations sent to Iraq over the past several years had done their work successfully and thoroughly (ElBaradei, 2011), that Saddam Hussein had no weapons of mass destruction, and that the Bush administration's 'evidence' to the contrary was fraudulent (Pincus and Milbank, 2003). ElBaradei eventually demanded a war crimes tribunal be set up in order to try the US administration for violations in Iraq. In the 2007–2009 period, when the US was accusing Iran of developing nuclear weapons, ElBaradei again articulated the voices of post-cold war internationalism, insisting that Iran's nuclear program was consistent with international nonproliferation law and had no military aims or potential, and that those in Israel demanding military intervention against Iran were 'crazy' (Cohen, 2009).

In October 2005, he was awarded the Nobel Peace Prize for his efforts. Also in 2005, US Ambassador to the UN John Bolton and Secretary of State Condoleeza Rice targeted Dr ElBaradei (EGY Leaks, 2011). The US tried again to use its influence to fire a prominent Egyptian UN official, but by this time, opposition was mounted. Russia, China, and the Non-Aligned Movement refused to let the US remove ElBaradei, and he was reappointed until he decided to retire in November 2009 (EGY Leaks, 2011). Soon after this, he reentered Egyptian politics and became one of the leading figures in the Egyptian Revolution, perhaps the only leader that during 2011 enjoyed influence and legitimacy on all sides of this polarized struggle. ElBaradei had a degree of 'Tahrir credibility' among youth movements, was trusted by the Muslim Brothers, was supported by the judicial establishment, was considered a patriot by many in the military, and maintained international credibility and recognition.

The 'Human Security' Age

More recently, from the late 1990s through 2011, developmentalism and internationalism were brought back together, and the Egyptian military turned outward again. In this period, the Armed Forces gradually reclaimed their military and coercive identity from the police and security apparatus and reengaged in global-scale and UN-system missions. But this rearticulation of military-driven developmentalism with internationalist interventionism did not proceed along the same lines as it did during the Third Worldist era. In the period of 'human security globalization' and militarized humanitarianism, the Egyptian military adopted a more humanitarian discourse characterized by moralizing, paternalistic, and civilizing aspirations rather than radical world-systems visions or emancipatory social-justice aims. This new kind of humanitarian discourse accompanied an increasingly paramilitarized and oligarchical set of practices and institutions.

During the late 1990s and the 2000s, the contradictions of the Egyptian military's involvement in neoliberal business and development projects intensified as clashes became apparent between military leaders' roles as protectors of the people and as self-interested mega-contractors or men of big business (Blumberg, 2011; Frisch, 2001; Gotowicki, 1997). This increasingly troubling and visible contradiction did not lead the military to back away from economic activities. To the contrary, they were able to take advantage of emerging countries' increasing interest in Egypt's large markets, workforce, resources, and infrastructure, as well as Egypt's access to the Gulf, Mediterranean, and Africa. Thus military leaders leveraged increasingly lucrative deals and increased their strategic centrality in the state and economy (Al-Khalsan, 2011). While it pursued these economic deals, the military did not ignore the changes happening in the discourses of intervention at the international level. Thus, during this period, the military began tentatively to return to active mobilization, projecting its capacity through humanitarian and 'human security' interventions that allowed it to expand its visibility and return to duty without threatening its commitments to the Camp David framework.

The first major reentry of Egypt's military into more than an 'observer' role was in its participation the ill-fated UN mission to Somalia, UNOSOM II (UNOSOM II, 2003). In June

1993, UN peacekeeping forces, led by US and Pakistani troops, received the order to launch direct attacks on rebel warlord Mohammad Farah Aidid. After generating substantial civilian casualties, becoming identified as foreign interlopers, and suffering military setbacks, the UN mission retreated. After the Somalia debacle, Egyptian interest in humanitarian internationalism continued to wane after it had supported the UN authorized US action against Iraq in Kuwait in 1991. But Egyptian military interest revived again with its highly visible participation in peacekeeping activities in Bosnia, where, for a change, it seemed the UN humanitarians and a Muslim civilian population were on the same side.

From 1992 to 1998, Egypt's TABA battalion in Sarajevo, originally launched as part of UN peacekeeping operations, became a model for remaking Egyptian military and humanitarian identities on the international stage. Although Egypt's Boutros-Ghali was not a supporter of the NATO bombing of Serbian forces in Bosnia-Herzegovina in 1995, he had enthusiastically backed previous Arab participation in international peacekeeping and humanitarian activities in the province to avert civil war (Said, 2003, p. 190). Egypt's TABA battalion patrolled Sarajevo's northern frontier, kept warring factions separated, and hosted the meetings of the Serb, Croat, and Bosnian presidents (Said, 2003, p. 190). And TABA, a full infantry battalion, provided regular food, supplies, and medical care to the population of Sarajevo for several years, earning them the gratitude of local officials. 'The hospital of the TABA battalion treated 57,876 patients. Additionally, they were instrumental in the restoration of 18 km of gas pipeline in Sarajevo, 2 km of water pipes, and they provided over 13 tons of food to the locals' (Said, 2005). The spectacle of the UN and Egyptian troops working together again, this time to provide assistance to Muslims, helped restore the reputation of the international agency in the eyes of the Egyptian media. And this process allowed for the Egyptian military to return to the field of battle in its reappropriated role as a leader in the transnational rescue industry. Egypt's role in Bosnia also served as a laboratory for reestablishing the Mediterranean as a sphere for regional and international security and humanitarian cooperation on a significant scale (Said, 2003, 2005). In the context of this increasing visibility and interest of the military, the Cairo Center for Training in Conflict Resolution and Peacekeeping was established in 1995, and a new program for humanitarian diplomacy and peacekeeping operations was established at the Nasser Military Academy.

After the Bosnia mission, Egypt's more visible military operations included the hybrid UN/African Union peacekeeping mission in Darfur, Sudan (UNAMID), and the UN peacekeeping mission in Sudan, UNMIS, that oversaw the referendum and separation process between north and south (UNMIS, 2011). UNMIS was overseen by Indian and Nigerian generals, but Egypt played a key role providing military troops, police brigades, and military-engineer personnel in charge of building projects. Although Egypt was not in a very good position to serve as a neutral peacekeeper since it had served as a colonial occupier of the Sudan between 1899 and 1956 (Daly, 2004). Also, Egyptian officials made statements indicating that they thought a Western conspiracy was behind the independence movement in South Sudan. In July 2011, in the Nuban mountain region of oil-rich South Kordofan (a province just on the north side of the new border with South Sudan), Egyptian troops stood by and watched a massacre of Nuban civilians just outside the UN compound (Howden, 2011). Faced with accusations of serving the Khartoum government's attempts to crush 'southern' resistance in the province or of siding with 'Arabs' against 'Africans', an Egyptian captain claimed that they were there not to 'make peace' but to 'observe' (Howden, 2011). Egyptian participation in the much larger UN–African Union mission in Darfur was plagued by similar incidents of inaction and accusations of pro-'Arab' bias. But in Egypt, the missions in Sudan were very popular among military leaders, who celebrated them for reviving the solidarity between the Sudan and Egypt that existed in the wars of 1948, and reuniting the peoples of the Nile. After two Egyptian soldier-peacekeepers in UNAMID were killed in Darfur (Lavallee, 2010), their 'martyrdom' provoked an explosion of hagiographic press coverage in Egypt and they received military honors for their service (*Egyptian Gazette*, 2010). And in 2003 Egypt's military staged a large parade in Khartoum to honor the expansion of Egyptian humanitarian military activities in Africa (*Sudan Vision*, 2003).

In February 2009, Egypt decided to send 1,325 peacekeepers to the Congo, about half of the overall UN commitment. 'Egypt said . . . its contribution to the force would . . . includ[e] a motorised infantry battalion, paratroopers, special forces and military engineers. Egypt would also send an interior ministry police unit whose mission would include protecting individuals and employees of the United Nations and its institutions, assisting the Congolese police and conducting joint patrols with them in the east' (*Reuters*, 2009). In July 2011, Egyptian participation in the Sudan (UNMIS) ended and a large Ethiopian force was brought in (at the suggestion of the United States). Nevertheless, on 13 December 2011, Ahmed Fathallah announced that Egypt's military participation in other UN peacekeeping missions in Liberia and elsewhere in Africa would be greatly expanded (Egypt State Information Service, 2011).

In the context of neighboring Arab Spring uprisings in Libya and Yemen, Egypt's potential role as leader of a Pan-African or Pan-Islamic stabilizing or humanitarian intervention has been raised. The Arab League in 2011 found itself split into four factions: those grouped around Saudi Arabia and the GCC (Gulf Cooperation Council), those more sympathetic to Iran, those who identify as pro-Western monarchies, and the tumultuous republics of the Arab Spring. Thus the league was unable to provide clear leadership either on the humanitarian and military conflicts in Libya or Syria. The GCC did step forward to support NATO's Libyan air campaign, but did not supply any substantive hardware (O'Brian and Sinclair, 2011). The Egyptian military set up massive camps and hospitals on the border with Libya and sent planes inside the country to lift out stranded expatriate workers (AlertNet, 2011). Meanwhile, the The African Union stood more firmly behind Qaddhafi (*Reuters*, 2011), but could not mobilize a consensus behind a peacekeeping intervention. Such an AU mission could have included substantial Egyptian military participation and served as an alternative to the NATO campaign. Instead, immediately after the fall of Qaddhafi, Turkey and Egypt began developing a series of bilateral cooperation agreements around business development, oil drilling in the Mediterranean, and education (*Xinhua*, 2011). The two countries have launched a Supreme Council for Strategic Cooperation (*Xinhua*, 2011), which could be a vehicle for developing joint humanitarian military intervention, particularly in Libya, if civil strife or conflict should erupt, or an invitation from the new government in Tripoli should arrive.

Given the complex history of Egyptian revolutionary and 'humanitarian' military involvement in Yemen during the 1960s, the parties in Yemen associated with Saudi Arabia, the US, and the GCC resisted Egypt's participation in peacekeeping activities there in the wake of the mass uprisings of 2011. But they may be brought in or at least evoked at the behest of youth protesters, who still see the Egyptian military as their historical ally, a counterweight to Saudi influence.

Conclusion

For the Armed Forces of Egypt, the mass uprisings against Mubarak in January and February 2011 provided both a critical challenge and historic opportunity. On 11 February, army leaders made the bold move of siding with mass public uprisings in Cairo's Tahrir Square and throughout the country. The Supreme Council of the Armed Forces (SCAF) declared the end of the long reign of President Hosni Mubarak and forced the president to step down (Masoud, 2011). Soon after, the SCAF put President Mubarak, his sons, and his wife in jail and on trial for gross corruption, dismissed Vice President Omar Suleiman (chief of the Intelligence Services and a key CIA counterterrorism ally), absorbed the loathed 'SS' (State Security), turned against the terrifying, corrupt interior ministry (Amar, 2011b, 2011c), and allowed the public to storm and destroy police stations across the country (Amar, 2011a; Dawoud, 2011).

As this drama unfolded, the Egyptian military moved to swiftly retake many of the roles and influence it had in the 1950s and 1960s, before the Camp David Peace Accords with Israel (1979). The heart of these accords consisted of a bargain (Quandt, 1988; Telhami, 1992) in which the Egyptian military agreed to exchange wars abroad for business and development activities at home (Albrecht and Bishara, 2011; Safty, 1991). Thus, during the 1980s and 1990s, Egypt's military reidentified as a technocratic and entrepreneurial group of development contractors, launching infrastructure projects, and utilizing their combat training only in the context of limited peacekeeping and humanitarian operations (Frisch, 2001; Gotowicki, 1997). They were to serve as a force not for escalation but for demilitarization in the region, particularly in the Sinai, the Suez Canal, and at the border with Israel. In 2011, the Egyptian Army reentered and remilitarized the Sinai Peninsula, a move legitimized by Israel's repeated violation of the Egyptian border and by the IDF's most recent killing of Egyptian border guards on 19 August 2011 (*The Telegraph*, 2011). On 9 September, when youth protesters moved to occupy the Israeli Embassy, the Egyptian military did not intervene as the activists entered the diplomatic building, leading to the flight of the Israeli ambassador from the country (*CBC News*, 2011). However, army leaders condemned the youth the next day in a move that became the SCAF's hallmark: use the Tahrir youth to do their dirty work and then punish them savagely.

On the globalization front, the Armed Forces asserted themselves boldly in 2011, rejecting IMF and World Bank loans to sustain the country during its transition (Mekay, 2011), freezing the assets of some of Egypt's wealthiest capitalists and Mubarak's most corrupt cronies, and suspending or overturning the privatization of textile factories whose sale to Malaysian investors had been a major trigger of mass protests. But the military also revealed how invested it had become in the economic projects associated with 1990s neoliberal globalization as well as with twenty-first century business deals and bilateral contracts that had recently become the hallmark of the new 'BRICS' form of globalization. As privileged entrepreneurs, the Egyptian Army had redeveloped the huge swaths of desert 'military zone' land into tourist resorts (Blumberg, 2011), they had dug Toshka (Baker, 1997), an environmentally questionable 'new branch of the Nile' to support Saudi–Egyptian agribusiness partnerships, and signed oil and gas extraction deals and aviation and tank co-production contracts with Brazil and Russia. While international commentators focused on whether the US should withhold its $1.3 billion in aid much of which goes to the military, they ignored the fact that this figure may not be a powerful lever given that the armed forces generate more than $14 billion in revenue from their business activities annually (Mayton, 2011). As a super-organized expression of national capital and state capitalism, and as an arbiter of multivalent forms of globalization, the military was torn between the Arab Spring's resurgent populist spirit of Arab nationalism (its patriotic insistence that public sectors and states reclaim their sovereignty on behalf of their peoples), and the spirit of political risk management (to revive tourism revenues and stabilize its bilateral agreements and lucrative contracts).

On the humanitarian-intervention front, the Egyptian Armed Forces began to reassert and 'remember' their history as pioneers of internationalism and Third Worldism. The SCAF appointed Nabil ElArabi, a brilliant and well-respected international law specialist and World Court Judge (2001–2006) as the first post-Mubarak foreign minister and then as Secretary General of the Arab League (Ezzat, 2011). Egypt signed the treaty of the International Criminal Court (Human Rights Watch, 2011), and set Egypt and the Arab League at the center of new and urgent debates around the legitimacy of militarized humanitarian intervention in an age when human rights and democracy uprisings are ascending, and in which the Western 'imperialist' instrumentalization of humanitarian intervention is being challenged more stridently by Russia, China, Brazil, the African Union, the Bolivarian Bloc (Venezuela, Cuba, Bolivia, Nicaragua, and Ecuador), and other groupings that are explicitly reviving the spirit and legacy of the Non-Aligned Movement. These groupings reflect much of the doctrine that used to be called 'Third Worldism', but is now more likely to be portrayed as a history-less 'emergent Global South-centric' world order. In this context, the Egyptian military quietly cooperated with its fellow Arab Spring revolutionists, the Tunisian Military, to facilitate NATO support for insurgents and to provide their own humanitarian aid to displaced workers in Libya, but it also worked to reassure Chinese and Russian state and corporate investors that the Egyptian Armed Forces would help them reap the rewards of future oil and development deals in Libya. The Egyptian military signaled that it may offer large-scale 'humanitarian interventions' into Yemen or the newly partitioned Sudan if the GCC and US-supported agreements and mechanisms were insufficient in guaranteeing Egypt's interests, as the guardian of reborn Arab nationalism, and as the protector of the waters of the Red Sea (whose exit to the Indian Ocean is flanked by Yemen and Somalia) and the Nile River (which flows for 3,000 kilometers through North and South Sudan).

This study has offered an initial review of the legacies of Egyptian military and diplomatic globalism, tracing the processes that enabled the fusion, then splitting, then reuniting of developmentalist politics and internationalist advocacy during the transitions from Third World decolonization to neoliberal restructuring to the new era of humanitarian militarism and 'human security globalization'. Further work should continue to energize current discussions of Egypt's internationalist cultures and histories and the roles these revived legacies can play in challenging antidemocratic development models and authoritarian military governance practices in the region.

References

Abaza, M. (2006) Egyptianizing the American Dream: Nasr City's shopping malls, public order, and the privatized military, in D. Singerman, P. Amar (eds.), *Cairo Cosmopolitan: Politics, Culture, and Urban Space in the New Globalized Middle East* (Cairo: American University in Cairo Press), pp. 193–220.

Abdel-Malek, A. (1968) *Egypt: Military Society: The Army Regime, the Left, and Social Change Under Nasser* (New York: Random House).

Albrecht, H. & Bishara, D. (2011) Back on horseback: the military and political transformation in Egypt, *Middle East Law and Governance*, 3(1–2), pp. 13–23.

AlertNet (2011) Egypt army opens camps, hospitals on Libya Border, 21 February, http://www.trust.org/alertnet/news/egypt-army-opens-camps-hospitals-on-libya-border

Aclimandos, T. (2001) Regard rétrospectif sur la Révolution égyptienne, ou le 23 juillet 1952, *Egypte Monde Arabe*, 4–5, pp. 15–39.

Aclimandos, T. (2005) Revisiting the history of the Egyptian army, in A. Goldschmidt (ed.) *Revisioning Egypt 1919–1952* (Cairo: American University in Cairo Press), pp. 68–93.

Aclimandos, T. (2008) Officiers libres et officiers communistes: collaborations et confrontations, *Cahiers d'histoire*, 105–106, pp. 175–202.

Amar, P. (2011a) Why Egypt's progressives win, *Jadaliyya*, 8 February, http://www.jadaliyya.com/pages/index/586/why-egypts-progressives-win.

Amar, P. (2011b) Why Mubarak is out, *Jadaliyya*, 1 February, http://www.jadaliyya.com/pages/index/516/why-mubarak-is-out-.

Amar, P. (2011c) Turning the gendered politics of the security state inside out? *International Feminist Journal of Politics*, 13(3), pp. 299–328.
Amar, P. (2012) *The Security Archipelago: 'Human Security' States, Sexuality Politics and the End of Neoliberalism* (Durham, NC: Duke University Press).
Amin, S. (1990) *Delinking: Toward a Polycentric World* (London: Zed Books).
Beinin, J. (2001) *Workers and Peasants in the Modern Middle East* (Cambridge: Cambridge University Press).
Baker, M. M. (1997) Mubarak: Toshka Project opens way towards new civilization in Egypt, printed, *The Executive Intelligence Review*, December 1997, http://american_almanac.tripod.com/toshka.htm.
Barnett, M. & Levy, J. (1991) Domestic sources of alliances and alignments: the case of Egypt 1962–1973, *International Organization*, 45(3), pp. 369–395.
BBC News (2000) UN Peacekeeping record, 23 August, http://news.bbc.co.uk/2/hi/health/892592.stm.
Blumberg, A. (2011) Why Egypt's military cares about Home appliances, *NPR, Planet Money*, 4 February, http://www.npr.org/blogs/money/2011/02/10/133501837/why-egypts-military-cares-about-home-appliances.
Boutros-Ghali, B. (1963) *Contribution à une Théorie Générale des Alliances* (Paris: A. Pedone).
Boutros-Ghali, B. (1968) *L'Organisation de L'Unité Africaine* (Paris: A. Colin).
Boutros-Ghali, B. (1971) *Les Difficultés Institutionnelles du Panafricanisme* (Geneva: Institut Universitaire de Hautes Etudes Internationales).
Boutros-Ghali, B. (1993) *From Madness to Hope: the 12-Year War in El Salvador* (New York: United Nations).
Boutros-Ghali, B. (1995a) *An Agenda for Peace* (New York: United Nations).
Boutros-Ghali, B. (1995b) *An Agenda for Development* (New York: United Nations, Dept. of Public Information).
Boutros-Ghali, B. (1996) *An Agenda for Democratization* (New York: United Nations, Dept. of Public Information).
Boutros-Ghali, B. (1997) *Egypt's Road to Jerusalem: a Diplomat's Story of the Struggle for Peace in the Middle East* (New York: Random House).
Boutros-Ghali, B. (1999) *Unvanquished: a US–UN Saga* (New York: Random House).
Boutros-Ghali, B. & Shallalah, Y. (1958) *Le Canal de Suez, 1854–1957* (Alexandria: Société Egyptienne de Droit International).
Boutros-Ghali, B. (1969) *Le Mouvement Afro-Asiatique* (Paris: Presses Universitaires de France).
Boutros-Ghali, B., El Kosheri Mahfouz, A. & Duverger, M. (1972) *Socialisme et pouvoir en Egypte* (Paris: Librairie générale de droit et de jurisprudence; dissertation).
Brownlee, J. (2007) *Authoritarianism in an Age of Democratization* (Cambridge, UK: Cambridge University Press).
Carlsson, I. (1995) The U.N. at 50: A Time to Reform, *Foreign Policy*, 100, 25th anniversary issue, pp. 3–18.
CBC News (2011) Ambassador flees Israeli Embassy in Cairo, Associated Press, 9 September, http://www.cbc.ca/news/world/story/2011/09/09/egypt-protests-israeli-embassy.html.
Cleveland, W. L. (2000) *A History of the Modern Middle East*, 2nd ed. (Boulder, CO: Westview Press).
Cohen, R. (2009) Realpolitik for Iran, *New York Times*, 12 April, http://www.nytimes.com/2009/04/13/opinion/13iht-edcohen.html.
Cook, S. (2007) *Ruling but not Governing: The Military and Political Development in Egypt and Turkey* (Baltimore: Johns Hopkins University Press).
Cook, S. (2011) *The Struggle for Egypt: From Nasser to Tahrir Square* (Oxford, UK: Oxford University Press).
Daly, M. W. (2004) *Empire on the Nile: The Anglo-Egyptian Sudan, 1898–1934* (Cambridge: Cambridge University Press).
Dawisha, A. I. (1975) Intervention in the Yemen: an analysis of Egyptian perceptions and policies, *Middle East Journal*, 29(1), pp. 47–63.
Dawoud, K. (2011) The challenge ahead, *Al-Ahram Weekly* online, 29 December, http://weekly.ahram.org.eg/2011/1078/eg11.htm.
Dekmejian, R. H. (1971) *Egypt Under Nasir: A Study in Political Dymanics* (Albany, NY: SUNY Press).
Director General's Statements (1999) 15th Summit of Non-Aligned Movement First Ladies' Summit. Food and Agriculture Organization of the United Nations. http://www.fao.org/about/diouf/statements2009@148954/en/.
Durac, V. (2009) The impact of external actors on the distribution of power in the Middle East: the case of Egypt, *The Journal of North African Studies*, 14(1), pp. 75–90.
EGY Leaks (2011) Mohammad ElBaradei. http://anarchitext.wordpress.com/2011/03/29/mohamed-elbaradei/.
Egypt State Information Service (2011) Liberia: Egyptian UN peacekeeping mission to be expanded. http://allafrica.com/stories/201112141258.html.
The Egyptian Gazette (2010) Military funeral for 2 Egyptians killed in Darfur, Masress online, 8 May, http://www.masress.com/en/egyptiangazette/7465.
ElBaradei, M. (1982) *Model Rules for Disaster Relief Operations* (New York: United Nations Institute for Training and Research).

ElBaradei, M. (2011) *The Age of Deception; Nuclear Diplomacy in Treacherous Times* (New York: Metropolitan Books/ Henry Holt & Co).
ElBaradei, M. & Gavin, C. (1981) *Crowded Agendas, Crowded Rooms, Institutional Arrangements at UNCLOS III: Some Lessons in Global Negotiations* (New York: United Nations Institute for Training and Research).
ElBaradei, M., Franck, T. M. & Trachtenbert, R. (1981) *The International Law Commission: the Need for a New Direction* (New York: United Nations Institute for Training and Research).
El Kosheri Mahfouz, A. (1972) *Socialisme et Pouvoir en Egypte* (Paris: Librairie générale de droit et de jurisprudence).
Ezzat, D. (2011) Nabil El-Arabi—justice-based diplomacy, *Al-Ahram* weekly online, 19–25 May, http://weekly.ahram.org.eg/2011/1048/re5.htm.
Frisch, H. (2001) Guns and butter in the Egyptian Army, *Middle East Review of International Affairs*, 5(2), pp. 1–12.
GlobalSecurity.org in the News (n.d.) Operation Blue Bat—1958. http://www.globalsecurity.org/military/ops/blue_bat.htm.
Goodman, G. (2006) Suez and Fleet Street, *BBC News*, 1 November, http://news.bbc.co.uk/2/hi/middle_east/6082076.stm.
Gotowicki, S. H. (1997), The role of the Egyptian military in domestic society, Foreign Military Studies Office Publications, Fort Leavenworth, KA. http://fmso.leavenworth.army.mil/documents/egypt/egypt.htm.
Goulding, M. (1993) The evolution of UN peacekeeping, *International Affairs*, 69(3), pp. 451–464.
Hallberg, C. (1974) *The Suez Canal: Its History and Diplomatic Importance* (London: Octagon Books).
Harb, I. (2003) The Egyptian military in politics: disengagement or accommodation? *Middle East Journal*, 57(2), pp. 269–290.
Heydemann, S. (2000) *War, Institutions, and Social Change in the Middle East* (Berkeley, CA: University of California Press).
Howden, D. (2011) UN accused of standing by while Sudanese forces killed civilians, *The Independent*, 8 July, http://www.independent.co.uk/news/world/africa/un-accused-of-standing-by-while-sudanese-forces-killed-civilians-2308896.html.
Human Rights Watch (2011) Egypt: important commitment to ratify Rome Statute, 29 April, http://www.hrw.org/news/2011/04/29/egypt-important-commitment-ratify-rome-statute.
International Atomic Energy Agency (IAEA) (n.d.) Director General Dr. Mohammad ElBaradei: Biography. http://www.iaea.org/About/dg/elbaradei/biography.html.
Jones, C. (2004) *Britain and the Yemen Civil War, 1962–1965: Ministers, Mercenaries and Mandarins* (Eastbourne, UK: Sussex Academic Press).
Kyle, K. (1991) *Suez: Britain's End of Empire in the Middle East* (London: I.B. Tauris Books).
Lavallee, G. (2010) Two Egyptian peacekeepers killed in Darfur ambush, *Agènce France Presse*, 7 May, http://www.google.com/hostednews/afp/article/ALeqM5jyyFb8nL9uJBbR3_7pbMkzk5QM-Q.
Mansour, Z. A. (1977) *The United Nations Emergency Force* (New York: Mansour).
Masoud, T. (2011) The road to (and from) Liberation Square, *Journal of Democracy*, 22(3), pp. 20–34. Online at Project Muse, Johns Hopkins University, http://muse.jhu.edu/login?uri=/journals/journal_of_democracy/v022/22.3.masoud.html.
Mayton, J. (2012) The Egyptian Army's Invisible Hand, *The Jesusalem Post*, 16 January.
Mekay, E. (2011), Egypt rejects IMF conditions, IPS News, 30 June, http://ipsnews.net/news.asp?idnews=56304.
Mitchell, T. (1988) *Colonising Egypt* (Berkeley & Los Angeles: University of California Press).
Morphet, S. (2004) Multilateralism and the non-aligned movement: what is the Global South doing and where is it going? *Global Governance*, 10(4), pp. 517–537.
Nasser, G. A. (1962) *Historical Addresses on the Occasion of the Fourth Anniversary of the Union, February 22nd, 1962* (Cairo: Egyptian State Information Administration).
Nasser, G. A. (1966) *On Non-Alignment* (Cairo: Egyptian State Information Administration).
Newens, S. (2006) Memories of a seminal year, *International Socialism*p. 112, http://www.isj.org.uk/index.php4?id=252&issue=112.
O'Brian, E. & Sinclair, A. (2011) , The Libyan War: A Diplomatic History/February–August 2011. New York University Center on International Cooperation, http://www.cic.nyu.edu/mgo/docs/libya_diplomatic_history.pdf.
Owen, R. (2011) Military Presidents in Arab States, *International Journal of Middle East Studies*, 23, pp. 395–396.
Perlmutter, A. (1969) *Egypt, the Praetorian State* (New Brunswick, NJ: Transaction Publishers).
Pincus, W. & Milbank, D. (2003) Bush clings to dubious allegations about Iraq, *Washingtonpost.com*, 18 March, http://www.leadingtowar.com/PDFsources_claims_yellowcake/2003_03_18_WP.pdf.
Prashad, V. (2007) *Darker Nations: A People's History of the Third World* (New York: New Press).
Quandt, W. (ed.) (1988) *The Middle East Ten Years after Camp David* (Washington, DC: Brooking Institution Press).
Reuters (2009) Egypt to send more than 1,325 peacekeepers to Congo, Reuters Africa online, 18 February, http://af.reuters.com/article/topNews/idAFJOE51H05Q20090218.

Reuters (2011) Has the African League got Libya wrong? Africa News blog, 31 August, http://blogs.reuters.com/africanews/2011/08/31/has-the-african-union-got-libya-wrong/.

Robinson, D. (2011) Government crackdown kills 30 in Yemen, *New Statesman*, 18 March, http://www.newstatesman.com/blogs/the-staggers/2011/03/anti-government-yemen.

Safty, A. (1991) Sadat's negotiations with the United States and Israel: from Sinai to Camp David, *American Journal of Economics and Sociology*, 50(3), pp. 285–298.

Said, M. K. (2003) A southern perspective and assessment of NATO's Mediterranean security dialogue, in H. G. Brauch, P. H. Liotta, A. Marquina, P. Rogers, F. & M. E. Selim (eds.) *Security and Environment in the Mediterranean: Conceptualising Security and Environmental Conflicts* (Berlin, Heidelberg, New York: Springer-Verlag), pp. 181–194.

Said, M. K. (2005), Egypt's evolving role in peacekeeping: capabilities and cooperation prospects within the EMP, Al-Ahram Center for Political and Strategic Studies. http://acpss.ahram.org.eg/eng/ahram/2004/7/5/STUD14.HTM.

Saliba, N. E. (1975) The decline of Nasirism in Sadat's Egypt, *World Affairs*, 138(1), pp. 51–59.

Sayigh, Y. (1992) *Arab Military Industry: Capability, Performance and Impact* (London: Brassey's Press).

Sayigh, Y. (2011) Agencies of coercion: Armies and internal security forces, *International Journal of Middle East Studies*, 23, pp. 403–404.

Shupe, M. C., Wright, W. M., Hipel, K. W. & Fraser, N. M. (1980) Nationalization of the Suez Canal: a hypergame analysis, *Journal of Conflict Resolution*, 24(3), pp. 477–493.

Smolansky, O. M. (1965) Moscow and the Suez Crisis, 1956: a reappraisal, *Political Science Quarterly*, 80(4), pp. 581–605.

Springborg, R. (1989) *Mubarak's Egypt: Fragmentation of the Political Order* (Boulder: Westview Press).

Springborg, R. (2011) Egypt's Military barrier to democracy, 28 October, http://warincontext.org/2011/10/28/egypts-military-barrier-to-democracy/

The Southeast Asia Collective Defense Treaty (Manila Pact) (1954) 8 September. Avalon Project: documents in law, history and diplomacy; Yale Law Review, Lillian Goldman Law Library. http://avalon.law.yale.edu/20th_century/usmu003.asp.

Sudan Vision (2003) Africa in Focus: Consulate of Egypt honours Egyptian contingent in UNMIS, 31 July, http://www.sudanvisiondaily.com/modules.php?name=News&file=article&sid=59481.

The Telegraph (2011) Egyptian border guards killed during Israeli raid on militants, 19 August, http://www.telegraph.co.uk/news/worldnews/middleeast/israel/8710372/Egyptian-border-guards-killed-during-Israeli-raid-on-militants.html.

Telhami, S. (1992) Evaluating bargaining performance: the case of Camp David, *Political Science Quarterly*, 107(4), pp. 629–653.

Traub, J. (2006) *The Best Intentions: Kofi Anan and the UN in the Era of American World Power* (New York: Farrar, Strauss and Giroux).

UNMIS: United Nations Mission in the Sudan (2011). http://www.un.org/en/peacekeeping/missions/unmis/background.shtml.

UN ONUC (2001) Republic of the Congo—ONUC. http://www.un.org/depts/DPKO/Missions/onucB.htm.

UNOSOM II (United Nations Operation in Somalia II) (2003) Information Technology Section/Department of Public Information. http://www.un.org/en/peacekeeping/missions/past/unosom2.htm.

UNTSO: United Nations Truce Supervision Organization (n.d.). www.un.org/Depts/dpko/missions/untso/.

Vatikiotis, P. J. (1975) *The Egyptian Army in Politics: Pattern for New Nations?* (Westport, CT: Greenwood Press).

Vatikiotis, P. J. (1991) *The History of Modern Egypt from Muhammad Ali to Mubarak*, 4th ed. (London: Weidenfeld and Nicolson, first published 1969).

Vayrynen, R. & Ohlson, T. (1986) Egypt: arms production in the transnational context, M. Brzoska & T. Ohlson (eds), *Arms Production in the Third World* (London: Taylor & Francis), pp. 105–128.

Xinhua (2011) Egypt, Turkey boost relations for bigger influence. English.xinhaunet, 15 September, http://news.xinhuanet.com/english2010/indepth/2011-09/15/c_131140895.htm.

Paul Amar, Associate Professor in the Global & International Studies Program at the University of California, Santa Barbara, specializes in international security studies, political sociology, global ethnography, theories of the state, and theories of gender, race, and postcolonial politics. His research, publishing, and teaching focuses on the areas of state institutions, security regimes, social movements, and democratic transitions in the Middle East and Latin America, and traces the origins and intersections of new patterns of police militarization, security governance, humanitarian intervention, and state restructuring in the megacities of the Global South.

Index

Page numbers in *Italics* represent tables.